State, Peasants, and Land in Mid-Nineteenth-Century Egypt

State, Peasants, and Land in Mid-Nineteenth-Century Egypt

MAHA A. GHALWASH

The American University in Cairo Press
Cairo • New York

First published in 2023 by
The American University in Cairo Press
113 Sharia Kasr el Aini, Cairo, Egypt
420 Lexington Avenue, Suite 1644, New York, NY 10170
www.aucpress.com

Library of Congress Cataloging-in-Publication Data

Names: Ghalwash, Maha Ahmad, 1958- author.
Title: State, peasants, and land in mid-nineteenth-century Egypt / Maha A. Ghalwash.
Description: Cairo ; New York : The American University in Cairo Press, 2023. | Includes bibliographical references and index.
Identifiers: LCCN 2023006342 | ISBN 9781649032775 (hardback) | ISBN 9781649032782 (epub) | ISBN 9781649032799 (adobe pdf)
Subjects: LCSH: Land tenure—Egypt—History—19th century. | Land tenure—Law and legislation—Egypt. | Peasants—Egypt—History—19th century. | Egypt—Rural conditions.
Classification: LCC HD976 .G445 2023 | DDC 333.3/20962—dc23/eng/20230221
LC record available at https://lccn.loc.gov/2023006342

1 2 3 4 5 27 26 25 24 23

Designed by Westchester Publishing Services

To my parents
Ahmed A. Ghalwash and Samira I. Mansour

Contents

Tables

Abbreviations

1. House of Archives

DWQ	Dar al-Watha'iq al-Qawmiyyia
DMU	Dar al-Mahfuzat al-Umumiyyia
PRO	Public Record Office

2. Religious Courts

MKH	Mahkamat al-Khanka
MQ	Mahkamat Qalub
MT	Mahkamat Tanta

3. Civil Courts

DD	Diwan al-Dakhiliyya
DKH	Diwan al-Khidawi
MA	Majlis al-Ahkam
MS	al-Ma'iyya al-Siniyya

Preface

This study examines the rural history of Egypt during the mid-nineteenth-century years (1848–1863), a period that is most often glossed over, or altogether forgotten. Specifically, it examines the impact of state policy on the peasant land-tenure regime at this juncture. While the conventional wisdom on the rural history of nineteenth-century Egypt generally specifies an avaricious state whose policies disregarded peasant well-being and ultimately led to unremitting peasant impoverishment, I present a different interpretation for the mid-century period. My argument is composed of two points: state policy at mid-century was shaped by the dual economic principles of the Ottoman (or traditional) philosophy of statecraft, which centered revenue maximization and peasant welfare; and the workings of the related laws and regulations did not produce widespread peasant land loss and impoverishment. To recount this story, I tried to highlight peasants' voices, experiences, views, and agential power. Being an empirically driven study, it drew from a wide array of archival sources housed in the Egyptian National Archives (Dar al-Watha'iq al-Qawmiyyia) and the Ministry of Finance Archives (Dar al-Mahfuzat). I tried to examine these sources as carefully as was possible, after which I relayed my findings to the reader.

This study would not have been possible without the assistance of certain institutions and scholars. The bulk of my research was undertaken in the archival houses situated in Cairo, and would have been impossible had it not been for the friendliness and helpfulness of their staffs. I cannot forget that the Dar al-Watha'iq staff disregarded institutional rules and allowed me to keep piles of registers on my desk; if not for their kindness, I would have had to wait each morning until they were brought from the storage rooms. The Dar al-Mahfuzat staff granted me the opportunity to actually visit the storage rooms, where I was able to inspect registers and select what seemed the most complete and pertinent for my study. And although my study is based on Egyptian archival sources, I did want to see if something of interest could be found in the British diplomatic correspondence; hence my visit to the British National Archives in London (or the Public Records Office), made possible by a generous grant from Princeton University.

I owe a special debt of gratitude to two late great historians, L. Carl Brown and Charles Issawi, professors at Princeton University's Near Eastern Studies Department, for encouraging me to develop a study that focuses on the experiences of ordinary folks rather than on high politics. When developing my research plans, I kept in mind what Professor Issawi had said to me: "This cake will be baked in Cairo." So I prepared myself for several rather lengthy stints in the Cairo archives, for my aim was to undertake an empirically-driven study. While both read the entirety of the manuscript when in the dissertation stage, Professor Brown also read the version prepared for publication.

I am also indebted to the insights of several other prominent scholars, who had taken the time to read the entire manuscript: Abraham Udovitch, Kenneth Cuno, Khaled Fahmy, and Fred Lawson. And while the late Muhammad Hakim did not read my work, I cannot forget his assistance in the deciphering of nearly unreadable archival material. Here I feel I must send special thanks to the blind reviewers selected by AUC Press to review this study. For their feedback, insightful and quite thought-provoking, prompted me to rethink and refine several crucial aspects/ideas. Here too I feel I must express my gratitude to Nadia Naqib, Senior Acquisitions Editor at AUC Press, for without her support and encouragement, my manuscript would not have transformed into a published book.

My family has always been my most important support base; always giving me unconditional love, always cheering me on. So I thank my siblings Tarek and Mae for boundless moral support, while Mustafa often combined this with good advice. Finally, I know they will approve of my decision to dedicate this book to our beloved parents.

Note on Transliteration, Spelling, and Dates

This study, which focuses on the peasant land-tenure regime during the mid-nineteenth century, involved referring to a number of Arabic terms. I have transliterated these by following the system specified by the *International Journal of Middle East Studies*. Yet in order to encourage students and nonspecialists to read this book, I have tried to simplify the transliteration of the Arabic words by dropping all diacritical marks, except for the *ayn* (ʿ) and *hamza* (ʾ) when their place is in the middle of the word. Yet when referring to names and terms that appear more often in the literature, like Said and Ismail, I omitted even these. In addition, when the discussion necessitated referring to a date of the Islamic calendar, I have taken care to convert it into the corresponding Gregorian date.

Introduction

This book examines the relationship between the absolutist state of Egypt and the majority of its subject population, the peasant smallholders, during the middle decades of the nineteenth century. Contrary to conventional assumptions about this relationship, the story is one of a state that upheld a traditional notion of justice and of a resilient peasantry. In another sense, this is an account of domestic ideas, rural economic viability, and the agency of ordinary folk that is set against a backdrop of Western military, political, and economic preeminence and the Ottoman determination to "catch up."

The trajectory of Egyptian history during the nineteenth century cannot be examined without considering the impact of the world economic order—dominated by Europe—on Egypt. Prompted by its industrial needs, Europe searched the world for raw products, and thereby drew Egypt into the international economic order as a provider of agricultural goods. During the first half of the nineteenth century, Egypt was ruled by the visionary and resolute Muhammad Ali Pasha. Determined to modernize the country as well as extend his influence beyond the boundaries of Egypt into other Ottoman provinces (most notably Syria and Sudan), he realized that his plans required huge financial outlays. To obtain the necessary funds, he developed a system that enabled him to take control of the entirety of the peasantry's agricultural produce; this was the infamous monopoly system. By its rules, peasants relinquished their crops to government agents at fixed low rates, and then Muhammad Ali sold these to European merchants at very high prices, making huge profits. This system was disrupted in 1840, when the Great Powers, in alliance with the Ottoman sultan, forced the pasha to give up his dream of empire and sign the London Convention. As one of the terms of this agreement stipulated that the pasha comply with the conditions of the 1838 Anglo-Ottoman Commercial Convention, he was thereby required to refrain from obstructing free trade in the country.[1] What this really meant was that Muhammad Ali had agreed to dismantle his monopoly system and allow European merchants to deal directly with Egyptian peasants.[2] But what he actually did was develop several strategies that enabled him to bypass the 1838 stipulations.[3] Notwithstanding these strategies, though, the dismantlement of the monopoly system proceeded gradually during the 1840s. In turn, the peasantry was increasingly exposed to the effects of Egypt's integration into the world economy as a producer of raw goods, particularly grains and cotton. By mid-century, European socioeconomic penetration of the countryside had increased noticeably.

Earlier writers who had examined this phenomenon developed an account that relied on liberal and Marxist interpretations of European history. This included the referral to the "integration into the world economic order" model to explain the rural socioeconomic changes of this period. Their interpretation highlighted important changes. Specifically, they claimed that Egypt's increased trade with Europe resulted in the commercialization of agriculture and the rise of an active market in land, which further led to the emergence of socioeconomic stratification in peasant villages.[4] These ideas were modified significantly by Kenneth Cuno, whose revisionist study on Egyptian rural society attributes the major changes experienced by villages to state policy.[5] This is the starting point of my study: my account of Egyptian history during the middle decades of the nineteenth century specifies that change in rural society was largely brought about by state policy. But, unlike Cuno, I draw attention to the state "regulations which were accommodative of the interests of rural cultivators" at mid-century.[6] Put another way, I shed light on a dimension of state policy commonly overlooked by the current literature; this is the concern with the preservation of the economic viability of the peasantry.

State Policy at Mid-Century

This account of Egyptian rural society during the mid-nineteenth-century years covers the reigns of Abbas Pasha (1848–1854) and Said Pasha (1854–1863). It seeks to examine the impact of state policy on the peasantry during this juncture of Egyptian history. Accordingly, it might be useful to begin the discussion by identifying the major ideas and precepts that shaped state policy at mid-century. Upon Abbas Pasha's ascension to the throne, several European contemporary observers believed that a reactionary ruler intent on destroying all things modern and Western presided over Egypt. That he chose to abandon many of the ambitious modernization plans introduced by his grandfather, the illustrious Muhammad Ali, only confirmed their view. More recently, though, Ehud Toledano's study of Egypt during this period overturns this interpretation. Instead, we learn that Abbas Pasha was a wise and astute statesman who realized that his grandfather had pushed the country too hard, and that its capacity levels no longer allowed it to sustain fast-paced modernization. Thus, by abandoning many of Muhammad Ali's projects, Abbas did not "[drive] Egypt back 'to the age of barbarism'"; rather, he granted the country a much-needed time of recuperation, rest, and rejuvenation.[7]

Abbas Pasha's disenchantment with the West allowed for another politico-cultural orientation to take precedence. The Turco-Circassian elite ruling Egypt during the first half of the nineteenth century identified with the Ottoman Empire culturally.[8] As such, this group was familiar with the same politico-philosophical traditions as was the Ottoman ruling elite. Thus at mid-century, the circumstances of the time—that is, the new ruler's clear dislike of the West and the slowdown in the modernization drive—afforded the Egyptian-Ottoman elite the opportunity to rule "within time-honored Ottoman traditions" of government and society that subsumed a certain notion of justice.[9]

This meant that the government of the mid-century years sought to develop an environment of legitimacy and consent by couching its laws and regulations in a traditional notion of justice. This idea of justice, premised on the historical experiences of Near Eastern agrarian empires, was articulated in the propositions of the "circle of equity."[10] These propositions start with "a view of society divided into two functionally determined groups." The ruling group, made up of the sovereign and his military class, were expected to protect the polity's subjects from foreign military threats, establish and guarantee public order, and dispense justice. The ruled, or the *re'aya*, which consisted of the peasants, craftsmen, and merchants, constituted the group whose surplus was channeled as taxes to meet the needs of the ruling group. As such, a group's fulfillment of its duties was entirely dependent on the other group's performance; circularity and reciprocity characterized the relations between these two groups.[11] Huri Islamoğlu-Inan and Çağlar Keyder provide further elaboration of these propositions:

> The ruled owed absolute obedience to the sovereign and were required to pay taxes to maintain his might and authority so that

> the absolute sovereign might protect them against abuses, form armies, and institute an administrative apparatus to maintain public order. This apparatus existed in order to enable the class of rulers to establish control over the sources of revenue in the form of taxes, thus ensuring the prosperity of the state. The class structure so defined rested on an "idea" of state which is equated with the absolute authority of the sovereign and which regarded justice and maintenance of public order as essential for its endurance. Given this ideological structure of the state, its specific functions are posited in terms of the global one of perpetuating the eternal order and of protecting the interests of the subject population.[12]

Thus, according to this philosophy of statecraft, justice was a manifestation of the state's power. In exercising its power over the subject population, the state sought to protect the subjects' well-being while collecting the revenue sums that would ensure its continued reproduction and endurance.[13]

From Boğaç Ergene we learn that the political traditions of the early-modern Ottoman Empire included alternative definitions of justice. On one hand, some groups of the ruling elite, particularly military officials, liked to view justice as the "acknowledgement of the mutual rights and obligations of the ruler and his servants," meaning the ruler and themselves. Indeed many believed "it was the duty of a ruler to ensure that each man was content with his official status, that he received what was due to him, and that others did not infringe on his rights."[14] But the justice specified by the propositions of the "circle of equity" targeted the subjects, or the tax-paying population. Specifically, it referred to the duty of the ruler to protect his subjects from oppression, which in turn ultimately ensured the continued generation of surplus and justified the state's right to that surplus.[15]

Simply put, then, the Ottoman philosophy of statecraft regulated the relations between the state and the tax-paying subjects according to the precepts of the traditional notion of justice, which encompassed the following economic principles: the state was to maximize its revenues while also maintaining the productive capability of its subjects.[16] Here I highlight one of the major claims of my study: at mid-century, the economic principles of the traditional (or Ottoman) philosophy of statecraft shaped the state regulations that targeted the peasants and their lands.[17]

My focus on state policy necessitates highlighting another two points concerning law during the period under study. The first concerns the nature of law. From archival-based studies on legal reform in nineteenth-century Egypt, we learn that the courts implemented a rational and systematic *shari'a* law, and that the government's introduction of secular codes (and new institutions to apply these laws) involved its intention to complement, not replace, the *shari'a*. Furthermore, these new codes and institutions were largely locally inspired. And if we are looking for foreign or external influence, we would do well to look to Constantinople, not the Western capitals. Such reform and innovation can be attributed to the government's desire to rationalize, regulate, and unify judicial administration in Egypt—which in turn was part and parcel of the state's drive for modernization, bureaucratization, and centralization during the nineteenth century.[18] The findings of these studies, which successfully challenge earlier writings that had described Islamic law as arbitrary and capricious,[19] are also confirmed by my own research. Thus, an underlying premise of my work is the view of law at mid-century as orderly and rational.

My second point concerns my reliance on certain ideas of the "law as discourse" model. According to legal historians, this model specifies that the law constitutes a statement of the government's view of the proper society, including the proper position of each of the polity's groups and their relations with each other.[20] Regarding Egypt, the findings of Rudolph Peters confirm the validity of this model. In his discussion of the 1830 criminal code enacted by Muhammad Ali, Peters concludes that this legislation "can be read as an articulation of the perceived social distance between the Turkish-speaking ruling class and other groups in Egyptian society."[21] What this meant was that the government used the law to uphold the traditional division of society. In a similar vein, my research reveals that the government utilized and developed the land-tenure regime during the mid-nineteenth-century years to shape the polity according to the societal ideals of the "circle of equity." For the state was known to bestow land grants on members of the ruling class and to award these holders extensive rights, thereby maintaining the socioeconomic distance between them and the peasants; but regulated the peasant land-tenure regime in accordance with the economic principles subsumed in the traditional philosophy of statecraft (maximization of revenues while maintaining peasants' economic viability). Although the focus of this model is on the state's "statement," it is also sensitive to the attempts of members of other bodies to contribute to the "discourse."[22] My research reveals cases that shed light on such attempts in mid-century Egypt. For example, I found cases where provincial officials, village headmen, and even lowly peasants voiced opposition to the center's decisions. Yet it was opposition not in the spirit of rebellion, but with the intention of informing the center of "the inappropriateness of this decision for this area."[23] Sometimes, these messages to the center carried suggestions on how to resolve the problem at hand.[24] Humble peasants, too, sent their ideas.[25] When the government approved these suggestions, it turned them into law. That it allowed such "discourse" to take place can be attributed to the moral environment created by the traditional notion of justice. For its major principles were known, comprehended, and accepted by the main bodies of the polity, and it is in the spirit of upholding these principles that members of the periphery entered into discussions about law.[26]

My examination of law and rural folk at mid-century leads me to specify another important underlying premise of my work: peasants used their agency to "engage with the state."[27] Recent research on peasant politics during the nineteenth century reveals that peasant relations with the state were not limited to docility or, conversely, some form of opposition; for peasants were also known to wish to engage and deal with the state.[28] Indeed, my archival samples show that peasants frequently made use of formal legal channels at mid-century, a sure way to draw the state into their disputes in order to check abuse. When aggrieved or experiencing injustice, peasants sought redress, and so presented their complaints to an Islamic law court (*al-mahkama al-shar'iyyia*) or to the newly created legal arm of one of the different administrative bodies, or to the Council of Justice (*Majlis al-Ahkam*), which in effect was the highest court of the land. The relevant registers document all kinds of peasant-initiated complaints. These covered, for example, their marriages, divorces, child custody problems, inheritance rights, land and property disputes, commercial transactions, and their relations with local and state officials. All in all, such cases provide demonstration of peasant cognizance of three matters: they understood *shari'a* law and that it was being complemented by secular codes; they were familiar with the major principles of the traditional notion of justice and what this meant in terms of the state's responsibilities regarding their well-being;[29] and they were aware of the creation of new judicial bodies and had an idea of how these functioned.[30] Such legal entries reveal the peasants as individuals who knew their rights and boundaries, and who would protest when others failed to respect these.[31] In this study I try to write the peasants—while examining their disputes, rights, victories, and defeats—as individuals with agency whose decisions often involved drawing the state into their problems.

State, Peasants, and Land in Mid-Nineteenth-Century Egypt

In introducing the main ideas of this book, it might be useful to begin with a brief overview of the major political events of the period under study. Egypt's mid-century period was not a time of dramatic political events. It starts with the ascension of the dour Abbas I to the throne in 1848. Foremost among his concerns was the necessity of slowing the ambitious Western-inspired modernization program developed by his grandfather, Muhammad Ali Pasha, in order to grant the country the opportunity to enjoy a period of much-needed rest and recovery. He proceeded with his retrenchment plans while ignoring the views of the resident European community, thereby earning wide Western condemnation.

Next there was the matter of his tense relationship with his Ottoman overlord. Although Sultan Selim I conquered Egypt in 1517, and thereby turned it into an Ottoman province, local elites managed to establish a level of independence several times during the following two centuries. But the most significant challenge came from Muhammad Ali in the late 1830s, when the pasha fought to secure his dynasty's rights to the governorship of Egypt.[32] These were finally confirmed by the London Convention of 1840. In this way, Egypt was granted semi-autonomous status vis-à-vis the Ottoman government. This status was tested during the reign of Muhammad Ali's successor, Abbas I. At this time, the Ottoman sultan's government, the Sublime Porte, was in the process of implementing its famed Tanzimat reforms across the empire's domains, which involved specifying new directives for Egypt's new ruler. He was required to agree to the cancellation of his right to issue the death sentence in his realm and instead refer the relevant cases to Constantinople. Abbas, though, objected strongly, claiming that the implementation of these instructions would undermine his authority. Although viewing himself as a loyal vassal of the Ottoman suzerain, Abbas was nonetheless intent on preserving his autonomy. Realizing that this aim necessitated courting a Western power, he turned to Great Britain. In turn, the British made their support contingent on being granted the concession for the construction of a railway from Alexandria to Cairo. Abbas acceded to their request, and the British oversaw the settlement of the dispute in his favor in 1852.[33]

Abbas's reign ended two years later on one hot day in July 1854, when he was discovered dead in his palace at Banha, a town in the Delta region, apparently strangled by his slave attendants.[34] At this juncture, his uncle Said Pasha became viceroy of Egypt.[35] The new ruler was the polar opposite of his nephew. Contemporary foreign observers were particularly quick to highlight his appreciation of Western ways and ideas. The contrast between the two rulers can be generally seen in their treatment of the three major political issues of their reigns. First, their modernization programs. While Abbas I shut down many modernization projects in order to grant the country a period of respite, Said Pasha believed it was necessary to accelerate developmental efforts, with his primary focus being the improvement of the country's infrastructure. He initiated his most dazzling venture in July 1854, when he granted his friend Ferdinand de Lesseps the concession to construct an artificial waterway that would connect the Red Sea and the Mediterranean Sea through the Isthmus of Suez; in this way, launching the Suez Canal project. Second, whereas Abbas Pasha was generally suspicious of foreigners, and therefore disliked and shunned them, Said Pasha, having been educated in France, admired the West and courted foreign approval. Several contemporary foreign observers concluded that Said wanted to introduce Western-inspired reforms in Egypt. Said's positive relationship with foreign residents and diplomats also had bearing on his plans regarding the Ottoman sultan, the third important political issue of his time. While Abbas had wrangled with the Sublime Porte over his right to issue the death sentence, the new viceroy's relationship with his suzerain was generally free of thorny disputes. Yet resident British diplomats reported to London that Said Pasha gave serious thought to two matters that would have required unwavering Western support: one, changing the rules of succession to the throne of Egypt from the Ottoman system of primogeniture to the monarchical system, thereby allowing his young son Tusun to succeed him; and two, declaring Egypt's independence from the Ottoman sultan.[36] Although Said Pasha dwelt on these ideas with his confidants, he refrained from acting on them in a clear and resolute manner.

At this point in our discussion of governmental interests, we must pause to highlight the paramount state concern of the nineteenth century: modernization and development. This was even true for Abbas's reign; for although he reduced the pace and scope of the state modernization project, he by no means completely abandoned it. This might be attributed to his cognizance of the world around him. In the European regions, the major theme and goal of the nineteenth century was modernization, improvement, and development. In Constantinople, the Sublime Porte acknowledged this reality, and tried to follow suit as best it could. Central to the state modernization efforts in both these contexts was the attempt to subject "agricultural wealth, particularly land, to state regulation."[37] The same was true for Egypt.

This book seeks to examine the state's efforts to subject peasant landholders to more rigorous official regulations during the mid-nineteenth-century years, which involves investigating the relevant mid-century policies and laws and then determining their impact on rural society. In researching this project, I found it necessary to rethink three assumptions of the current literature: the state was alienated from and without mercy for the lowly producing groups; the peasants were helpless victims who shunned the state and never thought to engage with it; and the peasantry experienced widespread land dispossession during the middle decades of the nineteenth century. After consulting a wide array of archival sources located in Cairo, many of them hitherto unexamined, I was able to challenge these views. For these sources reveal an absolutist state that displayed concern for the lowly "base" of society; that peasants did exhibit awareness of official policies and the willingness to deal with the state; and that the majority of peasant smallholders retained their lands during the mid-century period, with some of the indigent rural folks even increasing their land possessions.

This book develops an argument that is composed of two major points: one, state policies and regulations dealing with peasant lands at mid-century were shaped by the dual economic principles of the Ottoman (or traditional) philosophy of statecraft (that is, maximization of revenues, preservation of the peasants' economic viability); and two, the workings of these policies did not bring about widespread peasant ruination.

The Institutional Context

The elaboration of the just specified first point of my argument involves the exploration of the institutional context that shaped, regulated, and governed the land-tenure regime during the "middle years" of the nineteenth century: namely, the major land codes, the tax impositions, and the system of tax collection. I start with my findings on the major land laws. Most writings on these laws argue that the state specified stringent land recovery criteria in order to disallow poor original holders from suing for the repossession of their lands, in this way enabling current landholders to retain these lands. This thinking further implies nearly complete governmental disregard for the plight of the impoverished peasants. I challenge this interpretation of the land laws of the mid-century period, and instead show that the officials who wrote the first two land codes of this period (1847 and 1855 codes) were guided in their work by the dual economic principles of the traditional philosophy of statecraft, which involved addressing the plight of the insolvent peasants. Here, I highlight commonly overlooked features of these laws: for example, along with the stringent land recovery criteria, these laws also included provisions that focused on insolvent land claimants who could not recover their original lands, entitling them to a small portion of their original lands or to subsistence-size plots of vacant village land. With the comprehensive 1858 land law, though, we see that official concern for poor village cultivators had diminished considerably. But this was not manifested by the specification of more stringent land recovery rules, as was assumed earlier, but by the stipulation of a fee for the receipt of land assignments (the chief mode of land acquirement during the first half of the nineteenth century, which did not require payment of fees before 1858).

Finally, my research also sheds light on the actual writing of the 1858 law. One of the important assumptions that can be drawn from earlier studies is that the provisions that make up this law were formulated at the center without input from the periphery. My research reveals the opposite. Specifically, it reveals cases where provincial officials and humble peasants voiced concern over problematic regulations and proposed alternative ideas, which the center subsequently accepted and incorporated into the new law. Such willingness to listen to peripheral voices clearly points to the writers' practical bent: by drawing on ideas proposed by knowledgeable rural folk, they were actually introducing regulations that would work in practice—which in turn would only parlay into more effective state management of the countryside.

The dual traditional economic principles also guided officials when they developed the regulations that dealt with the imposition of peasant taxes and their collection. While earlier writings generally highlight peasants' many and very high taxes, made all the more daunting by an oppressive tax-collection system, I depict a more nuanced picture. During Abbas's reign, official interest in increasing state revenues while maintaining peasants' economic capability is demonstrated by certain decisions: his plan to increase taxes pertained to a very small proportion of village lands; corvée regulations were modified so as to ensure peasants would be treated fairly; and tax arrears were wiped out several times. On the other hand, with the acceleration of state modernization plans during Said's rule, state revenue needs expanded tremendously. And as the highest revenue sums came from the agricultural sector, the state increased taxes on peasant-held lands several times during his reign: in 1855, 1858, and 1861. Yet such focus on state revenues notwithstanding, this did not mean complete disregard for peasants' well-being. This latter policy can be discerned in the following: each of the major tax codes of the period included the mention of hardship cases where certain villages were forgiven part or all of the required sums; the 1858 code for indirect duties specified the elimination of duties on many items; peasants could sell their crops to whomever they wished for whatever prices they could fetch rather than turning over their produce to government agents at low, fixed prices; and the operation (until 1858) of the land-assignment system, which allocated land to indigent peasants.

Peasants and Land

The second dimension of my argument challenges the widely held view that the Egyptian countryside witnessed extensive peasant land loss at mid-century. In a word, then, I posit that the state policies of the period did not lead to widespread peasant impoverishment. This involves examining five issues. The first pertains to large-scale peasant abandonment of land (referred to as the phenomenon of *matruk* land). While the current literature refers to this phenomenon to substantiate the view of extensive peasant land loss, I explain the *matruk* occurrence differently. My sources reveal that the peasants who petitioned the authorities for permission to abandon lands usually focused on the barren, difficult-to-cultivate, rather costly lands in their possession. By this strategy, smallholders were better able to retain the lands composed of black, fertile soil that were productive and profitable. Yet my sources also reveal that many peasant smallholders managed to retain the barren lands in their possession, handling the reclamation/cultivation costs as well as paying their taxes during the entirety of our period.

The second issue pertains to the phenomenon of surplus or undeclared (*ziyada*) lands. During the mid-1850s, the state sought to locate and oversee the placement of undeclared lands: upon discovery, tiny plots were placed automatically with the peasants who possessed adjacent plots, in reality their actual cultivators; and larger tracts were either sent to the auction block or turned over to the (usually poor) informants who had disclosed their existence. In practice, these efforts actually contributed to the amelioration of poverty in the village. The passage of the 1858 land law worked to buttress this development; for it expanded the amount of land actual cultivators could automatically retain (specifying that these could range from 1 up to 10 faddans). But this changed in 1861, when the standardization of the unit of measurement (called *qasaba*) employed in the survey of arable land fictively created surplus lands, which were subsequently to be sold by public auction. By the new regulations, both poor and rich peasants lost small portions of their lands, but only the more affluent could effectively compete for new lands at the auctions. And yet the cases of land loss involved very small land portions, which in turn meant they did not bring about widespread peasant ruination.

The third issue deals with the creation of large, privileged estates. While earlier writings on Egyptian rural history specify this phenomenon as a major factor in peasant land dispossession and impoverishment during the mid-nineteenth-century years, I present different findings. Here I show that the land grants conferred on high state officials and on members of the royal family (*ib'adiyya*s and *jiflik*s) were largely composed of barren tracts that needed heavy reclamation effort (in labor-hours and costs), which meant that the majority of peasant-held lands were left undisturbed. I also show that the number of insolvent villages placed in the care of state officials as tax farms (*uhda*s) decreased: while earlier writings highlight the cases of tax farm establishment during this period, my archival sources strongly suggest that the trend of tax farm termination, which entailed the reassignment of the village land to its peasant inhabitants, was far more preponderant.

The fourth issue concerns the introduction of the 1858 land law. As mentioned above, the writings examining the major land laws of the mid-century period focus on the increasingly stricter rules of recovery specified by each of the major laws. These argue that the harsh recovery rules aimed to ensure the stability of landholding relations by preventing insolvent peasants from recovering their original lands; for, in this way, these rules confirmed the current (and more affluent) holders in their land possessions. But my archival sources allow me to present a somewhat different interpretation. These show that peasants generally acquired their lands by inheritance, and more frequently by the land-assignment (*ramya*) system. On one hand, this system removed land from the possession of insolvent cultivators. On the other, this system had another, equally important, yet hitherto overlooked, feature: it also assigned land to poor peasants so as to enhance their ability to secure their livelihoods. Thus, what mattered more to the well-being of impoverished peasants was the continued operation of the land-assignment system, not the rules regulating the recovery of original lands. But the 1858 land law modified the workings of this system in a way that disadvantaged poor cultivators: it stipulated the payment of a transfer fee upon the receipt of a land assignment, whereas the original rules regulating the *ramya* system had not specified any type of payment. This very likely hindered many indigent peasants who had experienced land loss from acquiring new land plots. Thus, what this meant was that the 1858 land law disadvantaged poor peasants on two levels: by introducing stricter land-recovery rules and, more importantly, by modifying the rules of the land-assignment system. Still, the implementation of the new land code did not bring about extensive ruination of the countryside, largely because the rising crop prices of the time enabled many cultivators to pay their taxes and retain their lands. This is demonstrated vividly by the following issue.

This fifth issue focuses on the distribution of land in two sets of sample villages located in the Lower Egypt region. My examination involves looking at two periods: the first covers 1813–1814 through 1849–1850; and the second extends from 1849–1850 until 1862–1863. These data reveal that the countryside experienced a measure of impoverishment, indicated by the loss of land by peasants, during the first period (when Muhammad Ali reigned). Yet this trend was reversed during the latter period (the mid-century years): by the end of this period, the "small" stratum of holders (possessing between <1 and <5 *faddans*[38]), which really consisted of the majority in the village, had experienced improvement in the level of their land possessions. In addition, the majority of peasants managed to weather the demands of three tax codes while continuing to retain their lands during the mid-century period, which lends additional support for the claim that state policies did not cause widespread peasant impoverishment during the middle decades.

My examination of peasant land tenure would have been incomplete if I had not included a chapter on women. When consulting historical feminist studies, we learn that women experienced restrictions and coped with circumstances that were unique to them; and moreover, that without an understanding of this uniqueness, the analysis of the topic at hand would be incomplete.[39] I found this to be true for the case of peasant women who sought to acquire and/or retain lands in mid-nineteenth-century Egypt. For this story cannot be told without reference to the societal views and customary practices that generally opposed female land possession; and accordingly this chapter does not limit its focus to the workings of state policy. My research reveals that two general factors impacted women's access to land at mid-century: societal hostility to female land possession and state policy. This finding basically aligns with that of Judith Tucker, who similarly attributes peasant women's land acquirement to the combined workings of custom and the "will of local officials."[40] But I take issue with Tucker's second factor. For this latter factor carries the implication that the decisions made by the local officials were rather arbitrary—that their decisions were not informed by coherent state policies. I challenge this view and instead argue that official treatment of issues concerning women's lands were informed by the economic precepts of the traditional philosophy of statecraft. Finally, my research reveals that the combined workings of societal hostility and mid-century state policy frequently prevented female land possession: throughout the entire period under study, the proportion of women smallholders in a village varied roughly between 0 and 2 percent. Indeed, studies on subsequent periods, even those on present-day rural society, reveal the stubborn endurance of this phenomenon.[41]

Why the Mid-Nineteenth Century?

The literature on the Egyptian countryside during the nineteenth century is very rich, addressing a number of dimensions of rural society. The conventional narrative presents the following general depiction of the countryside: During the first half of the century, peasant society experienced dramatic change that included the emergence of cash crop agriculture, the commoditization of land, and socioeconomic stratification—all largely brought about by the integration of Egypt into the world economic order. At this time, the state developed ambitious modernization plans, which led it to introduce rigorous regulations that generally aimed to increase the revenue sums collected from the countryside. Thus, the major land laws introduced at mid-century specified stringent land-recovery stipulations that aimed to disallow insolvent peasants from repossessing their lands, thereby ensuring the retention of these by the current, more affluent, possessors. And although these laws included provisions for female land acquirement, the number of women smallholders remained abysmally low. State taxation regulations brought additional hardship to villagers, as these specified the imposition of numerous taxes, repeatedly ordered increases in rate levels, and further included oppressive rules for the collection of the required tax sums. This led to the characterization of the state as rapacious, showing no regard for the welfare of the producing groups. And in further alignment with this view is the assumption that the central government made decisions unilaterally, displaying no interest in suggestions put to it by the periphery. Providing additional confirmation of this (negative) depiction was the state's tendency to bestow land grants on the *dhawat* (elite) that were carved out of peasant villages. The peasants who worked the lands of the large estates were, for all intents and purposes, the landlords' serfs. The combination of these rules and practices caused many peasants to experience land dispossession and economic ruination. Thus, most peasants resented and mistrusted the state, often shunning it as best they could.[42]

Some of the ideas presented by this literature have been revised; I highlight the following six. The first deals with the nature of change experienced by rural society. From Cuno's work, we learn that peasant society of the eighteenth century already knew cash crop agriculture, land commoditization, and socioeconomic stratification, which means that nineteenth-century rural society witnessed the intensification of these features, not their actual appearance. In tracing the development of these as well as other important features of rural society, he reveals their link to state policy, thus identifying state policy as the more determinative factor in socioeconomic change during the six decades prior to the cotton boom.[43] In the same vein, Muhammad Hakim's examination of the countryside during Muhammad Ali's reign focuses on the stratified nature of villages and particularly highlights the increase in the number of landless peasants, attributing these aspects of rural society to state laws and policies.[44] Second, the state's focus on revenue maximization and complete disregard for the welfare of the producing base. Ehud Toledano specifies that the mid-century ruling elite sought guidance from the Ottoman philosophy of statecraft (which foregrounds state concern for peasant welfare and revenue enhancement) in managing the country. In turn, this allows us to see that the state was interested in both revenue maximization and the well-being of the subject population at mid-century.

Third, the situation of the peasants at mid-century. Here Toledano contends that "the position of the *fallahin* must have improved" during the mid-century period, and concludes that "most of the *fallahin* remained [at] subsistence level," though without making any reference to land possession. Thus, he seems to indicate that most peasants were economically viable at mid-century, not mired in insolvency and ruination. But his examination of this point is rather cursory, only ascribing peasant economic viability to the dismantlement of the monopoly system (but he does not give thought to the workings of the dual economic principles of the Ottoman philosophy of statecraft).[45] Ali Shalabi's examination of this issue focuses on the reign of Said Pasha (1854–1863), and seeks to present an unconventionally balanced picture. For while he points to the high tax increases imposed on peasant lands, he also maintains that "the peasants enjoyed a high level of freedom and prosperity during his reign."[46] This latter claim, though, is largely unsubstantiated, as he merely links it to general factors (like the dismantlement of the monopoly system) but does not attempt additional elaboration or analysis.[47]

Fourth, the unilateral dimension of the decisions of the central government. For a recalibration of the conventional view, we turn to Alan Mikhail's examination of irrigation in eighteenth-century Egypt. Here he describes the time before the state began to construct major canals (in the nineteenth century), which is when the Nile waters were managed locally by the peasant cultivators. The Ottoman state understood the role of the peasants in maintaining the country's irrigation structures, and accordingly based its decisions on peasant knowledge and labor contributions. Thus, he depicts an imperial state that realized that overarching governmental aims (ensuring the supply of grain to various areas of the empire) depended on the appreciation of local knowledge and capacities. But his examination of the nineteenth-century centralizing state that developed and managed grand irrigation projects aligns with the conventional view, for he specifies that state decisions were no longer reliant on local knowledge, and instead were made unilaterally without input from the periphery.[48]

Fifth, state-peasant relations. As indicated above, these relations were originally characterized in binary fashion: either peasants were docile and apathetic or they were rebellious. But more recent research argues that peasants made an effort to engage and deal with the state; specifically, peasants wished to draw the state into their disputes so as to alleviate abuse. This involved the reliance on petitions.[49] According to Imad Hillal, the petition constituted "one of the important indicators of modernization in Egypt"; though here he did not mean that it was a new instrument. Instead, he asserts that the state relied on this instrument to learn peasants' views, while peasants used it to "win additional rights." His assertion is developed in the context of his discussion on peasant crime during the second half of the nineteenth century, where he links the decrease in crime levels in the countryside to the existence of a strong, centralizing state. For when the state demanded that peasants disarm, they complied; not out of passivity or apathy, but because they depended on another instrument to win rights—the petition. Such dependence, claims Hillal, really meant that peasants trusted the state and its institutions.[50]

Hillal's discussion on peasant-state relations further includes mention of rebellions, which, he claims, occurred when peasants believed their petitions were ineffective. Thus, he asserts that there was a direct relation between the number of petitions and the number of times rebellions erupted during the second half of the nineteenth century: when the former was high, the latter was low.[51] He also observes that peasants who resided in the "peripheral areas," meaning the Upper Egypt region, often expressed their discontent by simply "fleeing to the desert." He concludes that most revolts that occurred in the countryside actually erupted in different parts of Upper Egypt.[52] Other writings specify the same finding. Zeinab Abul-Magd's study, which focuses on one province in Upper Egypt, Qina, over a period of five centuries, relates the story of different imperial powers interested in asserting their hegemony over the entirety of the country. In Qina, such efforts brought environmental upheaval and destitution for the local population, which in turn, rose in resistance a number of times.[53] At the same time, Ali Barakat's new study on peasant society during the nineteenth century, which largely focuses on Upper Egypt, relates the story of an avaricious, harsh state and a disgruntled, resistant peasantry.[54]

Sixth, peasant-landlord relations. This was examined by Raouf Abbas and Assem El-Dessouky in a study that focuses on the origins and growth of the large landowning class and their relations to the peasants from 1837 until 1952. According to these writers, the large landowners defended their interests against those of the state and the peasants within a capitalist, not a feudal, system. And so, they argue that the landowners' relations to the peasants on their estates was contractual, not feudal. Their aim was to challenge the narrative of the Nasserist regime, which had described social relations in the countryside as feudal so as to justify its land-reform program.[55]

Readers of this literature might easily conclude that many aspects of the conventional narrative on nineteenth-century rural society hold true for the entirety of the period. This would validate, for instance, the view that state policies were unremittingly harsh and persistently indifferent to the well-being of the peasants. While the literature does include some retraction of certain aspects of this narrative for the mid-century years, this is generally cursory and unsupported by archival evidence. On the other hand, my examination of several different types of archival sources ultimately allowed me to build on and expand the retractions (by Toledano and Shalabi) specified for the mid-century period. For my archival material enabled me to overturn several aspects of the conventional wisdom on peasant-state relations at mid-century: most significantly, I show that state policies were informed and guided by the precepts of the traditional philosophy of statecraft (which centered state concern for peasant well-being and revenue maximization) and that the workings of these enabled the majority of the peasants to remain economically viable during this time. In conclusion, this leads me to claim that the middle decades of the nineteenth century constituted a distinctive juncture in the history of rural Egypt.

A Note on Sources and Method

I try to address the issues mentioned above by consulting the rich materials in the Egyptian archives that document official directives and perspectives as well as capture peasants' voices. At the very outset, I specify that I consulted several different kinds of archival sources, as I believe this research strategy allowed for better discernment of the realities of rural Egypt at mid-century than would its alternative—focusing on only one or two major kinds of records. Thus, my work is empirically driven, my purpose being to understand the various developments of the period under discussion and to relay the stories depicted by my archival sources as best I can.

I found several different kinds of sources in the archives of the Ministry of Finance (Dar al-Mahfuzat al-Umumiyyia). First, the *athurat* registers.[56] The term *athurat* is derived from the word *athar*, which refers to the lands cultivated by a peasant family for generations. This type of register lists the names of all the landholders in the village, and further explains how each holder acquired his/her lands. Village holders' explanations generally covered a time span of roughly thirty to forty years. An *athurat* register was compiled only once for a village, and never again; the bulk of these registers were completed between 1859 and 1860. This is a rather unique source that provides insight into such issues as the "market in land" and the role played by male relatives in female land acquirement. A valuable source, it also has significant limitations: the most notable in my view was the rather infrequent mention of dates. My examination of this type of source involved selecting the registers of four villages situated in the Lower Egypt region for close study: two are located in the province of al-Gharbiyya (Ibyar, al-Jazira al-Khadra), and the other two are situated in the province of Qalyubiyya (Kafr al-Rajallat, Jazirat al-Aʿjam). I complemented this examination with the quick perusal of the registers of another five villages located in the same region.

Second, the village land-tax registers (*mukallifat al-atyan*). These were compiled annually, and specify the names of the village landholders, the amount of land in each one's possession, the location of each parcel of land (by identifying the name of the basin in which it was situated), and the rate of tax assigned to it. Thus, these registers allow us to monitor such developments as a peasant's fortunes over a period of time, the different types of taxes imposed on landholders, the frequency and extent of increases in their taxes, and the level of economic stratification in a village. My examination of this kind of source involved focusing on the same four villages I had selected when consulting the *athurat* files: Ibyar, al-Jazira al-Khadra, Kafr al-Rajallat, and Jazirat al-Aʿjam. I looked at a total of eight registers for each village: I started with the register of AH 1266 (1849–1850), then looked at that of every other year until AH 1278/1861–1862, ending this examination with that of AH 1279/1862–1863. In addition, I supplemented this work with the quick investigation of select registers of seven other villages situated in Lower Egypt.

Third, the tax-reassessment registers (*dafatir takmil al-dara'ib*). This type of register specifies the tax increases imposed on peasant-held lands and covers all the villages of a province. Under the name of the village, we see the following: a list of the different grades of land that made up the village arable area, the current rate of tax imposed on each land-grade, and the new (revised according to the project at hand) tax rate. I only found the registers that detail the tax increases imposed on the villages of Gharbiyya Province: these are two large volumes that detail the situation of roughly four hundred to seven hundred villages during the mid-nineteenth-century period.[57] I believe this was a fortunate find. Upon consulting a different set of registers, I learned that the state had placed the governor of Gharbiyya in charge of the first major tax-reassessment project of this period. The central government instructed him to draw up the guidelines for the reassessment exercise at hand, and then ordered the tax officials of the other provinces to observe these guidelines when undertaking their own reassessment tasks.[58] Thus, we might consider the Gharbiyya registers a kind of "blueprint" for this tax project. The same situation likely applied to the following two reassessment projects of this period; hence, the importance and value of this particular source. But these do not contain a record of the final tax-revaluation project of this period (that of 1862), for which I had to rely on the village land-tax registers described above.

Fourth, the religious court registers (*sijillat al-mahakim al-shar'iyya*). This is a highly valuable source that provides us with insights into the lives of ordinary people: from these, we learn about their values and grievances; how they reacted to oppressive local officials; how they viewed the state; and much, much more. In general, a court entry specifies the plaintiff's claim, the defendant's rebuttal, and the judge's reasoning and final ruling. Regarding my examination of this type of source, I looked at the registers of three courts located in two provinces of the Lower Egypt region. For Gharbiyya Province, I examined the registers of the court of Tanta covering the mid-century period; and for Qalyubiyya Province, I consulted the Qalyub court registers as well as those of the al-Khanka court. My method involved reading the entries of every other year pertaining to my period.

Here I point out that the registers of the Khanka court are not housed in the Ministry of Finance archives, but in the Egyptian National Archives (Dar al-Watha'iq al-Qawmiyya). These were not the only source I found at the latter house of archives, for it also stores the registers of the "secular" courts. During the first half of the nineteenth century, the state established a number of new departments/bodies, each of which included a judicial unit charged with adjudication duties.[59] Each department compiled registers that documented the cases it had investigated, categorizing them according to the issues under its purview; rural affairs being one of these issues. Due to its importance, it was handled by more than one department. My research strategy for the material of the "secular" courts involved reading the registers of every other year pertaining to the period under study, starting with the year AH 1266/1849–50 and ending with AH 1278/1861–62. My selection of the department to focus on depended on the completeness of its "rural affairs" set of registers. This resulted in the examination of the registers of four state departments for select years: the Department of Civil Affairs (Diwan al-Khidawi), the Viceregal Cabinet (al-Maʿiyya al-Siniyya), the Council of Justice (Majlis al-Ahkam), and the Department of Interior (Diwan al-Dakhiliyya).[60]

The system of adjudication developed by the "secular" bodies differed from that pertaining to the religious courts. The latter court dealt with a petitioner on a face-to-face basis and usually issued its ruling at the end of the session. On the other hand, the former only dealt with documents and did not issue the ruling immediately, instead referring the case to the ruler or to other administrative bodies. Thus while the religious courts dispensed justice quickly, the secular courts did not, which meant that the petitioners preferring the secular courts could not depend on the speedy settlement of their grievances. Yet peasants were cognizant of the higher authority of the secular courts vis-à-vis the religious courts, and increasingly turned to the former judicial bodies. Thus, the secular court registers constitute a valuable source that allows us to discern peasants' views on various state laws and regulations.

In ending this brief examination of my archival sources, I reiterate that each one of the above-specified sets of documents provides valuable information on peasant society in nineteenth-century Egypt. Using them together, though, rather than depending on one source enables us to address the limitations posed by each source and thereby to enhance our understanding of rural trends. By way of illustration, I specify that the comparison between the land-tax registers and the *athurat* registers of a village allowed me to discover several important discrepancies that ultimately shed light on certain phenomena in the countryside. One of these concerns women smallholders. The tax registers list very few women as landholders, while the *athurat* registers reveal that a much higher number of women acquired land than was previously thought. From here, I was able to discern the nature of the arrangement a woman entered into with a male relative regarding the care of her land, which generally included the registration of the land in the name of her kinsman—hence, the absence of the woman's name from the tax register. Here I conclude, as did historian Amy Singer when she undertook her research on Palestinian peasants during the mid-sixteenth century, that relying on a single source "may prompt a distorted interpretation of the regime and the peasants."[61]

This study on peasant land tenure during the middle decades of the nineteenth century focuses on Lower Egypt (wherein the best agricultural land in the country lies, and correspondingly, where the majority of the peasant population lived) and is divided into five chapters. Chapters 1–3 focus on the institutional context that regulated the peasants' rights to their lands.

Specifically, these show how the traditional economic principles shaped this context: chapter 1 examines the major land codes of this period; chapter 2 discusses the various taxes the state imposed on the peasants, and chapter 3 explains the mechanics of the system of tax collection. These chapters seek to show that the state tried to temper its interest in revenue maximization with policies that aimed to protect the economic viability of the peasantry during much of the period under discussion. Toward the end, however, the state's financial straits dictated the abandonment of the "revenue needs–peasant welfare" balance, as its great focus on its fiscal concerns allowed only minimal attention for rural livelihood problems.

The following two chapters look at how the peasantry fared in this context. Chapter 4 examines the impact of state policies on peasant land tenure, and argues that the majority of the peasantry did not experience debilitating ruination. Chapter 5 examines women's access to land, and shows that by the end of this period, families more readily recognized women's rights to land than they had in the past. At the same time, this development did not parlay into a significant increase in the number of women smallholders.

This study of mid-century Egyptian rural society relied on a wide array of archival sources. These rich records and documents not only enabled me to shed light on the lives of ordinary folk in the countryside and their relationship with the state. More importantly, these allowed me to highlight the propensity of humble peasants to speak up and put their grievances before state authorities; at times, actually influencing the decisionmakers at the center. Thus this book on peasant-state relations stands as a case study that depicts an absolutist state concerned with and willing to listen to lowly subject groups, and a peasantry that wished to engage constructively with the all-powerful state.

1

The Land Laws

Upon ascending the throne of Egypt in 1805, Muhammad Ali Pasha, dubbed by one scholar as the "Founder of Modern Egypt,"[1] set about building a strong and prosperous country. This led him to introduce a multidimensional program of modernization that necessarily included the attempt to reshape the economy. This largely involved enhancing the productive capacity of the agrarian sector and initiating industrialization. By these efforts, the pasha "was trying to lay the foundation for a balanced, diversified economy."[2] These efforts, though, were thwarted by the London Convention of 1840. One of its stipulations required the pasha to recognize all treaties signed by his overlord, the sultan of the Ottoman Empire, which further meant he was to oversee the implementation of the Anglo-Ottoman Convention of 1838, and thereby allow free trade in Egypt. Thus the pasha was compelled to abandon his monopoly system, which had required peasants to turn over their crops to his storehouses at below-market rates, and to abolish his trade embargoes, which had protected the Egyptian market from the competition of European industry. According to Charles Issawi, the combination of these two steps hindered the emergence of a diversified economy, and instead brought about an export-oriented economy that centered on the production of agricultural crops for European factories. At this juncture then, the country was in the process of being integrated into the European-dominated international economic system as a producer of raw goods.[3]

In this environment of free trade and rising demand for Egyptian crops, increasing numbers of peasants came to believe that agricultural activity could generate substantial profits, and so wished to return to farming. Peasants who had been absent from their villages for lengthy periods returned in "great numbers" in the hope of recovering their lands, often making untenable claims against the current possessors.[4] The ensuing chaos and uncertainty that permeated the land-tenure regime did not go unnoticed by the government, which tried to impose order in the countryside by issuing new regulatory legislation. This chapter examines this new legislation—the land laws of 1847, 1855, and 1858. It argues that the economic principles of the traditional philosophy of statecraft, the maximization of revenues and preservation of the peasants' economic viability, influenced the drafting of the major land codes of the "middle" decades. It contends that the writing of the 1847 and 1855 land codes involved balancing legislative support for affluent peasants (and the state's desire to maximize land revenues) with care for the plight of destitute peasants. By the time of the drafting of the 1858 land law, though, the state's interest in revenue maximization was a distinct priority, and the nearly complete neglect of indigent peasants cannot be questioned. Finally, this chapter also sheds light on another two essential and hitherto unexamined features of the 1858 law: its inclusion of previously issued land decrees and some of the suggestions made by members of the periphery.

The Demise of Monopoly and the Peasants' Renewed Interest in Farming

By 1841, Muhammad Ali Pasha was the focus of European diplomacy. He had warred against the Ottoman armies more than once, and each time his armies had performed brilliantly on the battlefield. After the Egyptian victory at Nezib in 1840, the pasha was poised to dictate his terms to the defeated Ottomans, but the British government would not permit this and decisively checked his bid for empire. In alliance with the Ottoman sultan, Britain convinced the other European powers to declare against the troublesome vassal, and their combined troops forced him to withdraw from Syria. The Egyptian–Ottoman terms of settlement were finalized in June 1841. By these, the pasha had to complete his armies' withdrawal from the sultan's territories and to reduce his troops to less than one-fifth their standing size. In return, he was granted hereditary rights to the province of Egypt and was to be succeeded by the eldest male in his family as was required by Ottoman tradition. In further confirmation of the pasha's subordinate position in the Ottoman hierarchy of power, all the sultan's treaties with foreign countries were to be applied in Egypt without reservation.[5] Here, what the British really wanted was to ensure the implementation of the 1838 Anglo-Ottoman Commercial Convention in Egypt, which among other things, required all commercial activities to observe the principles of free trade.[6] This meant that the pasha had to abandon his monopolies and embargoes, and in the process give up his industrial experiment, which could not possibly withstand the onslaught of cheaper and better-quality British goods.

True to form, Muhammad Ali refused to go down without a struggle. Winter crops were not an issue. In the 1830s, the "state-run system of distribution" broke down in the face of consecutive bad floods and a cholera epidemic; and the population, on the brink of starvation, became rebellious. At the time, the pasha had his hands full with the invasion of Syria, and tranquility on the home front was an imperative. He responded to this crisis by freeing domestic trade in the major foodstuffs: barley, beans, wheat, and maize. By the end of the decade, most winter crops were outside the purview of the monopoly system. But highly profitable summer crops, like cotton, rice, sugar, indigo, and opium, were an entirely different matter, as loosening his grip on these would impair his economic capacity.[7] This is when his grants of large land estates increased noticeably. To members of his family went *jifliks*, estates often carved out of the lands of (not necessarily insolvent) peasant villages. On high state officials grown wealthy in his service, the pasha bestowed *ib'adiyya* lands, or barren lands specified by the cadastral records as suitable for reclamation. The new holders were not always enthusiastic about their recent acquisitions, which necessitated heavy outlays. So to spark their interest, the pasha granted them virtually complete ownership rights to their *ib'adiyyas* by 1842.[8] At the same time, he saddled government officials, as well as rural notables, with another kind of estate. This was the *uhda*, a kind of tax farm made up of an insolvent village, whose overlord or tax farmer (*muta'ahhid*) was responsible for paying its arrears and future liabilities, and for ensuring that the lands were regularly tended.[9] But once the peasants had redeemed their debts, the *uhda* was to be terminated and they were to repossess their lands. Muhammad Ali expected all these estate holders to show their gratitude by obeying his instructions, thereby planting the summer crops he prized and agreeing to hand over their produce at the prices he fixed, which inevitably were far below market rates. For he fully intended to resell this produce to foreign merchants at the highest price it could fetch. In this way, the pasha hoped to preserve the essential features of his monopoly system.[10]

This scheme, though, was not a great success. The new proprietors discovered that agriculture was a profitable business. Over the roughly half century in which Muhammad Ali had ruled, he had succeeded in imposing a measure of security in the countryside, improving the irrigation system, bringing barren lands under the plow, introducing new cash crops, and expanding Egypt's export market.[11] All these factors not only encouraged the new proprietors to invest in agriculture, but also prompted them to make every effort to evade the pasha's restrictive policies concerning direct sales to foreign merchants.[12]

The pasha's strategy for controlling the country's agricultural produce did not focus only on the estate holders, having also targeted peasant producers. This primarily involved requiring peasant cultivators to pay their taxes immediately at harvest time. Due to the shortage of cash in the countryside (partly because foreign merchants, who possessed ready cash, had limited access to peasant cultivators), the peasants often found themselves forced to deliver their crops to the government storehouses and thereby pay their taxes in-kind. But it seems that taxes did not consume the entirety of the peasants' harvest, and some was left over for free trade. Here Nubar Pasha, a prominent state official, observed that the termination of the second military campaign in Syria (in 1840) and the ensuing reduction of the government's expenses led to a decrease in the peasants' tax load, which allowed some to enjoy a measure of economic recovery.[13] This economic improvement picked up pace in 1846, for in that year Great Britain abolished its Corn Laws, which in turn created a mini-boom in Egyptian grains. These crops were easier to cultivate than the demanding summer crops, as they required less capital and labor, and so large numbers of peasants switched to the cultivation of grains for export.[14] Thus, grains became the cash crop of the 1840s, and the lure of profit gave peasants added incentive to deal directly with foreign merchants and bypass the regulations that aimed to preserve state control of the country's agricultural produce.

In the early 1850s, Egypt's new ruler, Abbas Pasha (reigned 1848–1854), was too busy with high state affairs to pay much attention to peasant matters. In 1851, the Ottomans had published their second penal code, which included a problematic point: it stipulated that no murderer in any part of the Ottoman realm could be executed unless the sultan approved the death sentence. Abbas Pasha rightly saw this as an attempt to limit his authority, and together with the British, argued that the implementation of this directive would only lead to disorder and instability in Egypt. British support did not come free of charge, though: it was at this time that the British government requested and duly received authorization to construct a railway between Alexandria and Cairo. After months of protracted negotiations, the British suggested a compromise solution whereby

Abbas retained the right to issue death sentences in return for an increase in Egypt's yearly tribute to the Sublime Porte. Both parties saw the wisdom of these terms, although the Ottoman government had needed some additional coaxing, and both signed the final settlement in 1852.[15]

Now that Abbas Pasha was at leisure to contemplate the affairs of his realm, he decided to disavow the idea of free trade in the countryside in the belief that the activities of the foreign merchants worked to decrease state revenues. In February 1853, state officials observed that the "advances made by foreigners to Egyptian cultivators on the security of growing crops operate as a bar to the recovery by the government from the cultivators of the dues payable by them to the Egyptian Treasury."[16] In October of the same year, the government saw fit to remind the European consuls in Cairo that direct dealings between foreign merchants and the peasants were expressly forbidden, buttressing its position by pointing to the current "scarcity and to the rise of the prices of grain."[17] By May 1854 the government's position had not changed, and an irritated Abbas Pasha told British Consul General Frederick Bruce "that he was much annoyed by the operations of the Greeks and other small traders in the interior; that they went about 'with English guineas,' offering large prices to the cultivators, and depriving the government of the supplies it required for public purposes."[18]

That Abbas Pasha wished to revive the monopoly system, in violation of the 1838 Anglo-Ottoman Commercial Convention, was hardly a secret. British Consul John Green realized this, making the following comment to a compatriot: "In every act of the authorities the determination to establish a complete system of government monopoly in the produce of Egypt is observable."[19] In 1854, Abbas ordered the expulsion of the Greeks, who were "the principal purchasers of produce in the interior of Egypt."[20] In this way, explained Consul General Bruce, he aimed to be "rid of his foreign competitors in the interior, to leave the fellah no option but to sell it [that is, the produce] to him at the price he offers."[21] Abbas's efforts did not stop there: Green reported that the pasha would send his minister of commerce to the large foreign commercial houses to convince "them to purchase from him the produce they are not allowed to buy from the native boats lying in the canal."[22]

Despite all this, free trade persisted in the countryside. Some of the Greek merchants enjoyed the protection of the European consulates, and so did not leave Egypt and continued with their activities.[23] In July 1854, just a few days before Abbas Pasha's mysterious death, Bruce reported that state officials were no longer obstructive: "I am informed by various persons who trade in the interior that impediments have not been thrown in their way latterly by the governors of the provinces."[24]

It also seems that all the pasha's attempts to reimpose monopoly practices did not harm the peasantry. Indeed, rural society actually experienced some economic recovery during his reign. In 1850, Abbas issued a decree that ordered the termination of the *uhda* status of many villages, partly because he had learned that the *muta'ahhid*s had not paid the required taxes, and partly because he wished to strike against his grandfather's (Muhammad Ali Pasha) supporters by diminishing their wealth. This resulted in the reassignment of the village lands to the peasant inhabitants.[25] According to British Consul Charles Murray, this step involved two-thirds to three-quarters of all *uhda*s; while Nubar Pasha, a high-level official of the government of Egypt, believed it covered approximately one-seventh of the country's agricultural land.[26] This step also involved many peasants; that these kept their new land assignments meant they had sufficient wherewithal to cultivate their lands and pay their taxes.

It was only with Said Pasha (reigned 1854–1863), Abbas's uncle and successor, that the contentious issue of free trade was finally put to rest. Tutored to appreciate Western ways, Said did not resist the foreign consuls' arguments concerning the inappropriateness of the monopoly system. So he permitted foreign merchants to deal directly with cultivators; and also allowed the peasant to "grow, buy, and sell what, where, and as he pleased."[27] His reforms extended to taxes: henceforth taxes could be paid in coin; and he forgave the tax arrears that seemed too high for the peasants to pay.[28] Further wishing to give trade a boost, he "abolished the octroi, or duty on provisions brought into the cities from the country," reported American Consul General Edwin De Leon.[29]

During the time that Said Pasha was introducing his reforms, fighting raged in the Crimea, which triggered another surge in foreign demand for Egyptian cereals. The Ottoman, British, and French troops desperately needed provisions, and this enabled peasant cultivators to demand "fabulous prices" for their produce.[30] Although the war ended in 1856, these favorable circumstances did not evaporate. In 1857, Bruce commented that there was an "active demand at Alexandria" for Egyptian grains.[31]

Many peasants could not take advantage of this demand without borrowing. Although cereal cultivation necessitated a comparatively small capital outlay, still, peasants often found themselves short of funds. Some turned to tax farmers, or *muta'ahhids*, for loans,[32] while others resorted to native and foreign merchants. Here the creditor could make one of two offers. He could buy the peasant's crop while it was still in the ground, thereby proposing a price that was much lower than the market price at harvest time. That this price was so low meant that the offer really included a "hidden" high rate of interest. Or a creditor could propose a "conventional" loan, which the peasant was to redeem later at a specified (usually high) interest rate.

It seems that creditors often protected their rights by insisting on documenting their agreements.[33] This way, they could take recalcitrant debtors to court. In one case the creditor did not like the decision handed down by the judicial body he had originally chosen, so he took his complaint to the Council of Justice, the highest court in Egypt.[34] Some, though, provided their own insurance against defaulting debtors: one creditor insisted on holding pieces of the peasants' jewelry until the debtors redeemed their loans.[35] Such precautions notwithstanding, some peasants simply could not pay up.[36] On the whole, though, the boom conditions of the Crimean War apparently enabled most cultivators to repay money relatively easily, as was noted by British Consul Harris, who observed: "If the fellah has at any time occasion to borrow he repays with regularity."[37]

With the growing profitability of farming, more and more peasants wanted to recover previously lost lands. According to historian Imad Hillal, this was a distinctly new development, for his research reveals that peasants were not interested in land possession at the beginning of the nineteenth century simply because of the onerous responsibilities that came with it, "like taxes, the corvée and the different and endless demands of the state."[38] But by mid-century, the new politico-economic environment prompted many peasants to revise their original cost-benefit calculations and to seek to recover family lands. Many went to court believing that old customary rights would be recognized and honored: most notably, that a male heir's right to family land would be prioritized over other claims. In the same vein, returning absconders and military men who sued for their lands seemed unaware of the September 1838 decree, which upheld the rights of the current cultivators against theirs.[39] The courts overflowed with these and other kinds of groundless cases. Here the government attempted to regulate peasant land tenure by issuing a major land law on December 2, 1847.[40]

But uncertainty and confusion over tenure rights did not end. For example, in 1852, two petitioners based their claims on a confused, convoluted understanding of two different bodies of law, Islamic law and state law.[41]

During this time, the government noted that the incidence of land disputes did not decrease, simply because, it reasoned: "Land is now more desirable than before."[42] Its response to this situation was to try to impose order with the introduction on January 27, 1855, of the second major land law of the period.[43]

Not much time passed before the central government realized again that the new law could not effectively address many of the land disputes that awaited adjudication. In 1856, the head surveyor of Rawdat al-Bahrayn Province requested guidance on how to resolve the "disputes concerning land which the [1855] law does not address." His questions revolved around pawns, partnerships, rentals, gardens, and vacant land. The central government focused on these in the Memorandum of July 1856.[44] But the queries kept coming: over the next two months, provincial officials asked for additional clarification on land pawns and documentation procedures for land transactions. In September 1856, the government addressed these problems in the "Appendix to the [1855] law."[45]

These stopgap measures were not enough, though; and it seems that the settlement of land disputes continued to be problematic. On July 2, 1857, Said Pasha observed that the government's instructions pertaining to land conflicts were "numerous and unclear." On this basis, he directed all state officials to "refrain from resolving the land disputes that are [presented to you] after the receipt of this order; and instead to undertake the necessary investigations [which pertain to a dispute] and [then] to present [your report] to me; and [then] to adhere to my . . . decision."[46] These instructions remained in effect until August 5, 1858, when Said Pasha promulgated the most comprehensive land law of the middle decades of the nineteenth century. At this juncture we point out that the introduction of this law cannot be attributed solely to domestic pressures, but also to regional ones. For the Ottoman Empire had introduced a major land code just four months earlier with the aim of realizing "various economic, social and political aims";[47] and Said Pasha, who was known for his interest in reform and modernization, undoubtedly took notice.

And from here, we turn to an examination of the major land laws of this period.

The Major Land Laws

The literature on Egyptian rural history includes important interpretations of the land legislation of the "middle" years of the nineteenth century.

First, Gabriel Baer (1969), following earlier authors Ya'qub Artin and A. E. Crouchley, asserted that these laws granted new, extensive rights to peasant-held arable land. Of the comprehensive 1858 land law, known as Said's Law, Baer wrote that it "was a far-reaching change in relation to conditions of the past." This legislation was seen to contribute to the development of private ownership in land.[48] Later research shows that the main aim of these laws was not to grant new rights. For the rights at issue—like inheritance, sale, pawn, and rental—had long been practiced by villagers, and in turn, the government merely wished to codify these practices.[49]

Another interpretation maintains that this legislation supported current holders against the claims brought by original holders, effectively tipping the scales in favor of affluent peasants. In this regard, Kenneth Cuno wrote that these laws "aimed to stabilize tenures by making permanent the redistribution of land that occurred under Muhammad Ali."[50] This view is premised on the nature of the criteria claimants had to satisfy for land recovery, which became more rigorous with each new land law.[51] According to this literature, then, the government purposely ignored the predicament of the indigent peasants. Here, though, it is necessary to note that scholar Muhammad Hakim's examination of the 1847 land law does include mention of a provision designed to accommodate peasants unable to meet the cash criterion for land recovery; but as he does no more than merely mention it, the conventional interpretation holds.[52] This chapter challenges this interpretation of the land laws. It shows that the economic precepts of the traditional philosophy of statecraft (maximization of revenues while maintaining the peasants' economic viability) influenced the writing of these laws. As such, I argue that although the government did favor the affluent peasants, it did not completely neglect the indigent folks.

The received wisdom on nineteenth-century Egypt would also have us believe that the various laws and decisions issued by the government emanated solely from the top, from the viceroy and his advisers, with no input from the periphery. And although historian Zeinab Abul-Magd claims that the 1858 land law was partly brought about by "internal pressures by provincial bureaucrats and village notables [in order] to consolidate and legalize their properties," which really constitutes recognition of some input from the periphery to the legislative process, she does not include any explanatory details.[53] In order to shed light on this process, I rely on the "law as discourse" model; while helpful in understanding that the government uses the law to shape the polity according to its societal ideals, it also alerts us to the contributions of members of other bodies (not just the government) to the formulation of law. Here, then, I examine some of the reports and petitions that eventually contributed to the writing of the 1858 land law, as these allow us to track some of the "discourse" that took place between the center and the periphery regarding the formulation of laws.

Finally, while more recent discussions on the 1858 land code invariably refer to the government's codification of customary practices, this chapter argues that the codification process was broader than previously thought, and so should also refer to the state's incorporation of earlier official decrees into the new code.

The Land Laws of 1847 and 1855

At the time of the introduction of the new legislation, the land-tenure regime in Lower Egypt had certain features. The peasants held plots with fixed boundaries and were individually responsible for the corresponding taxes.[54] The ownership of this arable peasant land belonged to the state, and was accordingly labeled *miri*. At the same time, the cultivator enjoyed usufructuary rights as long as he farmed it and regularly paid the required taxes. When the holder died, his lands usually passed to his sons, as was specified by Ottoman law, or *qanun*. And if several generations of his descendants continued to tend the land, it became known as their *athariyya* or *athar*, terms denoting "that which remains." In actual practice, though, peasants paid little attention to the letter of the law, and instead viewed and treated the lands in their possession as private property (*milk*); inheriting, renting, selling, and pawning their lands as they wished.[55] These lands made up the "freeholder" villages and came under the jurisdiction of the provincial government. The official rubric "the villages that are under the administration of the provincial government" distinguished these from the large estates of the state elite (*dhawat*), where different rules governed the peasants' relations to the lands they cultivated.[56] The government created different tax categories for these two kinds of lands: the *kharaj* tax was imposed on peasant lands, while elite lands (initially tax-exempted) bore the much lighter *ushr* tax starting in 1854. Thus the archival sources variably refer to peasant holdings as *miri* or *athar* or *kharajiyya* lands.

The 1847 and 1855 laws deal with these lands,[57] and their major focus is the recovery of land. Moreover, the 1855 law can be considered something of an amendment of the 1847 law, as it primarily addresses the same issues covered by the earlier law, and only modifies the original stipulations of the various articles. The most notable difference between the two laws is the later one's inclusion of a provision on inheritance of *athar* land.

Peasants had lost lands in a variety of circumstances, most particularly by *gharuqa* (land pawn), abandonment, and *ramya* (land redistribution or reassignment). And their repossession of former holdings depended on satisfying the stipulations specified by the new land laws.

Let us start with lands lost by *gharuqa*.[58] By this kind of land transfer, the original holder, or the *sahib al-athar*, handed over his land to another individual, who became known as the *wadi' al-yad*,[59] or the actual possessor/controller of the land, in exchange for an agreed sum. The pre-mid-nineteenth-century rules regulating this land transfer required the recipient to retain the land pawn, and thereby farm it for his benefit and pay its taxes until the original holder redeemed its debt. According to *qanun*, or Ottoman law, the latter could not reclaim his land after the passage of fifteen years; while Islamic law, preferred by the religious courts, extended this period to thirty or forty years. During this time, if one of the parties involved in the land pawn died, his heir automatically assumed his role and responsibilities. Thus, when pawn recipient Ali Hawwash passed away, his son Hassan became the controller, or *wadi' al-yad*, of the land pawn.[60] Furthermore, if a recipient no longer wished to retain the land, he had the option of transferring it to a third party, who thereby became the debtor's new creditor.[61]

Land pawns were the focus of Article I of the 1847 land law.[62] According to it, the claimant could retrieve his land if he had executed the pawn after the cadastral survey; and, if the land had been cultivated by several generations of his family and therefore was his family's *athariyya*. Thus, when the authorities consulted the survey records, the land at issue would appear under the name of an older (and perhaps deceased) member of the claimant's family. The question, here, is which cadastral survey did the 1847 law refer to? During the first half of the nineteenth century, the government had carried out several surveys starting with the 1813–1814 survey, then the 1819–1821 survey, and finally the incomplete one of the mid-1840s. The text of the law neglected to specify to which of these surveys reference was to be made, and Cuno concludes that "logically it was the most recent one, carried out in at least some villages in the mid-1840s."[63] However, the Memorandum of July 1856, issued in order to address the gaps of a later (1855) land law, indicates strongly that the cadastral survey in question was that of 1813–1814: it states that suits dealing with land pawns executed before "the survey were not to be heard because around forty years have passed" since the survey's completion.[64] So what the Memorandum had done, as will be shown, was simply to confirm in 1856 the cut-off point identified by the 1847 law—the 1813–1814 survey. Governmental preference for the records of this survey may be due to the belief that they were the most complete and accurate. Finally, that the authorities were to verify peasants' claims simply by referring to the 1813–1814 cadastral survey further meant that peasants were not to be burdened with the responsibility of supporting their claims with land titles.[65]

A successful claim to pawned land had to satisfy another condition; the possession of enough money for the redemption of the debt and the cultivation of the land without outside assistance. But if claimants could not fully satisfy these latter two requirements, they were allowed to recover a part of their land after redeeming the corresponding portion of the debt and affirming their possession of sufficient cash to cultivate it and pay its taxes independently. But their land was to remain permanently beyond their reach if they had ceded it, rather than pawned it, simply because cession resembles "sale and purchase."[66]

The combination of the various provisions of Article I highlights the government's concern to uphold the economic principles of the traditional philosophy of statecraft, in other words to maximize revenues while protecting and enhancing the peasants' productive capabilities. Thus, to increase agricultural revenues, the government placed land in the hands of peasants who possessed the wherewithal to maintain it, confirmed peasants' rightful possession of lands they had purchased, and consulted complete survey records to verify claims. At the same time, the government did not neglect the welfare of the indigent rural folks, as is most obviously demonstrated by its inclusion of a provision that permitted them to retake a portion of their land pawns when they were unable to claim the entirety.

Two other provisions similarly point to the government's commitment to maintain and improve the peasants' economic viability. First, by stipulating the 1813–1814 cadastral survey as the reference for peasants' claims, the state was essentially granting original holders a relatively lengthy period (more than thirty years) to redeem their debts and declare themselves solvent. This doubtlessly allowed many debtors sufficient time to regain a measure of solvency whereby they could recover at least a small portion of their land. Second, that the government did not stipulate the presentation of land titles when claiming pawned land, instead intending to rely on the cadastral survey for verification, shows that it was dispensing with a strategy often used to disqualify and restrict claims.[67] For the writers of this law certainly knew that few peasants possessed such documents, and that state reliance on the survey records would enable large numbers of peasants to reclaim their lands.

The economic principles of the traditional philosophy of statecraft continued to inform the thinking of the writers of the 1855 land law, as can be seen in the 1855 provisions pertaining to the recovery of pawned land.[68] These provide two scenarios for the recovery of such land. In the first, a claimant could win back his land if less than fifteen years had passed, if he could verify his claim with the proper documents, and if he possessed enough cash to both redeem his debt and cultivate the land and pay its taxes without depending on loans or other types of financial assistance.[69] But where these stiff money requirements prevented land recovery, claimants were permitted to repossess the portion of land that corresponded to their current cash supplies.[70]

The second scenario focused on peasants who claimed their lands after more than fifteen years had elapsed. For such a case to be heard, the current possessor had to admit that he had acquired the land by pawn.[71] In practical terms, the claimant's case would not hinge on the possessor's conscience or whim. Rather, claimants had to support their demands with appropriate evidence, which usually consisted of witnesses to confirm their story. So, for example, when one peasant in Jazirat al-Aʿjam Village armed himself with the corroborative testimony of witnesses, he was able to successfully contest his creditor/possessor's denial of having acquired the land at issue by pawn.[72] Thus, by this provision, the claimant could proceed with his suit upon securing the possessor's "acknowledgment" of the pawn. In many of these cases, peasants assumed that the specified time limit of "more than fifteen years" really was not a time limit at all, and on that basis sued for lands that had been pawned *before* the 1813–1814 survey. What this meant was that these claimants were operating as though in the days *prior* to the 1847 law. Upon discerning this situation, the state addressed it (among others) in the Memorandum of July 1856, where it merely reiterated the position of the 1847 law: it stated that "the limit that has been specified for disallowing the hearing of a suit is the cadastral survey." And to justify this cut-off, it explained that this was considered sufficient time for petitioners to act, as "approximately forty years had passed" since the survey.[73] This confirmation of the time limit observed by the 1847 law (that is, the 1813–1814 cadastral survey) allowed peasants much more than fifteen years to retrieve pawned lands, which certainly worked to the benefit of indigent peasants.[74]

In a word, then, the 1855 amendments for the recovery of pawned land by no means neglected the plight of poor peasants. Although the new law did specify stiff requirements that favored the comparatively wealthier holders, it also included provisions that considerably ameliorated the rigorousness of these requirements and thereby granted poor petitioners the opportunity to recover at least a portion of their lands. This interest in enhancing the peasants' economic viability notwithstanding, the state was careful to ensure that this did not come at the expense of revenue production and collection, as it stipulated that such recovery was to strictly correspond to the claimant's current cash supply.

The land laws of the mid-nineteenth century also addressed peasant deserters' desire to retrieve *athar* land they had previously abandoned. By the 1847 law (Article II), these claimants could repossess half their land if no more than five or six years had passed since their abandonment. In the case of the passage of ten or more years, claimants were to receive enough vacant village land to ensure their subsistence, but could repossess one-third of their land if the village lacked vacant lands. Petitioners who actually retrieved portions of their lands were further required to reimburse the current holders all pertinent arrears they had paid.[75] Although unspecified by the 1847 law, claimants were to satisfy yet another condition, as is disclosed by a case in the Council of Justice records. In a dispute concerning such land, this body, effectively the highest court in the land, declared the following: by "the [1847] law, lands are not to be handed over [to anyone] except to *ashab al-masaha* [original holders]."[76] This was an abbreviated way of stating that the authorities were to verify holders' rights to the lands they claimed by referring to the 1813–1814 survey. And since Article II specified certain time limits for the repossession of abandoned land, we cannot say that the council's directive concerning this cadastral survey actually worked to extend the time limit for such recovery to above thirty years. Rather this directive is reflective of the state's determination to refer to complete records, as these allowed for better official oversight of village land-tenure relations, which further facilitated revenue maximization.

While these stipulations, indicative of the state's interest in increasing its revenues, favored the current possessors by leaving a large chunk of the land in their hands, still, as occurred with pawned lands, the state did not neglect the predicament of the needy peasants. When these continued to be mired in insolvency, and when their village lacked vacant land that could be conferred on them, they could expect assistance from the governor of the province. For he was instructed "to devise a method using his discretion that would grant [the peasant a means] of livelihood in his village."[77] The archival sources suggest some of the plausible solutions: the governor might persuade a wealthy villager to release a minute portion of his land, perhaps a few *qirats*, into the indigent peasant's possession.[78] Then again, he might convince an affluent villager to enter into some kind of sharecropping arrangement with the needy peasant, or to hire him as a day laborer. Another distinct possibility was some kind of arrangement involving nonagricultural work (as in handicrafts or petty trade).

Another two points can be ascribed to the state's concern to improve the economic viability of disadvantaged peasants. One, although both scenarios specified for the recovery of abandoned land awarded a large part of such land to the current holder, the original holder also had the opportunity to retake a rather sizable portion of it. Two, the 1847 law required village headmen who had usurped land from powerless peasants, calling such instances "cases of forced land abandonment" brought about by the former party's greed, to return these to the original holders.[79] From historian Imad Hillal, we learn that the 1830 law regulating peasant agriculture (La'ihat ziraʿat al-fallah) included the very same provision, and that it did not specify the penalization of the perpetrators because of peasant disinterest in landholding at the time. But this changed with the issuance of the 1849 decree, which specified a three-pronged penalty for perpetrators that included corporal punishment.[80] The point I wish to highlight here is that the combination of the two laws (1847 and 1849) worked to prioritize the rights of the (usually poor) original holders over a status quo that involved successful land maintenance by capable cultivators.

The 1855 amendments regarding the retrieval of abandoned land, as was the case with pawned land, introduced tougher stipulations that allowed current holders to retain a large portion of the land as well as other conditions that accommodated poor peasants. According to the new law, the passage of five or six years since the abandonment of the land allowed the original holder, as the 1847 law had done, to reclaim half his land. All the other clauses pertaining to the recovery of abandoned lands were modified in 1855. Thus, for the recovery of one-third of the land, no more than ten years were to have passed. And in the case of fifteen years having elapsed, the suit was not to be heard; instead, claimants were to be assigned, either from vacant village land or from a wealthy peasant's holding, enough land to ensure their subsistence. The new law also revised its treatment of persistently insolvent peasants, aiming to ensure these folks' reintegration into rural society as smallholders. To this end, state officials were no longer to devise any solution of their liking (as was required by the 1847 law), but rather were to oversee the transfer of one-half to three *faddans* from a wealthy villager to the needy peasant, with the actual amount depending on the size of the latter's household.[81] Thus, in all these scenarios, poor peasants received some land.

Mid-century land legislation also included articles that regulated the recovery of *ramya* land. Article III of the 1847 law explains that this land had been "taken from the aforementioned [that is, the original holders] and assigned to others by *ramya* because of the inability of the original holders" to pay its cultivation costs and taxes.[82] Article IV expands this definition to include the lands removed from holders' possession because they lacked the wherewithal to cultivate costly summer crops and build water-lifting devices, as both activities were made mandatory by state decrees of the late 1820s and the mid-1830s.[83] For the recovery of *ramya* lands, petitioners had to prove their solvency, whereupon the province governor was to award them just enough of their original holdings to ensure their subsistence. And in their turn, current holders could expect reimbursement for all tax-arrears they had paid. Such cases of recovery were not bound by time limits, and so it did not matter whether the land assignment had been made "a short or a long time ago."[84]

Even the most cursory examination of the *athurat* registers, which detail how peasants acquired their lands, gives a good indication of the very large numbers of holders who had lost lands by *ramya*, and had had to stand by and watch as their lands were reassigned to others.[85] And as the 1847 law put the greater portion of claimants' lands beyond their reach, historians are justified in believing that the state favored the current, comparatively wealthier peasants at the expense of the numerous disadvantaged folks. These scholars, though, have overlooked the dual functioning of the *ramya* system, known in rural areas as early as the Muslim conquest of Egypt in the seventh century:[86] it awarded land to affluent peasants, as well as to indigent peasants for the explicit purpose of enhancing their economic viability. Thus, we might say that the writers of the 1847 land code understood that the relevant provisions of the new law would be operating in tandem with the *ramya* system. Indeed, it can even be said that they depended on the combined workings of both in order to promote indigent peasants' economic recovery.

Official concern with the economic predicament of poor peasants did not end here. For the 1855 law expanded some claimants' rights regarding the repossession of *ramya* lands. While the 1847 law did not specify a time limit for recovery suits, it only granted claimants subsistence portions of their previously lost land. But by the later law, petitioners could retrieve half their lands if five or six years had passed, and one-third if ten years had gone by; this being contingent, too, on the claimant's possession of sufficient cash to discharge cultivation costs and taxes, as well as to reimburse the current holder for all back-taxes he had paid. Suits were not to be heard, though, in certain cases: one, if petitioners had allowed fifteen years to elapse before making their claims; and two, if the land had been reassigned to an outsider and subsequently was made part of the latter's village area.[87] As before, the government counterbalanced these restrictive provisions with instructions for the conferment of subsistence-size plots composed of vacant village land on such petitioners.[88]

The 1855 law broke with the law of 1847 by explicitly addressing inheritance in land. For the earlier law had only indirectly recognized this mode of land transfer by inserting provisions that required the land to be the claimant's *athar* (or land that had been cultivated by multiple generations of the same family). But by the 1855 code (Article VIII), the sons of the deceased holder were to inherit the entire land legacy. These, though, had to share with their female relatives if the latter proved that they needed the land for their livelihood, if the relative's demise had occurred after the introduction of the 1855 law, and if they could provide a guarantor (*damin*)[89] to pay the land's taxes in case of insolvency. When women claimants satisfied these conditions, they would receive a portion of land that corresponded to their livelihood needs.[90]

Inheritance in land, whether by men or women, was hardly an unknown in rural society prior to the middle decades of the nineteenth century. In the case of male inheritance, writers and archival sources alike confirm that this had been a customary practice long before 1855, and had antecedents in Ottoman *qanun*. The argument is that the government had done nothing more than to codify a well-known feature of the land-tenure system. But it probably did so with the intention to preserve the economic viability of peasant households: for a *fallah*'s (male peasant) inheritance of his father's land really meant his retention of land he had been farming alongside his parent, uncles, and brothers and on which he had come to depend for his livelihood. And it is probably this very same intention that prompted the state to grant women provisional rights to inheritance of land. For another common feature of the peasant land-tenure system was the tendency of male relations to bypass women at the time of acquiring land inheritances, which likely led to the economic ruination of the peasant households that lacked male heirs in their majority.[91] Finally, by preserving the viability of the peasant household, the state was actually protecting its rural tax base and ultimately maximizing agricultural revenues.

It seems that the acquisition of land inheritances did not require the documentation of these transfers on official government paper. This did not mean that the village authorities did not keep track of these transfers, for the shaykhs certainly made note of these by specifying the heirs' names in the tax registers. On the other hand, the 1847 law required other transfers (specifically mentioning renting, ceding, pawning, and partnerships in land) to be recorded on official paper bearing the appropriate government stamps.[92] The 1855 law added other procedures for a cession transfer: it required state approval, which was to be obtained when the provincial administration ascertained that the land "rightfully belonged" to the prospective seller; the title deed was to be drafted at a recognized court of law; and the transfer was to be documented in the court and tax registers.[93] While it is easy to see that these measures expanded state supervision of village land-tenure relations, and thereby improved adjudication and taxation efforts in the countryside,[94] a closer look also suggests that these new measures probably protected poor peasants from land usurpation and concomitant ruination. For the state's attempt to supervise land transfers doubtlessly gave powerless holders some protection against unlawful land seizure by shaykhs and other provincial officials—something that the sources show had occurred often—and so probably resulted in the reduction of such cases.

To sum up at this juncture, this discussion on the 1847 and 1855 land laws has emphasized two points. One, the writing of these laws was informed by the economic principles of the traditional philosophy of statecraft, maximization of state revenues while preserving the peasants' economic viability. Two, the state's interest in protecting the economic capability of the peasants led it to address the plight of the indigent rural folks repeatedly. And yet such focus on impoverished peasants did not come at the expense of the state's interest in the enhancement of revenues: as indigent peasants could claim only the land portions that corresponded to the level of cash in their possession, this meant they would pay their taxes, and accordingly state revenue levels would not be impaired.

But state interest in the dilemma of the impoverished peasants did not hold for the entirety of the mid-century period; for as we will see below, this interest had waned noticeably by 1858.

The 1858 Land Law

The last major piece of land legislation of the mid-nineteenth-century period was the 1858 land law. Several factors made it the most important: it was comprehensive, its twenty-eight articles addressing land recovery as well as a number of other issues;[95] it superseded earlier legislation;[96] and along "with subsequent amendments and deletions became the basis of land law in modern Egypt."[97]

It was issued on August 5, 1858, just a few months after the Ottoman Land Code (promulgated on June 6, 1858). This led some writers to assume that the Egyptian legislators had merely emulated their Ottoman counterparts, thereby producing a noticeably similar code.[98] Gabriel Baer contests this view in his seminal article on the development of landownership in the Middle East, highlighting the significant differences between the two laws.[99] The most recent contribution to this discussion comes from Denise Jorgens, who argues that both the Ottoman Code and Said's Law aimed to ensure that the respective landholding systems conformed to "the basic principles of the Ottoman landholding system." She also recognizes that the "concept of state ownership of arable land," the most important of these principles, "was not an Ottoman invention," but came from "earlier Islamic traditions."[100] Thus, we see that the Egyptian 1858 law drew from Ottoman as well as Islamic traditions; a view that is confirmed by Cuno, who wrote: "The Egyptian land laws of the mid nineteenth century were more conservative, more 'Ottoman' in spirit, than modern scholarship has recognized."[101]

Huri Islamoğlu's study on Ottoman administrative practices and land legislation of the nineteenth century provides additional insight into the 1858 Ottoman Land Code, which I rely on for a brief comparison with the Egyptian code. According to Islamoğlu, the 1858 Ottoman Code aimed to confirm the state as the only claimant of land revenues and that the titleholders had exclusive rights over their lands.[102] The state's desire to establish individual property in land was strongly resisted by different groups in society, each of which insisted that the government address its concerns. The Ottoman government's attempts to resolve and mediate these conflicting demands can be seen in the text of the 1858 Land Code, one of the sites or "power fields" that "carried the stamp of the struggles carried out by different groups."[103] In comparison, Egypt's 1858 land law did not need to establish the state as the only rightful claimant to land revenues. Muhammad Ali had abolished the *iltizam* system in 1814, and with it the *multazims*' claims to land revenues. Thus, the state's right to land revenues was not a problematic that required confirmation by mid-nineteenth-century Egyptian legislation, for by that time it was a given. As for Egypt's interest in promoting individual property in land, the concern was to confirm titleholders in their land possessions and to extend peasants' rights to lands they were cultivating but to which they did not have title. The latter point, in particular, constituted a "site," where the center engaged in discussion with the periphery over appropriate legislation. While in the Ottoman context, a "site" involved the government's mediatory efforts between the claims of competing groups, in Egypt, the government engaged in discussion with the periphery over tenure problems, hearing its views and suggestions, and finally turning the best of these into law. Hence the Egyptian 1858 land law did not bear the imprint of struggles between competing groups. Instead, it reflected (as I will show in this section) the workings of "law as discourse," where society, including low-status groups, engaged in discussion with state authorities about existing tenure relations and whether proposed legislation was appropriate.

Two additional points require mention. The first pertains to the conventional view on the drafting of Egypt's 1858 land law, which specifies that the drafting process had included the codification of customary practices (like inheritance and cession). Instead my archival sources show that this narrative should be broadened to include the new law's incorporation of earlier administrative decisions and state decrees.[104] Second, while the drafting of the land code of 1858 was influenced by the economic precepts of the traditional philosophy of statecraft (maximization of revenues and protection of the peasants' economic viability)—as were the previously examined 1847 and 1855 laws—this time around the state was less concerned to alleviate the plight of disadvantaged peasants than it had been in the past.

This brings us to our examination of the 1858 law, which will highlight the points just mentioned.

The 1858 Land Law: Land Transfers

This law addressed different kinds of land transfers. As one of the most important of these constituted inheritance of land, we start our examination of land transfers with the new rules pertaining to land inheritance. The new law confirmed the "priority right" of peasant cultivators to the lands of their deceased relatives.[105] It also specified that the shares of the legal heirs, whether men or women, were to be determined by the Islamic rules of inheritance regarding personal property even though peasant-held land was state or *miri* land over which the peasants had usufructuary rights, not property rights. The text of the law explained that the decision to permit inheritance of land was motivated by the "concern for their [that is, the peasants'] livelihood and the [concern] not to deprive them of their usufructs."[106]

It is this very same reason (the concern to protect the peasants' economic viability) that prompted the law's drafters to instruct heirs to refrain from dividing the family land legacy. Instead heirs were to maintain the land patrimony as one holding, which further involved forming joint households where members pooled their resources; while an heir's exit required "a clear excuse."[107] Yet too, this official concern for the maintenance of the integrity of the family landholding and the extended household was not solely responsible for the inclusion of this provision; the concerns of the rural notables certainly played a role. For the rural notables (some of the writers of this law came from this group) wished to preserve their own favorable political and economic status in society—which was determined by the extent of their landholdings. As this was a time when the steady rise in agricultural prices could support smaller landholdings, they rightly worried that junior heirs might be tempted to break from the family household and claim their land inheritances—actions that would reduce the head's power and influence in society.[108]

That the formation of joint households constituted a strategy long known in the Egyptian countryside, whether adopted by the poor to overcome economic hardship or by rural notables to protect their economic and political status, is supported by the *athurat* register of Kafr al-Rajallat Village. Compiled before the implementation of this law (1857), this register shows that 15 percent of those who had inherited land over the previous thirty to forty years preferred to keep the family land legacy as one holding.[109] Accordingly, these heirs, and their respective families, continued to live in the same dwelling, while recognizing the eldest male (*al-arshad*) as the new head of the household. In this capacity, he placed the entire land patrimony in his name and supervised the division of the land's cultivation and tax responsibilities between the members of the household. Each heir's share of the land legacy, though, was rarely specified in a legal document, heirs tending to trust family members to acknowledge their rights. But the archival sources show that there were times when this trust was misplaced. To prevent such dispossession and an individual heir's economic ruination, Article II directed that the shares of the land patrimony were to be recorded in a legal document and notarized by a recognized Islamic court.[110]

In addition to inheritance transfers, the 1858 law recognized other types of land transfers: it granted holders of *miri* land the right to cede it, observing that this was "an ancient custom"; it permitted the rental of peasant land because this was "already taking place" in villages; and also allowed peasants to pawn their lands because this contributed to "prosperity and growth" in the countryside.[111] Together, these provisions show that the government took notice of the customary practices of rural society; and having deemed these beneficial for this society, included them in statute law in the interest of preserving and enhancing the peasants' economic viability.

But this did not apply to the most important kind of land transfer: the *ramya*, or land assignment, which was the chief mode by which peasants acquired land during the first half of the nineteenth century. Cuno's discussion of land assignments during Muhammad Ali's reign focuses on the placement of vacant land with the affluent villagers, which means he views these as no more than a strategy to ensure the regular payment of taxes.[112] But the sources, the *athurat* registers in particular, show that land assignments had also gone to landless (the poor) villagers, which is revealing of the government's interest in assisting indigent peasants.[113] In contrast, the 1858 law shows a noticeably waning interest in the welfare of disadvantaged villagers. Whereas in the past, the obtainment of *ramya* land was not contingent on the payment of a fee or tax, Article III specified that the receipt of a land assignment required the payment of 24 piastres per *faddan* (land measurement close to an acre).[114] This regulation most certainly put these lands beyond the reach of many indigent villagers, and resulted in their placement with the more affluent peasants who could take on additional payments.

Finally, that this rule targeted the chief mode of land acquisition in villages—prior to 1858, almost all peasant holders could attribute portions of their holdings to *ramya* transfers—reveals that lawmakers were no longer as concerned to balance between the two policies as they had been during the writing of the previous two land codes of our period; their interest in maximizing revenues having led to a stout disregard for the plight of indigenous peasants.

The 1858 Land Law: Land Recovery

Most of the provisions that addressed land recovery championed the actual holders of the disputed land. For it was these peasants that had steadily farmed the land and regularly paid its taxes over a lengthy period of time; and it was the reliability of this kind of tax base that enabled the state to maximize revenues. To this end, the 1858 law introduced stringent conditions for the recovery of *miri* land. According to Article VII, peasants wishing to retrieve land they had abandoned prior to the introduction of this new law had less than five years to present their suits. On the other hand, villagers who abandoned their lands after the promulgation of this law had until the next planting season to return; but if they had fled during cultivation or harvest time, thereby leaving important agricultural tasks undone, they completely forfeited their lands.[115] By Article VIII, pawned land could be recovered if fifteen years had not passed since the transaction. Claimants who met this condition had to satisfy yet another one: if the pawn transfers had not been recorded on official paper and documented in the provincial government's registers, these original holders were given one year to obtain the appropriate documents.[116] Article XIX addressed disputes that concerned partnerships in land. Holders formed these partnerships when they decided to discharge their farming and tax responsibilities with the assistance of a partner, which usually entailed registering their lands in their partners' names. Problems emerged when partners later claimed that these lands constituted their usufructs. The 1858 law examined five different partnership arrangements. In three of these, the partners (distinct from the original holders) contributed heavily to the land's maintenance, and, accordingly, Article XIX granted them the title to the disputed land; although the actual size of the land portion granted to the partner was to be determined by the extent of his responsibilities and the number of years the partnership had lasted.[117]

Together these articles show that the government sought to disqualify the claims of undependable farmers, for it loathed the removal of land from the control of "proven" cultivators. This policy can be further seen in the state's treatment of *matruk* (abandonment) cases. *Tasahhub* as well as *matruk* refers to the abandonment of land. In the first case, peasants' abandonment of their land necessitated its reassignment to other members of the village in order to ensure the continued payment of its taxes. In the second, though, reassignment was not required simply because the holders had been granted official permission to leave their lands, and the abandoned tracts were thereby deducted from the village's tax register and no longer constituted part of the village's arable area. The first time such requests to leave (*li-tarik*) land were put to the government was in 1854, when peasants from Buhayra Province informed the authorities of their inability to pay all their land taxes and asked to be granted permission to leave the problematic lands. The government acceded to these requests, as it did in the following year when similar requests were made by peasants from Daqahliyya and Sharqiyya Provinces. By 1857–1858, permission to leave land was being granted to peasants from all over the country.[118] By two entries (one dated November 1857 and the other July 1858) in the registers of the Department of Interior, we see that the government's instructions regarding the redistribution of *matruk* lands specified that officials were "forbidden by decree to give the aforementioned [*matruk*] lands to peasants of the villages that had abandoned the land";[119] thus, such peasants had no hope of recovering their lands. Later, the 1858 law incorporated this rule in Article XXII, explicitly stating that a peasant who abandoned land of his own accord could not later reverse this decision and try to recover it. In a word, these suits were not to be heard.[120]

Other requests, coming from more needy petitioners, though, were not disregarded. In an entry dated October 29, 1857, in the Department of Interior registers, the government observed that peasant conscripts released from military duty returned to their villages and demanded to be given portions of land to cultivate for their subsistence. This entry further informs us that this issue had been addressed earlier in the Draft Law (Article 35), and detailed some of the provisions of this article: specifically, rural conscripts who identified themselves as farmers, not as craftsmen, and who lacked land but possessed sufficient wherewithal to cultivate a land portion were entitled to a land assignment. Soldiers would receive two *faddan*s, and noncommissioned officers would take three.[121] The drafters of the 1858 land law did not have a change of heart toward this group, probably in recognition of their service to the state. Thus, the new law incorporated this earlier legislation, but added some stringent rules too, like forbidding military returnees to recover their original lands if they had spent more than five years away from the village (in military service). These lands were to remain in the possession of their new holders, while the petitioning conscripts were to be assigned vacant land according to the just-mentioned rules.[122]

That the writers (of this code) had decided that land recovery by needy peasants was not to involve the removal of land from the control of the current cultivators can easily be ascribed to the government's concern to ensure "proven" holders retained their land possessions, which in turn would promote stability and order in land-tenure relations, and ultimately translate into higher state revenues. Finally, we observe that the mid-nineteenth-century lawmakers consulted previous official decisions and legislation, and incorporated what they deemed was sound and effective into the 1858 law. Indeed, as will be shown below, the lawmakers relied on this method to examine several other issues aside from those pertaining to land recovery. For these officials did not work in a vacuum and, more often than not, looked to operational solutions for inspiration.

The 1858 Land Law: Eroded Land, Requisitioned Land (for Public Works)

Regarding legal treatment of eroded land, it seems that the writers of the 1858 law started their work with an examination of contemporary official efforts that had addressed the problems relevant to this phenomenon. Two entries, dated 1853, from the Council of Justice registers reveal the following case. When the floods eroded sections of a certain village's (name is indecipherable) land, thereby decreasing its cultivable area and simultaneously placing alluvial deposits close by, the peasants of this "impaired" village, led by their headman, Umda Muhammad Said, claimed the recently created land as theirs. Thus, they contested the legality of the nearby village's possession of this land. Here Umda Muhammad Said requested that official investigations should begin with a cadastral survey of his village, to determine the extent by which the village's agricultural area had decreased.[123] Another entry in the Department of Interior registers, dated November 6, 1857, gives us an idea of how this case was resolved: for it suggests that such information (the decrease) was subsequently recorded in the land-tax register of the relevant year, and that the disadvantaged peasants were relieved of the pertinent taxes. Also, whatever portions of the recently created lands (alluvial deposits) remained unclaimed (by the disadvantaged holders) were to be placed in auction.[124]

Together these entries suggest that provincial officials addressing eroded land problems before 1858 observed the following rules: villages that experienced land erosion were to be surveyed; the extent of the decrease in the village arable land was to be specified in the official registers and the relevant taxes were to be canceled; in cases where erosion occurred and further involved the formation of alluvial deposits, the new land was to be given as compensation to the peasants who had experienced land erosion; and whatever remained thereafter was to be placed in auction.[125] It seems that these rules allowed for the effective settlement of such disputes, and so were incorporated into the 1858 law with minor modifications.[126]

The pre-1858 rules regulating official treatment of land used in the construction of infrastructure necessary for farming, or indeed any kind of public works project (as a military fortress), particularly aggrieved the peasants, and they did not hesitate to present their complaints to the government. The archival sources help us to identify the problematic regulations. An entry dated January 31, 1854, shows us the following: a dispute over a portion of land revealed that "it was barren and the shaykh had used it in the construction of a canal and dike for the preservation and irrigation of his fields and those of his relatives . . . and that this land has been registered in his name for many years."[127] That this land portion had been registered in the shaykh's name means that lands utilized in this way were not tax-exempted. Moreover when holders experienced state requisition of their lands, they were not given new lands in compensation.[128] Peasants resented these regulations and petitioned the government for change. For example in December 1855, Shaykh Muhammad al-Sharqawi of Sandawa Village explained to the Viceregal Cabinet that the government had taken a section of his land for "the new dike," and so he wanted to take a portion of an uncultivated tract (*ib'adiyya*) in lieu of the requisitioned land-portion.[129] Another peasant in similar circumstances was so desperate for some kind of compensation that he requested a portion of waste land "despite the difficulty of bringing it under the plow;"[130] while another petitioner only requested tax remission for the land he had been compelled to relinquish.[131]

The writers of the new law certainly took notice of these suggestions: henceforth, requisitioned lands would be exempted of taxes, and indigent peasants would be compensated with vacant land.[132]

Finally, I mention that the just-specified provisions were noteworthy avenues or sites for the protection of the peasants' economic capabilities as well as for the maximization of state revenues. For what these provisions primarily aimed to do was to protect the economic capability of the peasants actually engaged in land cultivation—the proven cultivators whose work enabled the state to increase revenues.

The 1858 Land Law: Land Titles, Expansion of Taxable Land

The 1858 law included a number of other provisions that underscored official interest in the maximization of state revenues drawn from the countryside.

Specifically, these rules focused on granting titles to land and expanding taxable arable land, and thereby advantaged the more affluent village cultivators. In composing the relevant articles, the lawmakers examined accepted practices, previous legislation, and relevant "exchanges" between the center and the periphery; much of this, along with some modifications, was incorporated into the 1858 land code.

When a peasant took control of vacant land, and kept it cultivated and steadily paid its taxes, he became known as the *wadi' al-yad* of the land (literal translation of this process: "put his hand" on the land). The religious courts were known to grant such a cultivator title to the land if he discharged these duties for fifteen to twenty years.[133] The 1858 law similarly rewarded such a reliable taxpaying cultivator by granting him the title to the land, except that it reduced the period to five years.[134] The same applied to peasants who possessed *usya*s, land that had originally belonged to tax farmers, and *rizqa*s, originally tax-exempted land set aside for the upkeep of village mosques and clerics.[135] In addition, the law's drafters saw fit to introduce an entirely new rule: usufructuary rights to land were to be changed to full property rights when peasants dug wells, planted trees, or constructed buildings.[136] Doubtlessly, these provisions aimed to encourage investment in agricultural lands.

As specified previously, the state also wished to increase taxable agricultural land. One way was to encourage peasants to declare all unregistered lands in their villages. In 1854, Said Pasha made known his suspicion that peasant villages contained unregistered *ib'adiyya*s, known as *ziyada* (excess or surplus) *ib'adiyya* lands that were uncultivated or just recently brought under the plow.[137] Reports submitted by local officials supported this belief. This can be seen in one holder's attempt to explain to the pertinent officials how he had obtained his lands: "He had bought the aforementioned eight *faddan*s . . . and the fourteen *faddan*s appeared as excess when the *ib'adiyya* was surveyed, and were subsequently registered in his name."[138] This holder had probably requested that the excess *ib'adiyya* land be placed in his possession. Also, in 1856 the head of surveyors of Rawdat al-Bahrayn Province reported that peasants tended to make such a request when unregistered *ib'adiyya* lands were disclosed by a survey.[139]

Such reports convinced the government that unregistered *ib'adiyya*s disclosed by surveys required regulation, and accordingly, the following rules were specified in the Memorandum of July 1856. One, *ib'adiyya* lands that were less than a *faddan* were to be registered in the names of the holders of adjacent lands, and henceforth taxed at *kharaji* rates. Two, provincial governors were to supervise the placement of all larger tracts in public auctions.[140]

The implementation of the latter point proved problematic. In the spring of 1858, the officials of Qina Province informed the Department of Interior that when placing "two *faddan*s and three and four and more and less" in auction and advertising these "in province after province," takers could not be found for them. Thus Qina officials decided that advertisement for the small tracts would henceforth be limited to the village where the land was located and the neighboring villages.[141] Reports from other provinces disclosed additional problems. While some winning bidders became the actual controllers of the land (meaning it had become their *athariyya*s),[142] most became renters of the lands they had won, and were thereby told that they were to hold the land for a specified period only.[143] One disappointed individual complained to the Department of Interior that, "he had hoped to take the aforementioned land as an *athariyya*, a *milk*."[144] Furthermore, auction winners often had to accept tough conditions. For example, in the summer of 1858 Muhammad Musa was told that he had won the bid for 249 *faddan*s of *ib'adiyya* land, and so he was to pay the rates he had specified starting in the AH 1274 (1858) fiscal year; if, however, another individual offered to pay a higher rate for the AH 1275 (1859) fiscal year, then Muhammad Musa was to "choose" between paying the new rate or releasing the land to the new winner.[145] The preference for the second option may have been greeted with mixed feelings by this newest winner: for the new (higher) rate of tax he had specified was to cover the time during which the land was in the original winner's possession before he released it.[146] Bidders for *ib'adiyya* land could encounter yet another problem. Some individuals bid for *ib'adiyya* tracts without having first inspected them, only to discover after winning them that they were not composed of fertile land and their cultivation would require heavy outlays.[147] Often these disgruntled individuals petitioned to retract their offers, but their requests were rejected if other parties were not on hand to take these lands.[148]

The 1858 land law introduced four changes in the government's treatment of unregistered *ib'adiyya* lands destined for the auction block. First, it addressed peasants' disinterest in bidding for small *ib'adiyya*s; and accordingly stipulated that *ib'adiyya*s up to (but less than) 10 *faddan*s per basin were to be placed with the peasants holding adjacent lands, rather than being placed in auction. Second, it acceded to the peasants' demand to hold the land they won (in auctions) as *athariyya*s (that is, for as long as they could keep it cultivated and pay its taxes); meaning that the holding of land on a temporary basis in the capacity of renter was ruled out. Third, winners of land could no longer be plagued by higher bids, for the winner's bid was to be considered the final offer for the land, and the local authorities were instructed to ignore all later ones. Fourth, winners of *ib'adiyyas* were henceforth to be permitted to reverse their decision to keep the tracts if they realized these constituted bad investments.[149] The reason that prompted the government to introduce these four modifications to the original (and more onerous) rules is rather obvious: the state wished to encourage investment in *ib'adiyya* lands. Similarly, the methodology it followed for the drafting of the relevant provisions can be easily discerned: upon examining the peasants' requests as well as following the discussions between peasants and provincial authorities, it turned the best of their suggestions into statute law.

How did the state deal with the cultivators that avoided the declaration of their *ziyada*, or excess/unregistered, lands? Aware of such peasant disinclination, the state adopted the carrot-and-stick approach to convince them to do so. For example, in 1856, the central authorities instructed the top officials of al-Jiza wa-Atfih Province to hold a meeting with all shaykhs, when they were to ask them if their respective villages contained unregistered farmed lands. If a shaykh answered yes, the village agricultural area was to be surveyed, and the excess (or unregistered) land would subsequently be recorded in the land-tax register under the concerned cultivator's name. But if a headman said no, and a knowledgeable villager later proved otherwise, this informant would thereby win the excess, or *ziyada*, land he had exposed. And it was on the basis of this latter scenario that Muhammad al-Kirdasi turned informant and "asked to take fifty *faddans* from the [reticent] cultivator."[150] His request dovetailed with the current rules (pre-1858 land law) regulating excess lands disclosed by informants, for these specified that where the excess land constituted less than a *faddan*, the actual cultivator (rather than the informant) would automatically retain it, while larger land-portions were to be turned over to the informant.[151] That these instructions had generally proved appropriate is suggested by their incorporation into the 1858 law after some fine-tuning: it redefined the amount of land the actual/reticent cultivator could keep, specifying this as 1⁄24th of his holding.[152]

Official interest in the expansion of taxable arable land led the state to extend its focus beyond cultivable land to include *ib'adiyyas* composed of marginal lands (which often constituted *khirs* land[153]) that resisted ordinary reclamation efforts, and accordingly necessitated high labor-hours and huge outlays. Peasants' enthusiasm for the acquirement of marginal lands was minimal; and in response, the government specified relatively easy tax conditions for the holders of *khirs* lands. According to the decree of June 11, 1856/No. 83, holders would be exempted of tax payments for three years, would pay half the land's taxes during the following three years, and would thereafter pay in full.[154] And according to a November 6, 1857 entry in the registers of the Department of Interior, tax rates were set by the winning auction bid; but if the land was granted outside an auction, its tax was set at the same rate of the adjacent *ma'mur* (cultivated) land.[155] This attempt to increase investment in marginal lands was taken up by the 1858 law, as Article XV reiterated the tax conditions of the decree of June 1856/No. 83, and included other provisions that aimed to further decrease the hardship and riskiness of such ventures.[156]

The 1858 Land Law: Documentation of Land Transactions

In July 1857, about two and a half years after the promulgation of the 1855 land law, the central government issued a decree that disallowed the writing of title deeds for *athariyya* (commonly peasant-held) land. In this fashion, it attempted to stop peasants from engaging in transactions in land (the court entries specifically mentioned land pawns and partnerships) until a decree rescinding these instructions was announced.[157] Here the government had effectively passed sentence on its previous attempts to regulate the documentation process for transactions in land, deeming these inadequate. But this did not mean that the pre-1858 rules completely failed to serve their purpose (order and stability in peasant land-tenure relations). The archival sources reveal cases where land disputes were easily and neatly resolved because of the presentation of proper title deeds, as occurred with headman Hassan Jabra (in July 1854), who won the suit against him when the Council of Justice scrutinized the title deed he presented and affirmed its validity.[158] But such cases were too few for the government's liking, a situation that hardly allowed for order, security, and stability in peasant-held lands—an important prerequisite for the efficient collection of taxes and the maximization of revenues.

The 1858 land code addressed this problematic situation. It specified that henceforth suits would be heard only if these were supported by valid title deeds, and thus, claimants could not expect to win suits on the basis of oral testimony as they had in the past. Also, title deeds were to be issued by religious courts (or their deputies) of major towns only; the less significant courts were strictly forbidden from doing the same. And whereas the new land code retained the rule introduced by the 1855 law that stipulated that cessions had to have the approval of the provincial government, land pawns, rentals, and partnerships only required the writing of the pertinent title deeds. Regarding old title deeds (executed before the 1858 law) that were not issued by recognized courts, and where five years had not passed since the transaction, holders were granted one year to renew their deeds. But if five years had passed, the land was to be considered the possession of the controller on the basis of Article V of the new land code.[159]

Observing these regulations likely involved new costs: in addition to court fees, peasants bore traveling expenses in order to journey to the site of a recognized court. In turn, numerous (particularly, the poor) peasants were undoubtedly discouraged from properly documenting their land transactions, which compromised the state's ability to monitor village land-tenure relations. Thus, many peasants continued to execute land transactions in the customary method, depending on witnesses to verify the transfers. Part of the problem too can certainly be attributed to the religious courts, which did not closely observe the new regulations, and so would hear suits that should have been dismissed. This is suggested by the disputes over land that the Tanta religious court resolved on the basis of oral testimony rather than the required written evidence.[160]

This would change gradually: as the state's centralization drive picked up momentum in the second half of the nineteenth century, with what that meant for its ability to exercise more rigorous supervision over all the religious courts—both those near and far from the capital—the peasants learned anew about the long reach of the state and came to understand the wisdom of observing its laws.

Conclusion

State development efforts in the nineteenth century generally focused on standardization, uniformity, regulation, and the imposition of universalistic codes; in a word, on centralization. According to Michel Foucault, European states were driven by fierce interstate competition to develop governmental capabilities in a way that would ultimately allow for the enhancement of the country's productive capacity and greater state control over economic activity.[161] Islamoğlu found that centralization efforts in the Ottoman Empire took place during a time of commercial expansion; these efforts included state regulation of economic activity in a way that would increase productive capacity and taxable incomes.[162] Among the policies developed by the centralization project, whether in Europe or the Ottoman Empire, was greater state control over agricultural wealth.

These trends can also be discerned in the case of mid-nineteenth-century Egypt: the centralizing state wished to enhance its regulatory oversight of village land-tenure relations with the aim of preserving the peasantry's productive capabilities, and thereby enhancing agricultural productivity and revenue levels. To this end, the 1847 and 1855 land codes provided support for the three major groups with claims to village land: current holders were to retain the greater portion of the disputed land; solvent original holders were to take the smaller portion; and the original holders who had not satisfied all recovery criteria were to be granted vacant land. It is important to stress that this concern to assist the unproven cultivator did not compromise the state's concomitant interest in the maximization of revenues; as the extent of land such claimants would be permitted to possess was to correspond strictly to the level of cash at their disposal. On the other hand, the 1858 land law showed real interest in only one of these groups: the current, usually the more affluent, landholders. This support is particularly clear in the case of *ramya* land assignment, the chief mode of peasant land acquirement (both for the affluent and poor) prior to the introduction of this law. Originally free of charge, *ramya* assignments were henceforth to carry a fee of 24 piastres per *faddan*. This most likely prevented many indigent peasants from looking to the *ramya* system for land acquirement.

The 1858 law has another two features. One, the government incorporated a significant number of earlier decrees into this new law, leading me to claim that the narrative concerning the codification effort, which has focused on customary practices, should be broadened to include earlier official regulations. Two, there were cases where central government officials revised earlier decrees according to the suggestions that came from the periphery—from provincial administrators and lowly peasants alike. Together these characteristics clearly point to this law's pragmatic bent: the aim was to include ideas that worked on the ground and had proven to be sound. For these would contribute to the protection of the peasants' productive capabilities, and thereby bring about much-desired increases in state revenues.

2

Peasants and Taxes

During the middle decades of the nineteenth century, Egypt was ruled by two men who had different personalities and ambitions. The first, Abbas Pasha, was critical of his illustrious grandfather's (Muhammad Ali's) fast-paced modernization program. He was one of the very few who was brave enough to express this opinion during Muhammad Ali's reign.[1] Many of his contemporaries ascribed this censure to his political outlook, which they described in starkly negative terms, specifying it as "backward, reactionary, fanatical and opposed to Western ideas of progress."[2] Thus, when he ascended the throne in 1848 and ordered the dismantlement of a number of Muhammad Ali's projects, his critics lambasted him; as did Hekekyan Bey, an Armenian engineer hired by Muhammad Ali. After a particularly trying interview with Abbas, he confided to his diary that the pasha "is not regular in his ideas. He is the very emblem of inconsistency. He may be cunning; but he is very impolitic, and momentarily rash and headstrong."[3] On the other hand, historian Ehud Toledano persuasively revises this negative view of Abbas, instead presenting him as an astute and pragmatic ruler who understood that his grandfather had pushed the country too hard. This realization led Abbas to reduce the pace and scope of the reform program, not completely abandon it. Hence, what he had really done was to inaugurate a time of respite and recovery.[4] But it ended rather quickly. In the summer of 1854, Abbas Pasha died in mysterious circumstances after a final sojourn in the desert, at which time his uncle, Said Pasha, came to power. In contrast to the dour and conservative Abbas, the new viceroy was personable and a great admirer of Western ways. While contemporaries often commented on the great difference between the two rulers, the American consul general, Edwin De Leon, noted that Said himself liked to emphasize the dissimilarity, reporting that: "It is a point of pride with the present Viceroy to contrast his administration with that of his predecessor, whose memory he holds in abhorrence and whose enemies are his friends."[5] Among the most important points of contrast was Said Pasha's wish to resuscitate his father's (Muhammad Ali) ambitious modernization program. Here we might conclude that reform and improvement remained part of the state agenda during the mid-nineteenth-century period, though the nature and intensity of Abbas's efforts differed from those of Said.

The state modernization drive necessitated the replenishment of its treasury. And as much of state revenues came from the countryside, the government repeatedly found occasion to revise rural taxes. This chapter recounts the story of peasant taxes during the mid-nineteenth-century years. It starts with a focus on the three major tax codes of the period (those of 1855, of 1858, and of 1862), then turns to the extra taxes imposed on the peasantry, then the excise duties, and finally the corvée regulations. While much of the existing literature on this topic is of a negative slant, detailing high tax increases and how these brought added misery to the peasants,[6] I present an alternative interpretation. Specifically, my account focuses on three themes. One, I argue that the state observed the economic principles espoused by the Ottoman philosophy of statecraft, maximization of revenue while preserving the peasantry's economic viability, when reassessing and regulating taxes at mid-century. Such adherence meant that the new tax regulations were not always onerous, some even intending no more than slight increases in peasants' tax burdens. Two, in order to arrive at the "optimal" level of taxation, meaning the level that allowed the state to extract what it determined was its just due without pushing the peasants to abandon their lands, the officials at the center scrutinized the comments sent by various members of the periphery. Finally, the state's attempt to balance the two traditional economic principles was not uniform throughout the entire period under discussion. The sources show that this "equilibrium" was noticeable during the early years of the period (Abbas Pasha's reign), but gradually transformed into a distinct "disequilibrium," as Said Pasha demonstrated a growing interest in the maximization of revenues in the later years of his reign.

From Retrenchment to Modernization

The "theory of predatory rule" highlights the determinative role of the ruler in the formulation of state policy. The premise of this theory is that all individuals are interested in self-advancement, and this in turn means that we must expect rulers to seek to maximize their power and wealth.

No matter what the ruler's aims—increased wealth, more power, higher prestige, or the promotion of an ideological position—power and wealth are essential for their realization. Thus, to say that "rulers are predatory" is to say that they formulate "policies meant to maximize their own personal power and wealth."[7] Looking at the rulers of Egypt during the mid-nineteenth-century years, Abbas Pasha and Said Pasha, we note that each had developed different goals for himself, and more importantly, for the country; accordingly, they were not equally "predatory."

Dissension from the popular view of Abbas I—that identifies him as an "inconsistent," "imbecilic," and "rash" man—focuses on his practicality, wisdom, and competence.[8] By this alternative view, we see that his opposition to his grandfather's fast-paced modernization program was not due to unwarranted hatred of foreigners but rather to his astuteness, for "Abbas Pasha alone had the good sense to take up a position of his own." The contemporary observer who made this statement (Bayle St. John from Great Britain) went on to admit: "Let us be frank: Europeans have done more harm than good in Egypt."[9] According to Nubar Pasha, a prominent member of the ruling elite known to extol "Abbas's eminent qualities as administrator and his adherence to principles of order and economy," Abbas was highly capable of discharging the duties of governor of Egypt.[10]

Thus, Abbas Pasha's approach to matters of state focused on what was realistic and feasible.[11] This led him to assess Muhammad Ali's grandiose modernization program and conclude, as his grandfather himself had done toward the end of his reign, that it posed too much of a burden for the treasury. Respite and recovery became the order of the day. To this end, Abbas accelerated the process of retrenchment started by Muhammad Ali and continued during his son Ibrahim's brief tenure: he shut down several factories, stopped work on the Nile Barrage, dismissed many of the European advisers and technicians, closed several professional schools, and drastically reduced the army.[12] Reform and improvement, though, were not completely abandoned, but were scaled down to more modest and practicable proportions like paving roads, the establishment of the grand al-Sayyida Zaynab Mosque in Cairo, the construction of an administrative-military complex in Abbasiyya, and, most notably, awarding a concession to the British for the construction of a railway from Alexandria to Cairo.[13]

This concession, granted to the British to ensure their support in Abbas's dispute with the Sublime Porte concerning his right to issue death sentences in his realm, materialized because of Abbas's abiding passion, the preservation of his autonomy vis-à-vis his Ottoman overlord. The Porte repeatedly insisted on Egypt's full application of the Tanzimat reforms, promulgated in 1839 with the aim of modernizing the empire. As this would have compromised the viceroy's authority, Abbas demonstrated a measure of recalcitrance; so much so that he, generally seen as a loyal vassal, "declared himself ready to support his refusal by force." In this vein, British Consul J. B. Thompson reported, "He is already preparing to march a body of 8,000 men toward the frontier of Syria."[14] After some resistance on the part of the Porte, the matter was settled in 1852 in Abbas's favor. So when the Ottoman sultan requested assistance in the Crimean War in the following year, Abbas obediently dispatched a contingent of thirty thousand men.[15]

All in all, the combination of Abbas's activities brought about a reduction in the fiscal burdens of the state, and further allowed large numbers of proletarianized and conscripted peasants to return to agricultural production. The existent level of the state's funds, though, was not enough for the defrayal of all the state's expenses. To address this imbalance, Abbas attempted to reintroduce governmental monopoly over the export of cash crops during the final two years of his rule as well as to borrow from prominent merchants and firms operating in Cairo and Alexandria.[16] He did not think to raise land taxes except near the end of his reign.[17] His tax plan, had it been completed before he died, would have affected a small proportion of peasant lands. Thus, the tax rates imposed on peasant lands did not rise during Abbas Pasha's reign.

Said's accession to power in July 1854 was heralded as the beginning of a new age; the complete antithesis of the previous reign. Whereas Abbas had shunned foreigners, Said Pasha was French-educated, enjoyed the company of foreigners, and appreciated Western progressive ideas. Foreign observers easily discerned his wish to resuscitate Muhammad Ali's (his father's) modernization project. In July 1854, American consul-general De Leon reported that "those best acquainted with his previous character and career express the belief that it will be his ambition to tread in the footsteps of his father, in all save his ambitious projects for extension of Empire." This reign, predicted De Leon, would be "a blessing to Egypt."[18]

Said Pasha's modernization efforts, begun in the same year of his accession, largely focused on the improvement of the country's infrastructure. He oversaw the introduction of the electric telegraph in Egypt; ordered the continuation of work on the Alexandria–Cairo railway begun by Abbas, and after it was completed, added the Cairo–Suez line; gave directions for the improvement of Alexandria's streets and transportation facilities; and supervised the excavation of the Mahmudiyya Canal and the repair of the Suez Port. These projects were relatively successful, and bore fruit during Said's reign.[19]

Other ventures were inadequately planned, very costly, and rather quickly soured. Said Pasha's interest in improving water transport did not end with the repair of infrastructure, but further led to the formation of two steamship companies in cooperation with European businessmen: the Nile Navigation Company was to provide transport on the Nile and the Mahmudiyya; and the Medjidieh Company was to focus on the Red Sea and the Mediterranean. Neither company ever became a robust operation though, mostly because the European partners were too preoccupied with extracting huge money rewards from the government. Both enterprises failed just a few years after their inception, at which time the government had to pay investors handsome amounts in compensation.[20] Another venture aimed to stimulate agricultural production: this project intended to complete the construction of the Nile Barrage, and necessitated vast sums of money and thousands of peasant laborers. Said Pasha duly met these obligations—but only for a time. He preferred to busy himself with projects closer to his heart: he allowed his passion for fortresses and the related military accessories to interfere with and stall his plans for the barrage. In December 1859, British Consul Robert Colquhoun reported that the "Sadieh, the military work at the Barrage of the Nile . . . cost this year upwards of 550,000 [sterling pounds] and where no less than ten thousand fellahs have been employed daily on the undertaking." At the time of his death in January 1863, the barrage was still incomplete.[21]

The most dramatic of Said's ventures was the Suez Canal. This project was the brainchild of Ferdinand de Lesseps, a close friend of Said's from his boyhood days. According to Consul General Frederick Bruce, de Lesseps easily won the support of his royal friend, who "was dazzled with the grandiose nature of the scheme, which meets also with the approbation of his head-engineer, Linant Bey."[22] This approval parlayed into the Suez Canal concession of 1854 and the later one of 1856. Most writers view the terms of these concessions as having been unfavorable to Egypt, and accordingly ascribe their inclusion to such factors as Said's problematic character traits, which disallowed rational thinking, and de Lesseps's ability to charm and persuade.[23] On the other hand, Fred Lawson links the moot terms of the Suez Canal concessions to the "interests of powerful forces in mid-nineteenth-century Egyptian society," and persuasively shows how each of these groups stood to benefit from these. Thus he concludes that the "details concerning Sa'id's idiosyncrasies are incidental" to the final composition of the concessions.[24]

This interpretation leads to another assumption: that these powerful groups of Ottoman-Egyptian society were just as anxious as de Lesseps for the commencement of the Suez Canal project. Accordingly, they united with him in urging Said Pasha to accept the enormous financial obligations necessary for the establishment of the Suez Canal Company.[25] Thus in 1858, when subscriptions were opened to the public and only 56 percent of the company's four hundred thousand shares were purchased, Said agreed to acquire the remaining 44 percent. This was necessary because "under French law the company could not be regularly constituted until all the shares were effectively subscribed." Immediate payment to the company was out of the question, though.[26]

The state treasury also had to contend with the financial demands of other foreigners. The surly Abbas had reduced the European presence and activities in Egypt; however, when he died and Said, an open admirer of Western society, took the throne, the floodgates opened. According to David Landes, between 1857 and 1861, approximately thirty thousand foreigners arrived in Egypt every year.[27] In March 1858, British Consul John Green reported on "the numerous bad characters daily arriving in Egypt."[28] Many of these were Europeans of shady background, bold and shameless adventurers who had come to Egypt in search of quick wealth. Some were merchants who found their way to the provinces of Upper Egypt, where they traded in grains and the commodities brought by the Sudanese caravans, often paying "unfair prices" in order to enlarge their profits.[29] Their activities brought hardship to the locals. In Qina Province "resentment . . . grew . . . against the presence of foreign merchants," and bandits raided their steamships "almost every day"; and in Isna Province, an uprising broke out in 1858.[30]

In his easy and good-natured way, Said often gave these fast-talking businessmen a hearing, usually to his detriment. In one case where he had verbally committed to a project but later decided to reverse his decision, the result was that "the claim [was] raised by Messrs. Barker and Co. of Alexandria against the Egyptian Government [for] . . . damages said to have been sustained by them in consequence of the Viceroy having declined to ratify a promise made verbally by His Highness."[31] Also disadvantageous for Said was his desire to win the goodwill and support of the European powers in order to advance his plans vis-à-vis his Ottoman suzerain.[32] This made the foreign consuls weighty figures at his court, and they used this influence to persuade the viceroy to hear the demands of their compatriots and protégés who faulted the government of Egypt for their business losses—and although the claims were often exaggerated, some even preposterous, enormous indemnity payments were always expected.[33] Thus, members of this body pressed "claims which in any other country would tarnish the names of those bringing them forward, but which in Egypt seem to meet with official support as a matter of course."[34] By December 1862, Said was loudly complaining about this phenomenon, declaring that "he has been pillaged in a most shameful manner."[35]

Said Pasha's straitened finances can also be attributed to his own expensive interests and proclivities. The enhancement of the fighting capabilities of the country's military forces was considered something of a pet project, as indicated above. In the autumn of 1858, a contemporary observer noted that Said Pasha "has evidently a personal taste for military details. He is spending a large part of his revenue on the clothing, equipment and feeding of his troops; he is almost always in the field with them and commands personally."[36] In the following summer, British Consul Alfred Walne was reporting on the manufacture of ammunition, which was taking place "with great rapidity,"[37] and on the destination of this military equipment, which was being "sent to Saidieh, an extensive fortification raised between the barrages."[38] This effort also involved increasing the size of his forces; and to this end, Said issued instructions for the levying of military recruits, who were to receive military training for several months and then return to their villages. But they could be recalled; for the names of these recruits were recorded in government registers, and they were to be called for duty whenever the need arose. In July 1859, Walne reported: "There are not less than one hundred and fifty thousand men who have gone through drill and are thus, as it were, kept within call."[39] Said hoped "to infuse a national military spirit into them" during their time of service and training;[40] for he ultimately dreamed of creating a strong and loyal fighting force. Some believed that he intended to use his military to fend off an attack by a European enemy, while most believed that he needed it to win his independence from the Ottoman Porte.[41] That the latter opinion was the better-informed one is supported by Said Pasha's decision in January 1863 to send Egyptian troops to Mexico to assist the French military effort in that country.

Said probably hoped this act would cement his relations with France, and that he might later count on it to support his dreams of independence.[42] Needless to say, all these activities included a distinctly financial dimension.

In the midst of these major concerns, Said Pasha also had to address several other issues that similarly had a financial dimension: he was "pressed on all sides to discharge the debts left by Abbas Pasha's administration";[43] Ilhami Pasha's (Abbas's son's) financial ruin turned into a headache for the new viceroy;[44] to improve relations with kinsmen, he liked to give them handsome cash allowances;[45] and finally, as Said wished to live in the style befitting a prince, he spent extravagantly on the decoration of his palaces and purchased luxury items like the customized steam yacht built for him in Liverpool.[46]

The combination of these circumstances and concerns meant that Said Pasha never had sufficient funds at his disposal, and to resolve this pressing problem he tried a number of strategies. Among these was the issuance of bearer bonds of short maturities, with the result that "there were £2 million of government paper in circulation" by the end of 1859.[47] Also among these strategies were the following: in 1859, he tried to replace foreign employees in his administration with Egyptians because during times "of momentary pecuniary difficulty he stops three months pay";[48] in 1860, he acquired his first foreign loan, which was arranged for him by the Paris branch of Charles Lafitte et Cie and the Comptoir d'Escompte, and consisted of 28 million francs; also by mid-1860, he arranged for the reissuance of treasury bonds, which resulted in the increase of government paper in circulation to £3.5 million; in 1861, he tried to sell forty thousand Minié rifles to the American consul general, which the latter appraised as "probably as good as can be manufactured in any part of the world";[49] in March 1862, he arranged for another major foreign loan, this time arranged for him by the House of Oppenheim and Nephew of Alexandria, and consisted of £3,292,800.[50] In addition, he raised the *kharaji* land taxes several times, as will be shown below.

Peasant Land and Taxes: Tax Revaluations at Mid-Century

Peasants of the Ottoman Empire traditionally paid taxes on the crops produced by their lands; an instance of a state that taxed the wealth actually produced.[51] As the state's control over distant agricultural lands declined during the seventeenth and eighteenth centuries, feudal lords multiplied peasants' taxes far beyond the rate specified by the central government, sometimes taking up to half the crop in taxes.[52] The Tanzimat reforms of the Ottoman Empire, introduced between 1839 and 1876 with the aim of modernizing and strengthening the empire, sought to rectify such abuse; and accordingly, "a tithe of exactly one-tenth of the value was established as the sole tax on all produce of the land."[53] In contrast, the government of Egypt divided *miri* land, or state land held by peasants on a usufructuary basis, into different grades according to the quality of the land, which was determined by several factors, such as proximity to irrigation infrastructure, the type of soil, and the kind of crops produced by the land. Then officials specified rates of tax that reflected the grade or quality of the land. This is a case of "the capacity to generate wealth being taxed rather than taxing the wealth generated."[54] As will be seen below, the Egyptian land-tax changes introduced at mid-century consisted of specifying new rates of tax for the different grades of village agricultural land. This difference between the Ottoman and Egyptian taxation logic aside, we also point out that the Egyptian tax changes were to contribute to domestic modernization and centralization efforts—that moved in tandem with the wider Ottoman or regional drive for centralization and modernization—in two ways. One, nineteenth-century centralization efforts required enhanced official knowledge of village specifics, which also constituted the first necessary step in the assignment of new tax rates. Two, the new (and for the most part, higher) tax rates translated into higher levels of revenue, needed to pay for the various modernization projects.

During the middle decades of the nineteenth century, the state reassessed the tax rates of the village lands several times, thereby introducing the 1855, 1858, and 1862 tax codes.

The 1855 Land-Tax Code: Part One

Work on the first tax code began in the last few months of Abbas Pasha's reign. In November 1853, the Council of Justice instructed village authorities to prepare records that were to identify holders who possessed "*ib'adiyya* lands whose rate of tax was lower" than the tax rate imposed on the village *ma'mur* (fertile, cultivated) lands. Upon completion, these records were to be sent to the council.[55] However these instructions did not include an explanation of why the government requested these records.

The untimely death of Abbas Pasha in July 1854 did not terminate official investigations of village *ib'adiyya* lands. An entry dated February 3, 1856, in the registers of the Viceregal Cabinet reveals that these were completed under his successor, Said Pasha. It also reveals that these investigations were undertaken in order to allow the government to revise the taxes imposed on village *ib'addiya* lands, as these carried minimal rates or were tax-exempted.[56] These *ib'adiyya*s originally constituted barren, uncultivated lands, which the cadastral records of the early nineteenth century described as being suitable for reclamation. Muhammad Ali had encouraged peasants' interest in these lands by stipulating advantageous tax terms for their holders. By mid-century, the government believed that the productive capacity of village *ib'adiyya*s had reached the level of cultivated (*ma'mur*) land, and so decided to revise their tax terms.

Charged with this task was the governor of Gharbiyya Province, who was instructed to focus on Gharbiyya and Buhayra Provinces. This was a pilot project that was to serve as a model for all other provincial governors.[57] The completed tax-revaluation project had three facets or elements, with specific guidelines (developed by the Gharbiyya governor) for each one.

The first, and most important, facet constituted the adjustment of the *ib'adiyya* taxes, with the aim of aligning these with the 1854 tax rates of the village *ma'mur* lands.[58] This entailed the following:

A. When the *ib'adiyya* tract was situated in a basin comprising *ma'mur* land of only one grade, the *ib'adiyya* was to be assigned the same tax rate as the *ma'mur* land. For illustration, we turn to the village of al-Jazira al-Khadra. There, an *ib'adiyya* tract of 74 *faddan*s carrying a tax rate of 16 piastres, 35 para, was situated in a basin called al-Farsha, which also held 502.5 *faddan*s of *ma'mur* land taxed at 59 piastres, 34 para.[59] Accordingly, the *ib'adiyya*'s rate of tax changed from 16 piastres, 35 para, to 59 piastres, 34 para.[60]
B. In some cases, the *ib'adiyya* tract was situated in a basin that contained *ma'mur* land of different grades, with the various grades commensurately taxed at different rates. Here, the *ib'adiyya* was to be assigned the highest of the rates imposed on the *ma'mur* lands. The village of al-Jazira al-Khadra again provides illustration. The agricultural land of this village was divided into two basins, and one of these was al-Nakhil Basin, which contained *ma'mur* land of different grades (each carrying a different rate of tax) as well as an *ib'adiyya* tract composed of 2.5 *faddan*s. As the highest grade of *ma'mur* land in that basin carried a tax rate of 63 piastres, this

ib'adiyya's tax was accordingly raised from 40 piastres, 20 para, to 63 piastres.[61]

C. Some basins were composed solely of *ib'adiyya* land. Here the adjustment of the tax rate consisted of raising it "to the rate that exceeds the mid-point of the [average] tax-rate."[62] In practical terms this meant that the *ib'adiyya* was to be assigned the same rate carried by the poorest grade of *ma'mur* land in the village. Abnahas Village had a basin that contained only *ib'adiyya* lands; their taxes varied from 11 piastres, 10 para, to a high of 39 piastres, 15 para. All these were raised to 43 piastres, 35 para—the rate carried by the poorest *ma'mur* land in Abnahas.[63]

D. Some *ib'adiyya*s constituted wide expanses of waste land that could not be brought under cultivation without high levels of investment, and were referred to as *barriyya* (plural: *barrari*) land. The tax rate of this land type was simply to be adjusted to the rate carried by the nearest *ma'mur* tract. The village of Kafr al-Jarayda contained *barrari* lands, their taxes ranging from 4 piastres, 20 para, to a high of 13 piastres, 20 para. These taxes were raised to 33 piastres, 30 para, because the *ma'mur* land lying closest—this was situated in the basin of Kum al-Dabi—paid this rate.[64]

The second facet of this tax-revaluation project focused on the monetary system, by which provincial officials were to undertake the *takmil kusur al-para*,[65] or the reassessment of the fractions of the para denomination. The aim was to eliminate the lower denomination, the jadid, from the rate of tax; and henceforth, the tax rate would be specified only in the piaster and para denominations.[66] This was to be done by imposing slight increases in tax, as the following example shows: the rate of tax specified as 40 piastres, 20 para, 5 jadid would become 40 piastres, 21 para. Here, the former rate had been increased by 5 jadid, as 10 jadid constituted 1 para. The examination of a number of (I quickly inspected 15) village land-tax registers reveals that peasant lands were not subjected to this reassessment procedure, simply because their rates of tax were already specified only in the piaster and para denominations.

On the other hand, there certainly were other taxes that did include the jadid denomination and which landholders did have to pay; and it is on these that this monetary reassessment focused. Its inclusion in the tax-revaluation project may be attributed to the government's aim to withdraw the *jadid* coin from circulation in an attempt to combat inflation (which was probably caused by the persistent imbalance between government expenditures and revenues, as in the 1850s the former exceeded the latter by about 10 percent[67]). For with the increase in prices, the lowest denomination lost value. Such deterioration of value further meant that the cost of actually minting the *jadid* most likely exceeded its value, and thereby made its production superfluous and expensive.

The third concern of this tax-reassessment project was villages in a state of *aya*, translated literally as sickness. The authorities classified village lands in this way when these had experienced extensive ruination, like that caused by drought, destructive flood waters, high salinity levels, or the breakdown of the irrigation system. Here the government officially recognized peasants' inability to pay taxes and accordingly canceled some or all of the newly imposed taxes upon determining the level of hardship. Finally, it identified the following reason for this general policy: "in order to prevent their [that is, the peasants' economic] deterioration."[68]

What were the results of this stage of the 1855 tax project? First, most of the *miri* or *kharaji* lands, translated simply here as usufructuary lands, did not undergo an increase in taxes simply because the government had focused almost entirely on *ib'adiyya* lands;[69] and these usually constituted a small proportion of a village's arable area. For illustration, we look at Gharbiyya Province. In 1854, the total agricultural area of the peasant freeholder villages (referred to in the archival sources as "villages under the administration of the provincial bureaucracy," or in shorthand as the "province's villages"[70]) constituted about 404,985.5 *faddans*; only 11 percent of these constituted *ib'adiyya* land and accordingly incurred an increase in tax. The same applies to insolvent villages entrusted to the care of affluent individuals—most were high state officials who had become wealthy through government employment—known as *muta'ahhid*s and the peasant villages in their care as *uhda*s. It is to be recalled here that the change of category from freeholder village to *uhda* village did *not* bring with it a change from the *kharaji* tax category to the less onerous category referred to as *ushuriyya* (which generally pertained to elite-held lands); and so such insolvent lands remained *kharaji* lands while in the care of their *muta'ahhid*s. Of the *uhda* lands in Gharbiyya Province, 8 percent were *ib'adiyya*s, and it was these that underwent a tax increase (table 2.1).

On the other hand, the situation of the *jiflik* (or type of land grant made to members of the royal family) situated in Gharbiyya Province

Table 2.1: *Kharaji* Lands of Gharbiyya Province that Incurred Tax Increases: The First Stage of the 1855 Land-Tax Project

	Total *faddans*	*Faddans* that incurred tax increases		Proportion that is *ib'adiyya* land
		No.	%	%
Kharaji lands of freeholder villages	404,985.5	42,941.0	11	100
Kharaji lands of *uhda* villages	74,644.0	5,819.5	8	100
Kharaji lands of *jiflik* villages	10,858.0	2,677.0	25	69
Total	490,487.5	51,437.5	10	98

Notes:

(i) Computing the data for this table began by adding up the number of *faddans*, including all fractions of a *faddan* (facilitated by the table provided by Jirjis Hunayn, which specifies the meaning of the different symbols; see Hunayn, *Al-Atyan wa al-dara'ib*, 111–12). If the final sum included a fraction of a *faddan*, it was rounded accordingly:

- 17 *qirats*–23 *qirats*: rounded to 1 *faddan*
- 9 *qirats* < 17 *qirats*: rounded to half a *faddan*
- < 9 *qirats*: eliminated

(ii) The numbers pertaining to *faddan* areas (absolute numbers) in this table are slightly exaggerated; the reason for this lies in the difficulty in deciphering the different symbols. Despite my attempts to closely examine the different symbols, there must have been some misreading. In addition, there was another problem: there was one symbol (frequently used) that was not included in Hunayn's table; here I had to make an educated guess regarding its meaning. Nevertheless, I preferred this method (adding up the fractions, then rounding up only the final sum as explained above) rather than completely eliminating the fractions of a *faddan*, or turning each fraction into 1 *faddan*. I believe my method allowed for *less exaggeration of numbers.*

Sources: DMU, Daftar takmil al-dara'ib, rawdat al-bahrayn, 1271, 2209/109/22 (Part I).

(named Jiflik Sabat) was slightly different. This *jiflik* was composed of seven peasant villages; and at the time of its establishment, the grant recipient, Tusun Pasha (Said Pasha's son), decided to allow the peasant holders to remain on his estate as tenants, thereby allowing them to rent the land they had formerly held on a usfructuary basis.[71] The new tenure arrangement meant that the estate lands continued to be categorized as peasant land, which paid the *kharaj* tax, rather than elite-held land referred to as *ushuriyya* land because its taxes (*ushur*) were one-tenth of the harvest. As can be seen in table 2.1, a comparatively high proportion of this estate, 25 percent, experienced increases in tax. In six of the estate villages, the lands subjected to tax increases constituted *ib'adiyya*s, as occurred with the lands of the freeholder and *uhda* villages. That was not the case with the largest of the estate villages, called Dimira, composed of 3,119.5 *faddan*s: 36 percent of the agricultural area of Dimira incurred tax increases; however, of this area (that incurred tax increase) only 27 percent was *ib'adiyya* land while 73 percent was *ma'mur* land.[72] The tax-reassessment register does not explain why this exception was made, and in the absence of supporting evidence, we can only suggest that the irrigation infrastructure in this village had been greatly enhanced, leading to the improvement of the productive capacity of the surrounding *ma'mur* tracts. On the other hand, the evidence suggests that Tusun Pasha protested this decision, and may have argued that the tax increase did not reflect the productivity level of the land at issue, and so was too high. So it is probably for this reason that this same village (unlike others) enjoyed a very substantial tax decrease in the very next tax-reassessment exercise.

All in all, table 2.1 shows that this one exception did not modify one of the important features of this stage of the 1855 tax-reassessment project. Its focus was on *ib'adiyya* lands already under cultivation, which further meant that a rather small proportion of *kharaji* lands incurred tax increases.

Second, the new tax code generally stipulated very high rates of tax increase. Table 2.2 shows that 78 percent of the *kharaji-ib'adiyya* lands (of the freeholder, *uhda*, and *jiflik* villages) of Gharbiyya Province experienced increases in tax that ranged from 16 percent to a whopping 697 percent; the latter rate specified for a tract of 130 *faddan*s in Kafr al-Jarayda Village (a freeholder village.) A closer look at table 2.2 shows that a little more than half of the *kharaji-ib'adiyya* lands (52 percent) sustained extremely high tax increases that varied from 36 to 697 percent. In looking at the different components that made up the total area of *kharaji-ib'adiyya* lands, we see that this was true for the lands of freeholder villages (53 percent), and held true for the lands of the *uhda* villages (57 percent). In contrast, only 29 percent of the *kharaji* lands of Jiflik Sabat that were marked for tax increase[73] fell into this category of increase. This suggests that this estate was composed of some of the most fertile lands in the province that had already carried tax rates that reflected their high productive capacity—and hence a much smaller proportion of this land experienced such high tax increases. At the other end of the spectrum, tax increases of less than 1 percent were specified for only 0.3 percent of the *kharaji-ib'adiyya* area of Gharbiyya Province (table 2.2).

Table 2.2: Increases in the Tax Rates of the *Kharaji-ib'adiyya* Lands of Gharbiyya Province: The First Stage of the 1855 Land-Tax Project

Rate of increase	*Kharaji-ib'adiyya* lands of freeholder villages		*Kharaji-ib'adiyya* lands of *uhda* villages		*Kharaji* lands (marked for tax increase[a]) of *jiflik* villages		Total land	
%	*faddans*	%	*faddans*	%	*faddans*	%	*faddans*	%
< 1	18.0	0.04	130.5	2.24	—	—	148.5	0.29
1–5	1,377.5	3.21	612.0	10.52	—	—	1,989.5	3.87
6–15	7,679.0	17.88	1,001.0	17.20	424.5	15.86	9,104.5	17.70
16–25	7,557.5	17.60	499.0	8.58	1,067.0	39.86	9,123.5	17.74
26–35	3,516.5	8.19	338.0	5.81	407.0	15.20	4,261.5	8.28
36–50	4,421.0	10.30	735.5	12.64	202.0	7.55	5,358.5	10.42
51–99	5,890.5	13.72	1,090.0	18.73	341.5	12.76	7,322.0	14.23
100–199	9,743.0	22.69	639.0	10.98	—	—	10,382.0	20.18
200–299	1,563.0	3.64	464.0	7.97	—	—	2,027.0	3.94
300–399	305.5	0.71	293.5	5.04	235.0	8.78	834.0	1.62
400–499	572.0	1.33	8.0	0.14	—	—	580.0	1.13
500–599	56.0	0.13	—	—	—	—	56.0	0.11
600–697[b]	242.0	0.56	8.5	0.15	—	—	250.5	0.49
Total	42,941.5	100.00	5,819.0	100.00	2,677.0	100.00	51,437.5	100.00

Notes:

[a]The *jiflik* lands marked for tax increase consisted of both *ib'adiyya* (69%) and *ma'mur* land (31%).

[b]This (697%) was the highest rate of tax increase.

In computing the data for this table, I used the same method specified in the notes of table 2.1.

Source: DMU, Daftar takmil al-dara'ib, rawdat al-bahrayn, 1271, 2209/109/22 (Part I).

Finally, the tax revaluation effort in Gharbiyya Province produced an additional three results, which can be briefly summarized. One, the reassessment effort pertaining to the monetary system (that focused on the jadid denomination) was undertaken for 90 percent of the villages of this province; and here, the increases in tax were generally slight, ranging from several paras to 25 piastres (for an entire village.). Two, 6 percent of the peasant villages of this province did not experience any increase in their taxes. Three, the authorities had determined that 10 percent of the peasant villages had experienced some form of land ruination, and accordingly canceled some of the newly imposed taxes, which ultimately resulted in the remission of approximately 280.5 purses,[74] or 16 percent of the additional revenue that the new taxes were to generate from this province.[75]

In summation, the first of the tax-reassessment projects of the mid-nineteenth- century period, initiated by Abbas Pasha and completed by his successor Said Pasha, certainly aimed to increase government revenues. Yet the state was similarly concerned not to undermine the peasantry's economic viability, as is indicated by the project's focus on village *ib'adiyya* lands (which constituted a small proportion of peasant holdings), and its declared policy of adjusting rates so that they would equal (not exceed) the tax rates of the fertile *ma'mur* lands. Moreover, state interest in balancing the dual traditional economic precepts (revenue maximization, preservation of peasant economic capability) can be seen clearly in the official justification for the introduction of the new taxes. For the project supervisor had explained that the *ib'adiyya*s were originally barren lands, largely acquired by peasants during Muhammad Ali's reign and subsequently brought under the plow while carrying minimal taxes. By mid-century these reclamation efforts had greatly enhanced the *ib'adiyya*s' productive capacity, which meant that the original rates of tax no longer reflected real productivity levels. In short, the government terminated the "tax holiday" enjoyed by the holders of these *ib'adiyya*s because the productive capacity of the soil had improved and thereby generated higher profits.

The 1855 Land-Tax Code: Part Two

Upon the completion of the first stage of the 1855 land-tax project, which had focused on the reassessment of the taxes of village *ib'adiyya*s, the authorities specified the additional sum required of each village in taxes as well as the additional total required of each province. For Gharbiyya Province this additional sum amounted to 1,454 purses, 283 piastres, 17 para.[76] On December 26, 1855, the Viceregal Cabinet issued Decree No. 37, which specified that the payment of the revised tax sums would retroactively start from September 1854 (the beginning of the 1855 fiscal year).[77]

At the time of the preparation of this decree, the government had intended to introduce it for the purpose of specifying tax increases for *ib'adiyya* lands only. But when it actually introduced Decree No. 37, the original instructions had been modified, now specifying new taxes for the entire arable area of a village, both the *ib'adiyya* and the *ma'mur* lands. The modified instructions were generated by the second stage of the 1855 land-tax project.[78]

So how did the 1855 tax-revaluation project come to have a second stage? After the task of revising the *ib'adiyya* taxes for Gharbiyya Province had been completed, the central government ordered "the heads of districts, inspectors, *uhda* representatives, and village shaykhs and tax collectors" to convene at the seat of the provincial government in order to submit their registers, which detailed the results for each "district . . . and village . . . and the villages in *uhda* and [the villages] of Jiflik Sabat." These registers were sent to the Viceregal Cabinet for careful inspection, which was duly completed. "And after the writing up of the [province's tax-reassessment] register, the tax-reassessment file of Nisf-awal Batra Village, which was late, arrived." Upon its arrival, the authorities examined the rates specified for the various grades of the village's arable land—that is, both the *ib'adiyya* and *ma'mur* land—and found that some of these were inappropriate. This led to the decision to similarly examine the tax registers of all the villages of the province. "And because of this [a new tax-reassessment register for Gharbiyya Province] was composed." This rewriting included the specification of revised tax rates for the entirety of the arable area of each village of this province.[79]

This official account of the second stage of the 1855 land-tax project aside, we should not forget that this decision to increase the taxes of all the *kharaji* lands was made at the beginning of Said Pasha's reign—when he was afire with grandiose ambitions for the development and modernization of Egypt, all of which necessitated large sums of money. This most certainly contributed to the governmental decision to reassess, which generally involved increasing, village land taxes.

So what was the outcome of this second round of assessment? The results are specified in table 2.3, and are based on a sample that comprised 79 percent of the *kharaji* lands of Gharbiyya Province during 1854–1855.[80] To begin, the bulk of the *kharaji* lands experienced tax increase: this was the case with 98.28 percent of the sample lands. Also, the bulk of these lands incurred very high tax increases. This is confirmed by our sample, which shows that 98.04 percent of these lands experienced tax increases that ranged from 16 percent to the incredible 1,055 percent. At the other end of the spectrum, a very small, actually a miniscule, proportion of lands enjoyed a decrease in their taxes: only 0.45 percent of the sample lands enjoyed this scenario; although in one case, the *jiflik* village of Dimira, the decrease was a hefty 64 percent for a tract of 215 *faddans*.[81] And finally, a small proportion of lands did not undergo any change in their land taxes; this pertained to 1.27 percent of our sample.

Table 2.3: Tax-rate changes specified by the Second Stage of the 1855 Land-Tax Project for the *Kharaji* Lands of Gharbiyya Province[a]

Rate of change	*Kharaji* land of freeholder villages		*Kharaji* land of *uhda* villages		*Kharaji* land of *jiflik* villages		
%	M[c]	I[d]	M	I	M	I	Total land
I No change	4,820.0	—	—	—	—	93.0	4,913.0
II Rate of decrease[b]							
< 1–4	1,124.5	—	410.0	—	—	—	1534.5
28–30	3.5	—	10.0	—	—	—	13.5
48–64	—	—	—	—	215	—	215.0
III Rate of increase[b]							
< 1	—	—	—	—	—	235.0	235.0
1–5	138.0	—	—	—	—	—	138.0
6–15	521.5	—	—	—	—	15.0	536.5
16–25	45,438.0	561.0	3,539.0	—	—	287.5	49,825.5
26–35	65,962.0	2,302.0	23,126.0	26.0	8,542	93.0	10,0051.0
36–50	149,715.5	793.0	21,124.5	184.0	—	19.0	171,837.0
51–99	34,007.5	10,092.5	2,398.0	444.0	254	1,073.5	48,269.5
100–199	541.0	3,742.0	—	852.5	—	30.5	5,166.0
200–299	53.0	1,262.0	—	52.0	—	—	1,367.0
300–399	2,027.0	609.5	—	11.0	—	—	2,647.5
400–499	—	295.5	—	52.0	—	—	347.5
500–599	—	112.0	—	—	—	—	112.0
600–699	—	355.0	—	—	—	—	355.0
700–799	—	104.5	—	—	—	—	104.5
800–899	—	36.0	—	2.5	—	—	38.5
900–999	—	27.5	—	—	—	—	27.5
1,055	—	130.0	—	—	—	—	130.0
Total land	304,351.5	20,422.5	50,608.5	1,624.0	9,011	1,846.5	387,864.0

Notes:

[a]The data for this table were based on a large sample: specifically, this sample comprises approximately 79% of the *kharaji* lands of Gharbiyya Province in AH 1271, or 1854–1855. In computing the data, I used the same method specified in the notes of table 2.1.

[b]These unconventional categories best reflect the rates by which these lands experienced tax decreases/increases.

[c]M: refers to the number of *faddans* of *ma'mur* land.

[d]I: refers to the number of *faddans* of *ib'adiyya* land.

Source: DMU, Daftar takmil al-dara'ib, rawdat al-bahrayn, 1271, 2209/109/22 (Part II).

Unlike part one of the 1855 tax-reassessment register, which specified how the authorities determined the new rates for the *ib'adiyya* lands, the second part of this register does not inform us how the tax officials determined the new rates of tax that were to be imposed on the *kharaji* lands (both *ma'mur* and *ib'adiyya* lands) during the second round of tax reassessment. Nevertheless, a close reading of the sources allows for some suggestions. Let us begin with the *ma'mur* lands. In determining the new tax rates for lands already under the plow, tax officials probably depended on certain criteria common to any agrarian-based society. In Egypt, these were likely to have been set and developed centuries ago: whether the land had been cleared and leveled,[82] its quality, the distance between it and the Nile River, and the kinds of crops it produced.[83] Another factor was certainly added to this list in the early decades of Muhammad Ali's reign with the conversion from basin to perennial irrigation: the quality and extensiveness of the irrigation system that fed the land.

The reassessment of the *ib'adiyya* taxes was much simpler the second time around. The tax officials began by examining the results of the first stage of the 1855 tax project, or the revised *ib'adiyya* taxes (that corresponded with the 1854 rates of the nearby *ma'mur* lands.) These *ib'adiyya*s had transformed into *ma'mur* lands; and as such, they were subjected to a second round of tax increases, the same tax increases as were imposed on other village *ma'mur* lands. Thus, the revised tax rates specified by the 1855 land-tax code for the village *ib'adiyya* lands constituted the result of two reassessment processes, each process reflecting a stage of the 1855 tax-revaluation project.[84] It is for this reason that most of the *ib'adiyya* lands incurred much higher tax increases (these capped at 1,055 percent) than were experienced by the *ma'mur* lands, which capped at the much lower 319 percent (see table 2.3).

The 1855 tax-reassessment register hints at another factor that contributed to the determination of the new tax rates: the peasant holders. The smallholders of Kitama and Sirbay Villages (of Gharbiyya Province) complained to the Viceregal Cabinet about the inappropriateness of the revised rates specified for two land tracts: the 279-*faddan* tract and the 489-*faddan* tract situated in their villages, respectively. They claimed that the tax officials had mistakenly designated the tracts as *ib'adiyya*s; and as they "confirm that these are *ma'mur* . . . they complain about the unjustness of the tax increases." In turn, the council ordered an investigation into the matter, which began by "requesting the [villages'] cadastral registers." In the meantime, the government delayed the imposition of the problematic tax increases.[85] The tax-reassessment register does not reveal the outcome of the investigation, but it does state that the imposition of the disputed taxes was contingent on the villagers' voluntary acceptance of the idea.[86] By this, the state was most certainly *not* seeking approval for the introduction of new taxes; rather it merely wanted to ensure that the government officials had performed the tax-revision tasks properly.

The 1855 Land-Tax Code: The Reality

Upon the completion of the second round of tax reassessment, the authorities had thereby finished the final version of the 1855 land-tax code. By this code, Gharbiyya Province was henceforth to pay 1,452 purses, 300 piastres, 26 para more than it had in 1854.[87]

This amount was 0.1 percent *less* than the sums specified by the first stage of this tax project—a puzzling result if we bear in mind that the first stage focused only on village *ib'adiyya*s, while the final stage focused on the entire arable area (both *ma'mur* and *ib'adiyya* lands) of peasant villages.

To unravel this enigma, let us start by comparing the final statements or results of the two stages of the 1855 tax-reassessment project. To begin, the statements were identical in several respects. First, both specified the same amount in additional taxes for the very same villages; this was true for 72 percent of the peasant villages of Gharbiyya Province. Second, both specified the remission of the same tax sums for the same villages. Three, both instructed the villages of Kitama and Sirbay to pay taxes at the 1854 rates while their complaints were being investigated.[88]

At the same time, the second round of reassessment generated some discrepancies. One, twenty-nine villages were eliminated from the statement for the second stage of the project because these were no longer part of Gharbiyya Province, but had become part of the province of Munifiyya after provincial boundaries had changed. Two, the villages of Jiflik Sabat were to pay an additional one-fifth of their 1855 *ib'adiyya* taxes. Three, the authorities finally obtained the tax-reassessment register of Nisf-awal Batra Village, and included its revised taxes in the second statement. Four, government officials discerned slight mistakes in the tax calculations for 28 percent of the villages of Gharbiyya Province during the first stage of the tax project, and rectified these in the second stage.[89]

This comparison of the results of the two stages of the 1855 tax-revaluation project suggests that the tax officials had worked hard to ensure that the results for each stage coincided as closely as was possible. For illustration, we look at Mit al-Harun Village. For the first stage of the 1855 project, tax revaluation had been restricted to village *ib'adiyya*s, which constituted 2 percent of the village's agricultural area. Here, the tax increases ranged from 5 to 17 percent, and generated a total land-tax increase of 65 piastres, 2 para. Also, currency reassessment produced another 10 piastres, 22 para in taxes. Thus, by these calculations, Mit al-Harun's taxes were to increase by a total of 75 piastres, 24 para, starting in 1855. Next, the second stage of the 1855 project specified the exact same increase in total taxes for this village, even though the second round of revaluation efforts had covered the entire village agricultural area and specified tax increases that went from 36 to 41 percent for the *ma'mur* lands while *ib'adiyya* taxes (for the two *ibadiyya* tracts) increased by 50 and 66 percent.[90]

As can be seen, the results of the second stage of the 1855 tax project consisted of the puzzling combination of high increases in the rates of tax for the agricultural lands of Mit al-Harun, and on the other hand, very small increases in the total sum of taxes due from this village. The explanation for this resides in the surcharge taxes; at the time, these were three. One was the "*dum al-ghirsh nisfayn*," commonly referred to as "*al-dum*," by which the government collected an additional 5 percent of the land's taxes.[91] The second one was called the "*suds*," meaning one-sixth, and generally consisted of an additional 17 percent of the land's taxes. Yet this proportion could vary between villages, perhaps in accordance with the quality of soil: for Sandbast Village, where soil quality was high, this tax constituted 21 percent; however, for al-Jazira al-Khadra, which contained large chunks of waste land, this tax constituted 14 percent of the land taxes.[92] Finally, there was the *wirku al-atyan* tax—a kind of counterpart to the tax imposed on artisans called *wirku al-karat*—which entailed the payment of a certain number of piastres for every *faddan* that was probably determined by land quality.[93]

The government had required the peasants to pay these surcharge taxes in 1854; and accordingly the tax officials included these taxes in the calculations relating to the first stage of the 1855 tax revaluation project. These, however, had been suspended by the time work on the second stage of the tax project had started.[94] We should recall that work on the second stage had begun under the auspices of the new, reformist viceroy, Said Pasha. European contemporary observers reported that his reform efforts that targeted rural society had entailed ameliorating the peasants' tax

Table 2.4: Increases in the Total Tax Sums of the Villages of Gharbiyya Province: The 1855 Land-Tax Code

Rate of increase	Villages	
%	No.	%
No change	6	1.6
< 1	241	64.1
1–5	83	22.1
6–10	23	6.1
11–15	10	2.7
16–25	10	2.7
30–45	2	0.3
64[a]	1	0.3
Total	376	100.0

Note:

[a]This was the highest rate by which the total tax sums increased in this province.

Source: DMU, Daftar takmil al-dara'ib, rawdat al-bahrayn, 1271, 2209/109/22 (Parts I, II).

burden: tax arrears were forgiven, and various octrois and customs duties imposed on local commercial exchanges were abolished.[95] Another reform, apparently missed or misunderstood by contemporary observers, was the decision (made in the very early months of his reign) to abolish these surcharge taxes.[96]

This abolishment offset the effect of the high tax increases specified by the second stage of the 1855 tax project, and further meant that the total sum in land taxes specified for a village was only a little higher than that of 1854. This was the case for the overwhelming majority of the villages of Gharbiyya Province (table 2.4). This allows us to conclude that the tax increases specified by the new tax code for village landholders were hardly onerous.

As was stated above, the government completed the 1855 land-tax code in December of that year; then it introduced this new code in January 1856, when it specified the payment schedule for the new taxes. Briefly, payment was to begin in 1855, which really meant that the tax increases for that year were to be paid retroactively between January and July 1856.[97] These instructions meant that approximately 64 percent of the villages of Gharbiyya were to make tax payments that were slightly higher than those they had made in 1854: for the increase in these villages' total taxes amounted to less than 1 percent. Another 1.6 percent of villages did not experience any land-tax increases (table 2.4). Thus, these instructions probably did not trigger much peasant grumbling.

But the instructions of the next few months most likely did. By the decree of June 11, 1856, the government ordered the reimposition of the *suds* surcharge tax, which generally entailed the payment of an additional 17 percent of the land's taxes; and it was to be effective beginning September 1855—an additional retroactive payment.[98] Then on October 7 of the same year (1856), the government reinstated the *wirku al-atyan*—another surcharge tax that entailed the imposition of a certain number of piastres on each *faddan* of the village arable area—and then on January 12, 1858, reassessed its rate or level, with the likely result of increasing it.[99]

While the above instructions applied to all holders of *kharaji* lands, the holders of village *masmuh* lands were expected to abide by additional ones. There were two types of *masmuh* lands. The *masmuh al-mashayikh* consisted of tax-free lands that the government conferred on the village shaykhs in compensation for performing various official duties. According to Kenneth Cuno, the government modified this system after the 1819–1820 cadastral survey, and from 1821, turned the *masmuh al-mashayikh* into cash payments or tax credit—which meant that these lands were no longer tax-exempt.[100] On the other hand, the village land-tax registers show that some years later, certainly by mid-century, the government had reinstated the original form of the *masmuh al-mashayikh* system. The AH 1264 1847–1848 land-tax register of al-Jazira al-Khadra Village, situated in Gharbiyya Province, provides illustration. Shaykh Yusuf Marʿi, whose authority extended over "half the village," possessed a landholding of approximately 113.5 *faddans*; and of these, about 15 *faddans* were categorized by the land-tax register as *tanzil masmuh*, or deducted for *masmuh*, meaning that these lands were tax-exempt. Accordingly the government expected this shaykh to pay taxes on 98.5 *faddans*, as 13 percent of his holding was specified as *masmuh*, and so was tax-free.[101]

The other type of *masmuh* lands were referred to as *masmuh al-masatib*. These were granted to shaykhs or other prominent village elders in compensation for the provision of hospitality to travelers, and unlike the *masmuh al-mashayikh*, were not established in every village.[102] Cuno states that "only a certain amount of *masmuh al-masatib* remained untaxed" after

1821,[103] which implies that most holders of these lands henceforth received money payments for their services. However, several entries in the registers of the Viceregal Cabinet show the following for the mid-century years: in the Delta area, the *masmuh al-masatib* generally consisted of tax-exempted lands; in Upper Egypt, the *masmuh al-masatib* were based on cash payments rather than tax-free lands; in 1856 the central government insisted that the villages of Upper Egypt convert to the system of Lower Egypt.[104] Senior officials in Upper Egypt tried to contest this decision, explaining to their counterparts in the central government that the system of money payments was more suitable for their region, basically citing these reasons: one, "the *masatib* holders are unaccustomed to farming, so they would take the land and give it to others"; and two, "the cash payments [customarily] were not made until it was ascertained that the *masatib* services were dispensed, that the *mastaba* holder was identified and whether he was alive or dead . . . but if the *masatib* are based on land, the government will be unable to verify the aforementioned."[105] These arguments fell on deaf ears, though, for the central government roundly dismissed them, stating that *masmuh* lands are generally given to village "umdas and shaykhs whose livelihood is farming"; and two, when local officials passed through villages they were to ascertain "whether *mastaba* services were dispensed and whether holders were alive or dead." That the central government ended its instructions by declaring that henceforth all *masatib* in Upper Egypt were to be based on "land, not cash, as is prevalent in Lower Egypt,"[106] might be partly attributed to its interest in advancing standardization and uniformity in the countryside and partly to its determined insensitivity to the needs of Upper Egypt.[107]

This decision remained operative for approximately one year. In September 1857, the government abolished the entire *masmuh* system and specified that the lands were to be taxed at the highest rate in the village,[108] probably because the central authorities realized that the rural notables had chosen their *masmuh* from among the most fertile lands in the village. While the rural notables most certainly resented this decision, their dissatisfaction probably faded when the government awarded them usufructuary rights to their former *masmuh* lands in June 1858, thereby making these their permanent holdings.[109]

The 1858 Land-Tax Code

At the time of the abolishment of the *masmuh* privileges in the fall of 1857, senior government officials were preparing to reassess *kharaji* land taxes yet again; as their recent efforts to increase revenues generated sums that were too small for the state's many needs—which varied from the important and beneficial, like the maintenance and enhancement of the country's irrigation system, to the unnecessarily expensive, like the construction and decoration of royal palaces. Especially pressing in 1856 and 1857 was the part the viceroy of Egypt had been forced to play in the Ottoman loans of the 1850s; specifically the Sublime Porte had ordered Said Pasha to make some payments on its behalf.[110] It seems that these were somewhat burdensome. In September 1856, the British consul general reported that "such is the financial condition of Said Pasha's govt. that he has neglected to furnish the funds necessary to meet the dividends on the Turkish loan, payable October, and is obliged to borrow the amount from the mercantile houses of this place."[111] In February of the next year, Bruce reported that "the subject of the delay in the remittance to the Bank of England of the sums necessary to meet the dividends and sinking fund payable on the Turkish loans" continued to figure prominently in discussions on Egypt's financial problems.[112]

Among the strategies developed by the government to address its shortage of funds was the issuance of Decree No. 4 of September 17, 1857, here announcing that the *kharaji* land taxes would be reassessed fairly and justly, "so that each one will take his due, meaning the peasants and the government."[113] In other words, the writers of this decree felt the need to confirm the continued adherence to the basic economic tenets of the traditional philosophy of statecraft; and accordingly that the government intended to increase revenues while protecting the peasant's productive capabilities. This need to allude to these traditional notions may be partly explained by the timing of the new tax project: that less than two years had passed since the introduction of the 1855 tax code—not to mention the reinstatement of the surcharge taxes that had followed soon after—was certainly suggestive of official disinterest in the welfare of the subject-base, and by implication, the principles of traditional and legitimate government.

Acting on this decree, the governor of Rawdat al-Bahrayn (by that time, parts of Gharbiyya Province had been integrated with parts of Munifiyya Province, and renamed Rawdat al-Bahrayn) convened with the village shaykhs and umdas to examine the land taxes. This meeting enabled him to reappraise the land tax-rates effectively: the pertinent register makes clear that he took the rural notables' expertise into consideration, for it states that the new taxes were based on their "knowledge of the lands and what they considered to be appropriate tax rates." Shortly after, the governor received new instructions that urged him "to be even more meticulous in the reassessment of the taxes in order to prevent complaint." This led him to revise some of his work, which in turn led him to decrease the sum specified by his earlier reassessment effort by approximately 9,000 piastres.[114]

At this point, it seems that Cairo replaced the incumbent governor with another, and put this latter official in charge of the new tax project. And like the former governor, he consulted with all the provincial officials involved in this effort, asking them whether they believed the revised rates specified by his predecessor were "appropriate or not and if these would be problematic for the peasants or the government." Most confirmed his work, as did the new governor.[115] This meant there were only a few cases of dissension. Two umdas from al-Zifta District refused to approve the proposed tax rates for certain land tracts situated in four villages in their district, and instead declared their preference for the former (lower) rates. The new governor accepted their view, "for the purpose of ensuring that their [that is, the villages'] peasants do not experience ruination." Also, a landholder from al-Mahalla al-Kubra Village, who had earlier petitioned for the decrease of the rate imposed on 109.5 *faddan*s of his holding by 10 piastres, was granted his request by the new governor when the latter learned that it had already been officially approved (in January 1858).[116] Finally, the headmen of Kafr al-Batikh Village also took this opportunity to complain that their land taxes were too high: they pointed out that the tax rate imposed on their lands was "above 100 piastres *before* the recent [tax] increase."[117]

When these meetings and consultations had ended, certain issues remained outstanding. In response to the complaint put by the Kafr al-Batikh headmen, the new governor wanted to know if this high rate was the result of combining the *wariku al-atyan* surcharge tax with the original rate imposed on the land; finally terminating this discussion by requesting a report on this village. In addition, this report was to identify all other villages in this same situation, as well as to provide a more detailed explanation of the former governor's recommendation to deduct 9,000 piastres from the total tax sum specified for this province. That the final settlement of these matters was postponed did not prevent the central government from issuing Decree No. 37 of April 30, 1858, by which it introduced the 1858 land-tax code.[118]

The new tax rates specified by this code generally were much higher than the original ones. For illustration, we look at our sample of *kharaji* lands (which consists of approximately 75 percent of the *kharaji* lands of

Table 2.5: Tax-rate changes specified for the *Kharaji* Lands of Rawdat al-Bahrayn Province: The 1858 Tax Code[a]

Rate of change	*Kharaji* land of freeholder villages	*Kharaji* land of *uhda* villages	*Kharaji* land of *jiflik* villages	Total lands
%	*no. of faddans*	*no. of faddans*	*no. of faddans*	*no. of faddans*
I No change	8,013.0	679.0	25.0	8,717.0
II Rate of decrease				
<1	24,771.5	3,502.0	—	28,273.5
1–10	24,023.0	2,315.0	—	26,338.0
11–20	530.0	8.0	—	538.0
21–30	1,062.0	—	—	1,062.0
31–39	437.5	—	—	437.5
III Rate of increase				
<1	10,215.0	368.5	5,748.5	16,332.0
1–5	50,922.0	11,741.0	1,563.5	64,226.5
6–15	98,634.0	25,566.0	1,406.0	125,606.0
16–25	46,612.0	1,060.5	725.5	48,398.0
26–35	25,168.0	2,893.0	451.0	28,512.0
36–50	18,157.5	1,558.5	488.0	20,204.0
51–99	17,531.5	511.0	—	18,042.5
100–199	2,726.0	43.0	308.0	3,077.0
200–242[b]	94.0	—	142.0	236.0
Total land	328,897.0	50,245.5	10,857.5	390,000.0

Notes:

[a]The tax-reassessment register of AH 1274 (1857–1858) categorizes all *kharaji* lands as *ma'mur*.

[b]This (242%) was the highest rate by which *kharaji* land taxes increased in this province.

In computing the data presented by this table, I employed the method described in the notes of table 2.1.

Source: DMU, Daftar takmil al-dara'ib, rawdat al-bahrayn, 1274, 2210/109/22.

Rawdat al-Bahrayn Province). Of these, 62.6 percent experienced high tax increases that varied from 6 percent to a very high 242 percent. On the other hand, a rather large proportion of the lands (20.9 percent) were treated comparatively gently by the new code: 2.2 percent of the lands maintained their original tax rates; 14.5 percent experienced a taxation decrease—which in some cases was quite substantial, ranging between 20 and 39 percent; and finally, 4.2 percent experienced a minimal tax increase of less than 1 percent (table 2.5).

For the most part, then, it seems that most peasant villages endured substantial increases in their land-taxes. This was the case for the villages of Rawdat al-Bahrayn Province, as a little more than half (51.5 percent) saw the total sum in taxes allotted to their villages rise by rates that varied from 6 to 124 percent.[119]

In reality, the results of 1858 tax code were probably more onerous than is suggested by these figures, simply because the new rates most probably did not reflect the productive capacity of most of the lands, but were too high. This can be attributed to the decision of the tax authorities to begin the process of tax revaluation by integrating several grades of arable land into one. The village of Sharanis provides illustration. In 1855, the agricultural area of Sharanis Village was composed of six different grades of land. Our concern here is with four of these, all located in the same basin: the first grade comprised 68 *faddan*s and was taxed at 81 piastres, 17 para per *faddan*; the second comprised 136 *faddan*s and carried a tax of 80 piastres, 2 para per *faddan*; the third, 5 *faddan*s that bore a tax of 69 piastres, 1 para per *faddan*; and the fourth, 90.5 *faddan*s that were taxed at 66 piastres, 11 para per *faddan*. The 1858 tax code integrated these four land grades into one, which thereby consisted of 299.5 *faddan*s and carried a tax rate of 85 piastres per *faddan*.[120] This new rate was probably most reflective of the productive capacity of only one of the original land grades—the superior land grade, which pertained only to the 68-*faddan* tract. And as this tract constituted the best in its basin, the surrounding (inferior) lands—of which this basin was largely composed—were given the same tax rate despite their inferior quality, making the new rate doubly onerous for these lands.

This was not the first time the government had adopted this method for the reassessment of land taxes. As shown above, during the first stage of the 1855 tax project, the tax officials partly relied on this strategy to align the original tax rates of the *ib'adiyya* lands with those of the *ma'mur* lands. While the government could justify the earlier use of this method by confidently stating that the productive capacity of arable lands had vastly improved since the reign of Muhammad Ali, it could not—and did not—make any such claim in 1858. For the improvement in land fertility and productivity realized between 1855 and 1858 by no means matched or outstripped that which had occurred between the 1830s and 1855. Yet the government seemed to ignore this fine detail, prompted by the need for higher revenue, and subjected much more land to this method in 1858 than it had in 1855.

State revenue needs did not diminish in the 1860s; and so on July 17, 1861, the government reimposed the *al-dum* surcharge tax of 5 percent on *kharaji* lands.[121] By this decision, all the surcharge taxes that had been in existence in 1854 (prior to the introduction of the tax codes of the mid-nineteenth century) had been reinstated, making the peasants fully cognizant of the extent their land taxes had increased since that year.

The 1862 Land-Tax Code

It was at this time (summer 1861) that Said Pasha approached European banks about the possibility of another loan. By the first European loan, raised for him by the Comptoir d'Escompte and the Charles Lafitte et Cie, the viceroy received a nominal sum of 28 million francs, collecting the first installment in September 1860; its terms had further required him to refrain from issuing Treasury bonds to meet government obligations. But old habits predominated, and by the summer of the following year the floating debt was estimated to have been between 7,000,000 and 10,000,000 sterling pounds. Moreover, governmental overspending created a rather unmanageable budgetary deficit of 3,000,000 sterling pounds. This financial morass necessitated another loan. Thus, in 1862 Said Pasha concluded an agreement with the House of Oppenheim and Nephew of Alexandria, whereby he was to borrow 3,292,800 sterling pounds, which would be repaid over thirty years at 262,735 sterling pounds per year.[122] To guarantee the new loan, Said had put up the revenues of the Delta as collateral.[123] It was probably at this stage of his negotiations with the European bankers that Said thought to issue instructions to his government to introduce a new increase in *kharaji* land taxes.

The urgency of this matter did not allow government officials enough time to develop a set of guidelines for the reassessment of the land taxes. As was shown above, the work on the earlier tax codes had resulted in different tax-rate changes for different land tracts, which indicates that the concerned officials had given some thought to the diverse circumstances of the different villages in the province and how best to deal with these. On the other hand, the 1862 tax code issued strikingly simple instructions that seemed to completely overlook difference and diversity: it simply stipulated a uniform tax increase of 5 percent for all *kharaji* lands that was to take effect at the start of the fiscal year of 1862. That these succinct instructions did not necessitate the compilation of detailed records that would have documented the results of the implementation of the new code may explain why I could not find an "1862 tax-reassessment register" among the archival collections housed in the Dar al-Mahfuzat. What I mean to say is that such a register probably does not exist.

Indeed, I had discerned the 1862 land-tax increase when investigating the extent of economic stratification in villages, which had necessitated examining a different set of archival sources, the village land-tax registers. After discovering that the village of Ibyar had experienced an increase in its land taxes in 1862, I proceeded to examine the land-tax registers of seven additional villages, all situated in the same province, Rawdat al-Bahrayn. While this sample is admittedly small, it is fairly representative of the villages of this province. It includes villages composed of high-grade lands, such as Ibyar Village; villages that contained both good and marginal lands, like al-Jazira al-Khadra; and villages, like Kafr al-Jarayda, that were basically made up of low-grade lands. Table 2.6 shows that all the tracts—no matter what their land grade—of each of the sample villages incurred a uniform tax increase of 5 percent in 1862. In comparison with the impositions of the previous tax codes of the mid-nineteenth-century years, this one was relatively mild.

By the end of Said's reign of approximately 7.5 years, *kharaji* land taxes had increased by enormous proportions since the time of his predecessor, who, it should be remembered, only started a tax-reassessment project but did not complete it (and thus the tax rates imposed on *kharaji* lands did not increase during Abbas Pasha's reign).[124] To get an idea of the extent of these tax increases, we start by remembering that at the beginning of Said's reign in July 1854, the three major surcharge taxes (the *dum*, *suds*, and *wirku al-atyan*) were in place. These were abolished in the early months of his reign, maybe the fall of 1854. Such abolishment largely offset the increases in tax rates specified by the 1855 land-tax code and further meant that the peasants' land-tax burden did not change much, becoming only slightly heavier. This began to change in 1856, when the government reinstated two surcharge taxes (the *suds* and *wirku al-atyan*). Thus, for the next four years, peasants had to cope with a large part of the surcharge tax regimen in combination with the land-tax increases specified by the 1855 and 1858 tax codes—making this a time when peasants' tax load increased significantly. The last two years of Said's reign (he died in January 1863) saw additional land-tax increases: in July 1861 the government reimposed the last of the major surcharge taxes, the *dum*, and in the following year (1862) introduced the final land-tax code of the mid-nineteenth-century period.

Table 2.6: Rate of Increase in Land Taxes of Eight Peasant Villages in Rawdat al-Bahrayn Province: The 1862 Tax Code[a]

Village	Land tracts[b] (as specified by 1861 tax register)	1861 tax rate	1862 tax rate	Rate of increase
	no. of faddans[c]	*paras*	*paras*	%
Mahallit Abu Ali al-Gharbiyya	680.0	3,600	3,780	5
	358.0	3,120	3,276	5
	100.0	2,800	2,940	5
Al-Hayatim	2,463.0	3,400	3,570	5
	1,566.0	2,800	2,940	5
Al-Jazira al-Khadra	404.5	3,200	3,360	5
	51.5	3,300	3,465	5
	663.0	3,000	3,150	5
	146.5	3,240	3,402	5
Kafr al-Jarayda	490.0	3,000	3,150	5
	802.5	2,040	2,142	5
	211.0	1,660	1,743	5
Al-Qini wa Bani Bakr	781.0	3,440	3,612	5
	208.0	3,000	3,150	5
Ibyar[d]	3,711.0	3,954	4,152	5
	74.0	3,733	3,920	5
	322.5	3,622	3,804	5
Kafr al-Rajallat	650.5	3,320	3,486	5
Jazirat al-A'jam	63.0	3,000	3,150	5
	376.0	2,600	2,730	5

Notes:

[a] This table specifies the 1861 and 1862 tax rates in the para denomination, rather than in the combined piaster and para denominations (which was how tax rates were usually specified in the sources). When converting the tax rates into paras and calculating the proportion of increase, the result was a uniform 5 percent increase for all the land tracts of the eight sample villages. Yet, when examining the tax rates in the combined piastre and para form and calculating the proportion of tax increase in 1862, the results varied between 4.3 and 5.0 percent; more importantly, no clear pattern or reason for the differences in the rate of increase could be discerned. Based on this, I lean toward the idea that the village tax accountants (*sarrafin*) converted the tax rates into paras and raised taxes by a uniform 5 percent in 1862.

(*continued*)

[b] The village land-tax registers distinguish between the different land tracts (composed of different land grades) by two criteria: number of *faddans*; tax rate. This table does the same.

[c] These numbers were rounded by the same method described in table 2.1.

[d] The figures in the first and second columns for this village are based on the 1860 land-tax register (rather than the 1861 register), as the 1861 register could not be found on the archive shelves. Here, two additional points must be mentioned: (i) Based on my examination of the land-tax registers of the other sample villages, I maintain that the 1860 and 1861 land-tax rates for Ibyar Village were the same, which is why I relied on the 1860 register when I could not locate the 1861 register. (ii) The total registered area of Ibyar Village in 1860 constituted 4,149.5 *faddans*, yet this table specifies only 4,107.5 *faddans* for this village, less 42 *faddans*. These were omitted from this table because they constituted *ziyada* lands, which did not carry the *kharajiyya* tax rates.

Sources: DMU, Mukallafat atyan, mahallit abu ali al-gharbiyya, 1277–8, 22080–1/361/22; DMU, Mukallafat atyan, al-hayatim, 1277–8, 7202–3/176/22; DMU, Mukallafat atyan, al-jazira al-khadra, 1277–8, 3988–9/135/22; DMU, Mukallafat atyan, kafr al-jarayda, 1277–8, 17008–9/305/22; DMU, Mukallafat atyan, al-qini wa bani bakar, 1277–8, 6255–6/164/22; DMU, Mukallafat atyan, ibyar, 1276, 2922/121/22; DMU, Mukallafat atyan, ibyar, 1278, 2924/121/22; DMU, Mukallafat atyan, kafr al-rajallat, 1277–8, 8211–2/110/20; DMU, Mukallafat atyan, jazirat al-aʿjam, 1277–8, 4579–80/61/20.

That the major surcharge taxes were operative both at the start and the end of Said's reign means that the three land-tax codes of the period had a tremendous impact on peasant landholders, for this meant that they were fully cognizant of the massive proportions by which land tax-rates had increased between 1854 and 1862. This is illustrated by table 2.7, which shows, for example, that the tax rate imposed on a tract of 212 *faddans* of *ma'mur* land (situated in Kafr al-Jarayda Village) increased by 85 percent over this period. Again, the tax rate of a land tract of 130 *faddans*, originally denoted as *ib'adiyya* in 1854 and then designated as ma'mur in 1855, increased by a stupefying 1,167 percent.

Other Rural Taxes

The government of Egypt imposed a host of additional taxes on the rural population during the middle decades of the nineteenth century. The thinking of the ruling elite on this issue may have been influenced by ideas from both the Western capitals and Constantinople.

Western views on taxation during the seventeenth and eighteenth centuries included mention of the role of laboring groups. In Brandenburg-Prussia taxation was shaped by mercantilistic-cameralistic ideas, which

Table 2.7: Increase in Land-Tax Rates between 1854 and 1862: Kafr al-Jarayda Village

Land tracts[a] in 1854	Category of peasant land in 1854	Rate of increase between 1854 and 1862
no. of faddans[b]	*ma'mur or ib'adiyya*	%
22	*ma'mur*	53
169	*ma'mur*	59
33	*ma'mur*	74
212	*ma'mur*	85
6	*ma'mur*	40
12.5	*ma'mur*	60
636	*ib'adiyya*	303
24	*ib'adiyya*	491
130	*ib'adiyya*	1,167

Notes:

[a]The village land-tax registers distinguish between the different land tracts by relying on two criteria: number of *faddans* and tax rates. In this table, I rely only on the first criterion.

[b]These numbers refer only to the taxed lands of this village. They were rounded according to the method described in table 2.1.

Sources: DMU, Daftar takmil al-dara'ib, rawdat al-bahrayn, 1271, 2209/109/22, fol. 28 (Part I); DMU, Mukallafat atyan, kafr al-jarayda, 1278, 17009/305/22.

meant that the "tax systems were designed for the benefit of an absolutistic state; it was a forced saving in the case for an absolutistic governmental, military, administrative, and police machinery, with the aim of shaping and maintaining the socioeconomic structure in the right and 'just' proportion." In this scheme of things, the laboring groups shouldered a heavy part of the tax burden that was justified by the need to preserve the social order and prevent "the lower order from becoming idle, disobedient and demanding."[125] In Britain during the mid-seventeenth century, the Long Parliament ended the Elizabethan and Stuart tradition of exempting the poor groups of society from taxation. The first to introduce excise taxes in Britain, the Long Parliament disregarded the view that advocated the restriction of these duties to luxuries and instead expanded the list of taxed items to include necessary commodities to ensure that the poor would share in the payment of excise taxes.[126]

Muhammad Ali's taxation regime bore the imprint of these ideas. His tax system was designed to benefit the state, not the population of the country; and more importantly the producing groups, especially the peasantry, carried the heaviest part of the tax burden, paying a multitude of taxes.[127] That some contemporary foreign observers shared his belief that Egyptian peasants inclined towards laziness[128] suggests that they probably approved of the onerous tax load imposed on the peasantry. Their opinions were likely based on the Western views that highlighted the poor groups' penchant for idleness, and which advocated that the state should impose heavy taxes on them to force them to choose between working and starving.[129] While these views certainly did not guide Muhammad Ali's decisions on peasant taxation, they probably constituted something of a supportive backdrop for his own ideas.

The Tanzimat reforms of the Ottoman Empire moved in the opposite direction. Rather than excessively taxing the rural folk as did the government of Egypt, the Tanzimat statesmen chose to "shift the tax burden from the land to urban wealth." This involved establishing the tithe as the sole tax on the produce of the land as well as "replacing the excise taxes, which were levied mainly on households and land plots regardless of ability to pay" with the requirement that merchants, artisans, and peasant heads of households pay an income tax. This tax was to be determined by the profit level generated by their economic activities (outside of land cultivation).[130] In addition, all taxes traditionally imposed in accordance with Islamic law were abolished "with the exception of the head tax on sheep and other animals . . . and the head tax on non-Muslims."[131] That the Tanzimat statesmen streamlined and rationalized the tax load imposed on the peasantry did not mean that they expected and accepted a decrease in rural tax revenues. Quite the contrary: they simply reasoned that rationalizing taxation would enhance the peasants' economic capability, which would parlay into the improvement of the productive capacity of arable land and increased rural tax revenues.[132]

In reconsidering the Egyptian peasants' tax burden during the mid-nineteenth-century years, statesmen likely studied Muhammad Ali's tax system, which was firmly undergirded by Western notions and the Ottoman Tanzimat reforms. Like Muhammad Ali, they imposed the land tax as well as an additional array of other taxes; while the impact of the Tanzimat reforms can be seen in the decision to streamline indirect duties and reform corvée regulations. Also notable is that this amalgam of ideas neatly dovetailed with the economic principles of the traditional philosophy of statecraft, upon which the statesmen of this period relied for guidance in the formulation of state regulations.

Other Taxes

As stated above, peasants living during the mid-century years were required to pay the land tax and a variety of other taxes.

Some of these other taxes constituted extraordinary surcharge duties. Besides the universal surcharge taxes discussed earlier—the *dum*, *suds*, and *wirku*—some peasant landholders paid additional ones. The land-tax registers of Abnahas Village disclose a certain surcharge tax by which the peasants of this village paid 12 piastres for every *faddan* in their possession during the fiscal year of 1272/1856. These sums were designated for the Sanduq al-Qubaniyya, or the company's treasury.[133] The examination of the tax registers of other years reveals that this tax was operative during the 1856 fiscal year only; while the comparison between the Abnahas tax registers with those of other villages shows that this extraordinary tax was not imposed on these other villages. Based on this evidence, we might assume that the company in question—its identity was not disclosed—had enjoyed governmental patronage, which included financial assistance. That the government chose to produce the required sums by imposing an extraordinary tax on Abnahas Village implies that Abnahas peasants stood to benefit from the company's establishment.

Thus the government tended to impose extraordinary duties on peasants when they benefited from a service or certain exceptional circumstances that others did not similarly enjoy. Abnahas Village seemed doubly advantaged during our period, for in addition to the anticipated benefits discussed just above, it may have enjoyed unique topographical circumstances, like particularly fertile soil and/or superior irrigation infrastructure and/or its land was better leveled and cleared of trees than was that of other villages. It was such advantageous physical endowment that may have prompted the government to impose an extraordinary tax of 125 percent on the lands of this village; the sources show this was operative in 1261/1845.[134] An entry in Abnahas's land-tax register for the fiscal year 1270/1854 discloses the impact of this tax on the peasant's land-tax load. In that year, villager Mustafa Hillal's landholding constituted 36 *faddan*s and 20 *sahm*s. The initial calculation of the taxes of this holding at its original tax rates brought the amount to 955 piastres and 29 para. Next, the 125 percent tax was imposed on this initial sum, changing it to 2,149 piastres and 19 para. Then, using this latter sum as the basis, the calculations for the major surcharge taxes (the *dum*, *suds*, and *wirku*) were made.[135] At the end of this, Mustafa Hillal's land taxes had increased by roughly three times the original amount. Finally, the land-tax registers of this village show that this extraordinary tax was abolished the following year;[136] and in the absence of an official explanation, we might attribute this decision to a noticeable deterioration of the unique circumstance that had set Abnahas apart from other villages.

Some peasant taxes were not land-related. There was a house tax, originally introduced by Muhammad Ali in 1822 and levied throughout his reign; and although later abolished, probably by Abbas Pasha, it was reimposed in 1856.[137] Also existent at mid-century was a tax on date trees that also went back to the time of Muhammad Ali. In the early 1820s, peasants made yearly payments of 0.5 to 2.0 piastres per tree, which increased to 1.0 to 2.5 piastres during 1836–1844.[138] Ya'qub Artin specified that the peasants of Munifiyya Province did not pay this tax, and on this basis concluded that the tax on date trees was not uniformly imposed across the countryside.[139] These rules for the taxation of date trees were replaced by those of the decree of August 1860. By this, the trees were to be counted and the value of their produce (dates, bark, fronds) was to be assessed. These calculations were to be undertaken in 1862 and again in 1863 because the amount and quality of a tree's produce differed from year to year. Then the average value of each tree's produce during these two years was to be specified, and peasants were to pay one-tenth of this value starting in 1864 and through 1869. Finally, this entire process was to be repeated at the end of every sixth year.[140] And although not quite a tax, peasants were also responsible for the remuneration of the provincial officials who served in their villages, a responsibility that certainly added to the sums earmarked for the government. In 1861, every village tax accountant, or *sarraf*, in the province of Girga, was to be paid 11 piastres and 4 para for every 1,000 piastres the village paid in taxes. Such an amount was to be "collected from the peasants, apart from the sums owed to the state treasury."[141]

Rural folk were also required to pay the capitation tax, *firdat al-ru'us*, though not for the entire period under study. Its first appearance during the nineteenth century was in 1823. Every economically active male in the towns was required to pay it, payment being on an individual basis; but in the rural areas payment was made the responsibility of the household, and the tax was correspondingly called *firdat al-buyut*. With the completion of the village censuses in the 1840s, though, villagers were similarly made to pay this tax on an individual basis.[142] Thus in 1850, when peasants left their villages without settling this tax, the authorities carefully tracked them down rather than shifting this responsibility onto other family members.[143] For the rural folks who were wage-laborers, this tax consisted of one month's wages.[144] On the other hand, peasant smallholders were to pay a kind of income tax that was based on the profits they had garnered from the various economic activities in which they were engaged.[145]

As indicated above, the capitation tax was abolished at mid-century. While Abbas Pasha completely spared the rural wage-laborers the payment of this tax,[146] smallholders were not treated as kindly. Yet, he sought to ensure that their payments corresponded to their economic capability. Thus, the 1847 land law required the adjustment of the capitation/income tax when the holder's lands had increased or decreased.[147] This situation greatly improved with the introduction of the 1855 land law, for by Article V smallholders were no longer required to pay this tax. The state reasoned that the capitation/income tax was in a sense being doubly imposed on peasant holders, as they paid both the *firdat* and the *wirku al-atyan* tax, the latter originally intended as a counterpart to the profits tax exacted from artisans called *wirku al-karat*. Hence, in 1855 the state decided that it did not need to collect both taxes from peasant holders, and that the *wirku al-atyan* was "enough."[148]

Indirect Taxes

Rural folks also had to pay a variety of indirect taxes during the mid-nineteenth-century period. On August 15, 1858, the Privy Council approved the introduction of a code that aimed to streamline indirect taxation rules. Specifically, this code identifies the items to be subjected to indirect taxation and those that were to be exempted.[149]

The Council of Justice, the government body charged with writing this code, began its work by compiling a list of the items that carried indirect taxes. The examination of this list allows for the depiction of the indirect taxation rules existent before 1858. To begin, the items that carried some form of indirect taxes can roughly be divided into seven categories: foodstuffs such as sugar and rice; inedible items necessary for subsistence purposes like candles and soap; spices and herbs; the yield of salt and mineral operations; raw materials required for handicraft production like flax and wool; the products manufactured by artisans like copperware, rugs, and blankets; and animals, which included cattle, camels, horses, mules, sheep, and poultry.[150] Two, some items were subjected to more than one indirect tax. This, for example, was the case with flax: when sold either raw or manufactured, an excise tax was paid; when turned into thread or linen, a seals tax was paid; and when exported as raw flax, custom duties were collected.[151] Three, some taxes were not levied across the entire countryside, but only in certain areas. Thus, for example, governmental officials "found that a duty was imposed on types of cheese and butter in some areas";[152] that silk carried an excise tax in Minya Province only; and that Rawdat al-Bahrayn Province charged transit duties when goods passed through its territory.[153] Four, sales executed in the rural markets and town shops included the payment of a sales tax. Five, the sales that involved boats, personal property, and immovable property were usually concluded outside of rural markets and town shops, which often meant that government officials were unable to collect the required duties for such sales. Yet it seems that the officials stationed in Buhayra Province and Cairo Governorate were better informed and more diligent, for they more regularly collected the pertinent sales duties.[154]

The 1858 code introduced significant changes to this system of indirect taxation. In tandem with the state drive for centralization during the nineteenth century, which further entailed the push for standardization and uniformity, the new code specified that its stipulations were to be uniformly implemented throughout all of Egypt. Accordingly the state would no longer condone the decisions of local officials to impose additional or different duties.

But the more important modification constituted the reduction of the items to be subjected to indirect taxation. For many items, this really meant the abolishment of one of the taxes they carried. For example, growers of flax paid the *kharaj* land tax (as flax was a product of the agricultural lands that paid this tax); then a seals tax was paid upon completion of the manufacturing process, a customs tax when exported, and finally an excise tax when purchased. Here the state chose to abolish the excise duty (for raw flax and its manufactured items), reasoning that the other three taxes were sufficient.[155] Thus, the state seemed to recognize it had "over-taxed" this item. This recognition and subsequent treatment covered many other items: a number of foodstuffs such as oils, butter, sugar, and cheeses; some of the items needed for basic living purposes like soap and candles; tobacco and most spices and herbs; salt and minerals; raw materials needed by artisans like wool; manufactured products like copperware and silk cloth. In addition, the duties on sales concluded at the town shops were abolished, because shop owners paid the income tax (*wirku al-karat*), considered sufficient by the state. Similarly, the duties on sales executed at the *furushat* (booths set up at the rural markets) were abolished, for the state reasoned that some of the goods on display were products of agricultural lands, which already carried the *kharaj* tax while other goods constituted products of the handicrafts industry, whose workers paid the income tax.[156]

Yet this concern over multiple taxation of a single item was not the only one that brought about the elimination of excise taxes. Foods like *firik* (rubbed/soft green wheat) were spared an excise duty because these were usually eaten by impoverished folk; and *tawaqi*, or small netted caps worn by men, were similarly spared because these were netted and sold by indigent women. In still other cases, the government's decision to eliminate this tax was explained by weak consumer demand for an item; while in yet other cases, the concerned tax had not been levied throughout Egypt but only on a narrow, local basis.[157]

All in all, the 1858 code for indirect taxes stipulated the elimination of the bulk of excise taxes; for approximately 90 percent of the items that had formerly carried this tax were no longer required to pay it. On the other hand, the list of items required to pay seals and customs taxes was not modified. Finally, this code specified the payment of duties upon the sale of private property (real estate, boats) that consisted of 25 piastres for every 500 piastres (or 1 purse); 5 piastres to be paid to the middleman who facilitated the sale, and 20 piastres to the government.[158] The decree of July 27, 1859, modified this last stipulation, specifying the payment of a reduced sales tax of 20 piastres/purse to the government treasury upon the registration of the sale and before the issuance of the title deed (which really worked to eliminate the middleman's commission). It further specified the extension of these instructions to include the sale of *ib'adiyya* and *athariyya* lands, as the Buhayra provincial officials had pointed out that these kinds of lands should be treated as property in this respect, and the central government readily agreed.[159]

The Corvée

The obligation to perform corvée duty, another kind of tax, was nothing new for rural society, as the steady cultivation of land depended on and required well-maintained village irrigation systems. This kind of duty, while a burden, was generally tolerated by peasants because of its immediate and beneficial effect on their fields, and by extension their very livelihoods.[160] Muhammad Ali, though, added a new dimension to corvée duty by launching projects that aimed to develop the country's productive capacities, like the Mahmudiyya Canal, and drew its labor from villages that were both near and far. Peasants resented these corvée stints: as many had to travel long distances, their farm routines were disrupted, and their families' subsistence abilities were seriously impaired.[161] Such corvée duty was not suspended after Muhammad Ali's reign had ended, but remained an element of rural life throughout the mid-century years. The state's plans for the enhancement of the country's infrastructure (roads, railroads, irrigation systems) could not be completed without corvée labor. At the same time, the Suez Canal Company started its excavation work in the spring of 1859, relying on the state to supply the necessary labor contingents. The state most likely reasoned that the successful completion of the various major public works projects would ultimately allow it to increase revenue levels in the near future. This interest in the maximization of revenues and all that it implied for official corvée policies notwithstanding, the mid-century state did try to regulate the corvée system in ways that showed concern for the peasants' well-being.

Mid-century corvee regulations specified that all peasant villages were to send their fair share of laborers to state project sites. In 1854, though, the central government realized that some villages endured much heavier corvée levies than others, and attributed this injustice to the tendency of scribes at the provincial seat to reduce their workload, as they liked "to avoid hardship," by not issuing the summons for corvée duty (that was to be based on the census records) themselves. Instead they foisted this task onto the district heads (singular: *nazir al-qism*), simply informing each one of the number of laborers needed from his district. Thus, it became the responsibility of each district head to ensure that all the villages in his area sent the same ratio of laborers for corvée duty. The problem, though, as discerned by central government officials, was that the district heads often did not perform this task as they should have, fairly and impartially. Instead they favored the village headmen who were their friends with rather light corvée levies, meaning that those outside the circle of friendship bore heavier levies: "and in this way, some are protected and some are betrayed." The government responded to this problem by issuing Decree No. 5/May 16, 1854. By it, the officials at the provincial seat were charged with the responsibility of consulting each village's census records, and on that basis were to specify the number of laborers each village was to recruit for corvée duty. These instructions were to be relayed to the district heads, whose only responsibility was to pass them on to the village heads.[162]

Village headmen were expected to select the individual peasants for corvée duty on a just and impartial basis; but often did not. In December 1851, Mansur Ajur complained that his shaykh, Ibrahim al-Far, sent him and all his sons to the al-Qanatar project site for corvée duty, where they spent several months "even though there are forty-nine individuals who have never been sent to al-Qanatar." This complaint was investigated by the Council of Justice: "And the shaykh was questioned about not treating the villagers fairly; and he swore to tend to the aforementioned and the others and to ensure all peasants were treated equally. And if there arises another such complaint from one of the peasants, he [the shaykh] will be punished according to the law." But the authorities did not end this case with only a stern warning. The governor of the province (al-Munifiyya) decreed that the shaykh was to receive one hundred lashes as punishment; but the Council of Justice overrode this decision and specified two hundred lashes "because forty-nine individuals had not been sent to the al-Qanatar project . . . and he is unfair . . . and because this kind of person treats the peasants in accordance with his ambitions and this is not right."[163] The threat of punishment notwithstanding, village headmen did not always observe the law: in December 1853, a petition was filed against a Shaykh Bakri, which stated, in addition to other complaints, that "there were 75 individuals under his authority that have never been sent out on corvée duty";[164] in February 1854, a village headman named Ali Ghanim was to be punished "because he did not select peasants for corvée duty on the basis of impartiality";[165] and in August 1859, one peasant complained that the headman of his village "always selects him for corvée duty."[166] Headmen's decisions to ignore corvée regulations, and even risk punishment, can be attributed to several factors. British Consul General Bruce believed that money was a primary consideration in such decisions: "The sheikh [*sic*] on whom the task devolves of providing the quota his village is to furnish, selects those whom he knows to be well-off, and only releases them on consideration of a heavy bribe."[167] Also, shaykhs who wanted to keep their tenants and laborers in the village and on their lands kept them from corvée duty; while others liked to bestow the "gift of corvée exemption" on relatives and friends; and still others resorted to the corvée to rid themselves of troublesome villagers.[168] Knowing they had violated the law, such headmen sought to prevent detection by the higher authorities. In one case, a village shaykh allied with a clerk at the provincial seat who agreed to "hide the petitions" that would have exposed the former's transgressions.[169]

The state's interest in the just treatment of the peasantry led it to exempt certain groups of rural society from corvée duty. These consisted of the elderly because of their inability to undertake strenuous physical labor, and the religious clerics and village barbers because their communities needed their services.[170] A new corvée law, issued on February 11, 1851, expanded this list to include pregnant women, women still breastfeeding infants, and children (whether boys or girls) under eight years. It further identified what was meant by the term "elderly," clearly describing these as men and women over seventy years.[171] Stiff punishments were specified for the different members of the provincial administrative hierarchy when they did not observe the new law.[172] For example, village shaykhs who violated these regulations were to be jailed for fifteen days, and twenty days when caught a second time, but were to spend a month on corvée duty in the event of a third transgression, and altogether dismissed from their posts in the event of a fourth.[173] While earlier writings that examine the corvée focus on the recruitment of men, and specify that women and children, indeed whole families, voluntarily trailed their male relatives to project sites in order to care for them,[174] the 1851 corvée law suggests that this was not the only reason these groups could be found at corvée sites. For it specifies the major problem it sought to address accordingly: that provincial officials did not limit corvée recruitment to able-bodied men, but often included women, young girls and boys, and the elderly and infirm. The preamble to this law describes these practices as "unacceptable," and accordingly disallowed them.[175]

Other groups believed they deserved exemption from this duty and accordingly tried to plead their case. In 1849, the *ashraf*, or the religious nobility, of Nabrawa, in Gharbiyyia Province, believed they should be treated as were the *ashraf* that resided in Tanta, close to the tomb of Sayyid Ibrahim al-Disuqi, and similarly be exempted from corvée work. The central government disagreed; and stated that the only members of these families who were to be exempted were the religious clerics and the elderly.[176] Military soldiers also wanted exemption from corvée duty and "submitted numerous petitions" to this effect. In response, the government issued the decree of March 14, 1857, which granted exemption to discharged soldiers and those still in the reserves if they had suffered bullet wounds and/or amputation of limbs and/or fifteen years of service.[177]

The state did not only grant exemptions to certain individuals or groups of rural society but also spared entire villages of this duty when they experienced economic ruination. It is probably for this reason that three villages in Daqahliyya Province had won official exemption from corvée work in 1859. And when the provincial officials disregarded this decision, the village headmen petitioned the Department of Interior, complaining "about the recruitment of their peasants for corvée even though an order had been issued which exempted them from being sent to major public works sites."[178]

The government's wish to ensure that corvée work was shared equally among peasants can also be seen in its insistence that large estate holders (not only the headmen of "freeholder" villages) observe corvée summons for public works projects. While these holders were known to ignore such summons during the 1830s and 1840s so that the peasants' work would not be disrupted, decisions the government usually condoned, they could not so easily do so at mid-century. Thus, in 1853, when a number of *muta'ahhid*s delayed in delivering the labor contingents specified for their *uhda* villages, immediate termination of the *uhda* ensued; and when one provincial official took responsibility for this delay, admitting that "he had made a mistake," he was punished according to the stipulations of the 1851 corvée code.[179] At the same time, *jiflik* estate holders as well as foreign landholders who did not comply with an official corvée summons received stern verbal reprimands.[180] While contemporary observers might attribute state insistence on corvée compliance to Abbas Pasha's desire to tame and control his enemies, specifically those who had served and had been loyal to Muhammad Ali,[181] still, the peasants' economic well-being likely figured in this new policy. But if not, we cannot deny that the enlargement of the corvée labor pool (by requiring estate holders to send labor contingents to public works sites) likely meant shorter work stints for ordinary peasants.

On the other hand, estate holders did have the right to request laborers from neighboring villages to service their lands.[182] Thus, when one estate holder made such a request in 1852, the central government approved it and commented that "this was an acceptable tradition that was recognized by the provincial [authorities]."[183] And although unauthorized, lower-level provincial officials, particularly village headmen and district chiefs, forced peasants to service their lands.[184] The peasants were known to clamor for relief when they felt overly exploited; or as in one case, if the shaykh failed to keep his end of the bargain. Here, the government advised these officials to refrain from overworking the peasants "so that they would remain in their villages."[185]

Despite all the government's attempts to regulate corvée work, so as to ensure the peasants remained economically viable, peasants' hatred of forced labor probably did not abate, but became more intense, at mid-century. For this was a time of free market rules, cash crops, and greater commoditization of land and labor—in a word, capitalism figured more prominently in the countryside—and the peasants resented losing the opportunity to profit from the favorable economic environment, whether by harvesting and selling their own crops or engaging in paid labor. The nebulous issue of remuneration for corvée work certainly added to their resentment.[186] It seems that they could expect payment during the Abbas reign. In 1849, the British consul (Charles Murray) reported that laborers were provided with food and paid 20 paras/day for their work on state irrigation projects.[187] Also a July 1852 entry in the registers of the Viceregal Cabinet "clarified that the laborers working on the railroad project [are paid] the wages commonly set for anyone [who undertook corvée work]," and historian Toledano asserts that the laborers who worked on the Mahmudiyya Canal in 1849 received 1 piastre/day and bread rations.[188] But under Said, laborers could not always expect cash reward. British Consul Bruce's explanation in 1857 of the corvée rules included this explanation: "The nominal wages, low as they are, are not paid to the laborers in money, but are deducted from the land-tax payable by the villages which furnish the men."[189] Neither could peasants expect cash payments when they serviced the lands of estate holders and provincial officials, as some liked to give foods in exchange for labor and others offered to cancel debts, and still others offered exemption from state corvée duty. At the same time, some avoided making any kind of payment at all.[190]

Conclusion

Official assessment of rural taxes at mid-century generally proceeded according to the economic precepts of the Ottoman philosophy of statecraft. This led the government to raise the peasants' land taxes several times. On the other hand, it also alleviated the tax burden carried by poor peasants and readjusted the indirect tax regime and the corvée regulations, all to ensure that the majority of the peasants remained diligent agricultural producers who kept their lands cultivated and regularly paid their taxes. Yet rural society, provincial officials as well as ordinary folks, did not always simply accept and implement the central government's instructions. And so, when instructions seemed inappropriate or unjust, members of the periphery liked to offer alternative suggestions and ideas. Such feedback was not discouraged because it allowed the central government to gain a better idea of the situation on the ground, which in turn facilitated governmental efforts to increase rural revenues while preserving the peasants' economic viability. But governmental interest in striking a balance between these two economic precepts did not hold for the entirety of the mid-century period—specifically, the reign of Said Pasha. Upon his ascension to the throne, Said wished to initiate grandiose projects that needed vast amounts of money. And toward the end of his reign, the problematic of revenue deficits became more pressing, thereby prompting his officials to pay less and less attention to the peasants' welfare.

3

System of Tax Collection

The nineteenth-century push for reform and modernization in the Ottoman Empire involved addressing taxation matters in the decree of February 23, 1838, which supplanted the system of tax farming, or indirect taxation, with the direct collection of taxes by salaried state agents. This effort failed partly because the new collection agents (singular: *muhassil*) were not sufficiently familiar with the affairs of rural society, and by 1840 rural revenue levels had decreased dramatically. This led, perforce, to the reintroduction of tax farming, and the government awarded two-year leases for tax collection to those who offered to submit the highest sums to the state treasury. In turn, the tax farmers sought to recover the money they had promised to the state as well as make a profit before the expiration of their leases by squeezing the peasants as hard as was possible. Since this meant the resurrection of the very problems the Tanzimat reforms had wanted to eradicate, the government issued the 1847 decree in yet another attempt to reform the system of tax collection. Here it extended the duration of leases to five years and further required tax contractors to agree to the following points: to provide loans to the peasants at interest rates of no more than 1 percent, to refrain from forcing cultivators to pay taxes before harvest time, and to evaluate in-kind taxes at the market rate. Finally, the government was to grant short-term leases only when tax farmers could not be found to agree to the 1847 terms.[1] The state hoped that these measures would encourage tax farmers to align their aims with the long-term interests of the cultivators under their jurisdiction, and in this way contribute to the enhancement of state revenue levels while preserving the economic viability of the principal tax base of the Ottoman polity.

In Egypt, taxation policy at mid-century also aimed to maximize state revenues while preserving the productive capabilities of the peasants. But here this did not involve the introduction of attempts to eradicate the abuses of tax farmers; for Muhammad Ali had destroyed the *iltizam* (tax-farm) system decades ago, in 1814, and introduced direct taxation that relied on village and provincial officials.[2] Instead the state tried to facilitate the process of tax payment with the aim of preserving peasant economic viability, which can be seen, for example, in the instructions that specified the payment of taxes at harvest times. Also, it introduced new measures that aimed to generate high revenues, as can be seen in the 1858 and 1861 rules for *ramya* acquirement. This attempt to balance the equitable and harsh features of the system of tax collection ended in 1861, though, when the latter features were more salient.

Responsibility for Taxes: Individual versus Communal Responsibility

Basing his conclusions on the views of contemporary observers of Egypt, Gabriel Baer wrote that Said Pasha abolished the collective responsibility of peasants for the payment of taxes, which meant that from the mid-1850s onward, the state would not transfer the debts of insolvent peasants to affluent neighbors.[3] He further draws attention to these observers' negative view of tax solidarity.[4] Kenneth Cuno contributes to this discussion by explaining that the kind of tax solidarity that comprised the transfer of arrears to solvent peasants occurred from the late 1820s to the mid-1830s. But beginning in 1829–1830, tax solidarity entailed the transfer of the lands of the insolvent peasants (by *ramya*, or land assignment) along with their arrears to the wealthier villagers. And from 1835–1836 onward, the state imposed only this latter type of tax solidarity.[5]

This section challenges these ideas. It reveals yet another "mode" of tax solidarity (the tax-credit system); and thus, it shows that two modes of tax solidarity were operative at the beginning of the mid-century decades, the tax-credit system and the *ramya* land process. It also argues, contrary to the assumptions of earlier writers about tax solidarity, that both of these worked to buttress the economic viability of the peasants. This favorable situation gave way starting from the mid-1850s, when the government modified both tax-solidarity systems in ways that abolished their communal dimension; and so rather than benefiting rural society as the literature implies, these changes essentially disadvantaged the peasants.

A discussion on the issue of responsibility for taxes in Egyptian villages at mid-century can start by confirming, as Cuno does when examining rural society between the 1740s and 1850s, that the state observed the principle of individual responsibility for payment of land taxes.[6] This is easily confirmed by a cursory examination of the village land-tax registers of the relevant years, which specify the names of the landholders, the amount of land each possessed, and the tax sum each was to pay.

At the same time, the tax-credit system could turn the payment of land taxes into a communal responsibility. The state directed peasant landholders to pay their land taxes in installments throughout the year; and specified the amount (or proportion) for each installment. Sometimes, a peasant liked to pay more than was officially specified for an installment. This excess or increment, termed *al-fa'id*, was accordingly credited to his name, and was to be accessed later for the payment of another installment. Peasants were known to defer the use of their tax credits for lengthy periods of time. For example, one peasant, Ahmad al-Karash from Munifiyya Province, made a number of incremental tax payments between 1241/1825–1826 and 1255/1839–1840, but did not claim this accumulated credit until early 1854.[7] Why peasants chose to pay incremental tax sums is explained by a report dated February 1, 1856, composed by officials of the Buhayra provincial government and submitted to the Viceregal Cabinet. It explained the following:

> Some of the peasants want to pay more than is specified for their [current] tax installments, by their desire, because this is the season of the summer harvest, and they wish to pay now what they owe for the ensuing months, for fear that they will spend [the profits obtained from the sale of their] crops and thus will experience difficulty [in the payment of their taxes] in the future.[8]

In other words, the tax-credit system granted peasants a measure of insurance against times of insolvency and the attendant inability to pay taxes.

Yet there were times when peasants found they could not access their tax credits to pay current tax installments simply because the village authorities had employed these to discharge the tax arrears of other individuals. This is illustrated by the following case. When the tax inspector for Sharqiyya Province was examining the provincial tax registers, he found that these specified that the village of Akyad al-Ghatawara had tax credits that amounted to 399 piastres, 22 para at the close of the 1855 fiscal year. But "upon examining the register of the village accountant, he found that [some individuals] had tax credits of 9,159 piastres, 18 para," while other individuals had tax arrears. Thus, some peasants had chosen to pay tax sums in excess of what was required for 1855; indeed these sums would have covered the creditors' future tax installments until December 1856.[9] It was not to be, though. For the village accountant, probably with the approval of the village headman, used the sums paid by the affluent individuals as tax credits to settle the accounts of the arrear-laden peasants—a step that consumed the bulk (8,759 piastres, 36 para) of the original sum of tax credits and left only 399 piastres, 22 para for the tax creditors.

Provincial governments, too, were known to adopt this same strategy in an attempt to settle tax debts of villages under their jurisdiction. In 1852, the Viceregal Cabinet learned that the tax arrears for Buhayra Province through the month of Rabi Thani (through February 21) constituted approximately 2,000 purses. This figure came about because the provincial authorities had

> deducted the tax credits of some of the *uhda* [villages] that had paid more than was required of them, and credited [these sums] to those *uhda* [villages] which are late in their payments and especially to the villages [under the jurisdiction] of the provincial government.[10]

Put another way, the Buhayra authorities had accessed the tax credits of the solvent villages in the province to cancel what they could of the tax arrears of the insolvent villages.

That this and the other tax-credit cases discussed above came to the attention of the central government was because the tax creditors had not been consulted about the employment of their tax credits to cancel the tax debts of other cultivators. For as the Council of Justice explained to one of these creditors, unhappy with this situation, such utilization of his tax credits was contingent on "his agreement."[11]

This allows us to conclude that there were some instances where tax creditors *did* allow their poorer neighbors to access their tax credits. Why? Peasants' decisions were most likely guided by the precepts of the peasant "moral economy," which disregarded calculations of profit and loss.[12] To begin, affluent peasants liked to make excess tax payments whenever they could—although they could not be certain that their accumulated credit would later be available for their own use—mainly because they considered them insurance against natural disasters, which caused bad harvests followed by dearth, poverty, and the inability to satisfy tax obligations. Here peasants also knew they could not expect tax assistance from similarly straitened neighbors and kinsmen. Thus, it was during such times of crisis that the authorities likely did not disappoint these tax creditors, and employed their accumulated tax credits to clear their tax obligations rather than those of their insolvent neighbors. But when tax creditors enjoyed a level of economic prosperity that enabled them to pay tax installments without utilizing their tax credits, they might allow their insolvent neighbors to access these in recognition of an important principle of village society, the principle of reciprocity. By this, individuals assisted impoverished neighbors when they could and in return expected aid when they experienced hardship. Moreover, tax creditors who gave their consent for the "bestowal" of their accumulated credit on penurious cultivators probably anticipated gratitude, deference, and submissiveness from the beneficiaries, all of which translated into enhanced social standing in their community.

To briefly recapitulate: when tax officials employed the sums of tax creditors to wipe out the tax debts of other individuals, they were, in essence, confirming the communal dimension of tax liability during the mid-nineteenth-century period. The comparatively affluent tax creditors did not resist such communal responsibility because of their right to ask for assistance when they experienced hardship themselves; and just as important, because of its positive impact on their social standing in the village. But the real beneficiaries of this system were the penurious peasants whose tax debts had been erased; for the archival sources do not indicate that the beneficiaries were required to redeem their creditors, which meant that they retained their lands without being compelled to pay all their tax debts. This certainly facilitated their economic recovery. Finally, this feature of the system of tax collection was reflective of the state's interest in ensuring that revenue collection did not drive the majority (that is, the poor) of the peasants into destitution.

When tax credits ran out, and it seems they often did, the authorities depended on another system to resolve the problem of peasant arrears; this was the land-assignment (*ramya*) process, which entailed the transfer of arrears-laden land from the possession of the insolvent possessor to that of a solvent individual. In this way the original possessor was relieved of the payment of accumulated land arrears, as these were henceforth to be taken up by the land recipient as well as all future related liabilities. Thus, the most important criterion *ramya* recipients had to satisfy was the possession of sufficient cash resources for the payment of cultivation expenses, arrears, and future taxes. This led some scholars to conclude that *ramya* distribution essentially resulted in the transfer of land from the hands of the insolvent poor to the village wealthy.[13] Indeed, as the exigencies of the land-assignment process necessitated that village authorities reassign the land quickly, so that tax-collection efforts experienced minimal interruption, the village wealthy did accumulate sizable land holdings through *ramya* distribution. For example, in 1860, the headman of Jazira al-Khadra Village, Umda Yusif Mar'i, possessed a total of 263.5 *faddan*s, of which approximately 66 percent had been acquired by *ramya* assignment.[14]

What about the poor peasants in the village? In a study that examines developments in land tenure during the first half of the nineteenth century in Egypt, Cuno's observations include the following statement: "The gains made by wealthy peasants could only have come at their poorer neighbors' expense."[15] While Cuno understood this to be the outcome of state policy, he did not identify the nature of this policy. Then in his (later) seminal study on Egyptian rural society, Cuno identifies the state policy at work, land assignment by *ramya*, but seems to stand by his earlier conclusion; for he wrote: "The redistribution of land by *ramya* and *tawzi'* was therefore another policy that favored the expansion of the holdings of the wealthier strata in the countryside."[16]

While the archival sources show that the *ramya* system enriched the affluent peasants at the expense of their insolvent neighbors, these also show that the authorities made *ramya* assignments to poor villagers. For example, from the registers of the religious court of Tanta we see that in December 1856, a village shaykh made a *ramya* assignment of 27 *qirat*s (a little more than 1 *faddan*) to an indigent peasant woman for "the purpose of assisting her"; meaning for the express purpose of providing her with a means of livelihood.[17] Also, the *athurat* registers show that the *ramya* system transformed landless peasants into holders of small plots. For example, in 1856, the entire holding of 6 *sahm*s (1/96 of a *faddan*) that belonged to Mansur Sulayman of Kafr al-Rajallat Village constituted a *ramya* land assignment. The same applied to the 18 *qirat*s (3/4 of a *faddan*) that constituted the entire holding of Abd al-Rahman from al-Jazira al-Khadra Village in 1859.[18] That these were neither sporadic nor rare instances is confirmed by the data culled from the Ibyar *athurat* register: this shows us that in 1859, the poor-peasant stratum (where each holder possessed less than 5 faddans) together possessed a total of 634 *faddan*s, and that approximately 60 percent of these lands had been acquired by *ramya* assignment.[19] What this meant was that peasants lost land to the *ramya* process when their tax arrears reached unacceptable levels, but that these same peasants could look forward to the receipt of new land when they demonstrated the possession of an adequate level of cash resources.

The favorable features of the two modes of tax solidarity discussed above, which contributed to the preservation of the economic viability of the peasants, did not remain operative throughout the mid-century period. The first change was introduced by the decree of January 8, 1856, and may have been prompted by high-level tax officials who wished to enhance the comprehensibility of village tax accounts. By it, provincial tax officials were "to refrain from collecting anything from the peasants that was in excess of their installments; deficient or excess amounts [were not to be accepted] so that there would not emerge any tax credits or arrears."[20] Thus, peasants were expected to pay their installments in full, no more or less. The officials of Buhayra government viewed these instructions as problematic. So they quickly submitted a report to the Viceregal Cabinet that emphasized the following: that during summer harvest times, the peasants who grew summer crops wanted to pay in excess of their tax installments because they feared they might spend their profits and then would not be able to pay future tax installments; at the same time, "some peasants had nothing in their hands and needed an extension [for the payment of current tax installments] until they harvested their crops in the winter." In the face of this, the central government relented its earlier position. Here it proclaimed that peasants could henceforth make incremental tax payments if they wished, but were to understand that these were to be used to cover installments of the same year, and so could not be carried over to a new fiscal year. By the same token, those peasants who had delayed payments were to pay their taxes at harvest time.[21] While these instructions could not prevent the accumulation of tax arrears, what they really did was limit the amount of money that affluent peasants would deposit as tax credit, for these advance payments were to cover relatively short periods. In turn, this meant that village accountants probably accessed these tax credits to discharge the tax obligations of the creditors rather than those of others, which further meant that tax credits were no longer employed to cancel the arrears of insolvent peasants. Thus, in this way, the state abolished the communal dimension of the tax-credit system, thereby disadvantaging the penurious holders, who were henceforth compelled to pay all their tax obligations themselves.

The second change concerned *ramya* land. By the traditional rules of *ramya* distribution, the receipt of a land assignment took place "*bidun muqabil*," or without the payment of fees.[22] But by the 1858 land law, this was made contingent on the payment of a fee of 24 piastres per *faddan*. What this meant was that the poorest members of the village community, the landless peasants, could no longer depend on the workings of the *ramya* system to provide them with a land plot. For the combination of low wages and an adequate labor pool (that depressed wage levels) likely meant that they were unable to save the required fee for the acquisition of *ramya* land.[23] Complete exclusion of the majority of the villagers (the poor peasants), though, from *ramya* distribution came three years later. The increase in crop prices during the late 1850s and early 1860s,[24] which gave an upward push to the market value of land, led the state to introduce Decree No. 12/ December 13, 1861, whereby it disallowed the assignment of *ramya* land to members of the village community. Henceforth, the placement of *ramya* land was to be by competitive bidding—which translated into higher government revenues. In this way, the state eliminated the land-redistribution feature of the *ramya* system, which had assigned vacant land to both poor and wealthy villagers, and effectively turned *ramya* acquirement into an activity and prerogative of affluent individuals, from both inside and outside the village community.[25]

A final point remains; this is the notion of the "dissolution of the village community" developed by Baer. In his development of this notion, he identified the collective responsibility for tax payment as one of the three phenomena that gave expression to the communal dimension of village society. He defined communal liability for tax payment as consisting of the imposition of the arrears of insolvent peasants onto their more affluent neighbors, and further argued that the abolishment of this policy by Said Pasha contributed to the dissolution of the village community.[26] On the other hand, this section showed that the type of tax solidarity Baer described was not operative during the mid-nineteenth-century period; instead two other types were: the system of tax credits and the land-assignment process. Both these were modified during the reign of Said Pasha in ways that disadvantaged the indigent peasants, and probably further triggered these folks' anxiety about "the dissolution" of their community. For when the state decreed that incremental tax payments were not to carry over to the next fiscal year, poor peasants could no longer depend on the tax credits of other members of their community for tax relief. Similarly, when the state disallowed the assignment of vacant village land to villagers, poor peasants could not depend on their community for land provision. Thus, attendant with their diminished opportunities for economic recovery, the indigent rural folks likely felt that their community had failed and abandoned them. This is not to say that the village community disappeared at mid-century, but rather to point to state decrees that disregarded the peasants' welfare and resulted in the dilution of village communal bonds.

Payment of Taxes: In-kind or Coin, Schedules

In a brief discussion on the collection of rural taxes during 1850–1882, Roger Owen observes that taxes were collected in cash, which "made it possible for the government to begin to raise taxes in advance of the harvest"; and the combination of these features "increased the opportunity for arbitrary exactions" and also involved the moneylender in the collection process.[27] The implication here is that these features of the process of tax collection greatly disadvantaged peasant taxpayers. Yet this interpretation includes no mention of the attempts of the government to address the problems peasants encountered in the payment of taxes. This section highlights the government's attempts to facilitate tax payment as well as its introduction of rigorous rules at mid-century.

During the reigns of Abbas and Said, taxes were collected partly in cash and partly in-kind. Upon becoming viceroy, Abbas, unappreciative of Western ideas on liberalism, chose to disregard the stipulations of the 1838 Anglo-Ottoman Commercial Convention and preserve the monopoly system as much as was possible. Thus, he required cultivators to pay their taxes in-kind, which meant they were to deliver their crops to government warehouses at low fixed prices. But this was a time of high market prices, particularly for grains, which prompted some peasants to ignore this directive, as was clarified by an entry in the registers of the Council of Justice dated November 30, 1851: "Regarding the crops which the peasants sold and did not deliver to the government," reported the Daqahliyya provincial administration, "we clarify that sales on the market take place at higher prices than those of the government." Yet this report also clarifies that the concerned official had not received instructions that directed him to "compel them [the peasants] to deliver their crops [to the state warehouses.]"[28] While this lapse might be attributed to bureaucratic inefficiency, it is also reflective of a diminished interest on the part of the central government to possess the entirety of cultivators' agricultural produce. By 1853, it required only partial payment of taxes in-kind: as the instructions for *uhda* holders to pay taxes "half in cash and half in crops" probably extended to all cultivators of state (*miri/kharajiyya*) land.[29]

Said Pasha, widely praised as an enlightened ruler interested in ameliorating the condition of the peasants in line with Western ideas, modified the system of tax collection soon after his assumption of power in July 1854. In the first few months of the new reign, taxes were collected as before. Thus according to an entry (dated October 16, 1854) in the records of the Council of Justice, the villages specified as *uhda* by the Daqahliyya provincial administration were to pay their taxes half in cash and half in-kind, just as Abbas had latterly decreed.[30] The first change to this system came in the following year: according to a December 15, 1855 entry in the Viceregal Cabinet registers, the central government instructed tax officials to collect land taxes at harvest time, for the cultivators were "completely free to sell them [the crops] at the appropriate prices to whomever they wish"[31]—which further suggests that peasants could pay their taxes in cash. This decision was partially reversed for certain cultivators. A report dated February 18, 1856, from Daqahliyya Province to the Viceregal Cabinet explains how the "collection of taxes from the villages of the districts of al-Jiza and al-Simbillawayn is undertaken, which involves [state] possession of their [the peasants'] crops and their sale and the payment of the taxes from [the sale proceeds]." This report further explains that crops were "sold at the appropriate [that is, market] prices," and that once taxes were paid, all remaining sums were turned over to the cultivators.[32] Here the Daqahliyya authorities had targeted the peasants who had taken loans from the provincial treasury (so as to meet the costs required for the cultivation of summer crops), seeking to ensure that they redeemed their loans and paid their taxes. Finally by 1858, it seems that all peasants were permitted to dispose of their crops as they wished, and accordingly, could choose to pay their taxes in-kind or in cash. An entry (dated July 11, 1858) in the registers of the Department of Interior shows that peasants could deliver to government warehouses whatever crops they wished, and that these were to be assessed at market rates.[33] Thus, at the end of the 1850s, the peasants' payment of taxes in coin or conversely in-kind was not restricted by official regulations but rather by the shortage of coins in the countryside.

When were peasants to pay their land taxes? In earlier times, the payment of taxes at different intervals during the year, meaning the payment of taxes in installments, was official policy. According to Lionel Casson, money taxes were paid in three installments during Byzantine rule.[34] In the early period of the Arab conquest, the government specified two payments for the year, but each one could be made in several installments. While several chroniclers of the medieval period report that taxes were collected in two or three installments, the agricultural calendar preserved by Ibn Hawqal in his geographic manuscript dated circa 970 suggests a system of eight payments during the year.[35] Richard Cooper studied this conflicting evidence and concludes that "the information given by Ibn Hawqal is not a reference to the number of installments."[36] Instead, it might have referred to the months when peasants could make their payments.

This official policy (that is, payment of taxes in installments) carried into the nineteenth century. During the reign of Muhammad Ali, peasants paid their land taxes at harvest time, for the rules of the monopoly system required them to deliver their crops to government warehouses as tax payment. Here the tax-installment schedule, particularly the number of installments, likely depended on the kinds of crops peasants grew and when these were harvested. That the government compelled peasants to grow the profitable summer crops, particularly cotton, in addition to the traditional grains probably entailed an increase in the number of installments beyond the two or three of earlier periods. By mid-century, peasants were required to pay their land taxes in eleven installments, as can be seen from the official instructions for the payment of land taxes in 1858 that included this statement: "It is the prevailing custom to divide tax [payments] over eleven months."[37]

The government used the Coptic calendar to organize the payment schedule. This calendar was preferred over the Islamic one as the former is based on the flood cycle of the Nile, meaning that the Coptic months correspond to the seasons of the year, while the latter is based on the lunar year, and the Islamic months do not correspond to the year's seasons. The Coptic year begins on the first day of the month of Tut, which usually corresponds to September 10.[38] The first tax installment of the year was in Tut (September), while the last was in Abib, or July. The final month of the year, Misra (August), was when tax clerks worked on the drafting and finalization of the annual tax statement. Upon the completion of this work, the fiscal year was closed.[39]

The majority of peasants apparently found this payment schedule to be rather arduous. For some tax installments came at times when cultivators had to cover various farming costs, and other times cultivators had not yet harvested their crops. This prompted some peasants to seek assistance in the payment of their taxes. A report dated January 15, 1852, submitted to the Viceregal Cabinet, explained "that when there were complaints [made by provincial officials] against the shaykhs of Sabwa village regarding their delay in the payment of taxes, they [the shaykhs] presented a guarantee given to them by merchants from Alexandria, who were their guarantors in the payment of taxes at the appointed times."[40] Thus, these merchants had agreed to stand surety for the Sabwa cultivators in the payment of their tax installments at the officially appointed dates; and so they were to make these payments when the peasants could not. This agreement probably required the peasants to turn over their crops to the merchants at undervalued rates when the latter actually paid the pertinent tax installments.[41] More often, though, peasants did not take this circuitous route for the obtainment of cash, but simply outright sold their crops while still in the ground at prices that were substantially lower than the anticipated ones of harvest time.[42] Cultivators probably hated engaging in such disadvantageous sales; and in one case this resentment prompted a group of peasants from Sharqiyya Province to renege on their agreement, neither releasing the pledged crops to the merchant lenders nor redeeming their debt, which consisted of a "substantial sum"—a little more than 7,030 purses.[43] It is worth mentioning that lenders often tried to preempt peasant betrayal by documenting their loans on official paper, and sometimes took the added precaution of demanding that the peasants hand over pieces of jewelry (as a form of pawn).[44]

Aware of the occurrence of such disadvantageous sales, the government tried to prevent them. In the winter of 1851, it issued a decree that "forbid merchants from giving cash to the peasants for crops before harvest time."[45] But this decree did not address peasants' need for cash during critical junctures, and accordingly many cultivators did not observe it.[46] A few years later the government attempted another approach. By the decree of February 11, 1855, it instructed the provincial government of Daqahliyya to assist rice cultivators by lending them, from the provincial treasury, the sums they needed to purchase livestock, seeds, and tools. These loans were to be repaid at harvest time, when the "sale [of crops] at profitable rates" was possible, which was better than "taking sums from merchants . . . and [being forced] to give up their rice crop at a devalued rate." Moreover, peasants were permitted to postpone the payment of tax installments until harvest times. The text of the decree ends with the belief that the combination of these measures would "enhance the economic capability" of the peasants and encourage them to remain in the countryside.[47] In December 1855, the central government ordered the universal application of these instructions. At this time too, it granted tax remission for accumulated arrears of past years so that peasants could focus on the payment of the taxes of the current year; and accordingly "peasants would not have the slightest reason to do this [engage in disadvantageous crop sales]."[48]

This official interest in the development of a payment schedule that would not threaten peasant productive capacities notwithstanding, the state also insisted that peasants meet the demanding payment schedules specified by the 1855 and 1858 tax-reassessment codes. Regarding the 1855 tax code, the government undertook the reassessment of peasant land taxes between 1853 and 1855, and initially planned to introduce the new tax code in September 1854, the beginning of the 1855 fiscal year. It was completed and approved, though, fifteen months later, in December 1855; by which time the 1855 fiscal year had ended and nearly four months of the 1856 fiscal year had passed. During these months, the peasants had, of course, paid their land taxes at the old or current rates. This being the situation, what did the government propose? It decided to stand by its original plan: the introduction of the 1855 tax code in September 1854. What this really meant was that between January and July 1856, the peasants were to pay retroactively the difference between the former and revised tax rates that pertained to the previous fifteen months (for which they had already paid taxes at the old rates). In addition, they were to pay their monthly tax installments (for January–July 1856) at the new rates[49] (see table 3.1).

These instructions were likely carried out in Rawdat al-Bahrayn Province only; for it was the first province to have completed all the necessary reassessment work. It seems that all the other provinces completed the related work in early June 1856, prompting the central government to issue the decree of June 11, 1856, which instructed peasants to pay their land taxes at the revised rates effective September 1855.[50] This meant that in June and July 1856, peasants were to pay retroactively the difference between the former and revised rates for the previous nine months, as well as pay the monthly tax installments for June and July at the newly revised rates. Thus, while the peasants of Rawdat al-Bahrayn paid higher sums in land taxes (as they paid retroactively the taxes pertaining to fifteen months, while the rest of the country retroactively paid the taxes pertaining to nine months),

Table 3.1: The Tax Payment Schedules for the Land-Tax Codes of the Mid-Nineteenth Century: Rawdat al-Bahrayn Province

Land-tax code	Date of completion & approval of reassessment work	Initial date of introduction of new taxes	Actual date of introduction of new taxes	Payment schedule for new taxes
1855 land-tax code	Dec. 1855	Sept. 1854	Jan. 1856	From Jan.–July 1856: - Retroactive payments; effective since Sept. 1854. - Paid Jan.–July 1856 tax installments at new rates.
1858 land-tax code	April 1858	Sept. 1857	May 1858	From May–July 1858: - Retroactive payments; effective since Sept. 1857. - Paid May–July 1858 tax installments at new rates.
1862 land-tax code	Possibly Aug. 1861		Possibly Sept. 1861	From Sept. 1861–July 1862: - Paid Sept. 1861–July 1862 tax installments at new rates.

Sources:

- **1855 tax project:** DMU, Daftar Takmil al-dara'ib, rawdat al-bahrayn, 1271, 2209/109/22, Part II, fol. 48.
- **1858 tax project:** DMU, Daftar Takmil al-dara'ib, rawdat al-bahrayn, 1274, 2210/109/22, fol. 69.
- **1862 tax project:** See, for example: DMU, Mukallafat atyan, kafr al-jarayda, 1278, 17009/305/22; DMU, Mukallafat atyan, mahalit abu ali al-gharbiyya, 1278, 22081/361/22; DMU, Mukallafat atyan, al-qini wa bani bakar, 1278, 6256/164/22; DMU, Mukallafat atyan, ibyar, 1278, 2924/121/22; DMU, Mukallafat atyan, al-hayatim, 1278, 7203/176/22.

those in the rest of the country had to meet tighter payment deadlines. All in all, peasants everywhere must have viewed the fiscal year of 1856 as a trying one. Table 3.1 shows that the same was probably true for 1858, when the government introduced the second major land-tax code of the mid-nineteenth-century period, as it also required retroactive tax payments.[51]

Tax Remission

The introduction of a tax-remission decree granted the peasants the opportunity to attain some level of economic recovery, and further enhanced the image and role of the head of the government as one who prioritized the welfare of his taxpaying subjects over short-term state revenue needs, which in turn ultimately contributed to the legitimization of his authority. If the decision to grant a tax pardon came about in response to peasant demands for tax relief, this meant that the ruler had converted his "financially bankrupt tax base" into a source of "symbolic capital"; and every success of the peasants in the exertion of this "symbolic power" over their ruler only served to validate his authority in their eyes.[52] For peasants seemed cognizant of the basic premises of the traditional ideology of government, particularly of their role in the smooth functioning of the state: they understood what was expected of them and what they could expect in return.[53] Thus, official recognition of the times and circumstances when peasants were unable to pay their taxes relayed a powerful message of governmental concern for the welfare of its subjects, which further served to enhance state legitimacy. During the period under study, remission decrees pardoned arrears or current taxes.

By an entry (dated December 15, 1855) in the registers of the Viceregal Cabinet, we see that official interest in the collection of current taxes could lead to the remission of back-taxes. In the context of a discussion on peasant inability to pay current (1856) tax installments, this entry refers to a recently issued decree for the remission of arrears pertaining to the fiscal year of 1855.[54] Thus, the pardon covered the tax sums specified for September 1854 through August 1855. But in December 1855, peasants were struggling to meet the installments of the 1856 fiscal year (which had started in September 1855); and learning of this problem, Said Pasha decided to address it. Here he issued a viceregal decree that specified that the recently issued tax pardon would *also* cover the remaining tax debts "so that they [the peasants] will not experience hardship in the payment of the installments of the current year"[55]—meaning the fiscal year of 1856.

Indeed, this interest in the collection of current taxes led the government to wipe out peasant tax arrears several times during the 1840s and 1850s. Some of these decrees targeted specific groups, like the 1854 directive, which addressed the arrears of the peasants who had joined the military, wiping out the sums they owed in the year of their recruitment. Also, in 1855 a decree was issued that focused on one province, by which the government forgave the peasants of Sharqiyya Province their back-taxes, which amounted to about 473 purses.[56] But the more important tax-remission decrees were those that were to be universally applied. An entry (dated November 10,

1853) in the registers of the Council of Justice refers to a tax pardon that wiped out the arrears accumulated in the fiscal year of 1257/1841,[57] which meant the cancellation of peasants' tax debts owed for the period of September 1840 to August 1841. My sampling of the registers of various governmental departments reveals that the state pardoned peasant arrears another four times during these decades.[58] Finally, that a tax pardon covered a certain fiscal year does not mean it was issued in that year. For example, the instructions for tax remission pertaining to the 1269/1853 fiscal year were issued by Decree No. 25/November 28, 1855.[59] This suggests that in the year that the tax pardon was issued, the government wished to alleviate the peasants' current tax burden by wiping out the arrears pertaining to a previous period.

Sometimes the peasants garnered additional advantages from a tax-remission decree; as can be seen from the February 1856 case put forth by a foreign merchant before the Viceregal Cabinet. This merchant claimed that he had paid the land taxes on behalf of the peasants of al-Shurfa Village, who in return pledged to turn over their crops to him at harvest time. The peasants, though, reneged on the agreement, prompting the merchant to claim that the money the peasants intended to turn over to the authorities in taxes should instead be given to him. At this point, the *nazir al-nahiya*, one of the village officials, stepped into the fray, and altogether forbade the merchant from attempting to recover his money from the villagers, "basing this on the decree that dealt with the remission of arrears through the [fiscal] year of 1267/1851." The entry ends with the following observation of the cabinet on the *nazir*'s reasoning: This sum "has no relation to, and is not analogous to arrears."[60] So here the central government reversed this village-level decision. This outcome notwithstanding, the decision of this local official likely worked to grant the villagers additional time to realize a modicum of economic recovery before they had to settle their debt.

While alleviating hardship for the peasants, tax-remission decrees could also bring rather disadvantageous instructions in their train. One, these decrees could include instructions that specified new impositions. In September 1850, the settlement of the tax accounts of a village in al-Jiza wa-Atfih Province included this clarification: the imposition of *al-thumin* "is in accordance with the decrees concerning the remission of arrears through 1260, and [its] imposition starts from the year 1261."[61] Here we learn that the government pardoned peasant arrears pertaining to the fiscal year of 1260/1844, and also ordered the imposition of a surcharge tax (*al-thumin*, which literally means one-eighth) of 12.5 percent on peasant lands, which was to take effect at the beginning of the new fiscal year, September 1844. The government increased this surcharge tax upon issuing the remission decree that specified the cancellation of the arrears of the 1853 fiscal year: for this decree directed turning the *thumin* surcharge tax into *al-suds* (literally meaning one-sixth), which really meant that the surcharge tax was raised from 12.5 to 17.0 percent. This increase was to take effect in September 1853 (the beginning of the new fiscal year, 1854).[62] Two, peasants were not permitted to access tax credits they had paid prior to the issuance of a tax-remission decree. Thus, both arrears and tax credits were wiped out by remission decrees.[63] Three, when a village paid the arrears pardoned by a remission decree, the government did not always oversee the peasants' reimbursement. In November 1853, the peasants of Kafr al-Tirʿa filed a complaint against their *muta'ahhid* for compelling them to pay their tax debts in contravention of the official declaration that pardoned peasant arrears of 1844. The governor of al-Gharbiyya Province investigated the case and found that the village's "1844 arrears were incidental; and the shaykh of the village affirmed that the sum had been settled and so a tax pardon was unnecessary." In turn, the Council of Justice simply dismissed the case.[64] On the other hand, the case of Shirnin Village shows us that when the arrears constituted a sizable sum, the government found for the peasants. For this time it declared that the decision of the *muta'ahhid* and shaykhs to ignore official instructions regarding the cancellation of peasant arrears that had accumulated in 1844, thereby forcing the peasants to settle their tax debt of 29,558 piastres and 28 para, constituted a violation of the law. Thus, it ordered these officials to return this sum to the peasants.[65]

At times, tax pardons targeted current taxes. The government granted such pardon when the peasants experienced economic hardship due to the ruination of their lands or the loss of their crops because of natural disasters: for example, when arable land had not been inundated by the Nile (and became *sharaqi* land); or when sea water covered the rice fields and destroyed the plants.[66] Other times, the government did not forgive taxes, but merely instructed its tax officials to deal with the disadvantaged peasants with compassion. In 1861, the Nile flood was excessive in some regions of the country, particularly Bani Suwayf Province, and this prompted the government to instruct its tax officials to refrain from unduly pressuring the peasants to pay their tax installments; instead they were to "collect what it was possible [to collect]."[67]

But the government was not so accommodating when peasant requests for tax remission concerned marginal lands suitable for reclamation. In August 1856, a report to the Viceregal Cabinet observed that the 100 *faddans* of *ib'adiyya* land that had been adjoined to the arable area of Kafr al-Rahmaniyya Village "were not suitable for cultivation because of their salinity, and the shaykh of the village lacked the capability to pay their taxes, which amounted to 2,589 piastres, 13 para, annually." On this basis, continued this report, he requested the permanent cancellation of the related taxes. In response, the government stressed that the *ib'adiyya* tract would not have been adjoined to the village area in the first place if its reclamation had seemed impossible.[68] In other words, it attributed the failure of the headman to bring this tract of marginal land into cultivation to his laziness; and although this entry does not specify the final outcome of the case, it is likely that the headman's request was denied. The case of al-Jazira al-Khadra Village lends additional confirmation for this assumption. The arable area of the village included about 71 *faddans* of *atil* (waste) land, all of which carried state taxes. This situation prompted the village headmen to refrain from assigning this land to the villagers by *ramya* distribution, the customary way of dealing with vacant land; probably because they knew the *ramya* recipients would default (rather quickly) on the payment of the taxes of the objectionable land portions. In the face of this, the headmen chose to undertake the distribution of this land among the village peasants on an annual basis, which, according to the *athurat* register of al-Jazira al-Khadra, was a strategy they had introduced around 1839 (at which time the authorities apparently made the village liable for this land).[69] The introduction of this strategy as well as its endurance suggests that the village authorities were aware of the view of the state on marginal lands—that such lands could be brought into cultivation only when the peasants intensified their reclamation efforts—and its disinclination to pardon their taxes.

Neither was the government moved to find for peasants requesting tax forgiveness for lands utilized by public works projects when they had amply demonstrated the ability to pay the disputed taxes. In August 1859, the government denied the request of one holder of *miri* land for tax exemption for the 3 *faddans* used in the construction of the Sharqawiyya Canal in 1816, explaining its decision by referring to the following points: the petitioner had known and accepted the situation of the problematic *faddans* when he had purchased his holding; he had regularly paid their taxes through 1851;

and moreover, the canal "runs through the lands of many others and they have not complained about this."[70]

All in all, it seems that the government granted tax remission when the economic capabilities of the taxpaying base were seriously imperiled, but jealously demanded its revenue sums when peasants seemed to try to shirk their responsibilities.

The Role of the Village Headman

The examination of the system of rural taxation in the different areas that made up the Ottoman Empire reveals that the central role of the village headman in the collection of taxes constituted a common feature.[71] The same applied to Egypt. And while most studies on the Egyptian context highlight the responsibilities and prerogatives of the village shaykh,[72] I seek to shed light on another dimension of this role: at times, it was a trying one.

The jurisdiction of a village headman extended over his *hissa*, or section. The arable land of a village was divided into 24 *qirat*s, or parts; and a headman assumed authority over a certain number of *qirat*s, which became his *hissa*. A village usually had more than one shaykh, and the *qirat*s were divided between them according to their wealth and social status.[73] The *hissa* also had its counterpart in the village area where peasants lived, denoted *hara*; and both were administered by the same shaykh. According to Cuno, members of the same clan cultivated land in the same *hissa*, lived in the same *hara*, and were under the jurisdiction of the same shaykh.[74] The responsibilities of a headman were numerous, but may be generally categorized under either one of their two major duties: to represent the peasants to state authorities, and to represent the state to village comembers.[75]

The primary responsibility of a headman toward his *hissa* was to ensure the land remained in cultivation and that holders regularly paid their taxes.[76] This further involved ensuring that all peasants capable of farm work actually possessed arable village land; indeed, according to historian Imad Hillal, this constituted "one of the most important of the headmen's responsibilities."[77] As for his supervision of tax payments, the headman along with the village *sarraf*, or accountant, kept track of payments: they documented actual payments, tax credits, and the names of cultivators whose payments were outstanding. According to an entry, dated October 1, 1849, in the registers of the Department of Civil Affairs, Shaykh

Ayad Ibrahim, premier headman of the village of al-Zawiya al-Hamra, compiled a list of the names of the cultivators whose payments were outstanding through August 1848; these were six, and together they owed the state treasury 3,437 piastres, 7 para. As these cultivators were not peasants, but "were *dhawat* (high state officials) as well as others," the headman had to call on state authorities to locate these individuals and oversee their payments.[78] On the other hand, when peasant cultivators defaulted on their tax payments, headmen often invoked the *ramya* process; whereby a shaykh removed the land from the possession of the insolvent peasant and reassigned it to another villager who possessed the requisite level of resources for regular tax payment. Many times, the headman himself assumed the role of recipient, as can easily be verified by a quick glance through the village *athurat* registers, which show that *ramya* distribution constituted the primary means by which village shaykhs accumulated land wealth. At this juncture it is necessary to emphasize that a shaykh's repeated assumption of the role of *ramya* recipient was not always motivated by greed. In his discussion on *ramya* assignments in Kamshish Village, scholar Muhammad Hakim rightly cautions us about attributing the headman's comparatively large landholding to the "abuse of his power"; that is, that the headman relied on his power to expand his landholding at the expense of the other villagers by repeatedly assigning *ramya* land to himself.[79] For these individuals possessed the wherewithal necessary to pay cultivation expenses and taxes; and when other villagers were unable to carry the burden of additional land, it was imperative for the responsible shaykh to assume this responsibility himself. When he did not, the village tax accounts showed that his *hissa* had outstanding sums in taxes.

This was a situation to avoid; for the government often punished headmen who had allowed peasants under their jurisdiction to accumulate tax arrears. Sometimes, it ordered the removal of the headman from his post, as is illustrated by the following November 1851 case. When several shaykhs of one village in al-Jiza wa Atfih Province allowed arrears to accumulate in their respective *hissa*s, the provincial authorities dismissed them, integrated their *hissa*s into one, and offered it to a wealthy villager named Ali Tarih "on condition that he pay the accumulated amount pertaining to the aforementioned *hissa*."[80] Other times, the government ordered the imprisonment of the offending headman, maybe because a member of his family could replace him. The Department of Interior examined such a case in early 1850. The case begins with a complaint filed in December 1849 by Yaʿqub, a merchant, against Ismail Hamad, premier headman (umda) of Billa Village in Gharbiyyia Province. The merchant claimed that the umda had failed to reimburse him for a loan of 32,000 piastres, and that this should have been settled by his brother Muhammad on his behalf, and as the latter had failed to do so, he (Muhammad) should similarly be imprisoned. The government did not approve this demand though, explaining as follows:

> Starting from 5 Dhu al-Qaʿda 1265 (22 Sept. 1849) Ismail Hamad has been in jail because of the [late] tax payments due from his village through the fiscal year of 1264/1848 . . . and his brother Muhammad is performing his [brother's] duties, of collection of tax payments and selection of peasants for corvée, etc . . . And if he is sent to prison with his brother, the state taxes through 1264/1848 will not be paid and additional arrears will accumulate.[81]

Thus the government had locked up Ismail because he had allowed the emergence of arrears in his village and because he had a brother who could perform his duties on his behalf; and it adamantly refused to jail this brother, who was officially charged with the collection of the village's late taxes, when learning of Yaʿqub's legitimate complaint. In a follow-up entry of March 27, 1850, the authorities informed the merchant (and his partners) that they could not collect their money from the brothers until all village tax debts had been paid to the state treasury. On the other hand, if they wished to secure the immediate recovery of their loan, they had the option of possessing the brothers' livestock and selling it.[82]

There were times, too, when the government responded rather mildly to cases of village arrears, probably in the belief that some bleak village situations were beyond the control of their headmen. An entry in the registers of the Department of Interior, dated October 26, 1859, suggests that it was this belief that had prompted the government to direct the headmen of a village in al-Fayyum Province to pay the tax arrears in installments over a period of four years starting from September 1858.[83]

Yet it seems that a sympathetic government response to the emergence of village arrears could hardly be taken for granted, and headmen realized this. Thus, when saddled with persistent arrears, headmen quickly devised alternative solutions. In October 1859, Abd al-Rahim Rajah and Jad al-Rab Ahmad, the two headmen of al-Qusiyya Village in Asyut Province, explained that each one of them was responsible for half the village, and they experienced hardship in the performance of their duties because "the pertinent arable lands were extensive, and because they performed [the related] duties alone . . . and they are paying taxes without the possession of harvests. And for this reason, they request either their removal from their posts and the appointment of other shaykhs in their place . . . or the division of the [village] into four sections." This latter option would have entailed the appointment of another two individuals in the capacity of headman. In response, the government issued instructions for the investigation of the case, stressing the importance of resolving the related problems in a way acceptable to the petitioners.[84] Thus, by admitting their dilemma and suggesting possible solutions to prevent its exacerbation, headmen could save themselves from punishment. Then again, when headmen completely despaired about the payment of the requisite taxes, they might resort to abandonment, which might be the reason why two shaykhs from central Egypt, identified in 1850 by the Department of Interior as runaways, had fled their villages.[85]

Conclusion

During the mid-nineteenth-century years, the government attempted to modify the system of tax collection so that peasants might pay their taxes regularly and the state might maximize revenue levels. Inspiration for the related decisions did not always come from high-level officials at the center; for the state took notice of the ideas and comments that came from the periphery and adopted the best of these—as occurred with its land-legislation and tax-reassessment efforts—like its modification of the January 8, 1856 decree according to the suggestions made by the officials of Buhayra Province regarding peasants' payment of their tax installments.

But by the late 1850s and early 1860s, government policy regarding tax collection (as in land legislation and tax revaluation) had become more oppressive, as this disadvantaged the indigent peasants—the majority of the rural population. The related governmental decrees and regulations may be linked to the contemporary strengthening of capitalism in the countryside. In a time of rising crop prices and the ascendance of free market rules, whereby peasants could sell their produce to whomever they wished at market rates, land cultivation became a profitable endeavor that led to the increase of agricultural output as well as to the market value of arable land. Aware of these developments, the state sought to acquire its share of the rising agricultural profits. Hence, it restricted the land-redistribution dimension of the *ramya* system (by the 1858 and 1861 regulations), specified demanding payment schedules upon introducing the 1855 and 1858 tax codes, repeatedly qualified its tax-remission policy, and often dealt harshly with local headmen when tax arrears emerged in their villages.

Finally, bureaucratic inefficiency could inadvertently make the system of tax collection more oppressive than was intended by the state. In a December 4, 1859 entry in the registers of the Department of Interior, state authorities reviewed a complaint made by a peasant from al-Daljamun Village (in Rawdat al-Bahrayn Province). This peasant had earlier informed the government that the construction of the railway had entailed the utilization of 10 *faddans* of his landholding, which meant that this land was no longer productive arable land, and had become "waste" land; and on this basis the government had exempted him from the payment of its taxes. Yet the local authorities continued to demand these taxes, which prompted him to submit another petition, when he wrote of the "injustice" of his predicament and emphasized that "orders had been issued regarding this matter." At this point, the central authorities ordered an investigation of these claims, asking: "If orders had been issued, how is it that they have not been observed?"[86] While I was unable to find other entries that specified the outcome of this case, it stands to reason that the government championed the petitioner. But the point to emphasize here is that the delay in processing the tax-exemption orders only served to exacerbate an already difficult situation.

Another form of bureaucratic inefficiency was the center's limited capacity to monitor the activities of officials in the periphery, for this granted lower-level officials the opportunity to benefit from their position at the expense of the peasants under their jurisdiction. For example, some officials carried out their taxation duties in ways that disadvantaged the peasants. This is demonstrated by the 1851 case of Mansur Ajur, who complained that his shaykh, Ibrahim al-Far, "compelled him to pay the 1267/1851 taxes early."[87] But the most common complaint made by peasants in this regard had to do with the imposition of additional, or unofficial, taxes by village headmen.[88] This can be seen in the 1859 case where a group of peasants from Bani Silliman Village complained that their umda had "imposed on . . . each *faddan* five piastres, as payment for his services."[89]

4

Land Tenure in Peasant Villages

The leading Ottoman reformers of the nineteenth century, having embraced the understanding that development and modernization were underpinned by high economic growth, further realized the necessity of enhancing the productive abilities of the population.[1] This made the peasantry a component of the state reform project. In order to improve the productive (and taxable) capacity of peasant producers, state officials tried to address some of their major problems. Three were particularly significant. First, taxes were unduly onerous, which prompted the state to reform the system of tax farming between 1838 and 1847. Second, peasants lacked secure title to their lands, which meant they could not be expected to improve their output or pay their taxes regularly. State officials addressed this problem when drafting the 1858 Ottoman land law, whereby they sought to "reestablish the state's legal right of ownership" of agricultural land as well as to grant peasants secure title to their lands.[2] Third, the indebtedness of peasants to moneylenders was a chronic problem, and stemmed from peasants' need for cash for tax payments and cultivation costs. This problem had grave consequences; most importantly, land dispossession. Scholars of Ottoman history point to a number of decisions and policies (like the 1858 land law) that reveal state interest in ensuring that peasants remained economically viable producers.[3] But the assessment of these efforts reveals that they were less than successful: For peasants had to continue to bear crushing tax loads; most peasants were too suspicious of the state to try to obtain titles to their lands; and while indebted peasants could count on state protection and intercession if they were at risk for dispossession, the general state approach toward their problems "around the middle of the nineteenth century was characterized by indifference."[4] And yet, with the outbreak of the American Civil War in 1861, peasants in the Anatolian heartland were able to meet the rising demand for crops, especially tobacco.[5] This easily allows us to conclude that the peasants in Anatolia remained economically viable producers during the mid-nineteenth-century period.

The same was true for Egyptian peasants. At the start of this period, official decisions were informed by the economic principles of traditional statecraft, leading the state to seek to balance between its revenue needs and the well-being of its production base. But this changed toward the latter years of Said Pasha, whose grandiose dreams and projects prompted him to demand higher revenue levels from his subjects. Thus, this juncture witnessed his government increasingly focused on the maximization of state revenues while disregarding the needs of the producing base. But this focus, which involved repeated increases in agricultural taxes, more stringent rules for land recovery, and more rigorous tax-collection rules, did not lead to widespread land dispossession and impoverishment of the peasants. In 1856, just two years after Said Pasha assumed power, British Consul Harris reported his findings on the condition of the peasants of Upper Egypt, stating: "The great landed proprietors are becoming rich, and the smaller ones are saving money . . . the dues of the govt. are collected without trouble, and they are not onerous, considering the rate at which the produce of the land is sold."[6] The comments of British Consul Henry Bulwer that were made in 1862, near the end of Said Pasha's reign, are strikingly similar. For he describes the peasants' taxes as "a sum which is not beyond his [that is, the peasant's] means," and then concludes with this appraisal of the general condition of the peasant smallholder: "and tho' poor and squalid in appearance, he is frequently in possession of a small capital which he turns to account."[7] This chapter, which examines the impact of state policy on peasant land tenure during the mid-nineteenth-century years, confirms the view of these British diplomats. It argues, contrary to the assertions of other writers, that the majority of peasants did not experience debilitating land dispossession. The discussion focuses first on the issue of peasant land acquisition, which involves examining the various modes of land acquirement. Then we turn to the issue of peasant land loss, which necessitates the investigation of the major trends/points that are considered part and parcel of the conventional story on peasant land dispossession: *matruk* land (large-scale abandonment of land); *ziyada* (surplus) land; the encroachment of the state elite on peasant lands; the impact of the major land law (1858 law) of the period; and land distribution in peasant villages.

Peasant Land Acquisition

Unlike private property, the holders of *miri* (state) land did not enjoy the two rights of ownership: the *raqaba* (absolute ownership) and the *tasarruf* (usufructuary rights). Instead, the right of absolute ownership rested with the state, as was explained earlier, while the cultivators enjoyed the right to the usufruct of the land. As long as peasants kept their lands (variously referred to as *miri*, *kharajiyya*, or *athar* in the archival sources) cultivated and regularly paid the required taxes, their holdings remained in their possession, and they were assured of its transmission to their heirs upon passing away. But they also knew that the accumulation of tax arrears would lead the authorities to remove the arrear-laden lands from their possession and reassign these to solvent peasants. During the mid-nineteenth-century years, the state depended on these two modes of land transfer (inheritance and land assignment) to ensure that *miri* land remained cultivated and thereby continued to generate the required tax revenues.

Inheritance of Land

That inheritance constituted one of the primary modes of peasant land acquirement during the period under discussion is verified by the *athurat* registers, which list the names of holders in a village, the size of each one's landholding, and the mode of acquisition. Compiled only once, this register reveals how the villagers had obtained the different portions of their holdings over the previous thirty to forty years. The register of Ibyar Village (its compilation was completed in late December 1859) shows that 41.50 percent of the peasant holders had acquired a portion of their holdings by inheritance over this period.[8] Table 4.1 shows the same importance of inheritance as a means of land acquirement for the peasants of the other three sample villages, though specifying even higher proportions for these.

Not only did the majority of village holders acquire land by inheritance, they also counted on this mode of land transfer for the acquirement of a sizable portion of their holdings.[9] This can be seen in the village of Kafr al-Rajallat. The examination of its *athurat* register, compiled in 1857, reveals that all three strata of village holders had obtained significant proportions of their holdings by inheritance: the small stratum acquired 29.59 percent of its land by inheritance; the medium, 25.05 percent; and the wealthy, 26.50 percent. A quick glance at table 4.2 allows us to discern the same

Table 4.1: The Proportion of Village Holders Who Acquired *Athar* Land by Inheritance

Village	Land heirs (%)
Kafr al-Rajallat	50.00
Jazirat al-Aʿjam	58.06
Al-Jazira al-Khadra	61.87
Ibyar	41.50

Sources: DMU, Daftar al-athurat, kafr al-rajallat, 1273, 3/1/20; DMU, Mukallafat atyan, kafr al-rajallat, 1274, 8208/110/20; DMU, Daftar al-athurat, jazirat al-aʿjam, 1274, 1/1/20; DMU, Mukallafat atyan, jazirat al-aʿjam, 1274, 4576/61/20; DMU, Daftar al-athurat, ibyar, 1276, 10/77/22; DMU, Daftar al-athurat, al-jazira al-khadra, 1276, 27/77/22.

phenomenon in the other three villages of our sample. Also, the figures for Kafr al-Rajallat, Ibyar, and al-Jazira al-Khadra Villages suggest that inheritance figured more prominently for the small stratum of village holders than it did for the medium and wealthy strata, whose numbers were lower; and in the case of al-Jazira al-Khadra much lower. Still, in three of the sample villages—Kafr al-Rajallat, Jazirat al-Aʿjam, Ibyar—these numbers do not cover the bulk of the poor peasants' holdings: for example, the small stratum of peasants in Ibyar acquired only 27.84 percent of their lands by inheritance, leaving roughly 72 percent of their holdings to account for.[10] Thus, even though poor peasants might have obtained larger proportions of their holdings by inheritance than did other strata, they depended on another far more important mode of land transfer (specifically, land assignment or *ramya*) in the acquirement of land—as had the other strata.

A final comment remains to be made: if table 4.2 had not included *masmuh* lands, which it does, it would have necessitated recording lower inheritance proportions for the affluent village strata than is specified here. As will be recalled, the government originally compensated village shaykhs for the performance of their duties by granting them tax-exempted lands, and when it abolished this system of compensation in 1857, it did not remove the lands from the shaykhs' possession but instead transformed these into their *athar* lands. These lands are not specified in the *athurat* registers of Kafr al-Rajallat and Jazirat al-Aʿjam simply because both of these registers

Table 4.2: The Proportion of Peasant Holdings Obtained by Inheritance

	Kafr al-Rajallat Village			Jazirat al-Aʿjam Village		
	Village land	Inherited land		Village land	Inherited land	
	faddans	*faddans*		*faddans*	*faddans*	
Stratum	no.	no.	%	no.	no.	%
Small < 5	218.0	64.5	29.59	79.0	19.5	24.68
Medium 5 < 20	271.5	68.0	25.05	158.0	45.0	28.48
Wealthy 20 and more	175.5	46.5	26.50	211.5	60.0	28.39

	Ibyar Village			Al-Jazira al-Khadra Village		
	Village land	Inherited land		Village land	Inherited land	
	faddans	*faddans*		*faddans*	*faddans*	
Stratum	no.	no.	%	no.	no.	%
Small < 5	634	176.5	27.84	118	80	67.80
Medium 5 < 20	1,144	255.0	22.29	448	130	29.02
Wealthy 20 and more	2,506	523.0	20.87	923	231	25.03

Totals	Village land	Inherited land	
	faddans	*faddans*	
Stratum	no.	no.	%
Small < 5	1,049.0	340.5	32.46
Medium 5 < 20	2,021.5	498.0	24.64
Wealthy 20 and more	3,816.0	860.5	22.55

Notes: In computing the data presented by this table, I employed the method described in the notes of table 2.1.

Sources: DMU, Daftar al-athurat, kafr al-rajallat, 1273, 3/1/20; DMU, Mukallafat atyan, kafr al-rajallat, 1274, 8208/110/20; DMU, Daftar al-athurat, jazirat al-aʿjam, 1274, 1/1/20; DMU, Mukallafat atyan, jazirat al-aʿjam, 1274, 4576/61/20; DMU, Daftar al-athurat, ibyar, 1276, 10/77/22; DMU, Daftar al-athurat, al-jazira al-khadra, 1276, 27/77/22.

were compiled in 1857, while the decree that recognized the shaykhs' *athar* rights to their *masmuh* lands was issued in June 1858. What this means is that, technically speaking, prior to 1858 these lands were not acquired by inheritance. On the other hand, village headmen—both the shaykhs of the different village sections (*hissas*) and the premier headman, or umda—often hailed from the same family, with the eldest son usually succeeding his father. Thus, in reality this land had been in the family for generations and had been transmitted by inheritance.[11] The significance of the inheritance of *masmuh* lands can most clearly be seen in Jazirat al-A'jam Village. Here the village headmen (the holders of the *masmuh* lands) belonged to the medium and wealthy strata, and this is why the inheritance figures for the medium and wealthy strata are higher than those of the small stratum (table 4.2).

State recognition of peasant inheritance of land being premised on its interest in ensuring cultivators remained economically viable, so that they could farm their land and pay their taxes—and ultimately increase governmental revenues—translated into state support for peasants with legitimate claims to their land patrimonies. On August 21, 1852, Mustafa Hassan from al-Ja'afira Village (in Qalyubiya Province) complained to the al-Khanka religious court about the usurpation of his land by a neighbor named Muhammad al-Jaky. Mustafa explained to the court that the disputed 2 *faddans* originally belonged to his father, and they had farmed the land together until his father's death, when it was transmitted to him. Here he specifically explained that he had acquired the land in accordance with Islamic inheritance rules: "*Bi-tariq al-istihqaq al-irth al-shar'i*," only to lose control of it in 1851, when Muhammad forcibly took it for himself. When the court asked Muhammad about the veracity of this allegation, he confessed his deed, and the court ordered the return of the land to Mustafa.[12]

Legal heirs could also count on state support of their rights even if the maintenance of their lands had been consigned to a caretaker for a lengthy period. In short, controllers of the land could not refer to this extended period of control to justify their attempts to dispossess legal heirs. On September 30, 1856, Bahnasawi, son of Bahnasawi Hamud, from al-Marij Village (in Qalyubiya Province) sued for the recovery of his inheritance from the control of its caretaker. Bahnasawi explained that when his father died, he and his three sisters and his mother constituted the legal heirs, but as he was a minor at the time of his father's death, the family's affairs (a sizable inheritance that included 9 *faddans* of *miri* land) were managed by a legal guardian, named Rifaʿi Omar, until he too passed away. It was then that relatives brought the family a servant who, explained Bahnasawi, "cultivated the land, took its harvest and paid its *miri* taxes in the name of our late father . . . and in return the servant and his family ate and drank with us." And when Bahnasawi reached his majority, he demanded that the servant relinquish control of the family inheritance, but the latter refused to comply, explaining "that the land and other inherited items had indeed belonged to the plaintiff's father, and upon his death were transmitted to the plaintiff, but I have had control for a lengthy period and [because of this] I thought I had become the rightful owner." However, the court did not accept this logic and informed the servant that "the long period along with your admission of the claimant's inheritance rights entitles you to nothing."[13]

But the state was not so accommodating when heirs neglected their land legacies for an extended period, as is illustrated by this 1857 case brought before the Council of Justice. The plaintiff, named Mustafa Salim, explained to the council that his father and uncle had shared the same dwelling, which further entailed having held their land jointly. After both had died, the uncle's widow had "requested [possession of] the *faddan* and a half, claiming these rightfully [belonged] to her," disregarding Mustafa's inheritance rights (he was the only male heir) to the disputed land. The land remained in her possession for fifteen years, at which time it seems that Mustafa returned to the village and claimed his legacy. The council issued its decision on April 23, 1857, ruling that "the aforementioned land is the right of the woman [because] she has possessed it for a period of fifteen years and [thus] the claimant does not have [any] right to it by inheritance." At first glance, it appears the council had applied Article VIII of the 1855 land law, which granted women inheritance rights when they proved to the authorities that the loss of their land legacies would cause them to live in destitution. Yet the entry makes no mention of this land law, and instead specifies the application of Islamic law, which upholds cultivators' rights against those of other claimants.[14] Mustafa's case was undoubtedly further undermined by Ottoman *qanun*, which stipulates that cases were not to be heard after the passage of fifteen years.

That the state liked to champion responsible cultivators can also be discerned in its treatment of cases dealing with the division of joint landholdings. Many times, heirs did not divide their land patrimony among themselves, but instead preferred to keep it intact as one holding. This further entailed continuing to reside in the family home and pooling their resources so that each coheir would contribute to the payment of farming expenses and taxes, participate in the various labor tasks involved in the cultivation process, and finally receive a share of the profits generated by the land. Peasants frequently described this arrangement as living in "one dwelling and [sharing] one income."[15] While rural notables liked this arrangement because it prevented land fragmentation through inheritance and thereby allowed the "reproduction and enhancement of their economic and political status," poorer villagers probably viewed it as a strategy for poverty alleviation.[16] Yet the decision to form joint households and joint holdings was not irreversible, for the archival sources disclose a number of cases where peasants insisted on the termination of such arrangements. Those peasants who requested official mediation found that the government treated such cases as it did inheritance disputes. Thus, coheirs were entitled to their shares of the joint landholding upon the dissolution of the joint household, which is precisely why one peasant decided to sue his brother on June 1, 1857. Bringing his case to al-Khanka religious court, this man explained that "since the death of my father I have [lived] with my brother, the aforementioned defendant, in one dwelling; and now he wishes to evict me and dispossess me of [my share of] the patrimony." The defendant, in turn, did not deny this, instead justifying his position by stressing certain aspects of their family history. The two men were stepbrothers, related through their father. It appears that the plaintiff's mother had assumed she was a widow at the time she had remarried. But the first husband presented himself to the family many years later, which invalidated her second marriage. This apparently led the defendant to consider his brother an illegitimate child, and on that basis believed that he had no rights to the family patrimony. However, the court ruled otherwise, granting the plaintiff one-half the disputed land, his legally recognized share, explaining that "the plaintiff is your brother and the son of your father."[17] Thus, when petitioners were able to prove their rights to their land patrimonies, further demonstrating that they had not neglected these lands, they could be certain of state support of their claims.

The Assignment of Land

Even more important than inheritance was land assignment, or the acquirement of land through the workings of the *ramya* system. Hardly a novelty of the middle decades of the nineteenth century, some form of this system existed in Islamic Egypt. According to Petra Sijpesteijn, the state developed two strategies for the enhancement of agricultural productivity in the early years of the eighth century: one involved the introduction of a new tax category for land recently brought under the plow, "while 'forced' land-assignments were needed to increase the acreage."[18] State reliance on this mode of land distribution can also be discerned for the first six decades of the nineteenth century, as the archival sources are replete with entries that reveal frequent and extensive governmental reliance on *ramya* assignment. This enduring interest in *ramya* assignment can be attributed to the state's wish to ensure that agrarian land was consigned to capable cultivators who regularly paid their taxes.

During the mid-nineteenth-century years, the *ramya* process began with the appearance of vacant land. At this time, the authorities assigned it to any individual who demonstrated the possession of the cash level—whereby the individual was viewed as "*qadir*" or had "pecuniary capability"—which would ensure the land was kept in cultivation and its taxes were regularly paid. The *athurat* registers show that peasants received this land free of charge, for receipt was not contingent on the payment of transfer fees.

Three circumstances called for *ramya* land assignment. First, when holders allowed the accumulation of tax arrears. In the examination of the history of Siliman Ibrahim al-Dib's holding in Kafr al-Rajallat Village, we learn that one parcel of land, roughly 2.5 *faddan*s, had originally belonged to a woman, but had then been reassigned to another villager, Mohammad al-Dib, for the following reason: "When there was delay in the cultivation of the land and the payment of the taxes, the land was distributed by *ramya*."[19] Second, when the holder died without issue, as was the situation of Uthman al-Badawi of al-Jazira al-Khadra Village, upon whose death in 1844 the land was reassigned to another villager, Rajab Amir.[20] This category can also include those cases where the heir of the deceased holder was listed as *mutasahhib*, or someone who had fled the village, at the time of the original possessor's death. This was the case with Muhammad and his son Umar of Kafr al-Rajallat Village: "The original holder of the land has died [but] his son Umar had fled the village and his whereabouts are not known, and he [Muhammad] has no other heir besides [Umar]." Here Umar's land patrimony was reassigned by *ramya* to other responsible cultivators in the village, one of which was Yusif Khalifa, who obtained roughly half a *faddan*.[21] The third circumstance involved the assignment of marginal land, which in the case of the 71 *faddan*s of wasteland in al-Jazira al-Khadra Village constituted a local strategy to cope with unwanted, virtually uncultivable, village land. But in the case of Jazirat al-Aʿjam Village, the assignment of marginal land constituted a governmental strategy to expand the arable area of this village, for by it the peasants were assigned barren land, which had originally lain outside the village boundaries.[22]

The Egyptian archival sources suggest that the majority of peasants relied on *ramya* distribution for land acquirement during the mid-nineteenth-century period. This is specifically confirmed by the *athurat* registers of the four sample villages, as these show that the majority of the peasant holders relied rather heavily on this mode of land acquirement roughly between the 1810s and the 1850s. Here we must note historian Ali Barakat's assumption regarding the high proportion of land classified as *ramya* assignments by village holders: when peasants were asked by the *athurat* committee to verify their right to the lands in their possession, but could not, they simply "claimed it was '*ramya*' land."[23] This suggests that the numbers pertaining to the frequency of *ramya* assignments are somewhat exaggerated, which further means that peasants generally expected the authorities to accept slightly exaggerated accounts simply because *ramya* assignments *did* occur on a frequent basis—thus, such "falsification" in the relaying of their land stories would not be noticed by the concerned officials. Whatever the case, the *athurat* registers show that the proportion of *ramya* land recipients could be quite high. For example, in January 1860, 79.82 percent of Ibyar Village holders attributed parts of their holdings to this mode of land acquirement, and while the corresponding figure for al-Jazira al-Khadra Village is not as high, it is still quite impressive (table 4.3).

Table 4.3: The Proportion of Village Holders Who Acquired *Athar* Land by *Ramya*

Village	Ramya recipients (%)
Kafr al-Rajallat	57.14
Jazirat al-Aʿjam	19.35
Al-Jazira al-Khadra	62.59
Ibyar	79.82

Sources: DMU, Daftar al-athurat, kafr al-rajallat, 1273, 3/1/20; DMU, Mukallafat atyan, kafr al-rajallat, 1274, 8208/110/20; DMU, Daftar al-athurat, jazirat al-aʿjam, 1274, 1/1/20; DMU, Mukallafat atyan, jazirat al-aʿjam, 1274, 4576/61/20; DMU, Daftar al-athurat, ibyar, 1276, 10/77/22; DMU, Daftar al-athurat, al-jazira al-khadra, 1276, 27/77/22.

While earlier studies on village land tenure in nineteenth-century Egypt recognize the significance of *ramya* assignment for peasant land acquirement, their view is rather narrow: for they only see it as a means whereby land was transferred from insolvent holders to affluent villagers. Thus, in this view the *ramya* system worked to enrich the affluent villagers at the expense of their poorer neighbors.[24] Yet the examination of the land-tenure registers of Kafr al-Rajallat Village reveals the following picture for the year 1274/1857–1858. The relevant land-tax register specifies 140 landholders for this village; of these, 107 holders belonged to the small stratum or the poor group of village holders. When comparing this land-tax register with the village *athurat* register, we see that 49.5 percent of the small stratum of holders acquired portions of their holdings by *ramya* assignment.[25] And while this is a very conservative estimate (the real figure certainly was much higher as will be shown below), these findings do confirm an important dimension of the *ramya* system: it often assigned *ramya* land to poor peasants. Indeed even landless peasants could aspire to receive *ramya* land, as was the case with Husayn al-Bayumi, whose entire holding of approximately 1.5 *faddans* was acquired by two instances of land assignment, the first one in 1844 precisely because "he was landless."[26] At the same time, these poor peasants were not penurious or destitute, for the acquirement of a land assignment was contingent on the possession of the level of funds that would ensure the payment of the land's farming expenses and taxes. Thus, the authorities took care to assign only that portion of land that the recipient's wherewithal could maintain. This is confirmed by the October 1853 response of the Council of Justice to a peasant who was unhappy with the amount of land assigned to him: the council rejected his request for a larger assignment because his resources did not enable him to maintain additional land.[27]

As is suggested by table 4.4, both the poor and the affluent peasants depended rather heavily on the system of land assignment for the expansion of their holdings during the mid-century period. That the numbers specified for the wealthy stratum are higher than those of the other two should not be surprising, for this group, quite simply, possessed the level of funds that allowed repeated assignments of *ramya* land.

Indeed, the workings of the *ramya* system led to the concentration of land in the hands of a few wealthy villagers. Thus, in early 1860, the wealthy stratum of Ibyar Village consisted of twenty-nine holders, who had together received 1,322 *faddans* by *ramya* assignment during the previous three to four decades. At the other end of the spectrum, the 217 holders who made

Table 4.4: The Proportion of Peasant Landholdings Obtained by Land Assignment: Totals of Two Sample Villages, Ibyar and al-Jazira al-Khadra

	Village land *faddans*	*Ramya* land *faddans*	*Ramya* land %
Stratum	no.	no.	%
Small < 5	752	406.0	53.99
Medium 5 < 20	1,592	766.5	48.15
Wealthy 20 and more	3,067	1,883.0	61.40

Notes: The numbers specified in the "Village land" and "*Ramya* land" categories were computed according to the system specified in table 2.1.

Sources: DMU, Daftar al-athurat ibyar, 1276, 10/77/22; DMU, Daftar al-athurat, al-jazira al-khadra, 1276, 27/77/22.

up the village small stratum (these constituted 49 percent of the village holders) had received 382 *faddans* by land assignment during this period.[28]

The above discussion on the patterns of *ramya* distribution during the mid-nineteenth-century period has refrained from closely examining what seems to be the anomalous situation of Jazirat al-Aʿjam Village. A quick look at table 4.3 reveals that the proportion of holders who received land assignments was much lower than that of the other villages, as can be seen by comparing its 19.35 percent to that of, say, al-Jazira al-Khadra's 62.59 percent. In addition, the *athurat* register of Jazirat al-Aʿjam Village discloses that each of the village strata attributed very small proportions of their holdings to *ramya* distribution: by 1857, the small strata had received 6.96 percent of its lands by *ramya* distribution, the middle 2.22 percent, and the wealthy 10.40 percent. But when comparing this *athurat* register (which was compiled in 1274/September 1857) with the land-tax register of the same year, we discern a huge discrepancy: the *athurat* register specifies that the village agricultural area was composed of 213.5 *faddans*, while the land-tax register puts this at 448.5 *faddans*.[29] That the government was known to expand the agricultural area of a village by compelling its peasants to accept barren lands originally situated outside the village boundaries helps to explain this discrepancy.[30] For the *athurat* registers documented only the village *athar* lands, or arable lands possessed by generations of peasants, and as the recently assigned barren lands hardly counted as *athar*, these latter were omitted from the village *athurat* register. For Jazirat al-Aʿjam Village, this omission concerned 235 *faddans*, or 52 percent of its arable area, and further covered 88 percent of the land distributed by the *ramya* system. Finally, this means that the figures pertaining to *ramya* acquisition in Jazirat al-Aʿjam Village are much higher than is revealed by its *athurat* register. Accordingly, the figure of 19.35 percent specified in table 4.3 is only a very conservative estimate; the real figure, though difficult to estimate exactly, certainly was much higher. This also means that the numbers specified just above for Jazirat al-Aʿjam regarding the amount of land each stratum received by land assignment are too low.

In addition, the comparison of the land-tenure registers of Kafr al-Rajallat Village suggest the same scenario for this village; as this comparison reveals that 33 percent of the land distributed by the *ramya* system is not mentioned by the village *athurat* register. Thus, although the *athurat* register shows that the small stratum of Kafr al-Rajallat received 25.69 percent of its lands by *ramya* distribution, the middle stratum 20.26 percent, and the wealthy 42.17 percent, the real figures are probably much higher.[31] This further allows us to deduce that the proportion of holders of Kafr al-Rajallat Village who ascribed portions of their holdings to the *ramya* system was higher than the 57.14 percent specified by its land-tenure registers (and by table 4.3). In conclusion, we might say that there was little variance in the general pattern of *ramya* distribution in these four sample villages.[32]

The combination of these findings allows us to discern the impact of the workings of the system of land assignment on peasant villages during much of the mid-nineteenth-century period. One, the majority of peasant landholders acquired some land by *ramya* distribution. Two, this allowed for the concentration of land in the hands of a few holders. Three, many poor peasants received small plots of land by *ramya* assignment. Finally, such workings of the *ramya* system dovetailed with and amply reflected the economic principles of traditional statecraft (revenue maximization and preservation of peasant economic viability), which helps to explain their endurance during much of this period.

The pattern of *ramya* distribution began to change in 1858, when the government focused more strongly on increasing revenue levels. Prior to this date, receipt of a land assignment was not contingent on the payment of transfer fees; however, by the 1858 land law, a land recipient was required to pay a transfer fee of 24 piastres per *faddan*. This was something of a forbidding sum for peasants who relied on wage-labor to augment small land profits, and for peasants whose very livelihood relied exclusively on wages, as wage levels were kept low by adequate labor pools from which landlords could easily replace recalcitrant workers. Then in 1861, the state disallowed the assignment of vacant village lands, instead directing that such lands were to be placed in auction and released to the highest bidder. For the most part, these two changes drastically reduced the opportunities of the indigent peasants to acquire land, and facilitated its concentration in the hands of affluent peasants.[33]

The Contribution of the Land Market to Peasant Landholding

Revisionist thinking about socio-economic stratification in peasant villages during the nineteenth century, having largely attributed this phenomenon to nonmarket modes of land acquirement (especially *ramya* assignment), is relatively silent on the workings of the land market except to link land alienation to peasant impoverishment.[34] This section examines the extent land-market activities contributed to peasant landholding during the middle decades, and further sheds light on how the state dealt with disputes over land transactions.

The first point on land-market activities can easily be gleaned from the previous discussion on inheritance and land assignment: that peasants acquired most of their landholdings by inheritance and *ramya* distribution can only mean that land-market transactions were infrequent and more importantly did not involve high numbers of *faddans*. Thus, for example, from the *athurat* register of Ibyar Village, a relatively large village made up of high-quality arable land, we learn that roughly between 1820 and 1860, the small stratum holders acquired 88 percent of their holdings by inheritance and *ramya* assignment, the middle stratum 72 percent, and the wealthy stratum 74 percent.[35] In turn, this suggests the following figures for acquirement of land by market transaction: the small stratum 12 percent, the middle stratum 28 percent, and the wealthy 26 percent. In reality, though, these latter figures are very likely even lower.

This is because peasants were known to rely on additional nonmarket modes of land acquirement. Some peasants decided on their own volition to bring idle land under the plow, and thereafter kept it cultivated and regularly paid its taxes, ultimately earning state recognition of their right to it. Thus, when the *athurat* committee that visited al-Jazira al-Khadra in 1859 learned that this was how al-Hajja Mina had obtained a particular 5 *faddans* of her holding, they noted in the village *athurat* register that these *faddans* had become "her *athar* by way of her own efforts."[36] Also, state recognition of cultivators' prescriptive rights to land extended to peasants who continued to tend the *usya* lands originally owned by *multazims* (or tax farmers). For many *multazims* were unable to maintain the *usya* lands they had been allowed to keep after the abolishment of the *iltizam* system in 1814 because they or their heirs had become impoverished; and in many cases *multazims* had died without issue.[37] In these circumstances the peasants already engaged in working the land continued with their farming tasks, thereby retaining the land portions that their resources could maintain. This situation existed in Kafr al-Rajallat Village: when the village *multazims* had died without issue, their *usya* lands became the *athar* lands of the peasant cultivators; this situation covered 99.5 *faddans*, roughly 15 percent of the village arable area.[38] Other times, peasants attributed plots in their possession to *badal*, or land exchange, whereby a peasant holder agreed to turn over a plot of land to another villager in exchange for a land plot in the latter's possession. Sometime between 1858 and December 1859, Ahmad Khatir of Ibyar Village had entered into such an arrangement, having agreed to turn over a plot that consisted of 21 *qirats*, 16 *sahms* to Ya'qub Jirjis in exchange for a land plot composed of 1 *faddan*, 12 *sahms*.[39] What is interesting about land exchanges is that they often did not involve land plots of the exact size, as can be seen from the example just mentioned—meaning that one party, in this case Ahmad Khatir, slightly augmented his holding at the expense of the other party. That peasants engaged in this mode of land transfer cannot be attributed to the mechanization of farming, which had not yet spread to peasant villages during the period under discussion. Thus, we cannot say that land exchanges aimed to consolidate holdings originally composed of land strips situated in different basins in order to facilitate mechanization of farming and thereby achieve economies of scale. Instead, we might say that peasants engaged in *badal* transfers in order to facilitate coordination efforts between themselves and their relatives/neighbors of onerous farming tasks like plowing, weeding, and harvesting.

The archival sources reveal two other nonmarket modes of land transfer. Some peasants chose to register their lands in the names of other villagers, and in this way the controller became the legal representative, or *wakil*, of the original holder. While controllers' responsibilities varied from one case to another, original holders, most of whom were women or minors, often relied on their *wakils* to discharge all the relevant tasks pertaining to the management of their lands.[40] For example, this is what Amuna expected of her husband, Ahmed Ramadan, when she placed her entire holding of 23 *sahms* in his hands, which, by the way, also constituted the entirety of land in his possession.[41] Finally some peasants obtained land by entering into partnership arrangements, the terms of an arrangement dependent on the level of contribution made by each partner. And in the case of Ahmad Jamush of Ibyar Village, the death of his partner, Ali Siʿda, without issue meant that the former was entitled to keep the entirety of the half *faddan* they had cultivated as partners.[42]

Thus, if the discussion on the nonmarket modes of land acquisition is limited to an investigation of inheritance and land assignment, we find that peasants acquired high proportions of their holdings by these kinds of land transfer: for example, in Ibyar Village roughly between the 1820s and the late 1850s, these transfers covered approximately 75 percent of its arable land; and as stated above, the small stratum acquired 88 percent of its lands by these means, the middle stratum 72 percent, the wealthy 74 percent. But if we also take into consideration the additional nonmarket modes of land transfer just mentioned above, we find that the numbers are significantly higher: for Ibyar Village, we find that the combination of these transfers covered about 83 percent of its arable land; and that the same applied to the different village strata, as the small stratum attributed 92 percent of its lands to nonmarket transfers, the middle stratum 80 percent, the wealthy 83 percent. In turn, the different strata of this village acquired relatively small proportions of their lands by land-market transactions: the small stratum, 8 percent, the middle 20 percent, and the wealthy 17 percent.[43]

Peasants resorted to the alienation of their lands for a variety of reasons. Some liked to circumvent the Islamic rules of inheritance by ceding land to certain relatives; some affluent landholders chose to rent small land plots to indigent villagers; and in one case, Abdalla Yusif of Kafr al-Rajallat Village freed himself of an undesirable land plot (it had come into his possession because he had paid its tax arrears) by pawning it to another villager (Muhammad) for 60 piastres.[44] But most often peasants sought to alienate their lands when they experienced a shortage of funds. For example, that 64 percent of the area that had been pawned in Kafr al-Rajallat Village between the 1830s and mid-1850s still remained in the possession of the creditors in 1857 strongly suggests that the debtors had originally engaged in the land pawns because of the lack of sufficient resources.[45] Again, we emphasize that while insolvent peasants may have liked to alienate their land, their neighbors often did not accept their alienation overtures, as they knew that the holders' cash shortages might likely lead to the accumulation of tax arrears and finally the activation of the land-reassignment system that involved the removal of the land from the possession of the insolvent holder and its reassignment to any individual with the necessary wherewithal. In short, holders' shortage of funds more often resulted in the activation of the ramya process, not the alienation of land—hence the comparatively low number of land alienation cases.

Those individuals who did acquire land by market transaction could count on the state to confirm them in their possession when these satisfied the relevant legal criteria. In July 1854, Ahmad al-Sharif of Mahallat Marsum Village complained to the Council of Justice that Hassan Jabra, a village headman, had taken possession of the legacy of land and trees left him by his father. The investigation of the allegation of usurpation revealed that Hassan Jabra had bought this land from Ahmad's father, and moreover "the father had died when he [Ahmad] was still a minor and he did not know the truth about the land, whether his father had sold it to Hassan Jabra or not." The religious legal experts called on to examine the case concluded that the land sale had been documented in the appropriate deeds and was legally sound, thereby confirming Hassan Jabra's right to the contested land.[46] State support for market transactions also meant that the parties were expected to respect the conditions of the transaction. Thus, peasants who had obtained land by pawn were expected to relinquish it to the original holder when the latter satisfied the legal criteria specified for the recovery of pawned land. In November 1854, two brothers sued for the retention of the 3 *faddan*s they had obtained by pawn from the original holder. They pointed out to the Council of Justice that "they had been cultivating it for a lengthy period," and further complained that the original holder's sons wanted to take possession of the land. Here the council ruled accordingly: "After investigations, it was clear that the plaintiffs have no right [to the land] as the land is the *athar* of [the defendants'] father and is listed in his name in the cadastral register and [the sons] paid the pawn debt and they are capable cultivators; and according to the land law they deserve their father's *athar*."[47]

A comparison between the land disputes resolved by the judicial councils of the government administrative bodies, like the one just examined, and those settled by the religious courts during the mid-nineteenth-century period reveals that the former usually recognized the viability of the land transaction on the basis of officially certified land deeds, which is not surprising given the emphasis of mid-century state legislation on the documentation of land transactions in official deeds. But the religious courts tended to settle disputes on the basis of the testimony of witnesses in accordance with Islamic law, as occurred in the land dispute al-Adli Ismail brought to the Tanta religious court on August 14, 1858, where he claimed that Ali Sadiq refused to return the land he had pawned him although he had offered to redeem its debt. Ali Sadiq premised his refusal on the claim that he had obtained the land by cession. The court investigated the veracity of the opposing claims by recourse to reliable witnesses, who testified in favor of al-Adli Ismail; however, it did not insist on the presentation of the deeds in order to examine them, nor did it otherwise mention them.[48] While we might say that the presiding judge (*qadi*) in this case may not have been aware of the promulgation of the 1858 land law (on August 5, 1858) and its stipulations regarding written evidence for land disputes, still he must have been aware of the stipulation specified by the 1847 land law that required the documentation of land transfers, and yet (as just stated) his queries did not include any mention of deeds. And although there were other cases where the claimants supported their stories by the presentation of deeds, still the religious courts often did not request written evidence, and settled the disputes in accordance with the testimony of credible witnesses.[49] For the most part, these findings strongly point to uneven implementation of state legislation in the Egyptian countryside. At the same time, other cases show us that the introduction of state legislation did not result in the replacement of religious law with "secular" law, but that the authorities drew from both bodies of law at the same time.[50] This is illustrated by the dispute brought to the Tanta religious court on December 11, 1860, when defendant Khalil backed his version of the story, that he had acquired the land legally by cession, with the presentation of the relevant land deed. Here the court examined its registers for evidence of this deed, and finding none, subsequently ordered Khalil to produce credible witnesses who would confirm his claim, which he did, thereby winning the suit.[51]

At this juncture, it might be helpful to briefly recapitulate the major points of our discussion thus far. State regulation of peasant lands during the mid-nineteenth-century years, largely informed by the economic principles of traditional statecraft, aimed to ensure that *miri* lands remained cultivated and thereby continued to generate the requisite tax revenues. To this end, the state recognized inheritance rights to *miri* land and granted legal heirs the right of possession so long as they farmed the land and regularly paid its taxes. But they lost their lands when they permitted tax arrears to accumulate, for this situation called for the activation of the *ramya* system and the assignment of the lands to other peasants. The authorities were careful to assign lands only to individuals whose cash levels would ensure their steady maintenance. These policies undoubtedly encouraged rural folks to view inheritance and land assignment as the primary modes of land acquisition, which meant that comparatively few individuals obtained land through market transactions. More importantly, state policies allowed affluent peasants to accumulate rather large land fortunes while further granting poor peasants opportunities to possess land. Finally, those holders who satisfied the terms of land possession (legal right, regular cultivation, and tax payment) very likely felt secure in their possessions, and fully anticipated state support in the event of dispute.

The Issue of Peasant Land Loss

Earlier examinations of peasant land tenure during the nineteenth century highlight the phenomenon of peasant land loss, and assert that it began during the time of Muhammad Ali and continued uninterrupted throughout the century. When looking at the mid-century period, this interpretation generally highlights the large-scale abandonment of the 1850s due to repeated tax increases, the continuation of large-estate creation, and the negative impact of the major land laws of the period on smallholders. Accordingly it concludes that the majority of peasant smallholders experienced impoverishment and destitution at mid-century.[52]

But the examination of the registers of various governmental administrative bodies as well as the land-tax registers of four sample villages allows for a more conservative interpretation. Specifically, I argue that the majority of peasants did not experience debilitating land loss during the mid-nineteenth-century period. My discussion involves looking at large-scale abandonment, the emergence of surplus lands in peasant villages, the creation of large estates, the impact of the 1858 land law, and ends with the examination of land distribution in peasant villages.

Large-Scale Abandonment of Land

The examination of large-scale abandonment of land should start with the differentiation between this phenomenon and that of *tasahhub*, which also refers to peasant flight from land. In the latter case, peasants' realization of their inability to maintain their land plots prompted them to simply flee their village, whereupon the village headmen were required to reassign their lands to whoever demonstrated the ability to cultivate them and pay their taxes. The former case emerged when the peasants and their headmen agreed that they could not maintain certain lands in their village and subsequently requested official permission to be relieved of them. When the government granted such a request, the unwanted lands were deducted from the total registered area of the village and were specified as *matruk* lands, thereby effecting a shrinkage in the arable area of the village. The land remaining in the peasants' possession was dubbed *al-marghuba*, or the desired, lands.[53] Another important difference between the two cases concerns the recovery of these lands: in the case of *tasahhub*, recovery was regulated by the three major land laws of the period; but in the case of *matruk*, the original holders were completely forbidden from recovering their lands.[54]

Large-scale abandonment of peasant lands began in the mid-1850s. According to Ya'qub Artin, this phenomenon first emerged in "1854 when the government allowed the abandonment of many lands in Buhayra" Province. He further asserted that the government permitted the peasants of al-Sharqiyya and al-Daqahliyya Provinces to leave a total of 46,866 *faddans* in 1855; though Jirjis Hunayn had put this number at 66,866 *faddans*.[55] Barakat wrote that the *matruk* land in al-Sharqiyya Province amounted to a total of 40,000 *faddans* in 1855. But his evidence for al-Fayyum Province relates to two villages only, Abu Kasaa and Abshway, which together consisted of 9,696 *faddans*: the peasants of these two villages abandoned a total of 8,139 *faddans*, or 84 percent of their combined lands, sometime in 1855–1856.[56] The registers of the Department of Interior show that Barakat's estimate of *matruk* land in al-Fayyum was hardly comprehensive. One such entry, dated October 24, 1859, examines the request of four villages—Shadmawa, Qalmashaa, Habthir, Azbat al-Munshaa—to abandon a total of 1,380 *faddans* of their combined lands;[57] with additional entries revealing similar requests made by other villages between 1859 and 1860.[58] These same registers disclose a number of *matruk* cases for al-Qalyubiya, Bani Suwayf, and al-Jiza Provinces, which earlier writers had not mentioned at all.[59] Thus, this leads us to note, in agreement with Barakat, that the reliance on the archival sources currently at our disposal makes the attempt to estimate the total number of *faddans* abandoned by the peasants as *matruk* quite a difficult undertaking.[60]

And yet, the archival sources suggest that the first appearance of this phenomenon centered on *ib'adiyya* lands (or originally barren land not yet fully brought under the plow),[61] most likely because these were comparatively new acquisitions that necessitated high outlays but did not yield high profits. At this juncture then, those peasants experiencing economic hardship chose to abandon costly barren lands in order to ensure their retention of their *athar/ma'mur* lands, or the prized black, fertile lands cultivated by successive peasant generations. It seems too that the government did not automatically grant abandonment requests. For if the petitioning villagers were seen to possess sufficient resources and so were viewed as "capable" cultivators, their request was denied. Such a situation unfolded in 1853 when the government reviewed the abandonment request put forth by the peasants of Quwaynisi and Sharanis Villages of Gharbiyya Province, as it had concluded that the concerned lands had long been liable for taxation and that "the peasants are highly capable and so there is no reason for" relieving the aforementioned peasants of these lands.[62]

In 1857, the government greatly modified the official approach to land-abandonment requests. Starting in August 1857, village holders could leave as many *faddans* as they liked no matter whether these consisted of the less fertile *ib'adiyya* or the prized *ma'mur* lands. It seems too that official consent of these requests was no longer to be contingent on official verification of petitioners' inability to maintain their lands. Instead permission was to be granted automatically and without question.[63]

This change in the government's attitude toward requests to abandon land can be traced to its growing inability to discharge its financial obligations during the late 1850s, brought on by Said Pasha's many development schemes and debts. This is suggested by its decision to give some state employees portions of *matruk* land "in lieu of their salaries," while other recipients were European creditors who accepted such lands in lieu of the government's reimbursement of its debts,[64] and still others were retired civil servants or military officers who were given such lands instead of money pensions.[65] Indeed, the government seemed particularly focused on pensioners in this respect: for in October 1857, the Department of Interior reserved 15,000 *faddans* of *matruk* land for this group;[66] and according to Barakat, Said Pasha was responsible for state conferment of a total of 70,414 *faddans* in lieu of pensions.[67] It is worth noting that recipients often expressed dismay at such land conferrals because of their poor quality. For example, upon receipt of such land in 1857, a military officer named Salih Bey "responded that he did not wish to take any of these [*matruk*] lands and he preferred to be given lands suitable for cultivation even if [the tract] was taxed at 100 piastres per *faddan*"—at the time, a very high rate of tax.[68]

The state disposed of *matruk* land in other financially advantageous ways. It awarded some of these lands by competitive bidding. Thus, in 1853, the advertisement of 280 *faddans* of *ib'addiya* land situated in three different villages in al-Buhayra Province resulted in different agreements between the state and the contracting parties. The first involved 80 *faddans*. These were awarded to Ali Abd al-Rahman Effendi who agreed to pay a tax rate of 10 piastres, 20 para per faddan for a period of six years that was to start in 1852 (with retroactive payments), while payments for the next ten years were to be at a higher (but undecipherable) rate. The second land conferment involved 150 *faddans* and went to Ali Shahat and Abd al-Mu'ti Siliman, who agreed to pay a tax rate of 10 piasters per faddan for three years, and pay the full (*kharaji*) tax rate afterwards. The third land award, which concerned 50 *faddans*, went to Ali Abu Zawyda, who agreed to pay half the village tax rate, which came to 15 piastres, 30 para per *faddan*.[69] As the auction process allowed the contracting parties to propose rates and terms that reflected the quality of the land, they probably deemed the final terms as fair. Accordingly, the new holders were likely to retain these lands, paying their taxes without begrudging the outlays necessary for the improvement of the soil. Such cases also worked to the advantage of the government, as it certainly appreciated the promise of regular tax payment. Here we note that the public land auctions did not only attract the attention of affluent rural folks, as members of the state elite (*dhawat*) also competed in these auctions. Thus, in November 1857, the al-Jiza provincial authorities reported on the outcome of the public auction of 2,777 *faddans* of *matruk* land, specifying that some "of the *dhawat* and others wish to take land at the full tax-rate."[70] That these privileged individuals tried to quickly and effectively secure their bid by offering to take these lands at the full *kharaji* tax rate instead of risking losing them (by suggesting lower rates) testifies to the growing profitability of agricultural activity.

The government was also known to reassign some *matruk* lands to peasant cultivators. In 1857, the Department of Interior reported that 22,122 *faddans* of *matruk* land situated in Rawdat al-Bahrayn Province were "assigned to those who wanted them"; it seemed to be referring largely to peasant recipients. Nearly half of these lands (10,205 *faddans*) were assigned to the recipients on the *athariyya* basis while the other half (11,917 *faddans*) was only leased to recipients on a temporary basis.[71] In the same year, peasants from al-Buhayra Province petitioned for permission to take possession of portions of abandoned *ib'adiyya* lands situated in their villages at the full tax rate. The government approved these requests and immediately assigned land to most of the petitioners.[72] What is particularly noteworthy about this case is that the just-mentioned approval actually violated the rule regulating *matruk* land, for the government had forbidden the conferment of *matruk* land on any member of a village that had originally abandoned it.[73] This easily suggests that the authorities worried about the disruption of the cultivation process (which entailed a disruption in tax payments); and this led officials to do whatever they could to prevent the emergence of such a situation.[74] In 1858, it probably was this concern that prompted the governor of al-Fayyum Province to force (in violation of state regulations) the members of al-Nazla Village to farm the lands they had previously abandoned.[75]

Nevertheless some abandoned lands remained vacant. So by the decree of November 14, 1861, the government included vacant *matruk* lands among the kinds that were to be sold by competitive bidding.[76] According to Gabriel Baer, buyers were granted full property rights over their lands and were to pay only one-tenth of the harvest in taxes, a rate that was substantially lower than the *kharaji* taxes imposed on peasant lands.[77] These decisions are indicative of governmental interest in boosting land sales; accordingly, it issued the decree of January 7, 1862, which extended the operation of these public auctions until the end of the Coptic month of Birmuda, or May 7, 1862.[78] For in this way, the state could oversee the sale of more lands, and win higher profits.

At the end of this discussion on large-scale land abandonment, we make a few general observations on the nature of this phenomenon. To begin, peasants generally and most often requested to abandon *ib'adiyya*, or poor quality, lands. My archival sample (of the registers of various governmental bodies) reveals a noticeable increase in abandonment requests in 1274/1857–1858, which is not surprising, given that large numbers of peasant smallholders experienced a significant increase in their land taxes at this time. It seems that most peasants reacted to this situation by giving up poor quality lands to ensure their retention of the prized *ma'mur* lands. Quite simply, these peasants probably reasoned that the tax increases imposed on the *ib'adiyya* and the *ma'mur* lands could push them into insolvency. At the same time, these same peasants might have retained their *ib'adiyya* lands had the government agreed to more suitable tax arrangements; as is suggested by the request put by peasants of al-Buhayra Province in November 1857 to take possession of abandoned lands situated in their villages on condition that they would be exempted from taxes during the first three years, and would pay half the village tax rate during the following three years, and afterwards pay the full tax rate. It seems, though, that the central government generally refused such requests, insisting that peasant landholders pay taxes in full.[79]

That most of the abandoned lands were poor quality *ib'adiyya*s is amply verified by the archival sources. For the provincial authorities repeatedly reported on the general "lack of interest in the possession of any of these lands."[80] Also civil servants who were offered land in lieu of money salaries/pensions often refused to accept *matruk* lands.[81] Two such recipients explained that "these lands necessitate huge outlays," and so "they requested different [land plots] that were suitable for cultivation."[82]

It is based on the just-mentioned evidence that we make our final observation, which is that the *matruk* land phenomenon cannot be viewed as an indication of extensive impoverishment in the countryside. For notwithstanding the two villages specified by Barakat (Abu Kasaa and Abshway Villages, mentioned above),[83] the archival sources strongly suggest that most peasant villages retained much of their prized *ma'mur* lands. At the same time, too, many peasants managed to retain their *ib'adiyya* lands during this period, as is demonstrated by the case of Kafr al-Jarayda Village. The arable land of this village consisted of 1,244.5 *faddan*s; and of this, 63.48 percent constituted *ib'adiyya* land. That the area of arable land remained constant during our entire period means that the peasants did not leave (*tarik*) their *ib'adiyya* lands, having continued to cultivate them and pay their taxes.[84]

*The Surplus (*Ziyada*) Lands*

That the countryside experienced the emergence of another phenomenon, *ziyada* or surplus lands, during the mid-nineteenth-century period, which paralleled the emergence of large-scale land abandonment—many case entries even referring to these two phenomena at the same time[85]—only lends additional confirmation to the just-specified conclusion: that the rural areas did not experience widespread impoverishment during these years. For had there been extensive ruination, most peasants would have distanced themselves from surplus lands and their attendant tax responsibilities; instead, many competed with each other to acquire these.

Cognizant of and concerned about the growing numbers of peasants who farmed unregistered lands for which they did not pay taxes—these were referred to as surplus or *ziyada* lands because they exceeded the number of registered, taxed *faddans*—the government relied on the emergence of certain circumstances for its discovery of such cases. These included the following: when the settlement of a land claim necessitated that the authorities survey the concerned area; when the peasants declared on their own volition that their villages contained such lands, most likely because they hoped to be awarded these very lands; and when peasants informed the government that their neighbors were surreptitiously cultivating such lands, again in the hope of some reward.[86] These peasants-turned-informants must have been fairly certain about the veracity of their information. For when official investigations revealed that they had misinformed government officials, they could incur heavy punishment—as in the case of Asʿad Atallah from Samadun Village, for instance, who was sentenced to one year in the Alexandria prison for misdirecting the authorities.[87]

The frequency of these latter two circumstances (peasant voluntary declarations and peasant informants) most likely increased when Said Pasha became viceroy (July 1854). Artin reports that the pasha came to the throne with the certain knowledge that "many landholders were in the possession of lands to which they had no right . . . and it was widely rumored that the original cadastral registers, compiled in 1813, were incomplete and contained many gaps." To remedy this situation, he gave orders for a comprehensive survey of the rural areas of Egypt.[88] The authorities did not manage to complete the 1854 survey, only completing the related work in some provinces; one of these was Bani Suwayf wa-al-Fayyum. This province was surveyed in 1854 for the first time since its cadastral survey of 1821; with the completion of the later survey revealing the existence of surplus lands in that province.[89] Such results notwithstanding, the survey efforts progressed too slowly for the impatient Said. Here Artin reports that his advisers suggested a different and speedier method for the discovery of surplus lands—to reward peasants who informed the authorities about the existence of these lands. The pasha liked this suggestion, and its adoption was quickly followed by a deluge of reports from peasants-turned-informants. This arrangement worked to the satisfaction of both parties, for the informant received a reward, unspecified by Artin, while the government "took control of the surplus lands."[90]

How did the government dispose of surplus lands? In an entry in the Department of Interior registers dated November 6, 1857, there is an examination of the results of the 1854 cadastral survey of Bani Suwayf wa-al-Fayyum Province that shows that the villages that contained surplus lands became fully liable for their taxes, set at the full *kharajiyya* rates.[91] Although this entry does not give us information about the actual possessors of these lands, it is likely that these were the peasants whose registered landholdings adjoined or were adjacent to the surplus tracts—moreover, these probably were the very individuals who had actually undertaken their cultivation for a period of time. Yet it seems that the authorities entrusted these lands to such cultivators on a temporary basis only, to ensure the regular payment of its taxes. Why? As the discovery of these surplus lands had not taken place with the assistance of and at the direction of the villagers themselves, they were ultimately destined for the auction block. Similarly, when the discovery of surplus land was attributed to the report of an informant, the actual cultivators also experienced the loss of this land—as can be seen in the examination of the order, dated December 3, 1856, issued by the Council of Justice to al-Jiza wa-Atfih Province. By this, the top-level provincial officials were instructed to convene with all the village headmen at the province seat and question them about the existence of surplus lands in their villages. Those headmen who responded in the affirmative would see their villages undergo a cadastral survey and the excess lands turned over to the peasant cultivators at the *kharajiyya* tax rates, to be retained as *athariyya* land. But if headmen denied that their villages contained such lands and the opposite was later confirmed by vigilant informants, the cultivators lost these lands to the informants.[92]

Thus, some surplus lands were turned over to those individuals who had uncovered their existence, for Said Pasha came to understand that informants might expedite the discovery of surplus lands, which worked to the latter's advantage. Prior to 1856, the government had completely denied informants the right to possess the lands they had exposed and instead preferred to award these by competitive bidding.[93] This certainly dampened the enthusiasm of many; and accordingly the government sought to remedy this situation by developing a new set of rules, outlined in the decree of June 11, 1856, for the disposal of surplus lands. By this, if the surplus consisted of fractions of a *faddan*, it was to be turned over to the cultivator who possessed adjoining land.[94] The governmental registers reveal what happened when informants disclosed the existence of surpluses that constituted large tracts of contiguous land. In a word, these were awarded to the informants, as occurred in the case of Ali Ali who had informed the authorities in 1856 that the headmen of al-Daljamun Village were surreptitiously farming an *ib'adiiya* tract. After official investigations verified that the surplus land was not made up of fractions of a *faddan*, and thus should not be awarded to the cultivators, the government decreed that Ali Ali had "greater right to it than anyone else."[95] This treatment of large tracts of surplus land was turned into law by the decree of July 16, 1857, which specified that "the surplus lands whose existence was discovered by informants are to be subject to immediate investigations and [then] are to be awarded to their discoverers."[96] Thus, while this decree seemed to instruct officials to award all surplus lands (big tracts and *faddan* fractions) to their informants, and thereby seemed to abandon the earlier just-mentioned decree (of 1856), what it really aimed to do is supplement, not rescind, the June 1856 decree.

Such official encouragement to declare unregistered lands notwithstanding, many cultivators continued to farm some lands clandestinely. Often the violators were village headmen;[97] for these were powerful enough to force others in the village to observe government regulations while ignoring these themselves. In the event that cadastral surveys exposed violators, the government authorities arranged for a public auction for these lands, while the village shaykhs were charged with the cultivation of the lands and the payment of its taxes until their new possessors claimed them.[98] When investors showed no interest in certain land tracts, the state utilized them to discharge pressing financial obligations, most frequently assigning them to retired state officials instead of money pensions.

Here it might be concluded that the rules regulating surplus lands during the mid- and late-1850s usually led to the placement of village lands in the hands of outsiders and so were the source of peasant impoverishment. Yet this assumption requires some modification. Many instances of surplus land discovery were not uncovered by official cadastral surveys, but actually constituted the work of vigilant informers; thus, the disposal of these lands did not necessitate the arrangement of public auctions, as these lands were to be awarded to the informers. On the one hand, some informants were not peasants, as the sources identify some of these as low-level bureaucratic officials, and in one case the informant was "Hassan Effendi of the military school."[99] But on the other, most certainly were, for none were as familiar with village affairs as its inhabitants. Not only were most informants peasants, they often came from the ranks of the village poor, as is suggested by the case of Ibrahim Awad al-Barbari, who complained that the headman of the village had beaten him when he had exposed his secret cultivation of an *ib'adiyya* tract.[100] Had this informant enjoyed the same socioeconomic status of his shaykh, he probably would have been spared this treatment. Based on this, we can conclude that the informant's receipt of the land he had exposed actually entailed its transfer from an affluent peasant to a poor one; also this transfer hardly impoverished the dispossessed (wealthier) party. The archival sources reveal another scenario for informants of unregistered land, which similarly undermines the peasant impoverishment assumption, as it, quite simply, worked to maintain the status quo in the village: this was the refusal of the original cultivator to turn over the land to the informant.[101]

The peasant impoverishment assumption is further undermined by the preferences of participants in the public auctions. Time and again, the provincial authorities noted that investors tended to avoid the *mutafarriqa* lands, or land lots that consisted of "two *faddans* or three or four or more or less."[102] In December 1854, the Daqahliyya authorities informed the Council of Justice about the existence of a surplus *ib'adiyya* tract that consisted of roughly 13 *faddans*. Investigations revealed that this land did not constitute a contiguous tract, but was composed of small lots that lay in different basins. On this basis, the local authorities proposed "the registration of these lots in the names of the peasant cultivators at the current *kharajiyya* tax-rates without advertising them in a public auction, as the interested [that is, auction participants] only take lands that lie in one basin."[103] On the one hand, it seemed that the central government did not accept this suggestion; but on the other, it still expected the provincial authorities to promptly remit the lands' taxes. In turn, this situation prompted the provincial authorities to place whatever lands had not been consumed by the auctions in the hands of the village cultivators at the *kharajiyya* tax rates, which ultimately meant peasant retention of small surplus lands at the village rates.[104]

Yet as noted before, the market value of agricultural land and its produce (and the possibilities of higher revenues) was hardly lost on the central government. For this was a time when crops fetched high prices and in turn made arable land a profitable asset, which can be seen in the outcome of the competitive bidding for a 17-*faddan* tract in 1856 that specified a yearly tax rate that was higher than the prevalent *kharajiyya* rate by an impressive 110 piastres.[105] This easily explains the instructions of October 29, 1857, which again ordered the arrangement of public auctions for big and small lots of surplus land;[106] though here the government chose to lease the land to investors for the fiscal year of 1858 only, rather than award it as *athariyya* land (which implied permanent possession) with the intention, certainly, of holding new auctions in the following years with all that meant for higher rent rates.[107]

The provincial authorities tried to relay to the central government the impracticality of this decree. In a November 4, 1857, report, the Asyut provincial officials explained that investors largely avoided the small (*muta-farriqa*) lots consisting of 1–5 *faddan*s advertised by public auctions.[108] The report from Jirja Province, dated a day earlier, contained the same observation and further tried to show the financial advantage of awarding the small lots to the current peasant cultivators, which simply was that these cultivators would be expected to pay both the 1857 and 1858 tax sums pertaining to these lands. In explanation it pointed out that these lands were in the possession of the village cultivators when the 1857 cadastral survey exposed their existence, and that these peasants were ready to farm the land in 1858.[109] The Qina authorities, though, merely requested further clarification of the 1857 instructions: they asked for clear confirmation of the rules pertaining to large and small plots; and also asked about the procedure to follow for the rental of the lands, pointing out that the planting season was at hand and that there was not enough time to arrange a public auction.[110] These reports and ideas notwithstanding, it seems that the central government would not abandon the idea of the conferral of small lots of surplus land by auction.

Such official insistence put the provincial authorities in an unenviable position, as they could not ignore the reality of investor preferences; which in turn prompted the Qina authorities to develop a compromise solution. They dutifully arranged public auctions for the small lots but "for now, restricted the advertisement of these among the members of the village where the lands lay and the neighboring villages . . . and no advertisement is made outside [this area] so as to facilitate [the auction process]." This, explained the Qina report of April 1858, ensures the placement of these lands "without delay."[111]

This debate was finally concluded in August 1858 with the introduction of the land law of that year, where there was a complete reversal of the official position regarding the placement of small lots of surplus lands. The explanation for this might be found in the practice of the writers of this law: they were known to examine the complaints and suggestions sent from the provinces, selecting the best of these in an effort to develop effective and meaningful solutions to problems on the ground. Thus, by this law, it will be recalled, the village cultivators were to retain automatically the surplus lands when these were small lots that ranged from 1 *faddan* up to (but less than) 10 *faddan*s per basin.[112]

At this point, we see that the linkage of the peasant impoverishment assumption to the phenomenon of surplus lands does not prove tenable for the 1850s. But this changed in the final two years of Said Pasha's reign. Hard-pressed to increase state revenues during these years, the viceroy gave instructions for the development of a number of strategies that aimed to increase the revenues generated by the country's prize economic asset, its agricultural land. This led to new focus on surplus lands; and the related new regulations, as will be shown below, carried significant disadvantages for the peasants.

To begin, there was the standardization of the length of the *qasaba*, the unit of measurement employed in the survey of land, in 1861. According to Artin, in the year that Said Pasha ascended the throne, "the length of the *qasaba* varied from one province to another."[113] Land measurement in Jirja Province was based on the *qasaba* that consisted of 3.50 meters, while Rawdat al-Bahrayn Province employed a *qasaba* that was composed of 3.55 meters.[114] The central government brought a level of uniformity to this situation with the introduction of the decree of May 25, 1861, which specified the *qasaba* of 3.55 meters as the official one.[115] In a March 11, 1862 entry in the registers of the Viceregal Cabinet, the provincial authorities of Jirja note the result of the resurvey of *ib'adiyya* tracts according to the new (for Jirja, it was a longer) *qasaba* measurement: "There will be changes in the [land] borders, and discrepancies with what is documented in the title-deeds [will appear], and also there will be a boundary decrease of 2 *faddan*s, 18 *qirat*s, 8 *sahm*s, for every 100 *faddan*s and for every 1000 *faddan*s [there will be a boundary decrease of] 27 *faddan*s, 14 *qirat*s, 16 *sahm*s."[116] In a word, this decrease in the size of land tracts resulted in the emergence of surplus lands.

How did the government dispose of the surplus lands generated by the standardization of the *qasaba* measurement? At first, it instructed that their cultivators be made liable for their taxes. In the case of al-Safiha and al-Shaykh Rusum Villages, situated in Jirja Province, the central authorities specified a tax schedule that included retroactive payments from 1273/1856–1857 to 1276/1859–1860. It explained the selection of the date of AH 1273 by pointing out that the 1861 survey results were measured against those of the previous survey conducted in these villages in 1275/1858–1859. And at the time of this earlier survey, the government had declared that the survey-exposed surplus lands were to be subject to the December 24, 1856 decree, which specified that their tax liability was (retroactively) to begin in 1273/1856–1857.[117] But this is not how the story ends for these two villages. For another entry in the Viceregal Cabinet registers reveals that these villages were the *uhda* of a Latif Pasha, that he refused to accept the 1861 survey results, and finally insisted that the survey authorities reexamine all the pertinent registers and documents.[118] This exercise revealed that the 1861 survey results were incorrect, and accordingly the 25 *faddans* specified by the 1861 survey as surplus lands did not exist, which entailed the retraction of the earlier orders pertaining to these villages (and the penalization of the officials responsible for the earlier, incorrect results).[119]

But this case of retraction notwithstanding, the standardization of the *qasaba* measurement led to the survey and subsequent emergence of a substantial number of *faddans*. This can be seen in another entry in the Viceregal Cabinet registers dated May 30, 1862, which focuses on 4,508 *faddans* of survey-exposed surplus lands in Jirja Province. The government chose not to impose these lands on the peasant cultivators, and instead sold these by public auction, in this way generating a total (rather substantial) sum of 1,672,378 piastres, 8 para.[120]

While the just-mentioned surplus lands were sold as *miri* (state) land taxed at the same high *kharajiyya* rates carried by village *ma'mur* lands, this was not always the case. Indeed, when the government first issued its instructions concerning the sale of survey-exposed surpluses, it had neglected to mention whether these were to be advertised as *kharajiyya* or *ushuriyya* lands. While the Jirja Province officials merely asked the central government to specify the status of the lands to be sold, the al-Jiza authorities warned that such neglect could result in disputes with purchasers who relied on this omission to insist on the registration of the lands as *ushuriyya*.[121] In response, the central government directed the various provinces to sell the survey-exposed surpluses as *ushuriyya* lands.[122] These new instructions included plots that measured less than 1 *faddan*, previously awarded automatically to the peasant cultivators.[123] It seems that these recent instructions contained some ambiguities about the lands that qualified for sale, bringing new queries and finally prompting the central authorities to issue the decree of November 14, 1861. This categorically stated that all surplus lands, both the large tracts and the small plots, discovered by survey were to be sold as *ushuriyya* lands. What was new about this decree was that it further included the sale of surpluses uncovered by informants, here annulling earlier regulations that specified the awarding of these surplus lands to those who had exposed their existence. Instead, informants were to receive a monetary reward of 5 piastres for every 100 piastres of the sale price of the land.[124] Thus, by sending all surplus lands to the auction block, the November 1861 decree worked to generate increased revenues for the government.

In April 1862, the officials of Rawdat al-Bahrayn Province took up the matter of revenue levels generated by the sale of surplus lands as *ushuriyya*. They began by informing the central authorities that their province had 310 villages that contained surplus lands, and that these amounted to a total of 6,853 *faddans*. If these lands were to be sold as *ushuriyya* lands, they would generate 374 purses a year in taxes; but if sold as *kharajiyya* lands, they would yield 1,175 purses in taxes, more than three times as much as would be collected from *ushuriyya* lands. Accordingly, they strongly recommended the sale of surplus lands as *kharajiyya* lands.[125] The logic of this recommendation was hardly lost on the central government, which, in its turn, turned it into law with the issuance of the decree of April 24, 1862.[126]

Thus, taken together, the 1861–1862 regulations worked to maximize the revenues generated by surplus lands by specifying these as *kharajiyya* lands that were to be sold by competitive bidding. These decisions certainly reflected official awareness of the growing profitability of agricultural produce with its attendant increase in the market value of arable lands. Top government decisionmakers, then, were certain that these public auctions would draw the attention of many from both rural and urban areas. While advantageous for the central government, these regulations did not benefit the majority of peasants, for most peasants lacked the wherewithal to outbid their richer competitors.

The 1861–1862 regulations concerning surplus lands, though, did contain an important caveat that granted some peasants better opportunity to acquire surplus lands. This pertains to the alluvial deposits that adjoined arable island lands; these constituted new lands (hence denoted as a type of surplus land) created by the force of the Nile floodwaters. By the 1858 land law, the authorities were to arrange public auctions for these lands, strictly limiting participation to the residents of the village where the surplus lay. Recipients were to register and hold this land as their *athars*, which entailed the identification of these surpluses as state (*miri*) lands that carried the *kharajiyya* taxes and were to be retained for as long as holders kept up with their tax payments. The tax rates were to be determined by the process of competitive bidding.[127] In some areas this led to some very competitive bidding, where peasants presented very high bids, some even specifying exaggeratedly high tax rates (specified by the Qina-wa-Asna provincial authorities as 200 piastres or more per *faddan*) in order to ensure winning.[128]

Yet another entry in the registers of the Viceregal Cabinet, dated May 1, 1862, shows that the auctions set up for these surpluses in Asyut Province were abused by the peasants in their attempt to acquire such lands: it was the belief of the Asyut provincial authorities that the peasants conspired to keep the bidding at low rates; and "that is because they know that the [1858] law does not permit the participation of individuals from distant villages." And here the Asyut governor asked for permission to widen the participation circumference, "at least to include the villages of the entire province," which would certainly lead to the specification of more "appropriate" tax rates and ultimately to higher revenues for the government.[129] While noting that the acceptance of the governor's suggestion would lead to this favorable outcome, the central government would not be swayed. It worried that "this might lead to discussions between the peasants who participated in the auction, [those who hailed from distant villages] and the inhabitants belonging to the villages whose boundaries are adjoined to the surplus land."[130] This entry amply reveals the desire of high state officials to prevent the assembly of large numbers of peasants who might share similar grievances and who might even think about coordinating some anti-government activities. Thus, in the thinking of the concerned state officials, this was a circumstance where the opportunities for revenue enhancement were not important enough to risk political turmoil in the countryside. At the same time, this was a circumstance that granted some peasants the opportunity to acquire new land portions on financially favorable terms.

The Large, Privileged Estates

Discussions on the formation of large estates during the nineteenth century often contain broad sweeping statements that highlight the detrimental impact of this phenomenon on the peasants. Alan Richards' examination of the growth of the area of *ushuriyya* land (of which the large estates were generally composed) involved his assertion that "the growth of this type of land can be taken as a lower-bound estimate of the growth of large landholding at the expense of the peasants." And Judith Tucker, similarly observes that "by mid-century, the best Delta land had passed entirely into the hands of the new grantees. The area of *athar* land had decreased." Even Barakat, whose own data suggest that this broad generalization should be tempered with some necessary reservations, states the following at the end of his discussion on this topic: "The establishment and growth of the large estates occurred at the expense of peasant land possession."[131] On the other hand, other scholars present different conclusions for the mid-century years. Baer, following Artin, specifies that there was "little change" in the area of *ib'adiyya* grants and *jifliks* between 1840 and 1863.[132] In discussing the growth of the large estates, Raouf Abbas and Assem El-Dessouky identify the kinds of land that made up these estates during the nineteenth century: these were the *ib'adiyya matruk* lands; the *usya* and *masmuh* lands; the entire arable area of some peasant villages. They specify that there were 18 *jiflik* estates by 1847 in the Lower Egypt region, and that these were composed of 843 peasant villages. Their discussion, though, largely focuses on the nature of the privileges granted to the estate holders by the state, and does not present data on the growth of these estates at mid-century. Instead, they show that the pace of such formation increased noticeably in the final years of the century, with the sale of the Da'ira Saniya lands and Royal Domain lands.[133] This section takes a different tack, for it addresses ideas from the interpretations of the two groups of writers just mentioned: specifically, this section traces the growth of the large estates during the mid-nineteenth-century years and shows that the pace of estate formation had slowed at mid-century, and moreover, that these estates generally were not carved out of prized *ma'mur* peasant lands. In turn, such growth did not involve wide peasant ruination during the period under discussion.

Muhammad Ali introduced the practice of conferring grants of land on high-level state officials in 1826, when he bestowed 62 *faddans* of *ib'adiyya* land in Qalyubiya Province on October 2 of that year on Muhammad Mahir Bey and followed this with the conferral on January 21, 1827 of 1,000 *faddans* of *ib'adiyya* land in Middle Egypt on Quja Ahmed Aga, the Chief of Doormen.[134] These *faddans* were composed of land that had been surveyed, in 1813–1814 or 1819–1821, but were not included in the cadastral registers because they were barren tracts. Although untouched by the plow, these lands were viewed as being "suitable for cultivation." While Artin believed that Muhammad Ali began this practice with the aim of creating a "class that would monopolize the land wealth," others more astutely attributed it to his desire to expand the area of arable land and further buttressed their view by pointing out that these free grants of land were exempted from taxes on condition that the recipients oversaw their improvement and cultivation.[135] By the end of his reign in 1848, Muhammad Ali had bestowed a total of 173,663

Table 4.5: Land Grants to State Officials and Bedouin Chiefs

	State officials			Bedouin chiefs		
	Ib'adiyya	*Ma'mur*	Total	*Ib'adiyya*	*Ma'mur*	Total[e]
Year	*faddans*	*faddans*	*faddans*	*faddans*	*faddans*	*faddans*
1848[a]	164,960	8,703	173,663	2,650		2,650
1854[b]	107,562	1,529[d]	109,091	14,450		14,450
1862[c]			66,758			

Source: Barakat, *Tatawwur al-milkiyya*, 75–78; 265–68.

Notes:

[a]This was when Muhammad Ali Pasha's reign ended.

[b]This was when Abbas Pasha's reign ended.

[c]This was when Said Pasha's reign ended.

[d]Barakat specifies the number of *ma'mur faddans* as 20,263. But then he states that this number includes the 18,734 *faddans* that made up Jiflik al-Wadi. As *jifliks* were grants of land conferred on members of the royal family only, I have excluded them from this table.

[e]The lands specified here were granted on the basis of a *taqsit*, or legal title.

faddans on prominent state officials. Table 4.5, based on the figures culled by Barakat from the nineteenth-century state registers, shows that the bulk of these land grants (95 percent) consisted of barren lands, or *ib'adiyya* lands, while only 5 percent constituted *ma'mur* lands, or peasant lands.

This pattern of land conferral continued during the mid-nineteenth-century years. Although Baer assumes that there was a general economic slowdown during the time of Abbas Pasha, which led the viceroy to desist making land grants, various sources prove him wrong on both counts.[136] Even though some peasants refused to grow the profitable cotton crop upon learning of Muhammad Ali's death in 1848,[137] it cannot be said that agricultural production declined dramatically during the reign of Abbas Pasha (1848–1854). For many cultivators had switched to wheat production, largely because of the increase in British demand after the repeal of the Corn Laws in 1846 and because of wheat's "positive advantages," which Owen sums up in this way: "Not only was it easier to cultivate, but it provided quicker returns and occupied the ground for a shorter length of time." Owen's data on wheat exports from 1840 to 1854 show that wheat production increased during this time: while average annual wheat exports constituted 485,021 *ardabs* in 1840–1843, when Muhammad Ali was in power, this climbed to 787,949 *ardab*s between 1848 and 1850, and climbed again to 949,023 *ardab*s for the final years of Abbas's reign (1852–1854).[138] This favorable agricultural climate, which undoubtedly made land grants an appreciated gift, probably encouraged Abbas Pasha to continue his grandfather's practice. Thus, in the space of only six years he conferred a total of 109,091 *faddan*s on prominent state officials (63 percent of what Muhammad Ali had given in the two decades since starting this practice). Additionally, as his venerable grandfather had done, the bulk (98.6 percent) of these lands constituted *ib'adiyya* lands, while 1.4 percent came from *ma'mur* village lands (table 4.5).

As most of these land grants were made up of *ib'adiyya* tracts, it might be helpful to recall the chief features of such land at this juncture. As just shown, when Muhammad Ali began the practice of *ib'adiyya* land conferrals, the related tracts were designated as "barren, but suitable for cultivation." Such conferrals were part of his plan to expand the arable land of the country. This same aim also prompted the authorities to offer peasant cultivators easy tax terms to encourage them to bring these tracts into cultivation. By late 1854, these *ib'adiyya* lands constituted roughly 11 percent of the total arable area of peasant villages in Gharbiyya Province.[139] Based on this finding, we might say that this kind of land generally constituted a small proportion of peasant-held lands in Lower Egypt at mid-century. The point I wish to highlight here is if Abbas did draw from these lands for his *ib'adiyya* conferrals, this did not involve heavy peasant land loss. Finally the combined evidence on this point allows me to state that like his grandfather, Abbas Pasha probably preferred to make his estate conferrals out of barren *ib'adiyya* tracts so as to expand the arable area of the country; but where his *ib'adiyya* grants did come from peasant-held *ib'adiyya* lands, these did not entail significant levels of peasant land loss.

This brings us to the land grants bestowed on prominent state officials during the reign of Said Pasha. Did these bring extensive ruination to the peasants? To begin, we point out that Said conferred 66,758 *faddan*s on esteemed state dignitaries, and that this number was significantly lower than those specified for the Muhammad Ali or Abbas reigns (table 4.5). One reason for this might be the government's need to set aside land for retired state officials (who were to receive these in lieu of monetary pensions). Some of these pension land grants were quite sizable. For example, in 1862, Khalil Bey, director of naval affairs, received 1,716 *faddan*s situated in al-Buhayra Province in lieu of a cash-based pension. Also in 1862,

Mustafa Pasha, a member of the prestigious Council of Justice, received a land grant of 1,104 *faddan*s situated in al-Minya Province when he retired. Barakat informs us that the government introduced a law for the dispensation of pension land grants toward the later years of the Said reign, and it was on this basis that it gave 70,414 *faddan*s to pensioners between 1860 and 1862.[140] And although Barakat does not specify whether these lands were *ma'mur* or *ib'adiyya*, the civil court registers contain a number of entries that reveal the despondence of recipients upon discovering that their land grants were poor quality *ib'adiyya*s.

Thus, the Said reign oversaw the bestowal of an approximate total of 137,172 *faddan*s on prominent state officials either because they had retired from state service or because the viceroy particularly valued them and wished to show his appreciation in this way.[141] And as his father and nephew had done before him, Said Pasha probably carved these land grants out of barren land so that he too might oversee the expansion of arable land in the countryside. But when a conferral was composed of peasant land, this most likely came from the *matruk* pool, which had emerged during his reign. Whichever the case, it seems likely that Said's land grants to state dignitaries did not involve extensive peasant land dispossession.

Neither can we say that the conferral of land grants on Bedouin shaykhs, also a practice initiated by Muhammad Ali, brought ruination to peasant cultivators at mid-century. According to Reuven Aharoni, these tribal heads had provided a variety of services to Muhammad Ali; having "taken part in his foreign wars, helped him to put down rebellions of other tribes, acted as watchmen in his public works projects, and executed logistic functions such as transport of food and equipment." By choosing to reward these shaykhs with sizable grants of land, Muhammad Ali aimed both to secure their loyalty to his regime and to enlist the assistance of the Bedouin groups in the expansion of the arable area of the country; this latter was confirmed by his conferral of tracts that were largely composed of barren lands in need of reclamation work in order to be brought into cultivation. The Bedouins, in their turn, preferred land grants composed of *ib'adiyya*s that were on the fringes of peasant-tilled lands, for this enabled the Bedouin recipients to possess land without abandoning their traditional migratory lifestyle.[142]

Bedouin shaykhs received different types of land grants. One type of land grant was composed of an *ib'adiyya* tract that was to carry half the *kharaji* tax rate. Here the actual payment of the taxes and the documentation of the relevant details in the state registers constituted a kind of proof of possession rights. In the second, the government conferred an *ib'adiyya* tract that was tax-exempt but withheld the *taqsit*, or legal title to the land.[143] Baer, basing himself on Ali Mubarak's records, informed us that these land grants could be quite sizable, here mentioning the case of Shaykh Muhammad Shawaribi of Qalyubiya Province, who received 1,700 *faddans*, which carried half the tax rate of *kharaji* lands. This grant came with an added bonus of an additional 400 *faddans* of tax-exempted land for the entertainment of guests.[144]

Barakat's archival research reveals a third type of land grant conferred on Bedouin shaykhs: this involved the bestowal of *ib'adiyya* tracts along with the requisite legal titles. From this research, we see that Muhammad Ali granted 2,650 *faddans* with their titles and that Abbas Pasha conferred 14,450 *faddans* on the same basis (table 4.5). This huge increase in land conferrals to Bedouin chiefs by Abbas might be traced to his anxiety over the possible formation of some kind of alliance between Bedouins and village shaykhs, and his subsequent decision to secure the loyalty of the Bedouins in this way.[145]

Said Pasha also paid attention to the issue of Bedouin land grants, but did not increase them. The early years of his reign witnessed a Bedouin rebellion that involved the al-Jawazi tribe as well as others. This was crushed in 1856, and afterwards, the pasha ordered the confiscation of the lands of the insurgents. The other notable decision regarding Bedouin lands was based on Said's realization that many of the Bedouin grant recipients had held their land for more than a decade, and accordingly, had managed to improve the soil quality of their *ib'adiyya* tracts and were enjoying high agricultural profits, but paid half the taxes imposed on *kharaji* lands or none at all. This led him to issue decrees in 1854 and in 1855, ordering the taxation of Bedouin lands at the same rate as peasant-held *kharaji* lands.[146]

Thus, based on this evidence, we conclude that the state land conferrals at mid-century on esteemed personages, whether state dignitaries or Bedouin chiefs, most often involved *ib'adiyya* tracts made up of barren lands or poor quality lands abandoned by the peasants. In turn, these mid-century land conferrals were rarely carved out of peasants' valuable *ma'mur* lands; and so generally did not involve heavy peasant land loss and attendant ruination.

My argument further extends to the *uhda* lands. Some writers assume that the *uhda* system, established by Muhammad Ali in March 1840 for the purpose of resolving the problematic peasant tax arrears, enabled their holders (*muta'ahhids*) to form large, privileged estates, and that this phenomenon also contributed significantly to peasant land dispossession and impoverishment.[147] This assumption might apply to the Muhammad Ali period. Baer's figures, drawn from the British consular dispatches, reveal that by the end of 1844, roughly one-third of Egypt's cultivated area had been turned into *uhda*.[148] By this system, the *uhda* holder was put in charge of the village entrusted to his care—which generally involved paying its arrears, guaranteeing its future tax liabilities, providing the peasants with the agricultural inputs they needed, and overseeing police and judicial matters. To ensure that the village paid its taxes on a regular basis, the very raison d'être for the *uhda* system, the *muta'ahhid* was to take charge of the insolvent lands. This involved the redistribution of these lands among the village cultivators according to the subsistence needs as well as the economic capability of each one.[149] The *uhda* status of a village was to be terminated when the peasants reimbursed the *muta'ahid* for any payments he had made on their behalf, and when they could demonstrate to the authorities that the level of their resources enabled them to cultivate their lands and pay their taxes without outside assistance. In compensation for his services, the *muta'ahhid* was entitled to a small portion of village land for the duration of the *uhda*, to be cultivated on a tax-free basis, using free corvée labor provided by the village peasants. There were those few *muta'ahhid*s who did not consider their *uhda* villages a means for the accumulation of wealth. This seems to have been the case with one Ahmad Pasha. For from an entry (dated November 7, 1853) in the Council of Justice registers, we learn that the *uhda* status of the villages in his care had been terminated, and more importantly, "that he had not cultivated any lands in these villages, as his assumption of the *uhda* responsibility had been based on his wish to assist."[150] But other *muta'ahhid*s were unhappy with the officially specified compensation, and so helped themselves to the village lands under their control. In an entry, dated July 17, 1856, in the registers of the Viceregal Cabinet, the peasants of Banha Village, which at the time was an *uhda* of Ilhami Pasha (son of Abbas Pasha), complained that they numbered above 2,100 individuals, and despite that, they had received a total of 400 *faddan*s, which was inadequate for their survival, while the *muta'ahhid* kept 1,133 *faddan*s for his own use.[151] It seems that the latter type of case recurred far more frequently than had the former.[152] While these cases occurred after the Muhammad Ali period, it is very likely that they reveal the same trends that had prevailed during the pasha's reign. Indeed, given the pressing financial straits of the 1840s, the government very likely turned a blind eye to the abuses of *muta'ahhid*s as long as they paid all the required taxes.

In 1850, Abbas oversaw the termination of the *uhda* status of a large number of villages. This decision can be partly attributed to his desire to strip his grandfather's supporters of their wealth and power, and partly because he had learned that these *muta'ahhid*s had failed to keep up with their tax payments. According to British Consul Charles Murray, this decision covered roughly between two-thirds and three-quarters of all *uhda*s.[153] Thus, Abbas permitted some villages to remain *uhda*s, and further allowed certain *muta'ahhid*s to retain their *uhda*s on a lifetime basis, while conferring on others the lands of their *uhda*s as *rizqa-bi-la-mal* estates, or tax-free estates.[154] Here, we easily conclude that the latter two cases *did* involve the land dispossession of the peasant inhabitants. At the same time, we should recall that Abbas's 1850 decision *did* result in the termination of the *uhda* status of the majority of the related villages.

While Barakat questions the veracity of the official statements that specify the return of the lands of abolished *uhda*s to the peasant villagers, instead contending that peasant repossession did not actually take place,[155] the archival sources do not bear him out. In 1853, the peasants of one village managed to prove that their shaykhs had lied about the state of their economic capabilities. For the latter had affirmed, in conspiracy with the legal representative (*wakil*) of their *muta'ahhid*, that they lacked sufficient resources for the cultivation of the village lands and the payment of the required taxes, and thereby prevented the termination of the *uhda* status of the village. In response, the government ordered the dismissal of these men from their positions as village headmen and further specified two hundred lashes for each. More importantly, it ordered the termination of the *uhda* status of the concerned village; and further specified that at the time of the return of the land to the peasant inhabitants, each one was "to take control of his original lands and wells."[156] That the peasants retook possession of their lands upon the abolishment of the *uhda* status of their village is also confirmed by the *athurat* registers of four villages in Gharbiyya Province—Ayjul, Abstu, Abtu, and Billa—which document the reassignment of the village lands to the peasants, and accordingly show how much each peasant had received.[157] All in all, officials charged with the reassignment of *uhda* lands to the peasants took into consideration their *athariyya* rights (as specified above), as well as "livelihood needs and levels of capability."[158]

Some *muta'ahhids* did retain land in the village after the *uhda* had been abolished. Yet the archival sources suggest that such retention was hardly an easy matter, as the peasants were known to valiantly fight the attempts to unlawfully retain village lands. Thus the August 1854 attempt of a former *muta'ahhid* to keep the land he had cultivated in his capacity as *uhda* holder of Bashway al-Rumman Village met with firm opposition from the peasant cultivators, who emphasized to the Council of Justice that "his *uhda* has been abolished; and so according to custom, he is not allowed to cultivate land in our village, as we are capable of undertaking its cultivation and the payment of its taxes."[159] Although the official response to this petition was not specified by the relevant entry, other entries suggest that governmental support of this *muta'ahhid* would depend on his ability to prove legal right to the land. This is demonstrated by the May 1854 entry in the registers of the Council of Justice, which examines the attempt of a former *muta'ahhid* to retain village land on the basis of having purchased it from the peasants. But when investigations clarified that "the cession by the holders of the 236 *faddans* was not viable," the *muta'ahhid* was ordered to return this land to the original peasant holders.[160] On the other hand, a *muta'ahhid's* petition to retain land in his former *uhda* was likely to be accepted if it was couched in a legitimate and attractive offer. The December 1855 case of former *muta'ahhid* Selim Bey al-Hejazi shows that he petitioned the government to retain an *ib'adiyya* tract situated in the village of Lamhudiyya, his former *uhda*. He had previously learned that a village inhabitant by the name of Sa'ad Hassan wanted to take control of this *ib'adiyya* tract, offering to pay the full *kharaji* rate. Selim Bey emphasized that he had a greater right to this tract, for it had originally been composed of barren lands that he had successfully brought into cultivation by spending huge sums of money. Then he offered to pay a tax rate that was 12 piastres higher than the *kharaji* tax imposed on the *ma'mur* lands of the basin in which the tract was situated. It was an offer that secured governmental approval of his petition.[161]

For the most part, the examination of the archival sources suggests that such cases of *muta'ahhid* retention of village lands did not occur frequently; and where these did, they often involved *ib'adiyya* tracts that had originally constituted barren lands. Moreover, *muta'ahhids'* retention of recently improved lands generally did not involve peasant dispossession.

That Abbas Pasha had terminated the majority of the *uhdas* did not mean that the system had been abolished. Indeed, he continued to view *uhda* entrustment as a reliable strategy by which to address the problem of peasant tax arrears; accordingly, in 1851 he placed insolvent villages in Sharqiyya Province in the *uhda* of Burhan Pasha.[162] Said Pasha held the same view, for he issued the decree of October 1, 1855, which ordered the placement of the insolvent villages of more than five provinces in the care of *muta'ahhids*.[163] Still, this does not mean that the 1850s witnessed a significant increase in the establishment of *uhdas*. Indeed, evidence concerning the situation of al-Gharbiyya Province during this decade suggests that the total number of *uhdas* continued to decline: in 1854, 13 percent of the villages of this province were in *uhda*, while in 1858, *uhdas* constituted 9 percent of the total.[164] And with this decline came the peasants' repossession of most of the village lands.

Now we turn to the examination of *jiflik* estates, which Baer considers "[p]robably the most important factor in the formation of large estates" during the nineteenth century.[165] Starting the practice of such estate bestowal in 1838, Muhammad Ali limited these bestowals to himself and members of the royal family.[166] Barakat's examination of the relevant archival sources reveals that these estates were primarily composed of village *ma'mur* lands, that their creation had involved the exclusion of the village *ib'adiyya* lands (or the poorer-quality lands), that they were tax-exempt, and finally that they were enormous, for an estate frequently exceeded 10,000 *faddans*. He further concludes that these lands were probably worked by the peasant villagers, whose status had changed from *athariyya* holders to mere tenants. By the end of the reign of Muhammad Ali, the *jiflik* estates covered 334,286 *faddans*, or roughly 9 percent of the arable area of the time.[167]

This rapid pace of *jiflik* creation did not continue into the mid-nineteenth-century years. For the most part, Abbas and Said were content to focus primarily on the *jiflik* lands Muhammad Ali had set aside for himself, which amounted to 249,426 *faddans*, redistributing much of this to members of their own families while reserving some for themselves. Thus, between 1848 and 1862, few new *jifliks* were created, for the total number of *jiflik faddans* increased by 41,310 *faddans* only.[168]

Not only was there a slowdown in *jiflik* creation during this time, but just as importantly, we also see the creation of *jiflik* estates that contained large tracts of barren lands. This, in turn, necessitated the installation of landless peasants who were charged with the responsibility of bringing these lands into cultivation. Such peasants fought hard to retain these lands. In 1861, the peasants of Jiflik Mit Sandub objected to the proposed arrangement of a public auction for the rental of the estate lands. They stated that "since their possession [of these lands] in 1855 until now, they have been engaged in the improvement of the lands bit by bit. And if the auction takes place, the winning bidders will not take a tract in its entirety, but will take the choicest [portions] and leave the bad [portions]." Here they offered to pay substantially higher taxes; meaning that starting in 1862 they would pay the *kharaji* taxes and the *ushuriyya* taxes, as well as the required extraordinary taxes.[169]

In addition to the slowdown in *jiflik* creation, this period also witnessed the dismantlement of some *jiflik*s. In 1849, Abbas Pasha ordered the dismantlement of Jiflik Kafr al-Shaykh and Jiflik Nabrawah, most likely because their holders had committed unforgivable deeds. Thus, these lands were placed in the names of the peasant cultivators who thereby retained them on the *athariyya* basis, "just like the province's villages that had never been part of a *jiflik*."[170]

Thus, by the above discussion we see that *jiflik*s constituted the most important component of large estate formation during the Muhammad Ali reign, but that the formation of these estates slowed quite perceptibly during the mid-century years. Why was that? To begin, it should be recalled that the great pasha was under pressure to abandon his monopoly system, and that his acquiescence would have deprived him of the huge profits it generated. Accordingly, one of the primary reasons that led Muhammad Ali to establish the large *jiflik* estates was to ensure the delivery of agricultural produce to his warehouses (which he intended to resell to foreign merchants). That most of Muhammad Ali's *jiflik* conferrals took place between 1840 and 1846 provides support for this interpretation.[171] While Abbas and Said also worried about state revenue levels, they understood that the *jiflik*s would not contribute significantly to the enrichment of the state. For the country was slowly but surely returning to free market rules, which meant that landholders were no longer required to deliver their agricultural produce to government warehouses at fixed low prices. Also Egypt's mid-century rulers could not expect (unlike Muhammad Ali) *jiflik* holders to prioritize state approval and state profits and accordingly sell their produce to the government at below-market prices. Instead these holders wanted to keep whatever profits could be made from market sales of agricultural produce for themselves. Neither would jiflik holders contribute significantly to the state treasury by paying high taxes. Thus, one important way to maintain or increase state revenues involved refraining from transforming peasant land, which carried the high *kharaji* taxes, into large *jifliks*, which were tax-exempt until 1854, at which time they usually began to carry the comparatively lower *ushuriyya* tax.

All in all, official interest in the expansion of the area of arable land and the maximization of revenues at mid-century generally worked to ensure that the formation of large, privileged estates did not entail the dispossession of large numbers of peasants of their lands.

This examination of the formation of large estates would be incomplete without a brief consideration of peasant reaction to governmental decrees that *did* require them to turn over their lands to state dignitaries. On one hand, the literature strongly suggests that the "unlucky" peasants had little room for maneuver, and simply did as they were told, and then adapted themselves as best they could to their new, and often impoverished, conditions. Yet the archival sources reveal that the peasants did not always accept their "fate" quietly and passively, as some waged rather spirited resistance against such governmental attempts to please dignitaries at their expense.

The first step protesting peasants might take was the presentation of their grievances to the civil courts. In July 1856, peasant Asaʿad Abd al-Mallak of Izbat Farnawy Village (in al-Buhayra Province) submitted a petition to the Viceregal Cabinet to protest the seizure of his land and its transformation into an *ib'adiyya* land grant for the wife of Officer Raghab Agha. He explained that this land, which constituted 45 *faddans*, had been given to him while the village was still in *uhda* by the representative of the *muta'ahhid*. By the terms of their agreement, Asaʿad was to rent this land from 1846 until 1864, while paying half the *kharaji* tax rate, after which he was to pay the *kharaji* taxes in full. The retention of this tract had required that Asaʿad improve its soil quality and bring it into cultivation; that he had done so was confirmed by the village headmen. Here the government ordered the provincial authorities to conduct a survey of the area of the land grant (500 *faddans*) to ascertain whether the disputed 45 *faddans* had been taken in excess of the area specified by the grant; in other words, by mistake. If that was the case, the disputed land was to be returned to Asaʿad; at that time too he was instructed to begin paying the full *kharaji* rate immediately, rather than the 50 percent specified by his original contract.[172] Thus, Asaʿad's chances regarding the recovery of his land seemed to depend on whether or not the land had been mistakenly seized.

Other petitions reveal that some *ib'adiyya* grantees knew exactly what they were doing when seizing the peasants' lands. In December 1855, the headmen of three villages—Shubra Babal, Abu Jir, and Kafr Hijazi Villages—in Gharbiyya Province, complained to the Viceregal Cabinet about the actions of two dignitaries. Briefly, these two men had received *ib'adiyya* land grants that fell in the area of the aforementioned villages, whereupon they demarcated the area of their *ib'adiyya*s "so that parts were composed of *ma'mur* lands and in compensation gave to the peasants barren land that had never undergone cultivation . . . and all this was against their [that is, the peasants'] wishes."[173] This case ends with these instructions to the governor of the province: he was to examine carefully the details (that is, the area boundaries of the *ib'adiyya* tracts) specified by the grant title deeds to ascertain whether the grant recipients had taken land to which they had no right.

These two cases suggest that the legal route could be a lengthy process and that outcomes were uncertain. In short, peasants could not always be certain that land seizures would be reversed. This led some of the more imaginative rural folks to dispense with the legal route and instead protect their lands by resorting to subterfuge, sabotage, and deceit—or the "weapons of the weak"[174]—and sometimes, to outright force.

That the archival sources reveal cases of peasants' recourse to the "weapons of the weak" as well as to force to protect their interests allows us to discern something of a varied response on the part of the peasants to land seizures by state elite. Yet these cases cannot allow us to comment with much certainty about the frequency of a certain type of response, simply because of the anecdotal nature of the evidence—except to say that if any of these were very frequent, they would have changed the course of Egyptian history. Hence the following discussion seeks only to draw attention to the existence of some cases of peasant opposition and their varied nature.

At times, peasants boldly defied the land-grant instructions and simply took the disputed tract. In May 1858, Mahmud Sultan complained to the Department of Interior about an *ib'adiyya* land grant composed of 1,128 *faddan*s (in Qalyubiya Province) that had been bestowed on him in 1268 (1851–1852). The problem was that the peasants of the nearby villages had "trespassed on this land and have been cultivating it from that time until now."[175] Another petitioner who had endured the exact same situation insisted that the peasants pay him rent for the eleven years they had unlawfully cultivated his land; here too the peasants had brazenly ignored the rights and demands of the *ib'adiyya* grantee.[176]

Peasants were also known to sabotage the attempts of *ib'adiyya* grantees to cultivate their lands. In August 1852, Qaymaqam Ahmad Shawqi

Effendi complained that his summer crop had been ruined and that he was unable to prepare the land for the winter season because the village shaykhs had terrorized his labor force.[177] In the same month, the French consul put forth a similar complaint on behalf of a French *ib'adiyya* grantee. That petitioners could not expect immediate relief is confirmed by the fact that the consul filed another petition roughly six weeks later to make the exact same complaint.[178] In turn, the peasants were probably familiar with the sluggish movement of the machinery of government, and this certainly encouraged them to stay their course. The archival evidence shows that the peasants' sabotage repertoire also included interfering with the irrigation system so that the water resources did not reach the lands of the disputed *ib'adiyya*s, and the refusal of village headmen to send the required corvée labor contingents.[179]

Finally, peasants could thwart land dispossession by the resort to deceit and cunning. In December 1857, a dignitary put forth a complaint to the Department of Interior that concerned a land grant of 500 *faddan*s that had been bestowed on him in 1269 (1852–1853). He pointed out that 45 *faddan*s of his estate were situated in Banayus Village, and his problem concerned this particular tract. For when the *nazir*, or the supervisor of his estate, went to the village headmen in 1269, "they did not give him the aforementioned lands in their entirety; and what they revealed and gave to the *nazir* was 30 *faddan*s and some fractions and they hid the remainder from him."[180]

The Implementation of the 1858 Land Law

On January 29, 1860, the presiding *qadi* (judge) of the Tanta religious court observed that a state decree had ordered *shari'a* (religious) courts to adjudicate land disputes in accordance with the 1858 land law.[181] This meant that land-tenure problems were not to be the sole province of the "secular" courts, that is, the judicial branches of governmental departments—which in turn meant that peasants could take their land disputes to a religious or a secular court. The first course of action of disputants most likely was to put their cases before the religious court, for its system of adjudication involved face-to-face contact between the *qadi* and all concerned parties, and just as important, cases were usually concluded quickly, often on the same day peasants presented their petitions. The immediacy and speed with which cases were concluded in the religious courts contrasted with the system of the secular courts, for the latter did not deal with disputants in person, only with their written petitions, and further required a space of time for the issuance of rulings, certainly more than a day. Hence peasants probably approached the secular courts when they rejected the decisions of the religious court, as they knew that the former had the authority to overrule the latter; and too they might have preferred to bypass the *shari'a* courts altogether when their problems seemed particularly complicated and intractable. What this meant, as just stated above, was that the first recourse of a rural petitioner was to approach the religious courts. This preference of peasants for the religious courts necessitates an examination of how these courts dealt with the 1858 land law during the early years of implementation (1858–1862).

One of the most noticeable features of this early stage of implementation had to do with the degree of compliance with the injunctions of the new law by the religious courts; in a word, the religious courts did not always observe the stipulations of the 1858 law. For the central government's control over the countryside had waned in the late 1840s and the 1850s, and this undoubtedly gave the *qadi*s some latitude regarding the interpretation and implementation of new legislation.[182]

This can particularly be seen in the way the religious courts dealt with evidence; probably something of a sticky point for the courts because of the emphasis on oral testimony in Islamic law. As mentioned before, the 1858 law stipulated that all land transactions were to be recorded in legal documents issued by a major court, and further granted landholders a period of one year to renew invalid documents. Henceforth, land disputes were to be decided solely on the basis of written evidence. Yet, the Tanta religious court registers show otherwise. On November 21, 1859, a woman named Zaynab and her son Yusuf, both of al-Jawhariyya Village, filed a complaint against Muhammad Ayad from Mahallat Marsum Village, demanding that he return the land he had been renting from them for the past three years. The case was continued two days later, when Muhammad was asked to relate his version of the story: he completely denied that he had received the land from the original holder (Yusuf's father) on a rental basis, and instead declared that the land had been ceded to him in exchange for the sum of 1,450 piastres. The claimants did not accept this story, and so the presiding *qadi* required Muhammad to "produce *shar'i* [legal] evidence that would support his declaration." By this Muhammad was required to produce the two credible witnesses specified by Islamic law; which he did, and accordingly the court informed the plaintiffs that the land rightfully belonged to Muhammad.[183] What is noticeable here is that the court did not ask to examine written evidence as was required by the 1858 law, but rather preferred to resolve the land dispute in accordance with Islamic law.[184]

Other cases suggest the religious courts might consult both Islamic law and the 1858 law when examining evidence. In a December 21, 1858 case brought before the Tanta religious court, the suing party (Ghurbal al-Zinawy) claimed that the land in the possession of the controller (Asaʿad Qudsi) was a pawn and demanded its return, while the controller asserted it had been ceded to him and further supported his claim with a legal document (dated August 29, 1845) that carried the signature of the *shar'i* representative in the village, Shaykh Hassanayn Taj al-Din. The document, described as "unregistered," was read to the plaintiff, who denied its contents. That the court read this document aloud meant that it had accepted it as viable written evidence; maybe because the one-year period stipulated for the renewal of invalid deeds had not yet passed. But rather than decide the case solely on the basis of this evidence, it also examined the oral testimony provided by the witnesses. As both kinds of evidence supported the claims of the controller, the court, in turn, championed this controller.[185]

The tendency of the religious courts to consult both bodies of law in the adjudication of land disputes might result in the prolongation of cases and in the failure to issue clear rulings. This is illustrated by the following case. On August 4, 1861, Umda Ibrahim al-Fiqi, headman of Mahallat al-Labban Village, filed a petition at the Tanta religious court against his brother Umda Hifnawi al-Fiqi, headman of Qalib Ibyar Village. Ibrahim's petition clarified that the land at issue consisted of 60 *faddan*s, that these lay in Mahallat al-Labban Village, that these had originally constituted part of their deceased father's estate, that his brother Hifnawi had relinquished his rights to this land and thus recognized Ibrahim as the sole and rightful holder, that this was recorded in a document dated March 13, 1849, and that this land had been in his (Ibrahim's) control from that time until 1860, when Hifnawi had unfairly and without right retaken possession of the 60 *faddan*s. Ibrahim further clarified that his own possession of the land had been uncontested for "nearly twelve years and that the [1858] law specified that whosoever controlled land for a period of five years without dispute would be recognized as the rightful possessor." Hifnawi, in turn, admitted to retaking possession of the disputed land, and moreover explained that he had placed this land "in the hands of the aforementioned claimant for safekeeping, as was specified in the previously mentioned deed of which each [brother] had a copy, and he brought it forward, and it was read aloud before the court." This document corroborated Hifnawi's version of events; and on this basis the court ruled that the twelve years Hifnawi had spent away from his land were not to be "viewed as a case of land abandonment," and therefore the land rightfully belonged to him.[186]

At this point the disputants agreed to consult a legal scholar about their case, and so the *qadi* adjourned the adjudication proceedings to accommodate this decision. Examination of the case resumed fifteen days later, on August 19, 1861, when the legal scholar Ali al-Baqli appeared before the court and stated the following: if it has been proven that the land had been placed in the hands of the claimant (Ibrahim) for safekeeping, as was specified in the aforementioned deed, then the claimant cannot refer to the previously mentioned twelve years as a pretext for his permanent retention of the land. Al-Baqli further insisted that this agreement between the two brothers (recorded in the March 13, 1849 deed) could not be verified solely by written evidence and that it had to be corroborated by *shar'i* evidence, that is, oral testimony. Hifnawi duly produced the required witnesses, who effectively verified the main points of the 1849 deed, and thereby corroborated his version of the case.

By this time, Hifnawi had satisfied the legal criteria specified by secular law and religious law. And the court most likely would have ruled in his favor, but did not do so because of a new development in the case. For at this juncture Ibrahim modified his story, and claimed that after the deed had been issued, his brother had voluntarily relinquished his right to the 60 *faddans* at issue.[187]

Thus, the court was bound to investigate Ibrahim's claim. And when the case proceedings resumed on September 9, 1861, the court demanded that Ibrahim provide oral evidence of this latest modification of his account. The witnesses who came forward on his behalf provided somewhat conflicting accounts of Hifnawi's alleged relinquishment of his land; one specifying that this had occurred six years ago and that he did not know where the land tract was situated nor its size, while the other asserted that Hifnawi had declared in front of witnesses "that he had no right to the disputed land and these constituted sixty *faddans* and this was in 1851."[188]

The case proceedings do not specify the court's assessment of Ibrahim's claim nor of the accounts provided by his witnesses. But it seems that it did not dismiss them as untrue; neither did the court issue a clear ruling in the case, seemingly paralyzed by the conflicting claims of the disputing brothers.

The final entry regarding this case was on November 15, 1861, and it specifies that the fighting between the two brothers ceased on that date;

for that was when they agreed to divide the 60 *faddans* equally between themselves.[189] At the end, the dispute was resolved according to Islamic law, which allows for the resolution of disputes by *sulh*, or amicable settlement.[190]

In parallel to this tendency of the religious courts to consult both secular and Islamic law in the adjudication of land disputes—and aside from the sticky matter of written documents as the sole basis of evidence—these same courts were also known to observe closely the stipulations of the 1858 law.

What did this mean for peasant disputants? To begin, it meant that they could count on state support for legitimate inheritance claims. In March 1860, Sayyid Shusha from Kafr Abu Dawud Village filed a complaint at the Tanta religious court on behalf of himself and his brother Basyuni against their paternal uncle Ahmad Shusha. The claimant explained that his late father and his two brothers, Ahmad Shusha and Ali Shusha, had lived in one household, that this arrangement had involved their having worked together, and that their combined profits had allowed them to acquire land. After the death of their father (twenty years ago) and their uncle Ali (thirteen years ago), Sayyid and Basyuni (the claimants) continued to reside and work with their uncle Ahmad. But they resented his control of their share of the land, which constituted one-third of the family patrimony, and they demanded its removal from his possession. In his turn, Ahmad Shusha confirmed his nephews' account before the court, explaining that their share of the family patrimony was 7 *faddans*.[191] Thus the nephews won their case because it had rested on viable claims, and what was just as important, because the court viewed them as responsible individuals capable of keeping their land cultivated and of paying its taxes.

This further meant that the courts did not stand by poor claimants who did not demonstrate an adequate level of capability. This official position can be discerned in the cases that involved land recovery, for the courts observed the new recovery criteria closely. This can be seen in the following case. On January 29, 1860, the peasant Amir filed a petition against his brother Muhammad for the recovery of his land. Amir explained that their deceased father had left them a land patrimony of 14 *faddans*, and that they divided their inheritance between themselves six years ago. At the time of division, Amir took control of roughly 4 *faddans*, rather than the entirety of his share, because of the deficient state of his resources, leaving the remainder of his land with Muhammad. Amir explained that his financial abilities had improved to the point where he could maintain all his land and thus demanded that Muhammad release the remaining 3 *faddans* to his control. Here the Tanta court summarily ruled that Article V of the 1858 law, which stipulated that the controller's possession of land for five years renders it his permanently, invalidated Amir's inheritance rights; for it should be remembered that Amir's poverty had forced him to place his land in the care of his brother, and in a sense he had "abandoned" his land. Thus, the fact that he did not reclaim it before the five-year period stipulated by the new law meant that his story ended badly, for he had forfeited his land.[192] Then again, insolvent peasants who had entered into partnership agreements in order to ensure the defrayal of their land's cultivation costs found themselves similarly disadvantaged. This was the case with al-Shaf'i Jalabi, who had established a partnership with Marzuq Khamis in 1855 for the cultivation of his 38 *faddans*. By the terms of their agreement, the two men shared everything on a fifty-fifty basis: they divided the land between themselves, as well as the cultivation costs, the tax payments, and the profits. But in 1861, al-Shaf'i wanted to terminate the agreement and sued for the recovery of his land before the Tanta religious court, which ruled that "by Article XIX [of the 1858 law] the right to the usufruct of half of the aforementioned 38 *faddans* belongs to the petitioner and to the defendant belongs the other half."[193]

But what mattered more to poor peasants than stringent recovery criteria were the new rules regulating the assignment of *ramya*, or vacant, land. As mentioned before, the most important of these specified that the receipt of a land assignment was contingent on the payment of a transfer fee of 24 piastres per *faddan*; whereas in the past, recipients possessed their land assignments without the payment of any fees. The 1858 law further encouraged peasants to expose neighbors who failed to pay these fees, awarding the land assignments to their informants when they demonstrated the possession of sufficient resources and so could ensure the steady maintenance of the lands. While impoverished informants were denied access to the land they had exposed, they were given a money reward that was to consist of 1 piastre per every 100 piastres of the tax sum owed by the land for that year.[194] These rules were to apply to all cases of *ramya* assignment, except where the recipients were soldiers or noncommissioned officers newly returned to their villages and in need of land for their subsistence; for in these cases, the transfer fee was to be waived.[195] That the transfer fee was an onerous sum that penurious folks tried to avoid is suggested by the attempts of military men to help their families avoid its payment. It was probably for this reason that in October 1859, a soldier named Siliman Jadid, still on duty at one of Said Pasha's military complexes, demanded that the authorities "give his father and siblings land for their subsistence."[196] That this petition was rejected is highly likely, and Siliman may have anticipated this outcome, for the law explicitly referred to land provisioning for soldiers, not for their families. Yet it seemed worth a try, for success would have spared his family the payment of the transfer fee.

For the most part, then, these rules most probably worked to limit the number of beneficiaries of the *ramya* system, for it is likely that these often worked to bypass indigent cultivators. The significance of this development can be discerned by recalling (shown earlier in this chapter) that prior to the 1858 law, land assignment constituted the most important means of land acquirement for village cultivators since both the poor and the affluent peasants attributed sizable portions of their landholdings to *ramya* distribution. Moreover, many landless peasants had joined the ranks of village smallholders precisely because of the land-assignment system.

Thus, earlier writers are right to say that the 1858 land law advantaged the affluent village holders at the expense of the penurious peasants. But the major reason for this cannot be sought in the stringent criteria for land recovery, or more specifically, in the reduced time periods in which recovery was possible. Here we should recall that the *athurat* registers show that relatively few peasant holders engaged in market transactions in land, and thus relatively few would need to worry about the recovery of lands they had previously transferred to others by some market transaction (like land pawn). And while numerous peasants (prior to 1858) lost their lands to the *ramya* system largely because of accumulated tax arrears, and many did try to recover their original holdings, far larger numbers did not, simply looking to and depending on the workings of the *ramya* system to provide them with new lands. This changed with the implementation of the 1858 law, for its modification of the *ramya* system meant that many peasants, most especially the village poor, could no longer depend on it for the acquirement of new land. The final blow to this system came in 1861 (shown earlier in this chapter), when the government forbade the assignment of vacant land to the villagers, and instead ordered its placement in auctions. Henceforth, villagers were to compete among themselves as well as with outsiders for the land. That this process particularly disadvantaged the impoverished village stratum hardly needs to be mentioned.

The Distribution of Land

To what extent did the distribution of land in the peasant villages of Lower Egypt change during the mid-nineteenth-century period?

The investigation of this question necessitated examining the land-tax registers of our four sample villages at the beginning of our period, those of 1266/1849–1850, and then the registers pertaining to the end of our period, those of 1279/1862–1863.[197] Our discussion focuses on "freehold" peasant villages, or those villages that were not part of a large estate (*jiflik* or *uhda* estates), and accordingly were identified by archival sources as "villages under the administration of the provincial bureaucracy." As specified earlier, the overwhelming majority of villages in the countryside during this period belonged to this category, as do all our sample villages.

The land-tax registers of a village specify the amount of land registered in the names of the holders, the rate of tax imposed on each plot, and the tax sums each holder owed. These lands were viewed as *athariyya* lands, or those lands farmed by generations of peasants and which carried the full *kharaji/miri* tax rate. Thus, where the registers identified certain plots as *usya* or *rizqa*, they intended nothing more than to refer to the earlier status of these lands (when they were held by the village *multazims* on a tax-free basis); as by the mid-nineteenth-century period, these lands were held by villagers and were considered peasant *athariyya* land. But the land-tax registers, unlike the village cadastral registers, did not distinguish between cultivable and marginal lands. Hence, tax liability extended to all lands in the possession of the smallholder, even if part of the holding was made up of wastelands.[198] Another difference between cadastral and land-tax records had to do with the focus of each of the registers. While the former registers focused on the lands within the village boundaries (which includes specifying the barren tracts lying on the fringes of the arable area that were suitable for cultivation), the latter's purpose was to record the entirety of the lands in the possession of holders (so as to facilitate the tax-collection process), which also involved specifying whether holders had been assigned arrears-laden land belonging to a neighboring insolvent village.[199]

This discussion on distribution of land in peasant villages cannot proceed without a brief comment on mode of landholding. Oftentimes, peasants did not divide their land patrimony, as male heirs preferred to cultivate their land together and reside in the same dwelling. This way they formed a joint household, each performing his share of the cultivation tasks, paying his share of farming costs, and paying his share of the taxes. The entirety of the holding, though, was registered in the name of the oldest male of the household, referred to as *al-arshad*. Accordingly, the land-tax registers (unlike the *athurat* records) specify only the name of the registered holder, making no mention of the rights of other individuals. In our examination of the land-tax registers, then, the use of the term "holder," which suggests the land belonged exclusively to one individual, does not allow for the possibility that the landholding may have belonged to more than one person. Thus, for the purposes of the following discussion on distribution of land, which relies almost exclusively on the land-tax registers, I prefer to substitute the term *holding* for *holder*.[200]

This brings us to the examination of tables 4.6 and 4.7, which show the distribution of land in four peasant villages in Lower Egypt: two in Gharbiyyia Province (al-Jazira al-Khadra and Ibyar Villages), and two in Qalyubiya Province (Jazirat al-Aʿjam and Kafr al-Rajallat Villages). These tables divide village landholdings into three: the small holdings consist of less than 5 *faddans*, the medium holdings of 5 to less than 50 *faddans*, and the large holdings of 50 and more. I point out that the tables presented in the earlier chapters of this study defined two categories differently; there medium consisted of 5 through less than 20 *faddans*, and large consisted of 20 and more *faddans*.[201] The reason for the reliance on this latter set of categories for previous discussions was to capture more effectively the level of economic stratification in small villages like Jazirat al-Ajam (which in 1850 consisted of approximately 385.5 *faddans*), where the most powerful individual in the village, its premier headman (Shaykh Abd al-Aal Hassan), possessed 38 *faddans*, 16 *sahms*.[202] But for the discussion on land distribution, I preferred to use the conventional categories in order to allow for comparison with earlier studies (that have relied on these categories when presenting their data).[203]

The landholding data of the four sample villages in 1849–1850 are presented in table 4.6. We start with some basic observations. For two of these villages, Ibyar and al-Jazira al-Khadra, the total arable/taxed area was well over 1,000 *faddans*, making them the largest of the sample. In three of the sample villages, the three landholding categories were found; only Jazirat Al-Aʿjam lacked large holdings. In these same three villages, the small holdings constituted the largest proportion of total holdings (between 65 and 72 percent); while the relevant figure for Jazirat Aʿjam was 45 percent. All four villages, though, shared one important characteristic: the small holdings category possessed the smallest proportion of the village land. These two features of the small holdings category were hardly a new phenomenon.

Table 4.6: The Distribution of Land in Four Peasant Villages: AH 1266/November 1849–November 1850

	<1–<5 *faddans*				5–<50 *faddans*				50 *faddans* and more				Total	
Village	Total holdings	% of holdings	Area in *faddans*	% of area	Total holdings	% of holdings	Area in *faddans*	% of area	Total holdings	% of holdings	Area in *faddans*	% of area	Holdings	Area
Ibyar	222	65.29	442.5	10.90	105	30.88	1,362.0	33.56	13	3.82	2,253.5	55.53	340	4,058.0
Al-Jazira al-Khadra	88	65.19	107.0	7.20	41	30.37	655.5	44.08	6	4.44	725.0	48.72	135	1,487.5
Jazirat al-Aʿjam	18	45.00	43.0	10.80	22	55.00	354.0	89.20	—	—	—	—	40	397.0
Kafr al-Rajallat	71	71.72	138.0	21.30	26	26.26	329.0	50.77	2	2.02	181.0	27.93	99	648.0
Total	399	64.98	730.5	11.08	194	31.60	2,700.5	40.98	21	3.42	3,159.5	47.94	614	6,590.5

Notes: In computing the data for this table, I used the same method described in the notes of table 2.1.

Sources: DMU, Mukallafat atyan, ibyar, 1266, 2913/121/22; DMU, Mukallafat atyan, al-jazira al-khadra, 1266, 3978/135/22; DMU, Mukallafat atyan, kafr al-rajallat, 1266, 8203/110/20; DMU, Mukallafat atyan, jazirat al-aʿjam, 1266, 4571/61/20.

Table 4.7: The Distribution of Land in Four Peasant Villages: AH 1279/June 1862–June 1863

	<1–<5 *faddans*				5–<50 *faddans*				50 *faddans* and more				Total	
Village	Total holdings	% of holdings	Area in *faddans*	% of area	Total holdings	% of holdings	Area in *faddans*	% of area	Total holdings	% of holdings	Area in *faddans*	% of area	Holdings	Area
Ibyar	294	66.67	638	15.36	136	30.84	1,636.0	39.41	11	2.49	1,879	45.23	441	4,153.0
Al-Jazira al-Khadra	76	56.30	102	8.00	55	40.74	770.5	58.00	4	2.96	457	34.00	135	1,329.5
Jazirat al-Aʿjam	34	53.97	76	14.73	29	46.03	440.0	85.27	—	—	—	—	63	516.0
Kafr al-Rajallat	108	77.14	227	34.08	31	22.14	388.0	58.26	1	0.71	51	7.660	140	666.0
Total	512	65.73	1,043	15.65	251	32.22	3,234.5	48.53	16	2.05	2,387	35.82	779	6,664.5

Notes: In computing the data for this table, I used the same method described in the notes of table 2.1.

Sources: DMU, Mukallafat atyan, ibyar, 1279, 2925/121/22; DMU, Mukallafat atyan, al-jazira al-khadra, 1279, 3990/135/22; DMU, Mukallafat atyan, kafr al-rajallat, 1279, 8213/110/20; DMU, Mukallafat atyan, jazirat al-aʿjam, 1279, 4581/61/20.

Next, we examine Kenneth Cuno's findings. Cuno's discussion of the distribution of land in peasant villages during the nineteenth century starts with a focus on 1813–1814; for this was when Muhammad Ali carried out his first cadastral survey, and as such the relevant cadastral records provide "the earliest statistical evidence for the distribution of peasant-held land in Egypt." Cuno's examination relied on this source as well as the land-tax registers of four sample villages in Daqahliyya Province (in Lower Egypt). And from it we learn the following: in three of his sample villages, the small holdings constituted the greatest number; and in three of these villages, this category controlled the smallest proportion of the village land. The only exception was al-Qubab al-Sughara Village, for 7 percent (the smallest proportion) of the village land was controlled by one (large) holding—which, needless to say, only aligns with the skewed nature of land distribution in villages in 1813–1814.[204]

Now we look more closely at the different landholding categories of our sample villages. Regarding the small holdings category, the next point of focus is the average size of a holding: for al-Jazira al-Khadra the average size of a holding for this category was roughly 1 *faddan*, while for the other three villages this was about 2 *faddans*. The comparison of this picture with that of the four sample villages located in Daqahliyya Province in 1813–1814 reveals significant similarities. For the small holdings category constituted 63 percent of all holdings in 1813–1814, and constituted 65 percent in 1849–1850; and thus was the largest of the three categories. This same category controlled the smallest proportion of the total area in 1813–1814 (18 percent), as was the case for 1849–1850 (11 percent). The latter set of figures also indicate that the intervening three decades had brought a small reduction in the total area of land in the possession of these holdings, which further entailed a slight reduction in the average size of a holding, having gone from 2 to 3 *faddans* in 1813–1814, to 1–2 *faddans* in 1849–1850.

This period also witnessed a reduction in the land area pertaining to the medium holdings category. In 1849–1850, the medium holdings of the two larger villages (Ibyar, al-Jazira al-Khadra) constituted one-third of village holdings, and possessed between one-third and roughly two-fifths of the total taxed area. The figures for the two smaller villages were more skewed: the medium holdings of Kafr al-Rajallat constituted 26 percent of total holdings, and possessed 51 percent of village land; and in Jazirat al-Aʿjam, which had no large holdings, the medium holdings constituted 55 percent of total holdings, and controlled 89 percent of the village land. Taken together (the four sample villages combined), this category accounted for roughly one-third of holdings and possessed two-fifths of the total area of land. The average size of the medium holdings for these villages ranged from 13 to 16 *faddans*. In 1813–1814, the aggregate numbers for this category were better: for the medium holdings constituted 33 percent of all holdings, these controlled 58 percent of the land, and the average size of a holding was 13–20 *faddans*. Thus, when comparing the 1813–1814 aggregate figures with those of 1849–1850, we see that this category had experienced a rather significant reduction in the total area of land, roughly losing one-fifth of its area; and as regards the average size of holding, the upper boundary had dropped by 4 *faddans* during the intervening three decades.

The large holdings category existed in three of the 1849–1850 sample villages, and in each of these it accounted for the smallest proportion of holdings. This category controlled most of the village land: it controlled roughly half the land in the two larger villages, al-Jazira al-Khadra and Ibyar, with the average size of a holding at 121 and 173 *faddans*, respectively. As for Kafr al-Rajallat, a mere two holdings possessed nearly one-third of the land, with the average size of a holding at about 90.5 *faddans*. The data at the aggregate level show that 3.4 percent of holdings possessed nearly half of the land. The comparison of these findings with the aggregate data pertaining to the 1813–1814 sample villages shows that the proportion of holdings basically stayed the same over the next three decades (3.5 percent in 1813–1814; 3.4 percent in 1849–1850), while the land under their control nearly doubled (24.4 percent in 1813–1814; 47.9 percent in 1849–1850).

The changes specified for these three categories can be attributed to the major policies of the Muhammad Ali era—particularly conscription and the corvée, which removed able-bodied men from the land; and high taxes and the monopoly system, which combined with the former factors to bring about extensive rural indebtedness. This set in motion the workings of the system of land assignment (*ramya* system), which removed arrears-laden land from the possession of insolvent holders. These same poor peasants later received land assignments of a few fractions of a *faddan*, for the logic of the *ramya* system included provision for needy peasants. But the *ramya* process more often focused on the placement of land plots with reliable and proven taxpayers, which meant that much of the insolvent land was assigned to the affluent holders. In general, then, the large holders weathered the vicissitudes of the Muhammad Ali era quite nicely.

So this brings us to table 4.7 and the examination of the distribution of land in peasant villages at the end of the mid-nineteenth-century period, 1279/1862–1863, as well as the discernment of the changes that occurred since 1849–1850. The 1862–1863 data pertaining to the sample villages reveal that in all four of these villages the small holdings category constituted the greatest proportion of all holdings; and in two of these villages (Ibyar and Kafr al-Rajallat) this category was well over 60 percent. In three of these villages, this category controlled the smallest proportion of the village taxed area. The aggregate numbers (the four villages combined) for 1862–1863 reveal that the small holdings category constituted the greatest proportion of all holdings (65.7 percent), that this category controlled the smallest proportion of the taxed land area (15.7 percent), and that the average size of holding was 2 *faddans*. As the 1849–1850 aggregate data reveal that the proportion of holdings was 65 percent, the land they controlled came to 11 percent, while the average size of holding was 1.8 *faddans*, we can conclude that the intervening thirteen years brought positive change for this group—which, although slight, should be noted because most members of this group possessed minuscule land plots. Indeed, the most important change to note here is the fact that the number of holdings had increased by 28 percent during these thirteen years, while the area under their control had increased by 42.8 percent, resulting in a slight increase in the average size of holdings. This significant discrepancy between holdings and area increases suggests that some members of this category managed to expand their holdings (probably by obtaining *ramya* land).

The 1862–1863 data for the sample villages show that the medium holdings category constituted a significant proportion of all holdings, and it controlled significant proportions of the taxed arable area. In the largest village, Ibyar, the proportion of holdings was roughly commensurate to the proportion of land: for this group constituted 31 percent of holdings, and controlled 39 percent of the land. As for the smallest village, Jazirat al-Aʿjam, the relevant figures were still (also noted above for 1849–1850) rather skewed, as this category accounted for 46 percent of holdings and possessed 85 percent of the land. Finally, the aggregate data (the four sample villages combined) show that 32 percent of holdings possessed 48.5 percent of the taxed area, and the average size of holdings was approximately 12.9 *faddans*. The comparison between these aggregate figures and those of 1849–1850 shows that the pattern of holding for this category broadly remained the same: as mentioned above, in 1849–1850, this category constituted one-third of all holdings and possessed two-fifths of the land, and the average size of holding was 13.9 *faddans*.

The examination of the pattern of holding for the large holdings category reveals the concentration of land in the hands of a few. In 1862–1863, this category constituted the smallest proportion of holdings in the village; indeed, in Kafr al-Rajallat, it was only one holding. In the larger villages (like Ibyar), much of the taxed area (45 percent) was controlled by this category. Though this was not true for the smaller villages, nevertheless, this very small group controlled disproportionately large areas; thus, al-Jazira al-Khadra's four holdings possessed 34 percent of the village land, and the one holding just specified for Kafr al-Rajallat possessed 7.7 percent. The aggregate figures for the sample villages show that 2.1 percent of holdings controlled 35.8 percent of the taxed land, and the average size of a holding was 149.2 *faddans*. These figures do not differ much from those of 1849–1850, when the holdings constituted 3.4 percent, the area 47.9 percent, and the average size of a holding was 150.5 *faddans*.

The changes specified for these categories support the assumption that state policies of the mid-nineteenth-century years did not cause widespread rural impoverishment. The majority of the peasants of these four villages (an admittedly small sample) remained viable and solvent landholders. This even held for those years that witnessed the imposition of the three major tax codes. The impact of the first land-tax code (1855 code, which was introduced in 1856) on Ibyar Village can serve as an example. In order to better present my findings, I point out here that the proceeding discussion reverts to and relies on the conventional meaning of the terms "holding" and "holder". The comparison of the 1270/1853–1854 land-tax registers with those of 1272/1855–1856 shows that 44 percent of the 1853–1854 group maintained the exact level of their holdings in 1855–1856; that 26 percent had managed to increase the size of their holdings; and that another 18 percent experienced some impoverishment. Thus 88 percent of the holders specified by the 1853–1854 tax registers remained viable and solvent holders in 1855–1856. As for the 12 percent of the 1853–1854 group that could not be found among the 1855–1856 listing, it is important to note that the reasons for their "disappearance" may not only have been land dispossession. For death without issue was a very real possibility, as was the decision to ward off insolvency by the pooling of resources, which entailed the formation of a joint household and the registration of land in the name of the eldest man of the family. The story does not end here, though, for the 1855–1856 register lists new names among the village holders for that year; these were 115 holders, or 27 percent of the 1855–1856 group. The combination of this evidence allows us to conclude that the majority of the peasant holders of Ibyar Village paid their taxes at the new rates while remaining solvent and economically viable. The same was true for the 1858 and 1862 land-tax increases.[205]

This evidence as well as that provided by the other three sample villages suggests that the countryside did not experience extensive land dispossession and debilitating impoverishment during the mid-century period, in contrast to what earlier writers had specified.

This can be attributed to the broad characteristics of this period: It witnessed the rise in the prices of agricultural crops due to increased European demand (especially for grains), and the demise of Muhammad Ali's monopoly system, which meant that producers dealt directly with merchants and sold their crops at market prices. Added to this favorable economic environment was the interest of the state in preserving the productive capabilities of indigent peasants, which can be seen in its land legislation, tax codes, and the rules for tax collection. But then, in the later years of the 1850s, the state gave precedence to revenue maximization and accordingly its demands became more onerous. Yet even so, the favorable economic environment generally allowed peasants to cope with the new rules while retaining most of their lands.

The comparison of the data of the mid-nineteenth-century period as well as that of 1813–1814 with the "earliest landownership statistics available for all Egypt, compiled in 1896," reveals the crystallization of certain trends over the century.[206] Most important of these was the concentration of land in the hands of a few; and so in 1896, the large holdings category constituted just 1.5 percent of all holdings and controlled the greatest proportion of the taxed area, 44 percent. And at the other end of the spectrum, in 1896, the small holdings category accounted for the largest proportion of all holdings (80 percent) but controlled the smallest proportion of taxed area (20 percent). Accordingly, in the early decades of the nineteenth century as well as in the middle and at the end, the majority of peasant holdings belonged to the small holdings category. The average size of holding for this category in 1813–1814 constituted 2–3 *faddans*; in 1849–1850 it was roughly 1.8 *faddans*; in 1862–1863 it was 2 *faddans*; and finally in 1896 it was 1.5 *faddans*. Thus, for the majority of the peasant holders of Egypt, the mid-nineteenth-century years allowed for some interruption of the century-long trend of impoverishment.

Conclusion

The examination of the official decrees and laws that regulated peasant lands during the mid-century decades reveals a growing state interest in the maximization of revenues even if this came at the expense of peasant well-being—as can be seen, for example, in the repeated tax increases, the increasingly stringent rules for land recovery, the growing inflexibility of the process of tax collection, and the change in the unit of measurement (*qasaba*) employed in the survey of arable land. Contemporary observers, like the resident British diplomats, noted some of these state decrees and linked them to the cases of peasant ruination that had come to their attention. But the examination of the relevant archival sources—the *athurat* registers, the land-tax registers, and the records of the Islamic and civil courts—allows us to appraise these cases of ruination more effectively, and accordingly to argue that the majority of the peasants did not endure debilitating impoverishment during the mid-century years. This can be attributed partly to the favorable economic environment of these years, specifically to the return to free market rules and rising crop prices, and partly to the state's interest in maintaining the economic viability of the peasantry.

Indeed, this state interest worked to enable the peasants to retain their land so long as they kept it cultivated and paid all its taxes; and they also knew that when they died, their lands would be transmitted to their legal heirs. In addition, cultivators understood that if they defaulted on their land obligations, the authorities would activate the land-assignment system. That provincial officials could not tolerate delays in the collection of taxes often meant that much of the vacant village lands wound up in the hands of the affluent peasants. Yet too, this system also demonstrated a distinct concern for improving the economic viability of needy peasants, and accordingly, many poor peasants acquired *ramya* lands. Thus the workings of these rules and policies meant that peasants generally acquired land by one of two modes, transmission/inheritance and land assignment; which further meant that there was little room for peasant land acquirement by market transactions.

That most peasant holders continued to retain these lands during the mid-century years effectively undermines the "peasant ruination" assumption developed by previous writers for this period. These writers had largely attributed this phenomenon to certain factors, one of these being the emergence of large-scale land abandonment (*matruk*). While there is no denying the appearance of such cases, still most times the peasants wanted to leave the *iba'diyya* lands in their possession—too overwhelmed by the combination of high reclamation costs, high taxes, and low profits—in order to ensure the continued retention of their prized *athariyya/ma'mur* lands.

Also, the linkage of the "peasant impoverishment" assumption to the emergence of surplus lands is not tenable for the 1850s. This is because state rules specified the placement of tiny surplus plots (*faddan* fractions) with the actual cultivators, and the larger lands were placed either in the auctions or with the vigilant (usually poor village) informants that had uncovered their existence. This treatment of the surplus lands contributed to the amelioration of poverty in the villages. Such improvement was further bolstered by the 1858 land law, as it expanded the amount of land actual cultivators could keep, allowing them up to ten *faddans*. In addition, peasant smallholders could effectively compete for the surplus island lands that lay in their villages, as the 1858 land law specified the arrangement of very restricted auctions that would not consider bids that came from outside this circumference.

Neither did the formation of large privileged estates bring about extensive peasant impoverishment during the mid-century years. The land grants awarded to high state dignitaries were largely made up of barren *iba'diyya* tracts that did not involve peasant land loss; while the grants awarded to the Bedouin chiefs were composed solely of *iba'diyya* lands that lay outside the boundaries of sedentary communities in line with Bedouin preferences. At the same time, the *uhda* system did not pose a great threat to peasant land possession during this period. For peasants witnessed the termination of a great number of *uhdas*, which entailed their recovery of their lands; and while the *uhda* system was not entirely abolished during these years, peasants did witness a considerable slowdown in *uhda* estate formation. Finally, a similar slowdown took place in the creation of the *jiflik* estates. This was paralleled by the growing tendency of the viceroys of this period to create *jiflik* estates from barren *iba'diyya* lands primarily because the transformation of peasant *ma'mur* lands into *jiflik* estates often entailed changing the tax status of highly fertile and productive lands from *kharajiyya* to *ushuriyya*, which in turn would have translated into reduced state revenues.

The number of cases of peasant land loss during the mid-century years most certainly picked up toward the end of this period. The contribution of the 1858 land law to this phenomenon did not lie in the stringent rules for land recovery, as earlier writers have thought, but rather in the rules regulating the *ramya* land system. This was the most important mode of land acquirement for the peasants—affluent as well as poor—and the specification of a transfer fee for the receipt of such land most probably worked to disallow many needy peasants from requesting land assignments. But the coup de grâce to this system came in 1861, when the government disallowed the assignment of *ramya* lands to village members, and instead sent these to the auction block. In the same year, the government standardized the unit of measurement used in the survey of arable land (the *qasaba*), which subsequently generated surplus lands. All these surpluses, both the problematic small lots and the coveted large tracts, were to be sold by public auction as *ushuriyya* land; this continued until 1862, when the government decreed their sale as *kharajiyya* land. While this directive did not deter affluent investors, both rural notables and high state officials, from competing for these lands, it did mean that the peasants who had lost land because of the *qasaba* standardization could hardly think of winning these back at the public auctions.

Yet this increase in the cases of peasant land loss notwithstanding, the mid-century period was not a time of widespread rural impoverishment. This is confirmed by the examination of the land distribution data of four sample villages, which shows that between 1849–1850 and 1862–1863 the fortunes of the small stratum of holders, often the largest group in the village, actually improved (albeit slightly), and that the majority of peasant holders endured the tax increases specified by the three major tax codes of the period while remaining economically viable and solvent.

It is at this juncture that I must point out that there is one very large group that has so far received scant attention in my examination of peasant land-tenure patterns, and this is women. For in addition to the general rules for land possession that were endured and observed by the entire peasant community, peasant women also had to cope with important societal and official ideas that did not look kindly on female land acquirement. The following chapter shows that these ultimately worked to limit severely the numbers of women who possessed land during the mid-century decades; and it is to this discussion that we now turn.

5

Peasant Women and Inheritance of Land

That the majority of peasants managed to retain much of their lands during the mid-nineteenth-century years means that this period cannot be considered one of widespread rural impoverishment. And yet I do not mean to say that the peasant community coped with the state's demands—especially rising taxes, more rigorous tax collection regulations, and the increasingly disadvantageous land laws—easily, experiencing little difficulty. Indeed, many peasants struggled hard to retain their lands and remain solvent. This struggle often necessitated developing some kind of a coping strategy, like the decision to consolidate family land. One of the most common coping strategies, it entailed the placement of the natal family's land in the name of the eldest male, who was to manage it on behalf of the entire joint household. For the younger male members, their loss of control over their land was often temporary, as they could reclaim it once they chose to separate from the household. For women, though, this situation could result in outright disinheritance.[1] This led to ruination and destitution for some women, particularly those who headed their conjugal households in the absence of their husbands. The state's interest in preserving the viability of the peasant household prompted it to address this problem in 1855, by granting women provisional inheritance rights, and again in 1858, when it specified that women were to inherit land according to Islamic inheritance rules.[2]

But peasant women in Lower Egypt had acquired, retained, and alienated land long before the introduction of the 1855 and 1858 land laws. Egyptian archival sources reveal a number of cases that demonstrate women's acquirement and control of *miri/kharaji* land during the eighteenth century, and further suggest that this phenomenon was not a novelty of the time, but had originated in an earlier period.[3] It continued uninterrupted into the mid-nineteenth century. For example, in 1853, the peasant woman Ghazala complained to the Council of Justice about the removal of her land from her control; and her rather pointed description of this land as her *athariyya* suggests that it had been in her possession for a lengthy period.[4] In 1857, the dispute over the rights to a half *faddan* of *miri* land was resolved by the testimony of two men, who declared that it "constituted the property [*sic*] of the woman Hijaziyya [which] she had pawned to Ibrahim al-Sayyid . . . in exchange for seventy-five riyals."[5] As for Upper Egypt, Abul-Magd claims that at the beginning of Said Pasha's reign, "women enjoyed full rights to land inheritance according to shariʿa as well as state civil laws." She supports this rather sweeping statement by pointing to a number of cases in Qina Province, where the state courts championed women's claims to their land inheritances.[6] But the close examination of the cases that she presents reveals that the courts were probably not as concerned to uphold female land rights as they were to preserve the economic viability of the female-led households. Thus, we might say that when the courts realized that the economic viability of the peasant household was at risk, they tended to support women's land rights.

And yet cases of female land possession ran against the grain of rural society. For most people upheld views like "females do not cultivate land"; "women have no right to possess land"; and "there is no inheritance in *miri* land, so it is not to be divided according to the [Islamic] inheritance rules, but is to be given to the son of the deceased."[7] Thus, for example, the land-tax registers of Ibyar Village do not list the name of a single woman among the village landholders between 1850 and 1858.

This chapter starts by examining the factors that allowed such a negative view of female landholding to emerge and crystallize in rural society. In investigating the *athurat* registers, which document the circumstances in which women holders had obtained their lands roughly between the 1810s and 1850s, I learned that inheritance constituted the most important mode of land acquirement for peasant women—which is why it is the focus of this chapter. It argues that peasant women's actual obtainment of their land inheritances during the mid-nineteenth-century years largely depended on the consent or absence of their kinsmen. In the case of disputes between men and women over land, state officials were likely to support the latter when their claims dovetailed with the economic precepts of the traditional philosophy of statecraft (preservation of the economic viability of the peasant household; maximization of state revenues). Finally, the archival evidence from this period suggests that few peasant women actually came into their land inheritances.

Women and Secondary Rights to Land

As agrarian society arose in the Nile River Valley, Egyptian agriculture came to exhibit several features that would later be found in all traditional rural societies around the world. Most notable of these was a certain sexual division of labor in agriculture. While men performed the more strenuous tasks, especially traction plowing, their womenfolk generally took up the role of helpers in the cultivation of the land. In this capacity, women undertook the less onerous tasks, such as harvesting and winnowing, and also substituted for men during times of male labor shortage. In general then, men led and directed women's work in the fields.[8] Thus, as land cultivation (and food provision) essentially was a male responsibility, control of the household's primary economic resource (land) became a male prerogative.[9]

This prerogative was further strengthened by the structure of the peasant household. For the head of the household was a position assumed by the eldest man in the family, referred to as *al-arshad*; and was rarely held by the eldest woman. For example, when Muhammad Diyab of al-Jazira al-Khadra Village died, his son became the head of the household, not Saʿda, his widow and the mother of this son.[10] The *arshad* was expected to manage all family affairs, which often involved registering the family land in his name and supervising its cultivation and paying its taxes. Members of the household entitled to shares of the family land could not take control of their land shares without his consent. That the state recognized this structure can be seen in the 1858 and 1869 laws, as these sought, among other things, to strengthen the authority of the household head, both times identified as the eldest man, *al-arshad*.[11]

The pattern of devolution of land upon the death of the family patriarch was reflective of male dominance in land control. The inheritance of land by the sons of the deceased patriarch became the norm in Lower Egypt largely because agricultural production was managed by the household unit and was oriented to urban markets, and there was a high level of economic stratification. In this setting, agricultural land was divided into fixed plots that were individually held and were passed on to heirs upon the original holder's death. Individually held land could also be alienated because it could be easily priced.[12]

State law, based on Ottoman *qanun*, only confirmed the societal bias in favor of men. By it, arable land did not belong to the cultivator but rather to the state, and as such it was not to be treated as property. This meant arable land was not subject to the Islamic rules of inheritance. Upon the death of the cultivator, his sons had exclusive rights to the land, while his kinswomen might claim it in the event of the absence of male heirs. Thus, the division of the land patrimony by the sons of the family patriarch to the exclusion of the female heirs was a recognized juridical norm. So when the heirs of the peasant al-Shafʿi brought their dispute over their patrimony to the Khanka religious court on June 1, 1857, the two sons fought over the land estate to the exclusion of the women heirs. Once this disagreement was resolved, with the elder son recognizing the right of his brother to the land patrimony, the focus of the court turned to the other component of the estate, a well. Here it expanded the list of heirs to include the two widows and the two daughters, and specified the share of each man and woman in accordance with Islamic rules.[13]

The examination of and comparison between the different land registers of the four sample villages discloses the unique case of al-Jazira al-Khadra Village, which presents yet another dimension of male dominance in land control in nineteenth-century Egyptian rural society. The arable land of this village was divided into two basins, or *hawd*s. One of these was designated *hawd* al-Farsha and embraced the village's highest-quality lands. The other basin, called *hawd* al-Nakhil, contained large tracts of a problematic nature: in 1859, it contained 71 *faddan*s of marginal land, "parts of these having experienced soil erosion, while other parts constituted ruined sand," and also contained a number of trees, which complicated the clearing and leveling efforts necessary for the cultivation process.[14] Here we must point out that peasant holdings were generally divided into strips of varying sizes that often lay in different basins. For example, in 1859, Ismail Marʿi possessed 21 *faddan*s. These were divided into eleven plots of varying sizes, with ten plots (together consisting of roughly 15 *faddans*) in *hawd* al-Nakhil, and one plot (consisting of 6 *faddans*) in *hawd* al-Farsha.[15] And from the same source that detailed the holding of Ismail Marʿi (the *athurat* register for al-Jazira al-Khadra Village), we also learn that the village authorities denied women access to plots situated in *hawd* al-Farsha, explaining their village custom in this way: "*Hawd* al-Farsha is the right of men only, to the exclusion of women, because it is cleared for cultivation and has no trees, and [thus], women have no rights [in this *hawd* despite the 1858] land law."[16]

So by this village custom, a woman's share of the land patrimony would be confined to and come solely from the "sanctioned" basin, *hawd* al-Nakhil. This meant that the women heirs in Ismail Marʿi's household could claim their share of the family patrimony from the land situated in *hawd* al-Nakhil, but had no right to the land in *hawd* al-Farsha.[17] Thus, the case of al-Jazira al-Khadra suggests that where villages contained high proportions of marginal land, village leaders could deny women access to the basin containing the higher-quality land by pointing to a local custom that was clearly informed by the idea of male prerogative in land matters.

Women and Inheritance of Land

The death of Salim of Kafr al-Rajallat Village in 1248 (1832–1833) was followed by the transfer of his land to his heirs, his widow Khadra and his daughters. The relevant entry explains this transfer by specifying that "the land was given to the woman Khadra, wife of the original holder, in order to provide her and her daughters with a source of livelihood" and further notes that Salim had no other heirs besides these women.[18] The village of Kafr al-Rajallat witnessed only eleven other cases of inheritance of land by women between 1815 and 1854 (before the introduction of the 1855 law, which granted women provisory inheritance rights).[19] The combination of this evidence allows us to state that women's inheritance of land was hardly perceived as an unconditional right even when the deceased lacked male issue or agnatic heirs. Also one wonders whether the authorities might have denied Khadra the land estate if she had not needed it for subsistence purposes.

Thus, by this evidence we realize that peasant women rarely inherited land. But nineteenth-century Egypt was not unique in this regard. In Elisabeth Croll's examination of traditional China and its practices, she states that "the main form of property had been land," and then observes that "women did not inherit except in rare cases where not a single male member of the lineage survived."[20] When studying the Hatay Region of southeastern Turkey in the 1960s, Barbara Aswad noted that "women are also denied access to land through inheritance unless they are brotherless."[21] This tendency to bypass women might largely be attributed to families' anxiety over the loss of parts of the land patrimony upon the marriage of their daughters, when they separated from the natal households.[22] For families in these societies generally expected a wife to move to her husband's residence, thereby insisting on the virilocal residence ideal for young couples. At the same time, this gender bias in land inheritance was not observed exclusively in non-Western societies. In their examination of the inheritance norms of modern Western societies, Jacqueline Goodnow and Jeanette Lawrence realized that "land more often passes to sons than to wives and daughters."[23] They attribute this practice to tradition as well as to cultural images of men and land in certain countries, like Australia. There, "the traditional image of farming takes the form of a tough struggle against a harsh and unforgiving land: a struggle made possible only by the physical strength of men."[24]

While families in modern Western societies *often* place land inheritances in the hands of sons, which further implies that a fair number of inheritance cases involve conferring the land on women heirs, families in non-Western, nineteenth-century societies *rarely* turned over land to women heirs. In the latter societies, this very pronounced bias was not necessarily born of societal and familial contempt for women, but probably had more to do with male competition for scarce resources. In Egypt during the time under discussion, and indeed until the middle of the twentieth century, men's social and political status at the national and village levels depended on the amount of arable land in their possession. And in the scramble between families for land wealth, men viewed women heirs as conduits of land loss that enriched competing families at their expense.

This was because women heirs generally preferred to consign their land inheritances to the care of their male guardians. This course of action usually involved the registration of the land in the names of their kinsmen, who thereby became the women's legal representatives or *wakil*s. Here it might be noteworthy to mention that Islamic law did not compel women in their majority to take this course; unlike English common law, which specified the transferal of "the property of women to their husbands upon marriage."[25] Husbands operating under the latter set of rules could dispose of their wives' property however they liked, and were not penalized nor reproached when they contradicted the express wishes of their wives.[26] Islamic law, in contrast, expected male legal representatives to act according to the wishes of the female property owners. Often, though, they did not—something that women could not easily prove. Yet, this did not stop women from consigning their land to the care of their male relations.

Thus, in Lower Egypt, when a peasant woman married she liked to entrust her land inheritance to her husband, which involved registering it in his name; in this way contributing to the aggrandizement of the conjugal household's wealth and status in the village.[27] In the event of the death of her husband, a woman preferred to "live in her son's dwelling" and register her land in her son's name.[28] Thus, when daughters and sisters married, they usually put whatever lands they had inherited at the disposal of the men of their new families. This came at the expense of their natal families and households.[29]

Inheritance of Land: The Primary Mode of Land Acquisition

While research on land devolution patterns in developing countries has revealed that rural families rarely included women in the inheritance of land, on the other hand, Shahra Razavi observes that in six Latin American countries, "women tend to become landowners mainly through inheritance."[30] This generally means that neither the marketplace nor official land-distribution systems favor women. The same applies to rural women in Lower Egypt during the nineteenth century.

Indeed, on the one hand, the *athurat* registers, which document how the village holders had acquired each land plot in their possession, confirm that women in nineteenth-century Egypt rarely inherited land; but, on the other, these also show that inheritance constituted women's primary mode of land acquirement. Some figures illustrate both these points. For example, the *athurat* register of Kafr al-Rajallat Village, which roughly covers the period between the 1820s and 1857, shows that twenty women obtained land during this time and that fifteen had inherited the entirety of their holdings. An additional three cases can be classified as inheritance, as the woman heirs (Fatma, Fatuna, and Jawhara) claimed the lands on the basis of their inheritance rights, though they actually obtained these after redeeming the pertinent pawn debts. The *athurat* register of al-Jazira al-Khadra, which roughly covers the 1820s through the end of 1859, shows that thirty-three women acquired land during this time; and of these, twenty-nine acquired the entirety of their holdings by inheritance, while another woman obtained the larger portion of her land by this mode.[31]

Women's inheritance of their share of the land patrimony most often depended on two circumstances; one of these was the consent of their kinsmen.[32] For example, when Hassan Ajlan died in 1271/1854–1855, his heirs, presumably his sons (al-Hafiz and Ibrahim Ajlan), allowed their father's widow, Aisha, to take possession of roughly half a *faddan* of the land patrimony. They explained their decision accordingly: "They confirmed that they had given [it] to the aforementioned woman voluntarily in order to [provide her] with a means of livelihood."[33] In some of these cases, kinsmen liked to give the female heirs marginal land. When Salman died, his sister Kamla was permitted to take roughly 2 *faddans* in inheritance by their male cousins (as agnatic heirs they had a right to the land estate), which the latter described pointedly as *atil* (waste land). That these kinsmen classified this transfer of land as *ramya* (in this context meaning unwanted land) rather than inheritance, neatly reflects their indifference to this piece of land.[34]

If kinsmen permitted their female relatives to take possession of their share of the land estate, they could not reverse their decision later. The case of al-Jarfi Dawud from Sadur Village in Rawdat al-Bahrayn Province provides illustration:

> When his paternal uncle died, he left him one *faddan* and sixteen *qirats*; and he took control of these. And after a time, [a portion] of these was taken from him; for a woman named Aisha, his paternal cousin, asked to take her father's land. Al-Jarfi agreed, and gave her one *faddan* of arable land, recording this in an official document [in front] of a *qadi*, without having been forced. This being the case, he has no right to make this claim [that is, that the land rightfully belongs to him].[35]

So why did al-Jarfi have a change of heart? To begin, we see that he voluntarily relinquished a full *faddan* to his cousin. But had he followed the rules of Islamic law, he should have divided the land estate between them; for according to these rules when the deceased's heir consists of only one daughter, she takes half the estate, and the agnatic heirs take the other half. Yet he chose to disregard these rules, and gave her the larger portion of the land estate, which suggests that he lacked the level of resources necessary to maintain the entirety of the estate by himself. Thus, we might assume that he wanted to retake this *faddan* from his cousin because his economic circumstances had improved.

For the most part then, men allowed their kinswomen to share in the inheritance of the land patrimony when they had experienced impoverishment and could not maintain the entirety of the estate, or when they viewed the land in question with distinct indifference, or when they wished to provide the women with economic support.

The second circumstance that afforded women the opportunity to take control of their land inheritances was the absence of male heirs. In some cases, women heirs took control of a rather respectable number of *faddans*, at least by village standards. Thus, it was for this very reason that Fatuma of Kafr al-Rajallat Village came into 9.5 *faddans*; and two sisters who resided in al-Jazira al-Khadra Village together inherited 6.5 *faddans*.[36]

Women heirs could also expect to retain their lands if their control had been uncontested for a lengthy period by the male heirs, as the latter may as well have been absent from the village. In the presentation of his claim for his land inheritance before the Council of Justice, Mustafa Salim explained the following. His father had lived with his brother and sister-in-law in the same dwelling, and when the two brothers died, his uncle's widow took possession of the entire land estate, for she claimed that it "rightfully belonged to her." The court supported the widow, stating that "the land is the right of the woman because she has had control of it for fifteen years, and so the petitioner has no right to it through inheritance."[37]

Finally, it is worth mentioning that court appraisal of disputes between men and women over their rights to land inheritances certainly necessitated determining the legal viability of the claims. Yet the courts also took into consideration the controller's record in farming the land and paying its taxes. Thus, in the two cases just discussed (Jarfi and Mustafa), the court likely examined the legality of each plaintiff's claim as well as the (defendant) woman's record of tax payments when making its decision. And as this record was not a problematic in either case, the court found for the women.[38] For the state was loath to remove land from proven cultivators.

Women and the 1855 Land Law

Judith Tucker's examination of women's inheritance of land during the 1850s prompted her to conclude that the official tendency to leave land with the members of the natal family, composed of parents and children, was clearly stronger than the "stated official preference for male heirs to *miri* land." In other words, the courts often found for sons against female heirs, while the daughters and widows of the deceased could be certain of court support against agnatic heirs.[39] But there was a similar if not greater official tendency to award land to women claimants when these pleaded poverty, as occurred in January 1854, when a provincial governor explained to the Council of Justice that he had championed two women petitioners against their brother primarily because "they need this land."[40] The state's support for these women points to its realization that their households might face economic hardship without their land inheritances. This position, in turn, dovetailed with the state interest in ensuring the economic viability of peasant households. This position was given additional legal expression in the 1855 land law.

As mentioned earlier, the 1855 law granted women provisional rights to familial land inheritances. By its rules, women were to take possession of portions of the family land estate if the original holders had died after the introduction of the 1855 law, if the women heirs needed the land for their subsistence, and if they could name individuals who had agreed to stand surety for their tax payments.

At the outset, it is worth mentioning that the courts refrained from the activation of this law in the absence of a specific request from female heirs. After the introduction of this law, then, families generally continued to dispose of their land inheritances as they wished. Some families chose to abide by Ottoman law, which exclusively awarded *miri* land to sons. The June 1857 case mentioned above provides illustration, for it shows two brothers fighting over their father's land estate while their sisters and mothers watched in silence. It was only after the Khanka religious court resolved the brothers' dispute and turned to the remainder of the deceased's estate (a well) that it expanded the list of heirs to include the female heirs.[41] Other families acknowledged the rules of Islamic law, but chose to persuade the female heirs to turn over their shares of the land inheritance to the male heirs rather than allowing them to take control of the land. This arrangement most often involved the transfer of the land by cession in return for a money payment; this way, female heirs permanently relinquished their rights to the land patrimony. On October 18, 1857, Muhammad Awad petitioned the al-Khanka court for the recovery of his mother's (named Salma) land inheritance, only to be told that she had ceded it to her brothers in 1261/1845, and that the cession was binding.[42] And still other families distributed the land inheritances between the male and female heirs according to the Islamic inheritance stipulations. For example, on June 27, 1858, the children (a son and two daughters) of the deceased Muhammad Shalabi Uthman declared before the Tanta religious court that their father's land legacy consisted of 8 *faddans* and 10 *qirats*; and that the son of the deceased, Uthman, took his share of the legacy, which consisted of half the land, or 4 *faddans* and 5 *qirats*, while his sisters divided the other half between themselves.[43] In each of these cases, then, the courts did not insist on the application of the 1855 law because the female heirs did not express any interest in it.

But some women clearly viewed the 1855 law as an opportunity to recover land inheritances previously denied them, and used it to their advantage. What certainly helped these women was the courts' readiness to develop liberal interpretations of the law. This can be seen in the case examined by the Ministry of Interior on April 12, 1857. Here, the women heirs specified that they had not received any shares of their father's legacy upon his death in 1257/1841. So in 1855, they petitioned this court for portions of this land, and were subsequently awarded 30 *faddans*. The court's decision necessitated removing the land from the control of their paternal uncle, Ibrahim Effendi Jurbaji, and their brother, Muhammad Effendi Bahjat. Incensed, Ibrahim Effendi claimed that this decision was not legally sound, reminding the court of one of the stipulations of this law—that it was not to be applied retroactively, but only to "the lands whose holders died now [that is, in 1855] and afterwards." He concluded with the following: "according to the law, the aforementioned daughters do not have any right to this land because they did not take control of it at the time of their father's death in 1257 [1841]; and this right belongs to Ibrahim Effendi Jurbaji and Muhammad Effendi Bahjat." This was the second time he presented this complaint, for he had presented an earlier one to another governmental body, the Viceregal Cabinet, which had only confirmed the original sentencing issued on March 12, 1856.[44] That the courts had twice stood by the women heirs (the relevant entry does not specify the outcome of the second petition presented by Ibrahim) suggests that they had clearly demonstrated to the authorities that they needed this land for their subsistence. Thus, there were times when official interest in ensuring the economic viability of peasant households won out over the letter of the law (and the rights of the male heirs).

This official interest in ensuring that impoverished peasant households became economically viable seems to have emboldened women to demand portions of land to which they did not have inheritance rights. When (in 1857) two brothers complained to the Council of Justice about the removal of 3 *faddans* from their control, they explained that "these had been taken from them while the crops were still standing and given to their paternal aunt, the woman Khaduja."[45] Although they do not specify why the land was placed in their aunt's control, it is likely that she was able to convince the authorities that she needed it for subsistence purposes. As the new land law specifies the granting of provisional inheritance rights to the legal female heirs, Khaduja's petition should have been rejected. For the identification of these heirs was regulated by Islamic succession rules, and these specify that siblings (both male and female) do not share in the deceased's legacy when there are male heirs. Yet the official concern for Khaduja's subsistence needs overrode the concern to observe Islamic inheritance rules.

On the other hand, the courts were not so obliging when the women claimants could not demonstrate that they were enduring economic hardship and needed the land for their subsistence. When one woman petitioned, in 1857, for the possession of her land inheritance, the Council of Justice demurred, observing that her need for the land was not evident "as a *usya* of 28 *faddans* and [some] fractions in Mit Sahil Village is registered in her name."[46]

Finally, the introduction of the 1855 law may have convinced kinsmen to release land inheritances to the female heirs peaceably and without the mediation of the courts. This is suggested by the following case. On April 18, 1857, Siliman declared before the Tanta religious court that his father and his uncle Mustafa had together possessed 5 *faddans*. When his uncle died, leaving a daughter named Zaynab, his father took control of the entirety of his brother's estate (2.5 *faddans*). His father died four years later, whereupon the entire holding passed to Siliman, who remained in possession of it for eight years. Then in 1855, Zaynab questioned Siliman's right to control her land, and so he willingly relinquished to her 14 *qirats* "and in this way ended the dispute."[47] This account was confirmed by Zaynab and her husband as well as other witnesses. Thus, the two parties went to court in 1857 in order to document the land transfer, not to seek legal mediation.

This brings us to some final comments on women's reliance on the 1855 law for the recovery of their land inheritances. To begin, that this law states that female heirs were to receive amounts of land that would ensure their subsistence meant that the amounts of land women actually received varied between cases. More specifically, what this meant was that some female heirs received the amounts allotted them by Islamic law; but others received less, as had the just-mentioned Zaynab, who (in 1857) took control of 14 *qirats* of land, although by Islamic rules, her paternal cousin should have turned over 30 *qirats* to her.[48] Second, in line with how women generally managed the lands in their possession, female heirs who successfully recovered their land inheritances usually placed these in the hands of male caretakers, most often their husbands or sons. In the case of Khaduja (mentioned above), who had recovered three *faddans*, we see that the "land was registered in the name of her husband starting from Tuti 1272/September 1855."[49] This step meant that Khaduja had only designated her husband as her *wakil*, or legal representative, but did not relinquish her right to it. On the other hand, this step also meant that the authorities recognized the husband as the *wadi' al-yad*, or possessor, of the land, and held him responsible for its cultivation and the payment of its taxes. In the view of the government, then, the land rightfully belonged to the male possessor. Some men tried to take advantage of these circumstances and dispossess their kinswomen of their lands.[50] Third, kinsmen who agreed to relinquish parts of the land patrimonies to the female heirs did not always agree to a complete break with these lands. Thus, when Khaduja's nephews learned that she had registered her land in her husband's name, they insisted on forming a partnership with this husband, which would involve "taking half the wheat crop and in return they would farm the land and pay half its taxes to the husband." The husband agreed to this arrangement, and the nephews declared that they "had no cause for complaint."[51]

The 1855 land law regulated women's access to their land inheritances for a period of three years only, as it was superseded by the 1858 land law. This more comprehensive law specified the expansion of women's inheritance rights to *miri* land, and we now turn to the examination of its impact on female access to familial land patrimonies.

Women and the 1858 Land Law

By Article I of the 1858 law, the notion of sons' exclusive rights combined with provisional rights for women to the familial land inheritance was abandoned. Instead, the Islamic inheritance rules were to apply to *miri* land, which really meant that the rights of the male and female members of the family to the land patrimony were to be determined by their relation to the deceased. The new law seemed poised to significantly change the imbalance between men and women in peasant landholding.

While this did not materialize, as will be shown below, the archival sources show some change of attitude on the part of families regarding the recognition of the rights of female heirs. For indication of this change, we might turn to the *athurat* register of al-Jazira al-Khadra Village. Here we find the name of Muhammad Diyab al-Kabir, one of the village holders, and under it the following explanatory note:

> The entirety of the land lies in *hawd* al-Nakhil. He came and declared that it rightfully belonged to him and his brother Abdu and his sisters Yufdar and Aisha, and his mother Sa'da. It passed to them by inheritance from their patriarch Muhammad Diyab, father

of the controller of the land. His mother Saʿda is entitled to one-eighth of his father's estate, and as for the rest, the males are to receive twice as much as the females.[52]

By this entry we learn that when Muhammad Diyab died, his heirs did not divide the land legacy, which consisted of approximately 11 *faddans*, and instead preferred to register the entirety of the estate in the name of the eldest son (*al-arshad*), Muhammad Diyab al-Kabir. At the same time, his acknowledgment of the shares of his mother and siblings in the land inheritance was strictly in line with Islamic succession rules. That this family chose to keep their land legacy in one unit and register it in the name of the family *arshad* was reflective not only of village customs but also of the 1858 law. At this point, we might recall that Article II encouraged families to keep the land legacy as one holding and further required family heads to record the names and shares of all heirs in a notarized document.

This included, as just shown, the recognition of the rights of the female heirs to the land legacy. This recognition, and indeed the actual division of land patrimonies in accordance with Islamic rules, was not unknown in nineteenth-century rural society. The novelty here, then, can be found in the relatively high number of instances that included such declarations of kinswomen's rights—probably brought about by the new land law. This is revealed by the *athurat* register of this village: it shows us that roughly 34.1 percent of the holders of al-Jazira al-Khadra Village made such declarations at the end of 1859, while on the other hand only thirty women had actually inherited land over the previous three to four decades.[53] Although we cannot be certain that such declarations later led to the female heirs' actual acquirement of their inheritances, still, they probably did help to bring about a modicum of change in society's attitude toward women's rights to land, encouraging rural folks to view these more positively.

Perhaps it was this new climate of opinion that prompted Ismail Jawiyda to seek to retake no more than his share of the land from Mubaraka, his sister-in-law. He put his claim before the Tanta religious court on July 20, 1860, when he explained that he and his brother, Muhammad Jawiyda, possessed roughly 4 *faddans*, and that the problem began when his brother died (June 1860) and his sister-in-law took control of the entirety of this land on behalf of herself and her young son, Ismail. In her defense, Mubaraka explained that the 4 *faddans* belonged to her husband, and accordingly, these should pass on to his legal heirs, his son Ismail and herself. Asked to verify his claim, Ismail produced two witnesses who declared before the court that Ismail "owned the usufruct of half of these lands." In turn, the court ordered Mubaraka to turn over half the land to Ismail.[54] What is noteworthy here is that Muhammad (male agnate) did not contest the inheritance rights of his sister-in-law and his young nephew, and accordingly did not try to dispossess them of their land.

Some widows focused their efforts on obtaining and safeguarding the land inheritances of their young sons, overlooking their own inheritance rights.[55] This was the case with Amuna, who presented her petition to the Tanta religious court on March 28, 1860. She explained that her husband, al-Haj Shahawy, had four sons; and that the youngest of these was her own son, Ibrahim, who at the time of al-Haj Shahawy's death in late 1858 was a minor. Al-Haj Shahawy's land estate consisted of 84 *faddan*s, and when Amuna calculated her son's share of the estate, she simply divided the number of *faddan*s by the number of sons, and concluded that her son was entitled to 21 *faddan*s. She omitted, though, to count herself as an heir and ask for her share (according to Islamic law, this would have consisted of one-eighth of the estate, or roughly 10.5 *faddan*s). Instead she focused on the fact that Ibrahim's land was under the control of his half-brother and guardian, Abd al-Wahid, and that this latter was cultivating Ibrahim's land for his own profit and generally seemed untrustworthy. She worried that Abd al-Wahid would dissipate her son's land inheritance, and so requested the termination of his guardianship over her son and the appointment of another individual in his place.[56] That Amuna did not ask for her share of the land legacy might be explained by her status as the mother of a young son who was entitled to a relatively sizable land inheritance, and that this land would support her son as well as herself quite nicely. Thus, if Amuna managed to secure the land for her son, she would not have to worry about living in destitution. But had she been childless and indigent, Amuna's petition would surely have focused on her share of her husband's land legacy, and might even have explained her inheritance rights by reference to the 1858 law.

Yet peasant women did not rely on the 1858 law to address current problems only, for some took advantage of this new legislation to seek redress for old grievances. This can be seen in the case of the three daughters of Ibrahim Zidan from Kafr al-Qulash Village. In September 1860, these sisters came before the Tanta religious court and explained that their father had died more than twenty years ago, at which time his brother (their uncle) took control of their share of the land inheritance, which came to 1 *faddan*. "He undertook its cultivation and the payment of its taxes to the government until this year [1860], when the state land investigators came to their village and returned the aforementioned *faddan* to them in the presence of a group of shaykhs and religious personages; and then they [that is, the sisters] planted the land with *barsim*." The uncle was displeased with this decision, causing his nieces to worry that he might forcibly dispossess them of their land. So they demanded that the court compel him to desist from threatening them.[57] The point to emphasize here is that the nieces took the opportunity of the visit of the "state land investigators" (probably the *athurat* committee charged with documenting village landholding details) to their village and put their grievance before them. Moreover, these state officials approved the nieces' request even though the uncle had possessed the land for a lengthy period and the law was on his side. For according to *qanun*, claims to land were not to be heard after the passage of fifteen years, and too the 1858 law was not to be applied retroactively. This means that these two pieces of legislation were disregarded simply because the women seemed indigent and needed their land inheritance for their subsistence.

But female petitioners who wished to bring old grievances to the religious courts could not expect their demands to be upheld if they did not need their lands for subsistence purposes. On October 15, 1858, a woman from Kafr al-Zayat Village complained to the Tanta religious court that when her husband died, her son Nuʿman had taken possession of the entire land estate, to the exclusion of herself and his three sisters. She demanded that he relinquish control of her share of this estate, which roughly consisted of 3 *faddan*s and 6 *qirat*s. The son, in his turn, specified that his father had died in 1269/1852–1853, and at that time he had taken control of the entirety of his father's land estate, because "he had the most right to the land, to the exclusion of his mother and sisters, as his father did not leave behind a son other than himself." He further produced a *fatwa*, or religious ruling, issued by the Mufti of Cairo (Shaykh Muhammad al-Abbasi al-Mahdi) in 1271/1854–1855, which clearly supported his retention of the land; it stated:

> There is no inheritance in arable *miri* land . . . [and so] it is not to be divided among the heirs as inheritance. Rather the rights to it belong exclusively to the son when he is present. And as those in authority [that is, provincial officials] gave the deceased's son the

> control of the land, and as he has had control of it for two years, cultivating it and paying what it owes in taxes to the central treasury, he has greater right to it than the deceased's two daughters and wife.

After the reading of this ruling, the court confirmed that the "women had absolutely no right to the land; and that all rights belonged to. . . . the aforementioned Nuʿman."[58] Nuʿman's *fatwa* was most likely issued before the 1855 land law, which recognized sons' inheritance rights to *miri* land and granted female heirs provisional rights if they could demonstrate they needed their land shares for their subsistence. This helps to explain why the petitioner (Nuʿman's mother) did not bring her complaint to court in 1855, but instead presented it in 1858, roughly nine weeks after the introduction of the 1858 law, as this later law abandoned the 1855 law's conditions for female land inheritance and granted women their Islamic rights in full. Thus, it seems very likely that Nuʿman's mother brought her case to the attention of the Tanta religious court in the hope that it would invoke the 1858 law and accede to her demand for her share of her husband's land legacy. That the court found in favor of the son likely meant that it did not believe that the mother needed the land for her subsistence (but only wanted what she thought was rightfully hers); with the known reluctance of the authorities to remove land from the control of reliable taxpayers, like Nuʿman, certainly factoring into its decision.

State interest in confirming reliable taxpayers in their land possessions explains the uneven outcome of the following case. On April 5, 1861, Umar Musa Maghrabi and his two brothers, Mustafa and Abu Ahmad, complained before the Tanta religious court that their brother Ali refused to give them their share of the family land patrimony. At the time of their father's death (more than thirteen years ago), the four brothers had chosen not to divide their land inheritance, and thus they "shared together the same dwelling and the same work activities." In other words, they formed a joint household, which had entailed registering the entirety of the land estate in the name of their eldest brother, *al-arshad*, Ali. Yet all four shared in the cultivation of the land and all equally contributed to the payment of its taxes. Then in 1266/1849–1850, their paternal uncle (their father's brother) Ahmad Maghrabi died, and his land estate of 17 *faddans* "passed on to them and it was registered along with their own father's land in the name of their brother the aforementioned [Ali]." Here Ali explained that "at that time there was no inheritance in land and so he took control of this land and did not give the daughters [of Ahmad Maghrabi] a share of the estate." So in claiming their own land inheritances, the three brothers demanded the division of the land left by their father, excluded the 17 *faddans* that had been left by their uncle, and freely acknowledged that "these belonged to the aforementioned [Ali], and they had no right to it." Ali's right to his uncle's estate had been confirmed two years earlier (September 1859) when the daughters of Ahmad Maghrabi petitioned for their share in their father's land; for their request was dismissed on the basis that the land had been registered in their cousin Ali's name since 1267/1850–1851 and rightfully belonged to him. On the other hand, the 1861 complaint brought by the three brothers concluded with the division of the land left by the father, Musa Magrabi, between the four brothers.[59] Thus, while Ali was able to retain his female cousins' land because it had been registered in his name for roughly a decade, he was compelled to relinquish control of his brothers' lands even though it had been registered in his name for more than thirteen years. That the court supported the claims of the brothers undoubtedly had to do with the fact that they had contributed to the maintenance of the family land while it had been registered in the eldest brother's name, performing their share of the cultivation tasks and paying their share of the required taxes. Thus, the court had been won over by the fact that the petitioning brothers had proven themselves responsible cultivators and taxpayers. And it was probably on the same basis that Ali won the case brought against him by his female cousins.

Indeed, it seems that few women claimants enjoyed the advantageous position of "proven cultivator/taxpayer," and it also seems that indigent female land claimants rarely managed to convince the courts of their neediness. Thus, the courts most often did not believe that women's old grievances merited legal redress.

At the same time, the introduction of the 1858 land law did not lead to the widespread application of the Islamic rules of succession to family land patrimonies in the post-1858 period. And accordingly, the new law did not bring about a dramatic increase in the numbers of female smallholders in peasant villages (table 5.1). Before and after the 1858 law, then, the majority of landholders in peasant villages were men. This might be attributed to a combination of factors. First and foremost, social opposition to female inheritance of land remained formidable. In al-Jazira al-Khadra, for example, this meant that male holders refused to acknowledge female

Table 5.1: Male and Female Holders in Four Peasant Villages between 1850 and 1862

	Kafr al-Rajallat Village				Jazirat al-Aʿjam Village				Ibyar Village				Al-Jazira al-Khadra Village			
	M		F		M		F		M		F		M		F	
Year	No.	%	No.	%	No.	%	No.	%	No.	%	No.	%	No.	%	No.	%
1850	97	98	2	2	40	100	—		343	100	—		121	89.6	14	10.4
1852	96	99	1	1	41	100	—		352	100	—		129	93.5	9	6.5
1855	121	98.4	2	1.6	48	98	1	2	351	100	—		133	92.4	11	7.6
1856	130	97.7	3	2.3	52	98.1	1	1.9	423	100	—		130	94.2	8	5.8
1858	137	97.9	3	2.1	61	98.4	1	1.6	432	100	—		132	94.3	8	5.7
1860	137	97.9	3	2.1	60	98.4	1	1.6	426	99.8	1	0.2	128	94.8	7	5.2
1862	138	97.9	3	2.1	61	98.4	1	1.6	424	99.1	4	0.9	126	94	8	6.0

Sources: DMU, Mukallafat atyan, ibyar, 1266, 2913/121/22—1278, 2924/121/22; DMU, Mukallafat atyan, al-jazira al-khadra, 1266, 3978/135/22—1278, 3989/135/22; DMU, Mukallafat atyan, kafr al-rajallat, 1266, 8203/110/20—1278, 8212/110/20; DMU, Mukallafat atyan, jazirat al-aʿjam, 1266, 4571/61/20—1278, 4580/61/20.

inheritance rights to prize village land. Thus, in 1859, Mustafa Marʿi al-Saghir could inform the visiting *athurat* committee that the land registered in his name did not belong to him exclusively, bluntly specifying that the tracts in "*hawd* (basin) al-Farsha are the right of the male [heirs], to the exclusion of the female [heirs], because this is land prepared for cultivation and is clear of trees, and women have no right to it [despite the 1858] law." The tracts that lay in the less valuable al-Nakhil Basin, though, belonged to himself, his two brothers, his mother, and two sisters; the share of each member being specified in accordance with the Islamic inheritance rules: "To his mother belonged one-eighth from his father; and as for the other [family members], the male takes as much as two females."[60] That the state officials accepted this rather unique village tradition regarding female land inheritance even though it contravened the 1858 land law is particularly noteworthy. So too is the case of what seemed to be one of the village's wealthiest women. Her name was Mina Abbasiyya, and her possession of 35 *faddan*s meant that she was wealthier than many of the men in her village. According to the *athurat* village register, she did not inherit any of her land, but had acquired most of it by *ramya* assignment (roughly 24 *faddan*s), and the remainder by purchase (6 *faddan*s) and by *wadi' al-yad*, or the possession of barren vacant land (5 *faddan*s). What is significant here is that none of these lands lay in the prized al-Farsha Basin.[61] And based on this, we might say that the men of this village so loathed the idea of female control of coveted high-quality lands that they refused to partake in any kind of transfer of land to women if the tract lay in the prized basin. But away from the customs of al-Jazira al-Khadra Village, a November 1858 case shows that women still had to contend with the widespread view that stated that *miri* land "is not to be divided among the heirs as inheritance, rather the rights to it belong exclusively to the son when he is present."[62]

Second, that families in the post-1858 period (indeed for the entire nineteenth century and even the first half of the twentieth century) continued to view their land as their most valuable capital asset, upon which their economic, social, and political status in the village depended, meant that men continued to prefer to consolidate holdings. This usually disadvantaged the female members of the family, as they had to agree to the placement of their inheritance shares in the name of the family *arshad*; otherwise they would have taken their land shares to other families when they married, thus enriching the conjugal household/family at the expense of the natal one. As Article II of the new law, which encouraged the consolidation of family holdings, aligned with these male concerns, some family heads very likely referred to it to compel female family members "who already had agricultural land titles to change the status of their properties in accordance with the new law, even if they had fulfilled their tax obligations."[63]

Third, the cases where peasant women resented the consolidation of the family land inheritance (which worked to deprive them of their lands) notwithstanding, the archival sources suggest that the majority of peasant women did not seek to possess their land inheritances. Why? Peasant women were not as worried about land inheritances as they were about marital stability[64]—hence, the importance of retaining the goodwill of brothers. When women married and joined new families, they most certainly did not like to cut ties with their natal families, particularly their brothers, who could protect them in the eventuality of severe marital troubles, like divorce or death of a husband. So to ensure their brothers' goodwill, married women often chose to come to some kind of understanding with them, either agreeing to the land-consolidation arrangement or altogether relinquishing their lands to their brothers in exchange for movable property or cash. The point I wish to highlight here is that the workings of Article II ensured that women could have these options. For by it, family heads were to specify women's names and shares in a land roster that was to be notarized by recognized religious courts, which really constituted a kind of confirmation of women's rights to the family land inheritance.[65] This means that the new law aligned with men's desire to control the family land and also afforded women the opportunity to leverage their inheritance rights in a way that enabled them to secure their brothers' goodwill, which was more important to them than land possession. It seems that so many peasant women chose to develop an arrangement that satisfied their brothers that society came to expect this of them; it is an expectation that can still be seen at work in the Egyptian countryside today.[66]

Fourth, certain circumstances involved the inadvertent neglect of women's welfare. One of these had to do with the decision of some fathers to register their lands in the names of their sons during their lifetimes, which effectively involved transforming these lands into the possession of these sons. Thus, when these fathers died, their lands did not count as family patrimony, invalidating the claims of other heirs. This can be seen in the following case. In March 1861, a woman explained to the Tanta religious court that her husband, Ali Abd al-Ghafar, had died the previous winter, leaving a land legacy of 9 *faddans*. The problem was that his eldest son (her stepson, Sayyid) had taken control of the entirety of the land, disregarding the rights of the other heirs. Here she demanded her share of the land estate as well as that of her daughter. The stepson, in his turn, did not try to deny her inheritance rights, but instead elucidated some very important points that ultimately showed that his rights to the land overrode those of the other members of the family: "He confirmed that the usufruct of the land was [originally] owned by his aforementioned father. And in 1844, his father was unable to cultivate the land or pay its taxes, so he voluntarily left it to him until 1272/1855–1856. In that year, he ceded to him the usufructuary rights [to the land] and he registered it in his [that is, the son's] name, and accordingly, he [that is, the father] no longer has any right to it."[67] When learning these details, the female heirs simply withdrew their petition.[68] By ceding the land to his son, then, the father relinquished all rights to it during his lifetime, and so when he died, his other heirs could not lay claim to it.[69] While some fathers were compelled to relinquish control of their land to their sons because they lacked the ability to maintain it themselves, others liked to cede or bequeath large chunks of their holdings to the eldest son with the aim of preventing excessive fragmentation of the land and preserving the family's sociopolitical status in rural society.[70] Whatever the reason for the placement of land in the control of eldest sons, though, female heirs were invariably disinherited (as were younger male heirs.)

Fifth, court biases often disadvantaged female land claimants. At times, it seemed that the courts displayed greater readiness to recognize men's inheritance rights than they did those of women. This can be seen in the different conclusions of two very similar cases. In the first case (examined earlier to demonstrate another point), brought to the Tanta religious court on July 20, 1860, Ismail Jawiyda petitioned for the recovery of his land inheritance from his sister-in-law, Mubaraka. He explained that he and his brother, Muhammad Jawiyda, possessed roughly 4 *faddans*, which meant that each one was entitled to approximately 2 *faddans*. It seems, though, that Ismail had consigned his share of the land to his brother Muhammad's care for a rather lengthy (unspecified) period. Muhammad died on June 13, 1860, and here Mubaraka seized control of the entirety of the land, including Ismail's share. According to Ismail, she had done so "without right or a *shar'i* [legal] basis," and he demanded that she return his land to his control.

Mubaraka, in her turn, claimed that the entirety of the land had belonged to her husband, Muhammad, and that his death meant that it subsequently belonged to his rightful heirs, herself and their son Ismail (a minor, under her guardianship). At this point, Ismail Jawiyda, the petitioner, produced two witnesses who confirmed his right to his share of the land; and on this basis, the court recognized Ismail's right to half the land in Mubaraka's possession and ordered her to release it to him.[71] That Mubaraka initially believed that the entirety of the 4 *faddan*s had belonged to her husband exclusively might be attributed to Ismail's consignment of his land to his brother's care for many years. Indeed, the period seemed to have been so lengthy that Mubaraka was not aware that half of the land under her husband's control belonged to Ismail.

This brings us to the second case, brought to the Tanta religious court on August 7, 1863, by a woman named Filfila, who demanded that her sister-in-law, Maʿajiyya, recognize her right to possess the 2 *faddan*s she had inherited from her mother, Badawiyya. This story starts with Badawiyya's decision to consign her land (6 *faddan*s) to the care of her son, Ibrahim. Thereupon he took charge of the land, farming it and paying its taxes, until she died fourteen years later. "When she died, her estate became the legal right of her children, the aforementioned Filfila and Ibrahim and no one else." Yet Filfila did not insist on the actual possession of her land inheritance, instead preferring to have her brother continue to maintain the land as he had done while their mother was alive. Here the two siblings might have agreed to some kind of sharecropping arrangement, whereby Ibrahim would give his sister a portion of the harvest each year. But this brother died very soon (one year) afterwards; at which time his estate became the right of his legal heirs, his wife Maʿajiyya and his children from her: Hassan, Ibrahim, Sittata, and Fatuma. This time too Filfila seemed content to leave her land inheritance in the care of her brother's family, but subsequently regretted this decision. It seems that she argued with her sister-in-law, maybe over her share of the harvest. At this juncture, Filfila claimed that her sister-in-law wrongfully seized control of her land inheritance one year ago and further demanded that "she relinquish control over . . . the land . . . which she had inherited from her mother, Badawiyya." Being asked to review this case, the Mufti of the Council of Tanta ruled that the "woman plaintiff has no right to the land because it is *kharajiyya* [land]," which can be interpreted to mean that *kharaji/miri* land belongs to its cultivators. Accordingly, the *qadi*, or judge, of the Tanta religious court informed Filfila that "she had no right to the land."[72] Thus, Filfila left her land inheritance in the care of family members (her brother and then his family) for a short period (about one year) and in the process forfeited it, which meant that the legal experts did not recognize her inheritance rights to her mother's estate. In their view, the land rightfully belonged to Ibrahim because he had taken care of it for fourteen years, and accordingly it should pass on to his rightful heirs, his widow and children.

This contrasts with the treatment by the Tanta religious court of Ismail's case described above, where the petitioner's consignment of his land for a lengthy period did not transform it into the possession of the controller (his brother Muhammad) to be passed on to his heirs (widow and son). While Ismail's presentation of two witnesses to confirm his story (while Filfila had none) certainly helped his case, still the difference in outcome might also be linked to the worldview of the legal experts (men themselves), which undoubtedly included the notion that land control constituted a male domain.

The discussion of court biases might also include official support for reconciliation (*sulh*) efforts in the settlement of disputes, as permitted by Islamic law, even where these involved the contravention of the 1858 law. This is illustrated by a case deemed so problematic by the Qalyubiya provincial authorities that they sent it, on February 5, 1859, to the Ministry of Interior for review. The petitioner is a woman named Amna bint Mustafa, and she presented her case before the Qalyub religious court, where she claimed that the man, Hassan al-Barbari, to whom she had rented her land (about half a *faddan*), denied this arrangement and instead declared that she had ceded it to him. The court's investigation of these claims necessitated examining the cession deed, and it discovered the following:

> The deed presented by the man's sons which records the cession of the aforementioned portion of land was not [drafted by] an accredited [religious] court or a legal representative of a *qadi*. And this document does not bear the [state] stamp, and it is not registered, and it does not have a registration number.

What was being said here was that this deed did not satisfy the stipulations of the 1858 law pertaining to deeds for land transactions; in short it was not a valid deed. Yet the court refrained from ordering Hassan to return the land to Amna, and instead focused on the supposed wish of "the two parties to settle [the dispute] whereby the controller [Hassan] would give to the aforementioned woman 300 piastres." Based on this, the *qadi* specified to the ministerial authorities that if the two parties agreed to settle their dispute in this way, "they should return to him and he would supervise the reconciliation." The problem, though, was that Amna staunchly denied having agreed to the proposed settlement. This led the *qadi* to turn the case over to the ministry authorities, calling on them to investigate the details of the case and issue the appropriate ruling.[73] Thus, such court propensity to resolve disputes by resorting to reconciliation settlements might have caused Amna to lose her land; and it was only her determination to continue to fight for what was rightfully hers that prompted the *qadi* to send the case to a higher authority. Yet while Amna was a determined fighter, most women in her situation probably chose the easier route and simply accepted the reconciliation offers in lieu of their lands.[74]

The combination of these factors ensured that women's inheritance of land, and even land acquirement by other means, remained a rather uncertain and infrequent undertaking after the introduction of the 1858 law. This is confirmed by table 5.1, which shows that there was hardly any change in the numbers of women landholders in the four sample villages by the end of 1862 (the mid-century period closed with the death of Said Pasha in January 1863). This reality certainly was not lost on the members of village society: some landholders knew that when they died, their primary female relatives were at risk of being disinherited by male relatives, particularly agnatic relations, and took steps to preempt these attempts. It was most clearly this concern that prompted Ibrahim Sallam from Kafr Asam Village (Gharbiyya Province) to cede approximately 8.5 *faddans* to his only child, his daughter Balad, on December 9, 1861. His plan involved carefully satisfying the stipulations of the law regarding cession transactions: he applied to the provincial authorities for permission to execute the land transfer and after obtaining it, took care to use the official paper for the title deed; and in the drafting of the deed, he made sure to specify that he had received 2,962 piastres from his daughter for the land, for the absence of this statement would have rendered the cession invalid.[75] Later in the month, Ibrahim Sallam died, leaving five legal heirs: his daughter, three wives, and his brother Muhammad. At this point, Muhammad "forcibly seized the aforementioned land without right or a *shar'i* basis," and so Balad took him to court, on December 21, 1861, to demand the return of the land to her control. In court, Muhammad refused to recognize the cession, which prompted Balad to present her documents as well as a witness who confirmed her story. This evidence was sufficient to produce a ruling in Balad's favor.[76] Her father's careful planning had saved the day.

Conclusion

That Egyptian rural society was not enthusiastic about female land acquirement during the mid-century years is amply demonstrated by the comparatively rare appearance of women's names in the village landholding records of this period—indeed, this is true for the entire nineteenth century. These records (specifically, the *athurat* registers) also show that inheritance constituted one of the most important means of land acquirement in peasant villages. But while almost all male holders could attribute a portion of their lands to this mode of acquirement, which means that men counted on the inheritance of their shares of the family land patrimony, women could not.

Still, inheritance was the most important mode of female land acquirement. Women's actual possession of their land inheritances depended on one of two circumstances, the consent of their kinsmen or their absence. More often than not, kinsmen did not oblige. At the same time, the few women who did possess land were at risk for dispossession by resentful kinsmen. These women could count on state support when their claims dovetailed with the economic precepts of the traditional philosophy of statecraft (preservation of peasants' economic viability; maximization of revenues), which entailed convincing the court of their neediness and/or their ability to maintain their lands.

These restrictive circumstances generally worked to deprive women of their land inheritances. Even more problematic was the situation of the households headed by women, which faced economic hardship or complete ruination. The state recognized this problem, and in line with its interest in the preservation of the peasant household, tried to address it by including a clause in the 1855 land law that granted women provisional inheritance rights. It is this state interest in the continued viability of peasant households that encouraged some *qadi*s to interpret this law rather liberally, and thereby actually ignore certain stipulations in order to champion needy women claimants. On the other hand, the courts scrupulously observed the law when the women claimants did not show that their subsistence depended on the acquirement of their land inheritances. Operative for about three years, this law did not produce a noticeable increase in the numbers of women landholders.

This law was superseded by the 1858 land law, which specified that both men and women were to inherit land in accordance with Islamic rules. The new law encouraged families to recognize the rights of female members to their land patrimonies; for the notarized land rosters kept by family/household heads often specified the shares and names of both the male and female heirs. And although this did not mean that all these women heirs actually took possession of their inheritances, it likely caused rural society to view female land inheritance more positively.

This new climate of opinion probably emboldened some women to go to court to claim their land inheritances.[77] Also, some women invoked the 1858 law in an effort to seek redress for old grievances, winning their land suits when they were able to demonstrate their neediness.

But most women preferred to give up their land rights to their brothers, peaceably and willingly, as they tended to value social approval and good relations with their natal families over the possession of their land inheritances. The result was that the 1858 law did not bring about a dramatic increase in the numbers of women smallholders.

Conclusion

This book examined peasant land tenure in Lower Egypt during the mid-nineteenth-century years of 1848 through 1862, largely a forgotten period in the historiography of rural Egypt. And like had Ehud Toledano's study on this historical juncture, it highlighted several "dynamic processes," hitherto unrecognized and unappreciated, that might "alter the prevailing view of the middle decades as a dull and uninteresting period of Egyptian history."[1]

This discussion focused on the institutional context developed by the state for the regulation of peasant lands. This involved the examination of the major land laws of the period, the direct and indirect taxes imposed on the peasants, and the system of tax collection. It also sought to determine the impact of the workings of the related laws and regulations on the peasant land-tenure regime.

The argument developed by this book is twofold: it maintains that the state policies pertaining to peasant lands were shaped by the economic principles of the traditional philosophy of statecraft, and that the workings of these policies did not bring about widespread peasant land dispossession and ruination.

I will summarize the major findings of the two dimensions of my argument, and end with a brief discussion on the implications of this for the nature of peasant politics at mid-century.

State Regulation of Peasant Lands

While earlier studies attributed the changes that had occurred in Egyptian peasant villages during the first half of the nineteenth century to the country's integration into the world economy, Kenneth Cuno successfully challenged this view, attributing these changes to state policy. This study adopted the same view for the middle decades. At the same time, while previous writings depicted the state as revenue-hungry and without mercy for the base of its polity, I departed from this position, and instead drew attention to state regulations that sought to accommodate the interests of the rural cultivators. On the nature of state policy at mid-century, my position was informed by Toledano's research on the reign of Abbas Pasha, which specifies that the pasha looked to the high culture of Constantinople, especially the Ottoman (or traditional) philosophy of statecraft, for guidance in the management of the country. This study adopted this view, and further demonstrated its relevance for Said Pasha's reign.

Thus, one of the major claims of my study specified that the dual economic principles of the traditional philosophy of statecraft shaped the laws and decrees that regulated the peasant land-tenure regime at mid-century. To explore the relevant state policies, I examined the key dimensions of the institutional context that regulated peasant lands: the major land laws of the period, the direct and indirect taxes required of the peasants, and the tax-collection system.

There is a near consensus in the literature on the intent of the major land laws of the period. From this view we learned that the state aimed to confirm cultivators in their current land possessions by specifying stringent recovery criteria that would disallow large numbers of poor peasants from suing for recovery of their original lands. Such treatment disadvantaged these indigent peasants and ultimately locked them into poverty.

My study did not uphold this interpretation, and instead presented a different one. I maintained that the writers of the 1847 and 1855 land laws were guided in their work by the dual economic precepts of the traditional philosophy of statecraft, which led them to pay closer attention to the plight of poor peasants than had been assumed earlier. Regarding the 1847 land law, the first point of interest has to do with the time limits specified for land recovery, which are actually quite lengthy, varying from roughly thirty years for the recovery of pawned lands, to no time limit at all for the recovery of lands that had been assigned to others because of tax arrears. The second commonly overlooked feature of this law pertains to the stipulations that targeted indigent cultivators who were unable to satisfy all the land recovery criteria, as these entitled this group to the receipt of small portions of their original lands or of subsistence-size portions of vacant land. This interest in the peasants' economic viability notwithstanding, the state did not compromise its interest in revenue maximization. For each stipulation that entitled poor peasants to land further specified that the actual receipt of land was to be contingent on the possession of the resources required for its maintenance: the size of the land portion they were to receive was to correspond to the level of the resources at their disposal. In a word, the state expected all cultivators, both affluent and indigent, to farm their lands and pay their taxes. The combination of these two features (generous time limits and granting land rights to partially solvent peasants) very likely worked to benefit many poor peasants.

State interest in the plight of poor peasants continued with the 1855 law, as every article that specified a reduced period for the recovery of land also made provision for the penurious folks by allowing them to possess a portion of their original lands or subsistence-size vacant land. And in one circumstance of land recovery, specifically where more than fifteen years had passed since the execution of the pawn transaction, the 1855 law retained the same generous cutoff date for valid claims (1813–1814 cadastral survey) observed by the 1847 law, which effectively meant the extension of the time limit for this type of case to more than forty years.

With the introduction of the 1858 land law, though, state concern for the plight of impoverished peasants had diminished considerably. According to previous studies, the stringent rules for land recovery, and in particular the reduced time limits, severely disadvantaged indigent peasants. While my study confirmed diminished official concern for poor peasants, it did not view the new rules for land recovery as the major problematic for these peasants; instead it identified the required payment of a transfer fee (24 piastres per *faddan*) for the receipt of *ramya* land as the more crippling stipulation. My interpretation is based on the village *athurat* records, which show the great reliance of both rich and poor peasants on the *ramya* system for land acquirement.

My study contributed to the discussions on the 1858 law in two other respects. The first pertains to the idea of codification. The view that this law granted peasants new rights regarding the alienation of their lands was challenged by Cuno, who correctly argued that the relevant provisions merely codified well-known customary practices. But my archival sources show that the codification efforts went beyond that to include decrees and directives that had been issued earlier and had proved effective. The second point deals with the notion of top-down decision making by the central government, an underlying premise of much of the current literature on nineteenth-century Egypt. My research revealed instances where provincial officials, and sometimes ordinary peasants, took issue with an official decree or regulation, and offered alternative ideas. The central government, in its turn, examined these and incorporated some of them into the new law. These two features of the 1858 law clearly point to the drafters' wish to monitor closely the situation on the ground so that they might introduce regulations that would work in practice, all with the aim of preserving the productive capacities of the peasants, and, more importantly, increasing government revenues.

The traditional economic precepts also informed state regulations regarding the imposition of peasant taxes and their collection. This story, as related by previous studies, generally belabors one point: many and high taxes, made all the more onerous by an oppressive system of collection. On the other hand, I sought to modify this story by highlighting the instances of state interest in the preservation of the peasants' economic viability. *Kharaji* land and their peasant holders were a major source of state revenue, and this necessarily meant that the authorities had perforce to examine the fiscal rules that regulated this sector a number of times. Thus, my period starts with the intention of Abbas Pasha to increase the taxes imposed on village *ib'adiyya* lands; and as these constituted relatively small proportions of the total village arable area, the planned tax increases would have been relatively light. During this time too, the government streamlined the corvée regulations with the intention of bringing fairness and impartiality to the system. And finally, it tried to alleviate the hardship of arrears-laden peasants to better enable them to defray cultivation costs and current taxes by wiping out accumulated back-taxes more than once. This interest in the alleviation of peasant hardship was not renounced by Said Pasha at the time of his assumption of power; for the early months of his reign saw him abolishing the three heavy surcharge taxes imposed on *kharaji* land and canceling peasant tax debts at least twice.

But Said's ambitious development and modernization plans required huge amounts of money, and this led him to instruct his senior officials to reexamine state tax regulations several times in order to extract higher revenue sums from the agricultural sector. By the end of the mid-century period, the direct taxes imposed on the *ma'mur* lands of Kafr al-Jarayda Village, for example, increased by 40 to 80 percent since Said's ascension to the throne in 1854; though the reintroduction of the three surcharge taxes (which he had canceled in the early days of his reign) actually meant much higher increases.

And yet, while Said Pasha and his senior officials no longer focused on peasant economic viability, they did not completely ignore all the related problems. Their continued interest in the preservation of peasant productive capabilities can be discerned in a number of instances, like the mention by each major tax code of hardship cases whereby certain villages were forgiven part or all of the required sums; the 1858 code for indirect duties eliminated the duties on many items; peasants were no longer compelled to deliver their crops to government warehouses and instead could sell them to whomever they wished; and peasants were granted the right to pay their taxes at harvest time, which enabled them to sell their crops to merchants at market rates and realize a modicum of profit. But the more important factor for peasant well-being was the functioning of the *ramya*, or land-assignment, system: although this system aimed to dispossess insolvent peasants of arrears-laden land, it also functioned to assign them other land parcels so as to ensure they had a means of livelihood. This system was modified in the later years of the mid-century period—when revenue maximization was the dominant state policy—with the introduction of the 1858 and 1861 rules; for they prevented indigent peasants from obtaining land assignments.

This study also mentioned the favorable economic environment of the time, especially the rise in crop prices and the country's return to free-market rules, in which land cultivation was fast becoming a profitable endeavor. This situation undoubtedly formed the backdrop to governmental decisions. For senior state decisionmakers, appreciative of the necessity of protecting the productive capabilities of the peasantry—the goose that laid the golden egg—very likely reasoned that this favorable environment would to a certain extent offset the government's increasingly burdensome demands. Whether they made their decisions with this in mind or not, though, the point I wish to highlight now is that the combination of more rigorous regulations and rising taxes did not push the countryside into debilitating poverty. I present my findings on this point below.

Peasant Landholders at Mid-Century

The second part of my argument involved the investigation of the impact of state policies on the countryside. That state policies were informed by the economic precepts of the traditional philosophy of statecraft meant that peasants could expect to retain their land so long as they kept it cultivated and paid all its taxes. They also knew that when they died their lands would be transmitted to their legal heirs. In addition, cultivators understood that if they defaulted on their land obligations the authorities would activate the land-assignment system. That provincial officials could not tolerate delays in the payment of taxes often meant that much of the village vacant lands wound up in the hands of affluent peasants. In parallel, the *ramya* process demonstrated a distinct concern for improving the economic viability of needy peasants, and accordingly, many poor peasants acquired land assignments. Thus, the workings of these rules and policies meant that peasants generally acquired land by one of two modes: transmission/inheritance and land assignment.

But these findings, which only tell us how peasants acquired their lands, do not enable us to address the conventional view that identifies the mid-century years as a time of widespread peasant land loss. I challenged this view, arguing that the state policies of the mid-century period did not lead to extensive peasant impoverishment. This involved examining five issues.

First, the *matruk* lands. While the literature points to wide-scale peasant land abandonment to substantiate the view on widespread peasant ruination at mid-century, my position is different. Instead I showed that peasants usually petitioned the authorities to be allowed to abandon their *ib'adiyya*s, which often consisted of barren lands or lands that were recently brought under the plow and so were expensive to maintain. This strategy enabled petitioners to retain their *ma'mur* lands, which were made up of fertile black soil and often constituted their *athariyya* lands, or the lands that had been farmed by generations of cultivators and were prized by their holders. Thus, peasants retained most of the lands they valued. My sources also revealed that some peasants retained their *ib'adiyya* lands, continuing with both their reclamation/cultivation tasks and tax payments—which again serves to undermine the peasant-impoverishment thesis.

Second, the surplus (*ziyada*) lands. State regulation of these lands during the mid-1850s differentiated between tiny plots, which were to be placed automatically with their actual cultivators, and the larger tracts, which were either turned over to the (usually poor) informants who had revealed their existence or sent to the auction block. These rules really contributed to the amelioration of poverty in villages. The introduction of the 1858 land law, which expanded the amount of land actual cultivators could keep, boosted this development. The 1861 regulation that standardized the unit of measurement employed in the survey of arable land (*qasaba*) reversed it, though, by fictively generating surplus lands in many villages across the country that were to be sold by public auction as *ushuriyya* land,

and then as *kharajiyya* land starting in 1862. While these regulations really operated to dispossess peasant cultivators of small portions of their lands, rich and poor alike, the indigent peasants were particularly disadvantaged in regard to subsequent land acquirement because of the stiff competition they faced at the auctions from their wealthier neighbors as well as interested outsiders. This development notwithstanding, we cannot conclude that these regulations triggered extensive impoverishment.

Third, the creation of large, privileged estates. Previous studies point to this phenomenon as a major factor in peasant land dispossession. And again, my view is different. Regarding the land grants conferred on high state officials, I showed that the bulk of these lands were *ib'adiyya* tracts, while only a very small proportion had been drawn from the lands prized by peasant cultivators, the *ma'mur* lands. At the same time, the Bedouin grant recipients made clear their preference for *ib'adiyya* lands situated on the fringes of peasant-inhabited areas, and were accordingly indulged. The *uhda*s constituted the second type of large estate. Here we saw that Abbas Pasha terminated a large proportion of *uhda*s, but did not abolish the system altogether; and neither did his successor, Said Pasha, who also decreased the number of *uhda*s. Thus, while other writers highlighted the cases of *uhda* establishment, and further showed that some of these villages later became the property of their *mut'ahhid*s, I argued that the trend of *uhda* termination was more preponderant at mid-century. And too, contrary to the view of other writers, I further showed that *uhda* termination generally involved the peasants' repossession of their lands. The third type of privileged large estate, in fact the most important because of its huge size, was the *jiflik*. Here I showed that such estate establishment at mid-century was less injurious to peasants' well-being than previously assumed, and attributed this situation to three combined trends: there was a slowdown in *jiflik* estate creation; the new estates that were created during this time were often composed of barren *ib'adiyya* lands; there also was the dismantlement of old *jiflik*s, which entailed the return of the lands to the original peasant holders.

Fourth, the introduction of the 1858 land law. The conventional interpretation of the major land laws of our period emphasized the stringent criteria for land recovery: according to this view, these operated to confirm the current and comparatively more affluent holders in their land possessions by disallowing the poorer peasants from suing for the recovery of their original lands. Here too my interpretation is somewhat different. My examination of the *athurat* records revealed that the peasants generally acquired land by inheritance and, even more frequently, by the land-assignment (*ramya*) system. While this system worked to remove land from the possession of insolvent peasants, it also functioned to assign land to poor peasants in order to ensure their subsistence. Thus, so long as the *ramya* system continued to function, poor peasants could look forward to the receipt of new lands. So impoverished peasants very likely did not pay as close attention to the land recovery criteria specified by the 1847 and 1855 land laws as they did to the workings of the *ramya* system. The introduction of the 1858 land law modified this system in a way that disadvantaged the indigent peasants in the village; for, contrary to previous practice, *ramya* recipients were henceforth required to pay a transfer fee. This undoubtedly hindered many poor peasants from depending on the *ramya* system for the obtainment of new land—which really meant that these peasants could not hope to acquire new land at all. In addition, the fact that the 1858 law specified rigorous criteria for land recovery, which were observed closely by both the religious and civil courts, also meant that many poor peasants found they could not repossess the *athariyya* lands they had lost during earlier times of hardship. Thus, poor peasants, the majority in the village, found that the 1858 land law closed off two channels of land acquirement: henceforth, both the acquirement of *ramya* land (a new land parcel) and the recovery of family *athariyya* lands became more difficult. And yet, these aspects of the 1858 law did not bring immediate and widespread ruination to the countryside; most probably because the favorable economic environment (particularly rising crop prices) enabled many peasants to pay most of their taxes and thereby retain much of their lands. This is clearly demonstrated by the subsequent and final point.

Fifth, the distribution of land in four sample villages between 1813–1814 and 1849–1850, and then again between 1849–1850 and 1862–1863. While the data revealed a measure of deterioration in the level of landholdings during the first period (Muhammad Ali's reign) in these villages, the latter period (the mid-century years) witnessed the reversal of this trend. What is particularly noticeable was the situation of the small stratum holdings—the majority in the village—which had improved by the end of the mid-century period. Moreover, the examination of the land-tax registers of these villages also shows that the majority of the peasant holders endured the taxation increases specified by the three major tax codes of the period while retaining their lands. That the greater majority of the peasant smallholders remained solvent lends further support for the view developed here: that state policies did not engender widespread impoverishment in the countryside during the mid-century period.

The examination of peasant land tenure would have been incomplete without the investigation of the tenure patterns pertaining to women smallholders. And here, the focus was not on the question of peasant impoverishment caused by onerous state demands, but rather on the unique concerns that pertained to female holders; specifically on the problems related to land inheritance, the primary mode by which women acquired land. While peasant women did inherit land long before the nineteenth century, Egyptian village society was known to generally abhor the notion of female land possession. That the state chose to grant women inheritance rights to land at mid-century may be attributed to its adherence to the economic principles of the traditional philosophy of statecraft. For the state's interest in preserving the economic viability of female-led households prompted it to grant women provisional rights to land inheritance in 1855, and then their full Islamic rights in 1858. This meant that women who petitioned the courts for their shares of the family patrimonies could expect official support when their claims satisfied legislative criteria and/or dovetailed with the traditional economic policies. It seems that few women could satisfy these conditions, though. And while the 1858 law caused rural families to view women's inheritance of land more positively than before, still, societal opposition to female land possession remained formidable. Women understood this reality and used it to their advantage, offering their lands to their brothers in exchange for protection in times of marital crisis. Thus, what all of this meant was that the numbers of women smallholders remained negligible at the close of the mid-century period.

"Engaging the State"

My examination of the impact of state policy on the peasant land-tenure regime in mid-nineteenth-century Egypt involved addressing the conventional view developed by the current literature on the idea of the absolutist state.[2] And as mentioned above, most studies in Near Eastern history are premised on the view of the preindustrial state as exploitative, distant from, and unconcerned about the polity's producing base. Two more recent studies that focus on the region of Upper Egypt provide additional confirmation for this position: for both depict a distant state that imposed onerous burdens on the subject base, which in turn brought about hardship, resentment, and rebellion in the countryside.[3] Although my research focused on Lower Egypt, I did manage to examine some cases that pertained to Upper Egypt; and what little I found only served to confirm the general position of these studies.

But another trend in the literature casts the state differently. The writings by Linda Darling and Huri Islamoğlu-Inan on the Ottoman Empire during the sixteenth century highlight the state's interest in ensuring the peasants' well-being, and Alan Mikhail's examination of Ottoman Egypt highlights the state's appreciation of the peasants' knowledge and capacities in irrigation matters. This trend in the literature, to which my study belongs, further notes that peasants expected the state to ensure they lived in a land ordered by justice.

This modified interpretation of the absolutist state sheds light on why the rural areas of Lower Egypt were largely politically quiescent at mid-century. Discussion on this point might start with Gabriel Baer's examination of peasant revolts in Egypt and the two observations he made about the period under discussion. One, "apparently a number of the villages in Giza District revolted in the period between the death of Abbas and Sa'id's ascension to the throne." Two, immediately upon his ascension to the throne, Said introduced "special clauses" in the criminal-administrative law that aimed to punish peasant disobedience or revolt. At this point, Baer observed that "no other social groups' possible rebelliousness was mentioned in this law," thereby implying that the state was particularly worried about the outbreak of peasant revolt.[4]

According to Scott, peasant resistance constitutes the "constant struggle of the peasantry to thwart those who seek to extract labor, grain, taxes, rents and interest from them."[5] Here we might distinguish between different types of resistance. Rebellion, or wide collective action, involves organization and coordination of acts, the commitment to a single goal, and a recognized leadership that usually comes from outside peasant society.[6] At the other end of the resistance spectrum lie the kinds of actions that make up the weapons arsenal of the weak, or "the ordinary weapons of relatively powerless groups: foot-dragging, dissimulation, false compliance, pilfering, feigned ignorance, slander, arson, sabotage, and so forth."[7] At this end of the resistance continuum also belong the type of acts labeled "avoidance protest, by which dissatisfied groups seek to attenuate their hardships and express their discontent through flight, sectarian withdrawal, or other activities that minimize challenges to or clashes with those whom they view as their oppressors."[8]

So how can we characterize the mid-century attempts of Egyptian peasants to deal with their adversaries (usually the state and its officials) and attenuate their miseries? On the one hand, my examination of the archival sources did not reveal any instances of organized, coordinated collective peasant action that aimed to achieve a common goal and was headed by recognized leadership. This means that the revolts that had occurred in the Giza villages in the summer of 1854 (just referred to by Baer) can best be described as spontaneous local riots triggered by immediate village problems, not as outright, full-fledged rebellions. On the other hand, my archival sources reveal an abundance of cases of low-key forms of resistance like peasants' surreptitious cultivation of lands, and avoidance-protest activities like flight from the village.

These sources also show that peasant attempts to alleviate their hardships were not locked into one of two extremes, quiet subversion or outright revolt. John Chalcraft made the same observation when studying peasant petitions written in the 1860s and 1870s. Specifically, he found that these petitions evoked "sophisticated engagement and negotiation with state practice and discourse." Thus, his examination of these petitions led him to highlight peasants' interest in engaging and negotiating with the state in the two decades prior to colonial rule.[9] In the same vein, Hillal asserted that during the second half of the nineteenth century, peasants viewed the petition as an instrument that would enable them to "win additional rights."[10] Thus, peasant politics during this period often involved the reliance on petitions.

My research on rural society allows me to confirm the same finding for the mid-century years. That the civil and religious court registers of this period contain numerous cases that document peasant complaints against local officials, while some peasants even took certain official regulations to task, suggests that rural society generally viewed the option of "engaging the state," by the presentation of petitions to the appropriate legal institutions, as viable and meaningful.[11] Also, the mid-century period was a time, as I have tried to argue throughout this book, when the state sought to observe the major tenets of the traditional philosophy of statecraft, which involved balancing between its revenue needs and the peasants' well-being to ensure that the countryside remained productive. In turn, this strategy prompted the mid-century ruling elite to pay attention to peasant complaints, thereby listening to the criticisms and suggestions that came from the periphery. This was a time, too, when members of the ruling elite could *afford* to engage in such "discussions" with the periphery, simply because they did not deal with the kind of pressures that came with the fast-paced, ambitious plans initiated by Muhammad Ali.

The peasants, in their turn, had a strong sense of their place in the order of the polity, and accordingly of their right to just treatment. This further means that their outlook on life and society included a complex view of the state: for while it was their primary adversary and oppressor, they also depended on it to alleviate abuse and hardship.[12]

The examination of civil court registers, for example, shows that much of this abuse came at the hands of the local government officials. And in many of these cases, peasants chose to fight back, exposing their wrong-doings to their superiors and demanding some kind of redress. To see this, we might examine cases such as the following: the case of the peasants who described their shaykh's misdeeds and demanded his dismissal from his post; in another case, the peasants teamed up against their shaykhs, their umda, and the *sarraf* of their village, accusing them of malfeasance and theft; and in another, the peasants felt the *qadi* of their area was "ignorant in *shari'a* matters" and demanded his replacement; and in yet another, the peasants complained about "the dismissal of the shaykhs they wanted [as village head-men]," and given their reinstatement had been rejected, they then specified the names of the men they wished to see appointed as their shaykhs.[13]

But as mentioned previously, peasant engagement with the state was not limited to complaining about local officials. For many peasants took it upon themselves to voice opposition to state decisions when they viewed these as being particularly problematic. The *matruk* land phenomenon can be seen as an example of peasant engagement with the state about prob-lematic official requirements. Here we might recall that when peasants feared they would not be able to pay their taxes in full, they did not always choose to flee their villages. Rather many preferred to petition the govern-ment for the right to relinquish control over the problematic lands to the state. The state's acceptance of these petitions resulted in the emergence of the *matruk* land phenomenon, which meant that the peasant petitioners remained in their villages and continued with their farming activities. Had the state refused to pay attention to these complaints, it might have had to deal with different peasant responses: peasants might have simply fled their villages, which would have caused a shrinkage in the village labor pool and the decline in village productivity levels; or they might have participated in the type of uprisings (mentioned above) that had taken place in Giza in 1854. At this point, it might be instructive to recall Imad Hillal's observation on the relation between petitions and rebellions during the second half of the nineteenth century: when the number of petitions was high, the number of rebellions was low.[14]

The point I wish to highlight is the following: peasant actors viewed engagement and negotiation with the state as efficacious political activity.[15] And the state, in its turn, was known to scrutinize peasant petitions in order to keep abreast of rural affairs.[16] This resulted in a level of discussion and negotiation between the two parties that helped to make the countryside of the Lower Egypt region relatively quiescent during the mid-century years.

This study argued that the mid-nineteenth-century period was a time when the century-long trend of state indifference and widespread peasant impoverishment and discontent was temporarily reversed. For the state had chosen to govern its rural base in accordance with the teachings of the traditional philosophy of statecraft. This led it to try to balance between its revenue needs and the well-being of the peasant producers for much of the period. It was also a time of rising crop prices and growing international demand for Egyptian produce. The peasants, in turn, were able to take advantage of this favorable economic environment because new state policies permitted them to sell their crops at market rates and pay their taxes at harvest time. At this juncture, then, agricultural production constituted a profitable activity. So even when the state's pressing revenue concerns prompted it to disregard the welfare of the small peasant producers toward the end of the mid-century period, the majority of peasants remained economically viable, and the countryside remained relatively quiescent. This would change with the cotton boom and the ensuing scramble for arable land. Thus the mid-century period can be viewed as a distinctive juncture in the history of rural Egypt.

Appendix A

The Distribution of Land in the Sample Villages: Distribution of Land in Alternative Categories

This appendix shows the distribution of land in the four sample villages based on the following set of categories: the small holdings category consists of less than 1 *faddan* to less than 5 *faddans*; the medium holdings category consists of 5 to less than 20 *faddans*; the large holdings category consists of 20 *faddans* and more.

As explained in chapter 4, I used the conventional set of categories in my discussion on land distribution to allow for comparison with other studies that had relied on the conventional categories.

Yet the categories used in the tables below allow us to discern the wealth and power of the rural notables of the smaller villages, like Jazirat al-Aʿjam; and thus allow for a closer examination of the extent of economic differentiation in these villages.

Like the tables presented in chapter 4, these data reveal two major features of the distribution of land in the sample villages (that can be more easily discerned when focusing on the aggregate numbers). One, distribution was skewed, as the smallest group (the large category, in possession of 20 *faddans* and more) controlled the greatest proportion of the village arable area, while the largest group in the village (the small category, which possessed less than 5 *faddans*) controlled the smallest proportion of the village arable area. Two, the small holdings category experienced slight improvement during the mid-century period, as the average size of a holding went from 1.83 *faddans* in 1849–1850 to 2.04 *faddans* in 1862–1863.

Table A-1: The Distribution of Land in Four Peasant Villages: AH 1266/November 1849–November 1850

	<1–<5 *faddans*				5–<20 *faddans*				20 *faddans* and more				Total	
Village	Total holdings	% of holdings	Area in *faddans*	% of area	Total holdings	% of holdings	Area in *faddans*	% of area	Total holdings	% of holdings	Area in *faddans*	% of area	Holdings	Area
Ibyar	222	65.29	442.5	10.90	90	26.47	847.5	20.90	28	8.24	2,768	68.20	340	4,058.0
Al-Jazira al-Khadra	88	65.19	107.0	7.19	29	21.48	315.5	21.21	18	13.33	1,065	71.60	135	1,487.5
Jazirat al-Aʿjam	18	45.00	43.0	10.83	13	32.50	112.0	28.21	9	22.50	242	60.96	40	397.0
Kafr al-Rajallat	71	71.72	138.0	21.30	22	22.22	217.0	33.50	6	6.06	293	45.20	99	648.0
Total	399	64.98	730.5	11.08	154	25.08	1,492.0	22.64	61	9.93	4,368	66.28	614	6,590.5

Notes: In computing the data for this table, I used the same method described in the notes of table 2.1.

Sources: DMU, Mukallafat atyan, ibyar, 1266, 2913/121/22; DMU, Mukallafat atyan, al-jazira al-khadra, 1266, 3978/135/22; DMU, Mukallafat atyan, kafr al-rajallat, 1266, 8203/110/20; DMU, Mukallafat atyan, jazirat al-aʿjam, 1266, 4571/61/20.

Table A-2: The Distribution of Land in Four Peasant Villages: AH 1279/June 1862–June 1863

	<1–<5 *faddans*				5–<20 *faddans*				20 *faddans* and more				Total	
Village	Total holdings	% of holdings	Area in *faddans*	% of area	Total holdings	% of holdings	Area in *faddans*	% of area	Total holdings	% of holdings	Area in *faddans*	% of area	Hold-ings	Area
Ibyar	294	66.66	638	15.36	118	26.76	1,097.0	26.41	29	6.58	2,418.0	58.22	441	4,153.0
Al-Jazira al-Khadra	76	56.30	102	7.670	46	34.07	508.5	38.25	13	9.63	719.0	54.08	135	1,329.5
Jazirat al-Aʿjam	34	53.97	76	14.73	23	36.51	229.0	44.38	6	9.52	211.0	40.89	63	516.0
Kafr al-Rajallat	108	77.14	227	34.08	28	20.00	284.5	42.72	4	2.86	154.5	23.20	140	666.0
Total	512	65.70	1,043	15.65	215	27.60	2,119.0	31.80	52	6.70	3502.5	52.55	779	6,664.5

Notes: In computing the data for this table, I used the same method described in the notes of table 2.1.

Sources: DMU, Mukallafat atyan, ibyar, 1279, 2925/121/22; DMU, Mukallafat atyan, al-jazira al-khadra, 1279, 3990/135/22; DMU, Mukallafat atyan, kafr al-rajallat, 1279, 8213/110/20; DMU, Mukallafat atyan, jazirat al-aʿjam, 1279, 4581/61/20.

Appendix B
The Impact of the Major Tax Codes on the Four Sample Villages

A. The 1855 Land-Tax Code

I. The 1855 tax code (the first of the mid-century period) was implemented in 1856. Thus, to show how peasants coped with the tax demands specified by this code, I compared the land-tax registers of 1270/1853–1854 with those of 1272/1855–1856. The results are as follows:

- Ibyar Village: 44 percent of the 1853–1854 group maintained the exact level of their holdings in 1855–1856; and 26 percent of the 1853–1854 group increased the size of their holdings by 1855–1856. This means that 70 percent of this group coped well with the new tax demands. Another 18 percent of this group experienced some impoverishment by 1855–1856, but still remained solvent, viable holders. The remaining 12 percent could not be found among the 1855–1856 holders, and I have classified these as "Disappeared." The examination of the 1855–1856 registers also reveals the appearance of new holders; these numbered 115, or 27 percent of the 1855–1856 group.
- Al-Jazira al-Khadra Village: 40 percent maintained the exact level of their holdings; 22 percent increased the size of their holdings; 20 percent experienced some impoverishment; 18 percent disappeared. The new holders in 1855–1856 were twenty-one, or 15 percent of this group.

II. For the two smaller villages, I examined the land-tax registers of 1271/1854–1855 (the 1270 registers were not available) with those of 1272/1855–1856:

- Jazirat al-Aʿjam Village: 33 percent maintained the exact level of their holders; 35 percent increased the size of their holdings; 29 percent experienced some impoverishment; 3 percent disappeared. The new holders in 1855–1856 were fifty-three, or 6 percent of this group.
- Kafr al-Rajallat Village: 19 percent maintained the exact level of their holdings; 42 percent increased the size of their holdings; 32 percent experienced some impoverishment; 7 percent disappeared. The new holders in 1855–1856 were nineteen, or 14 percent of this group.

B. The 1858 Land-Tax Code

Between 1856 and 1858, the government introduced another round of tax increases, specifying an increase in the surcharge taxes as well as implementing the 1858 tax code. To examine the effect of these increases on peasant holders, I compared the land-tax registers of 1272/1855–1856 and those of 1274/1857–1858. The results are as follows:

- Ibyar Village: 89.36 percent of the 1855–1856 group maintained the exact level of their holdings in 1857–1858; and 3.31 percent of the 1855–1856 group increased the size of their holdings in 1857–1858. This means that 92.67 percent of this group coped well with the new tax demands. Another 5.44 percent of this group experienced some impoverishment by 1857–1858, but still remained solvent holders. The remaining 1.89 percent (eight holders) could not be found among the 1857–1858 holders, and I have classified these as "Disappeared." The examination of the 1857–1858 registers also reveals the appearance of new holders in 1857–1858; these numbered seventeen, or 3.94 percent of the 1857–1858 group.
- Al-Jazira al-Khadra Village: 53 percent maintained the exact level of their holdings; 20 percent increased the size of their holdings; 19 percent experienced some impoverishment; 8 percent disappeared. The new holders in 1857–1858 were thirteen, or 9 percent of this group.
- Jazirat al-Aʿjam Village: 21 percent maintained the exact level of their holdings; 19 percent increased the size of their holdings; 58 percent experienced some impoverishment; 2 percent disappeared. The new holders in 1857–1858 were six, or 10 percent of this group.
- Kafr al-Rajallat Village: 41 percent maintained the exact level of their holdings; 26 percent increased the size of their holdings; 27 percent

experienced some impoverishment; 6 percent disappeared. The new holders in 1857–1858 were fifteen, or 11 percent of this group.

C. The 1862 Land-Tax Code

Between 1858 and 1862, the government introduced new land legislation as well as the 1862 land-tax increases. To examine the effect of these new regulations on peasant holders, I compared the land-tax registers of 1274/1857–1858 and those of 1278/1861–1862. The results are as follows:

- Ibyar Village: 76 percent of the 1857–1858 group maintained the exact level of their holdings in 1861–1862; and 7 percent of the 1857–1858 group increased the size of their holdings in 1861–1862. This means that 83 percent of this group coped well with the new tax demands. Another 15 percent of this group experienced some impoverishment by 1861–1862, but still remained solvent, viable holders. The remaining 2 percent could not be found among the 1861–1862 holders, and I have classified these as "Disappeared." The examination of the 1861–1862 registers also reveals the appearance of new holders in 1861–1862; these numbered twenty-eight, or 6.5 percent of the 1861–1862 group.
- Al-Jazira al-Khadra village: 65 percent maintained the exact level of their holdings; 13 percent increased the size of their holdings; 19 percent experienced some impoverishment; 3 percent disappeared. The new holders in 1861–1862 were seven, or 5.2 percent of this group.
- Jazirat al-Aʿjam village: 68 percent maintained the exact level of their holdings; 13 percent increased the size of their holdings; 16 percent experienced some impoverishment; 3 percent disappeared. The new holders in 1861–1862 were two, or 3.2 percent of this group.
- Kafr al-Rajallat Village: 80 percent maintained the exact level of their holdings; 9 percent increased the size of their holdings; 7 percent experienced some impoverishment; 4 percent disappeared. The new holders in 1861–1862 were two, or 1.4 percent of this group.

Sources: DMU, Mukallafat atyan, ibyar, 1270, 2917/121/22; Mukallafat atyan, ibyar, 1272, 2919/121/22; Mukallafat atyan, ibyar, 1274, 2920/121/22; Mukallafat atyan, ibyar, 1278, 2924/121/22; DMU, Mukallafat atyan, al-jazira al-khadra, 1270, 3982/135/22; Mukallafat atyan, al-jazira al-khadra, 1272, 3984/135/22; Mukallafat atyan, al-jazira al-khadra,1274, 3985/135/22; Mukallafat atyan, al-jazira al-khadra, 1278, 3989/135/22; DMU, Mukallafat atyan, jazirat al-aʿjam, 1271, 4574/61/20; Mukallafat atyan, jazirat al-aʿjam, 1272, 4575/61/20; Mukallafat atyan, jazirat al-aʿjam, 1274, 4576/61/20; Mukallafat atyan, jazirat al-aʿjam, 1278, 4580/61/20; DMU, Mukallafat atyan, kafr al-rajallat, 1271, 8206/110/20; Mukallafat atyan, kafr al-rajallat, 1272, 8207/110/20; Mukallafat atyan, kafr al-rajallat, 1274, 8208/110/20; Mukallafat atyan, kafr al-rajallat, 1278, 8212/110/20.

Appendix C
Egyptian Archival Sources

Most of the research for this study was undertaken in the Egyptian archives: I examined several sources in the Ministry of Finance Archives, and others in the National Archives. The following list specifies these sources:

I. Ministry of Finance Archives (Dar al-Mahfuzat al-Umumiyya), Cairo

1. Village registers[1]

Ibyar Village registers

Land-tax registers

Year (AH)	*Number of register*
1266	2913/121/22
1268	2915/121/22
1270	2917/121/22
1272	2919/121/22
1274	2920/121/22
1276	2922/121/22
1278	2924/121/22
1279	2925/122/22

Athurat register

Year (AH)	*Number of register*
1276	10/77/22

Jazirat al-Aʿjam Village registers

Land-tax registers

Year (AH)	*Number of register*
1266	4571/61/20
1268	4573/61/20
1271	4574/61/20
1272	4575/61/20
1274	4576/61/20
1276	4578/61/20
1278	4580/61/20
1279	4581/61/20

Athurat register

Year (AH)	*Number of register*
1274	1/1/20

Kafr al-Rajallat Village registers

Land-tax registers

Year (AH)	*Number of register*
1266	8203/110/20
1268	8205/110/20
1271	8206/110/20
1272	8207/110/20
1274	8208/110/20
1276	8210/110/20
1278	8212/110/20
1279	8213/110/20

Athurat register

Year (AH)	*Number of register*
1273	3/1/20

Al-Jazira al-Khadra Village registers

Land-tax registers

Year (AH)	*Number of register*
1266	3978/135/22
1268	3980/135/22
1270	3982/135/22
1272	3984/135/22
1274	3985/135/22
1276	3987/135/22
1278	3989/135/22
1279	3990/135/22

Athurat register

Year (AH)	*Number of register*
1276	27/77/22

2. Tax-reassessment registers (for Gharbiyya / Rawdat al-Bahrayn Province)

Year (AH)	*Number of register*
1271	2209/109/22
1274	2210/109/22

3. Religious court registers

Tanta (in Gharbiyya Province) religious court registers

Number of register	*Period covered* (AH)
333/186/46	17 Jumada I 1273–1 Ramadan 1273
334/186/46, Part I	Dhu al-Qaʿda 1273–Dhu al-Hijja 1273
334/186/46, Part II	Dhu al-Hijja 1273–Rabi I 1274
335/186/46	13 Rabi I 1274–28 Rabi I 1276
336/186/46	29 Rabi I 1276–18 Rabi I 1277
337/186/46	19 Rabi I 1277–13 Dhu al-Hijja 1277
338/186/46	14 Dhu al-Hijja 1277–23 Rajab 1278
339/186/46	24 Rajab 1278–7 Jumada II 1279
340/186/46	7 Jumada II 1279–26 Rabi I 1280

Qalyub (in Qalyubiya Province) religious court registers

Number of register	*Period covered (AH)*
76/98/46	1 Dhu al-Qaʿda 1273–4 Jumada I 1277
77/98/46	6 Jumada I 1277–19 Safar 1280

II. National Archives (Dar al-Watha'iq al-Qawmiyya), Cairo

1. Civil court registers

These registers are categorized according to subject matter; and my research focused on the subject referred to as "the provinces." These registers are further divided into two groups: one records "incoming" documents, and the other records "outgoing" documents.

My research method involved starting my examination with the year AH 1266, and then looking at every other year through AH 1278 My selection of the civil court to focus on depended on the level of completeness of its records.

Diwan al-Khidawi (Department of Civil Affairs) registers

The main focus is the year AH 1266.

The following registers are categorized under "provinces, incoming":

Number of register	*Period covered (AH)*
S/2/8/16	22 Shawwal 1265–19 Shawwal 1266
S/2/8/17	6 Shawwal 1266–15 Dhu al-Qaʿda 1266
S/2/8/18	4 Dhu al-Qaʿda 1266–10 Shaʿban 1267

Diwan al-Ma'iyya al-Siniyya (Viceregal Cabinet) registers

The main focus is the year AH 1268.

The following registers are categorized under "provinces, outgoing":

Number of register	*Period covered (AH)*
S/1/8/16	15 Dhu al-Qaʿda 1267–9 Rabi II 1268
S/1/8/17	13 Rabi I 1268–8 Jumada II 1268
S/1/8/18	27 Jumada I 1268–4 Shaʿban 1268
S/1/8/19	8 Jumada II 1268–1 Shaʿban 1268
S/1/8/20	3 Shaʿban 1268–7 Shawwal 1268
S/1/8/21	5 Shawwal 1268–24 Dhu al-Qaʿda 1268
S/1/8/22	26 Dhu al-Qaʿda 1268–17 Safar 1269

Majlis al-Ahkam (Council of Justice) registers

The main focus is the year AH 1270.

A. The following registers are categorized under "provinces of Lower Egypt, incoming":

Number of register	*Period covered (AH)*
S/7/16/1	27 Dhu al-Qaʿda 1268–23 Safar 1269
S/7/16/2	12 Safar 1269–9 Jumada II 1269
S/7/16/6	8 Dhu al-Hijja 1269–17 Rabi I 1270
S/7/16/7	7 Rabi I 1270–8 Jumada II 1270
S/7/16/8	29 Jumada I 1270–5 Ramadan 1270
S/7/16/9	18 Shaʿban 1270–19 Dhu al-Hijja 1270
S/7/16/10	26 Dhu al-Qaʿda 1270–26 Dhu al-Hijja 1271
S/7/16/11	20 Dhu al-Hijja 1270–28 Rabi II 1271
S/7/16/12	28 Rabi II 1271–26 Dhu al-Qaʿda 1271
S/7/16/13	10 Dhu al-Qaʿda 1271–26 Dhu al-Hijja 1271
S/7/16/14	14 Rabi I 1273–23 Shawwal 1273
S/7/16/15	23 Shawwal 1273–20 Muharram 1274
S/7/16/16	21 Muharram 1274–9 Rajab 1274

B. The following registers are categorized under "provinces of Lower Egypt, outgoing":

Number of register	*Period covered (AH)*
S/7/6/2	30 Safar 1269–24 Jumada I 1269
S/7/6/7	19 Rabi I 1270–7 Jumada II 1270

Diwan al-Maʿiyya al-Siniyya (Viceregal Cabinet) registers

The main focus is the year AH 1272.

The following registers are categorized under "provinces, outgoing":

Number of register	*Period covered (AH)*
S/1/8/41	5 Rabi II 1272–14 Jumada II 1272
S/1/8/42	25 Jumada I 1272–19 Rajab 1272
S/1/8/44	17 Rajab 1272–24 Shawwal 1272
S/1/8/45	21 Shawwal 1272–6 Muharram 1273
S/1/8/46	10 Dhu al-Qaʿda 1272–8 Muharram 1273

Diwan al-Dakhiliyya (Department of Interior) registers

A. The main focus is the year AH 1274.

The following registers are categorized under “provinces of Lower Egypt, incoming”:

Number of register	*Period covered (AH)*
L/19/21/1	14 Rajab 1273–29 Jumada I 1273
L/19/21/2	27 Dhu al-Hijja 1273–11 Jumada II 1274
L/19/21/3	23 Muharram 1274–22 Rabi II 1274
L/19/21/4	18 Rabi II 1274–9 Rajab 1274
L/19/21/5	2 Rajab 1274–13 Shawwal 1274
L/19/21/6	10 Shawwal 1274–22 Dhu al-Hijja 1274
L/19/21/7	17 Dhu al-Hijja 1274–26 Rajab 1275

B. The main focus is the year AH 1276.

The following registers are categorized under “provinces of Lower Egypt, outgoing”:

Number of register	*Period covered (AH)*
L/19/15/5	25 Dhu al-Hijja 1275–12 Safar 1276
L/19/15/6	13 Safar 1276–8 Jumada I 1276
L/19/15/7	27 Rabi II 1276–22 Shaʿban 1276
L/19/15/8	28 Rabi II 1276–7 Ramadan 1276

Diwan al-Maʿiyya al-Siniyya (Viceregal Cabinet) registers

The main focus is the year AH 1278.

The following registers are categorized under “provinces, incoming”:

Number of register	*Period covered (AH)*
S/1/21/52	30 Dhu al-Qaʿda 1277–7 Rabi I 1278
S/1/21/53	28 Safar 1278–5 Shawwal 1278
S/1/21/54	6 Rabi I 1277–23 Jumada I 1278
S/1/21/55	20 Jumada I 1278–9 Jumada II 1278
S/1/21/56	1 Shaʿban 1278–18 Shawwal 1278
S/1/21/57	14 Shawwal 1278–19 Dhu al-Hijja 1278
S/1/21/58	19 Dhu al-Hijja 1278–20 Safar 1279

2. Civil Court: Mahafiz (Cartons)[2]

Majlis al-Ahkam (Council of Justice) Boxes

The following boxes are categorized under "Decrees" or *Awwamir*:

Number of carton	*Period covered (AH)*
6	3 Muharram 1269–8 Dhu al-Hijja 1270
7	2 Muharram 1271–30 Dhu al-Hijja 1273
8	17 Muharram 1274–29 Dhu al-Hijja 1279

Diwan al-Khidawi (Department of Civil Affairs) Box

The following box is categorized under "Decrees" or *Awwamir*:

Number of carton	*Period covered (AH)*
1	—

3. Religious court registers

Al-Khanka (in Qalyubiya Province) religious court registers

Number of register	*Period covered (AH)*
1	5 Dhu al-Qaʿda 1268–30 Shawwal 1273
2	15 Shaʿban 1272–26 Shawwal 1273
3	2 Dhu al-Qaʿda 1273–26 Shawwal 1276

4. Additional registers (that focus on agricultural affairs)

Title of register	*Number of register*
Nizam Umur Ziraʿiyya	5004

Notes

Introduction

1 For a copy of this treaty, see Issawi, ed., *The Economic History of the Middle East*, 39–40.
2 For a landmark study on Muhammad Ali's rural policies, see Rivlin, *The Agricultural Policy*.
3 One such strategy: Muhammad Ali was known to bestow land grants on members of the elite, and then order them to relinquish their crops to his agents at low rates. See Owen, *Cotton and the Egyptian Economy*, 61.
4 Baer, *Studies in the Social History*, 29; Issawi, "The Economic Development of Egypt," 359–61.
5 Cuno, *The Pasha's Peasants*.
6 I borrow this phrase from Islamoğlu's discussion on the policies of the early-modern Ottoman state. Islamoğlu, "Politics of Administering Property" (for quoted phrase, 283).
7 Toledano, *State and Society* (for quoted phrase, 122).
8 Fahmy, *All the Pasha's Men*; Toledano, *State and Society*.
9 Toledano, *State and Society*, 153 (for quoted phrase, 153).
10 Ottoman thinker Mustafa Naima articulated the major propositions of the "circle of equity" accordingly: [As cited in Singer, *Palestinian Peasants*, 10]:

> There is no *mulk* [sovereignty] and no *devlet* [state] without the military and without man-power.
> Men are to be found only by means of wealth [*mal*].
> Wealth is only to be garnered from the peasantry [*re'aya*].
> The peasantry is to be maintained in prosperity only through justice.
> And without *mulk* and *devlet* there can be no justice.

11 Islamoğlu-Inan and Keyder, "Agenda for Ottoman History," 43 (for quoted phrase, 43).
12 Islamoğlu-Inan and Keyder, "Agenda for Ottoman History," 43–44.
13 Islamoğlu-Inan, *State and Peasant in the Ottoman Empire*, 6. For additional discussion on this philosophy, see İnalcik, "The Ottoman Economic Mind," 217–18; Itzkowitz, *Ottoman Empire and Islamic Tradition*, 88–89; Mardin, *The Genesis of Young Ottoman Thought*, 94–102; Darling, *Revenue-Raising and Legitimacy*, ch. 9; Darling, *A History of Social Justice*, ch. 1.

14 Ergene, "On Ottoman Justice," 52–87 (for quoted phrases, 73, 75).
15 Ergene, "On Ottoman Justice," 52–69.
16 İnalcik specifically identifies these economic principles. See his "The Ottoman Economic Mind," 218.
17 A brief comment on the extent of my reliance on the "circle of equity" propositions to interpret Egyptian rural history at mid-century is in order. My focus, quite simply, is on the dual economic precepts included in these propositions: maximization of state revenues while preserving the economic viability of the subject population. That the "circle of equity" propositions are grounded in the traditional view of society (which divides society into two groups, the ruling group and the ruled) does not mean that my study should be read as a kind of commentary (orientalist/essentialist or otherwise) on the nature of Egyptian society at mid-century. Thus, I do not mean to suggest that Egyptian society was made up of simple homogenous units, and by extension, that peasant villages were inhabited by homogeneous groups, to the exclusion of artisans, merchants, money-lenders, Bedouins, foreigners, and the *dhawat* (the Turco-Circassian elite). Indeed, my sources reveal the opposite, and accordingly, I refer to peasant contact and dealings with members of these groups in my text a number of times.
18 Peters, "For His Correction," 164–92; Fahmy, "The Anatomy of Justice," 224–71; Goldberg, "On the Origins of *Majalis Al-Tujjar*," 193–223.
19 For example, see: Weber, *Economy and Society*, 978; Turner, *Weber and Islam*.
20 See Humphreys, "Law as Discourse," 251–59; also see Gerber, *State, Society and Law in Islam*, 55.
21 Peters, "For His Correction," 164.
22 See Humphreys, "Law as Discourse," 254–57.
23 DWQ, MS, S/1/8/46, fol. 48 (no. 118) 4 Dhu al-Hijja 1272. Also see: DWQ, MS, S/1/8/46, fol. 95 (no. 127) 29 Dhu al-Hijja 1272.
24 For example, see: DWQ, MS, S/1/21/58, fol. 181 (no. 430) 7 Safar 1279; DWQ, DD, L/19/21/5, fol. 167 (no. 112) 28 Sha'ban 1274.
25 For example, see: DWQ, Daftar nizam umur zira'iyya, no. 5004, fol. 37.
26 For a useful examination of the moral framework of law, see Corrigan and Sayers, "How the Law Rules," 21–53.
27 Chalcraft, "Engaging the State," 303–25.
28 Chalcraft, "Engaging the State"; Ghalwash, "On Justice," 523–40.
29 Singer makes the same observation for Palestinian peasants during the mid-sixteenth century. For she writes that "peasants also seemed to have absorbed formal Ottoman rhetoric about safeguarding the peasantry as a source of wealth for the state." Singer, *Palestinian Peasants*, 9.
30 See Fahmy, "The Anatomy of Justice." Also, Mine Ener's examination of the state's management of the poor during the nineteenth century highlights ordinary Egyptians' awareness of the relief options provided by the state, which provides further confirmation of ordinary people's familiarity with state bodies and their roles and functions during this period. See Ener, *Managing Egypt's Poor*, 61. For a different view, see: Reilly, "Women in the Economic Life," 92.

31 In a similar vein, Imad Hillal asserts that the view that specifies that the Egyptian peasant was unaware of his rights is incorrect. See: Hillal, *Al-fallah wa al-sulta*, 344.
32 While earlier writers had specified that Muhammad Ali aimed to win his independence from the Ottoman sultan, Khaled Fahmy shows convincingly that his aims were more modest, only wishing to secure recognition of his dynasty's rights to the governorship of Egypt. See: Fahmy, *Mehmed Ali*.
33 Rivlin, "The Railway Question," 365–88.
34 For additional details on his death, see: Toledano, *State and Society*, 123, 280 (no. 34).
35 Succession to the throne of Egypt was regulated by the Ottoman rule of primogeniture, not by the rules of the monarchical system (which granted succession to the deceased ruler's son). Thus, although Said Pasha was Muhammad Ali's son, he took the throne *after* the reign of his nephew, Abbas I, had ended because he was younger than him.
36 For changing the system of primogeniture see, for example: PRO, FO 78/1675, Cohen for Colquhoun to Russell, May 10, 1862. For declaring independence, see, for example: PRO, FO 195/618, Cowley to Malmesbury, June 17, 1859; PRO, FO 78/1467, Walne to Malmesbury, May 16, 1859; PRO, FO 78/1467, Walne to Russell, July 10, 1859.
37 Islamoğlu, "Property as a Contested Domain," 24.
38 Arable land in Egypt is measured by the *faddan* (which is slightly larger than an acre).
39 For a short and readable examination of the major trends in gender history, see Green and Troup, *The Houses of History*, ch. 10.
40 Tucker, *Women in Nineteenth-Century Egypt*, 49.
41 For example, see: Rouchdy, "Change and Continuity," 225–44.
42 See: Barakat, *Tatawwur al-milkiyya*, ch. 4; Baer, *A History of Landownership*, 28–38; Richards, "Primitive Accumulation in Egypt," 232–34; Baer, *Studies in the Social History*, 17–29; Issawi, "The Economic Development of Egypt," 359–61; Cuno, *The Pasha's Peasants*, 189–97; Abbas and El-Dessouky, *The Large Landowning Class*, 9–11; Richards, *Egypt's Agricultural Development*, 37; Owen, *The Middle East in the World Economy*, 142; Brown, *Peasant Politics*, ch. 1; Tucker, *Women in Nineteenth-Century Egypt*, 43–52; Hunter, "State-Society Relations," 156–57.
43 Cuno, *The Pasha's Peasants*.
44 Hakim, *Ayam Muhammad Ali*, ch. 2.
45 Toledano, *State and Society*, 286 (no. 7).
46 Shalabi, *Al-Rif al-misri*, 209.
47 Shalabi, *Al-Rif al-misri*, 76, 81, 209–11.
48 Mikhail, *Nature and Empire*, chs. 1 and 4.
49 Chalcraft, "Engaging the State"; Ghalwash, "On Justice."
50 Hillal, *Al-Fallah wa al-sulta* (for quoted phrases, 343–44).
51 Hillal, *Al-Fallah wa al-sulta*, 344.
52 Hillal, *Al-Fallah wa al-sulta*, 344–45 (for quoted phrases, 344).
53 Abul-Magd, *Imagined Empires*.

54 Barakat, *Al-Qarya wa al-sulta*.
55 Abbas and El-Dessouky, *The Large Landowning Class*.
56 I had relied on this source to write two earlier articles; but at that time, I had misread the term *athurat*, and mistakenly specified it as *aturat*. See: Ghalwash, "Land Acquisition by the Peasants," 121–39; and "Peasant Women and Rights," 26–53.
57 In 1855, Gharbiyya province was composed of 403 villages; for this see: DMU, Daftar takmil al-dara'ib, rawdat al-bahrayn, 1271, 2209/109/22. By 1858, parts of Munifiyya province had been integrated into Gharbiyya province, thereby expanding the boundaries of al-Gharbiyya, which was renamed Rawdat al-Bahrayn Province. The modified province was made up of 753 villages; for this see DMU, Daftar takmil al-dara'ib, rawdat al-bahrayn, 1274, 2210/109/22.
58 See DWQ, MS, S/1/8/42, fol. 413 (no. 65) 26 Jumada I 1272.
59 See Hunter, *Egypt under the Khedives*.
60 This led me to focus on the registers of the following state departments for these years: for the year AH 1266/1849–1850, I consulted the registers of the Department of Civil Affairs (Diwan al-Khidawi); for AH 1268/1851–1852, those of the Viceregal Cabinet (al-Ma'iyya al-Siniyya); for AH 1270/1853–1854, the Council of Justice (Majlis al-Ahkam); for AH 1272/1855–1856, the Viceregal Cabinet; for AH 1274/1857–1858 and AH 1276/1859–1860, the Department of Interior (Diwan al-Dakhiliyya); and finally, for AH 1278/1861–1862, the Viceregal Cabinet.
61 Singer, *Palestinian Peasants*, 17.

Chapter 1

1 Dodwell, *The Founder of Modern Egypt*.
2 Issawi, "The Economic Development of Egypt," 362.
3 Issawi, "The Economic Development of Egypt," 363.
4 For example, see: DWQ, DD, L/19/21/3, fol. 91 (no. 27) 11 Rabi I 1274.
5 For an excellent but brief review of Muhammad Ali's reign, see Marsot, *A Short History of Modern Egypt*, 54–66. For a revisionist view of the major aim of Muhammad Ali's policies, see Fahmy, *Mehmed Ali*. Fahmy argues that the pasha did not aim to secure independence from the Ottoman sultan or to build an empire; rather he wanted hereditary rule of Egypt. Thus, the 1841 agreement was a testimony to his success, not his failure, for by it he was able "to pass Egypt on to a dynasty whose legitimacy had been acknowledged by all the leading powers at that time" (for quoted phrase, 126.) For the text of the 1841 agreement, see Hurewitz, *Diplomacy in the Near and Middle East*, 121–23.
6 For the text of this agreement, see Issawi, *The Economic History of the Middle East*, 38–40.
7 Cuno, *The Pasha's Peasants*, 143–44 (for quoted phrase, 143); Shalabi, *Al-Rif al-misri*, 59; Barakat, *Al-Qarya wa al-sulta*, 36.
8 Owen, *Cotton and the Egyptian Economy*, 61; Hamid, *Al-Nizam al-ijtima'i*, 16, 30; Abbas and El-Dessouky, *The Large Landowning Class*, 22–23.

9 Baer, *A History of Landownership*, 13; Cuno, *The Pasha's Peasants*, 158.
10 Owen, *Cotton and the Egyptian Economy*, 60–63; Tucker, "Decline of the Family Economy," 250–51.
11 Rivlin, *The Agricultural Policy*; Abbas and El-Dessouky, *The Large Landowning Class*, 32–33; Al-Hitta, *Tarikh Misr*, 58–59.
12 Owen, *Cotton and the Egyptian Economy*, 62–67.
13 Cuno, *The Pasha's Peasants*, 160.
14 Cuno, *The Pasha's Peasants*, 181–82; Richards, "Primitive Accumulation in Egypt," 225–26; Owen, *Cotton and the Egyptian Economy*, 74.
15 Baer, *Studies in the Social History*, 113–19; Rivlin, "The Railway Question."
16 PRO, FO 141/23, Russell to Paget, February 1, 1853.
17 PRO, FO 141/21, "Translation of the Circular Addressed to the European Consuls at Cairo," October 23, 1853. For the 1853 decree that banned the export of grain to Europe because of domestic scarcity see: Najm, *Dafatir Majmu Idara*, 401; also see: Barakat, *Al-Qarya wa al-sulta*, 46.
18 PRO, FO 78/1035, Bruce to Clarendon, May 31, 1854.
19 PRO, FO 78/1035, Green to Bruce, May 5, 1854; also see Bruce to Clarendon, May 16, 1854.
20 PRO, FO 78/1035, Bruce to Clarendon, May 16, 1854.
21 PRO, FO 78/1035, Bruce to Clarendon, May 30, 1854.
22 PRO, FO 78/1035, Green to Bruce, May 5, 1854.
23 PRO, FO 78/1035, Bruce to Clarendon, May 16, 1854; also see Bruce to Redcliffe, May 2, 1854.
24 PRO, FO 78/1036, Bruce to Clarendon, July 5, 1854. According to Barakat, the nature of foreign merchants' dealings in the countryside changed between 1840 and 1858: In the 1840s, foreign dealings with peasants were mediated by local merchants; direct dealings between foreigners and the peasants began in the 1850s; finally, the introduction of the 1858 land law brought about intensive foreign penetration of the countryside. See Barakat, *Al-Qarya wa al-sulta*, 44–45.
25 For Abbas's attempt to strip his grandfather's supporters of their power by terminating their *uhda*s, see Toledano, *State and Society*, 64–65. For the attribution of this decision to his realization that many *muta'ahhid*s had failed to keep up with their tax payments, see Barakat, *Tatawwur al-milkiyyia*, 104–105; Barakat, *Al-Qarya wa al-sulta*, 24. Technically, when the government gave orders for the termination of an *uhda*, it explained its decision by one of two reasons, either the peasants had shown they were solvent or the tax farmer (*muta'ahhid*) had failed to satisfy his tax requirements. See DWQ, MA, S/7/16/6, fol. 12 (no. 8) 14 Jumada I 1269; DWQ, MA, S/7/16/6, fol. 12 (no. 9) 14 Jumada I 1269; DWQ, MA, S/7/16/6, fols. 14, 19 (no. 14) 16 Jumada I 1269; DWQ, MA, S/7/16/6, fol. 14 (no. 11) 14 Jumada I 1269; DWQ, MA, S/7/16/6, fols. 5, 12 (no. 7) 14 Jumada I 1269; DWQ, MA, S/7/16/6, fol. 40 (no. 3) 19 Muharram 1270.
26 Cuno, *The Pasha's Peasants*, 160.
27 Landes, *Bankers and Pashas*, 79.

28 Merruau, *L'Egypte contemporaine*, 60–65. Although Merruau claims that all peasant arrears were forgiven, the archival sources suggest Said's instructions did not cover all cases. (For further discussion on tax remission during this period, see chapter 3 below.)
29 U.S., Department of State, De Leon to Marcy, no. 16, vol. II, September 18, 1854, p. 73. Also see Barakat, *Al-Qarya wa al-sulta*, 38.
30 Senior, *Conversations and Journals*, 131.
31 PRO, FO 78/1313, Bruce to Clarendon, February 2, 1857.
32 DWQ, MA, S/7/16/8, fol. 98 (no. 139) 26 Sha'ban 1270.
33 For example, see: DWQ, MA, S/7/16/11, fols. 27, 52 (no. 27) 10 Safar 1271; DWQ, MS, S/1/8/17, fol. 375 (no. 102) 27 Jumada I 1268.
34 DWQ, MA, S/7/16/11, fols. 27, 52 (no. 27) 10 Safar 1271.
35 DWQ, MS, S/1/8/17, fol. 375 (no. 102) 27 Jumada I 1268.
36 For example, see: DWQ, MA, S/7/16/11, fols. 27, 52 (no. 27) 10 Safar 1271.
37 PRO, FO 78/1222, Harris to Bruce, December 19, 1856.
38 Hillal, *Al-Fallah wa al-sulta*, 164.
39 For this decree, see DWQ, Daftar nizam umur zira'iyya, no. 5004, fol. 40.
40 Some writers assert that this law was issued in 1846. See Jorgens, "A Comparative Examination," 114 (no. 3).
41 DWQ, MKH, Da'awi wa ashhadat, no. 1, fol. 6 (no. 22) 11 Muharram 1269; DWQ, MKH, Da'awi wa ashhadat, no. 1, fol. 7 (no. 24) 3 Safar 1269.
42 DWQ, Daftar nizam umur zira'iyya, fol. 39.
43 Some writers assert that this law was issued in 1854. See Jorgens, "A Comparative Examination," 114 (no. 3).
44 DWQ, MS, S/1/8/45, fol. 84 (no. 864) 9 Dhu al-Qa'da 1272.
45 DWQ, Daftar nizam umur zira'iyya, fol. 49.
46 DWQ, MA, Mahafiz, 7, (no. 71/89) 10 Dhu al-Qa'da 1273.
47 Jorgens, "A Comparative Examination," 95.
48 Baer, *Studies in the Social History*, 25–26, 68 (for quoted phrase, 68); Baer, *A History of Landownership*, 8–9; Artin, *Al-Ahkam al-mar'iyya*, 57–60; Crouchley, *The Economic Development of Modern Egypt*, 127. There is disagreement regarding the time when land-alienation rights to peasant land were granted. According to earlier scholars, these rights were granted by the 1858 land law. Shalabi, however, contests this view, and asserts that these were granted earlier, by the 1847 law: as the 1847 law specified the land transfers (rental, cession, pawn, partnerships in land cultivation), which were to be documented on official paper, it was, in effect, indirectly recognizing peasants' legal right to alienate land. See Shalabi, *Al-Rif al-misri*, 74.
49 Cuno, "The Origins of Private Ownership," 245–75.
50 Cuno, *The Pasha's Peasants*, 189; also see: 194, 197.
51 Cuno, *The Pasha's Peasants*, 192, 194, 197; Barakat, *Tatawwur al-milkiyya*, 66–69; Shalabi, *Al-Rif al-misri*, 94–101; Abbas and El-Dessouky, *The Large Landowning Class*, 9–11.
52 Hakim, *Ayam Muhammad Ali*, 109.
53 Abul-Magd, *Imagined Empires*, 101.

54 This system existed in Lower Egypt because the area of arable, irrigated land basically remained the same over the years. In Upper Egypt, the land was more elevated, and this meant that the irrigation process caused significant changes in the area of cultivable land each year. This land, referred to as *kilala* land, was distributed annually by the village leaders according to the recognized cultivation rights of each family. (See Cuno, *The Pasha's Peasants*, 66.) According to Rivlin, "This land was designated *bi'l-masahah* or land by the measure." (See Rivlin, *The Agricultural Policy*, 23.) Thus in this latter system, what the peasants owned were fixed rights to shares of the village land; and so it can be argued that here too, there was a form of individual responsibility for land. In examining this system, Hakim highlights the role of village headmen in the yearly redistribution process, and their tendency to concentrate village lands in their hands. See *Ayam Muhammad Ali*, 113–16.

55 Yet they could not turn their land into a *waqf*, a foundation created for the support of a religious or charitable activity, while property owners could.

56 For example, see: DMU, Daftar takmil al-dara'ib, rawdat al-bahrayn, 1271, 2209/109/22.

57 The only exception is Article VII in the 1855 land law, which deals with *usya* land. When Muhammad Ali abolished the *iltizam* system, he permitted the *multazims* to retain a portion of the land (referred to as *usya*) as compensation, and did not require them to pay taxes. He also granted them the right to bequeath and sell their *usya* lands. (See Al-Hitta, *Tarikh Misr*, 67.) By the 1850s, many *usyas* had been turned over to the village cultivators and reclassified as peasant land. Yet, some of the old *multazim* families continued to hold their *usyas* on a tax-free basis until 1854, when Said Pasha imposed the (comparatively light) *ushr* tax.

58 This discussion is based on the *athurat* registers. For example, see: DMU, Daftar al-athurat, kafr al-rajallat, 1272, 3/1/20, fols. 1–6; DMU, Daftar al-athurat, tant al-jazira, 1274, 29/127/15377, fols. 36–48. The court registers also contain many relevant entries, as will be shown below.

59 I point out that these two words make up this one term (*wadiʿ al-yad*); and as it is one term, I include the relevant diacritical mark for the *ayn* (ʿ) although it comes at the end of the word *wadiʿ*. (Recall that I specified that I would not include the *ayn* (ʿ) if it came at the end of the word.)

60 DMU, Daftar al-athurat, kafr al-rajallat, fol. 3.

61 DMU, Daftar al-athurat, kafr al-rajallat, fol. 1; also see Cuno, *The Pasha's Peasants*, 83–84.

62 For a complete copy of the 1847 land law, see DWQ, Daftar nizam umur ziraʿiyya, no. 5004, fols. 38–43. The text of this law can also be found in Al-Hitta, *Tarikh al-ziraʿa*, 359–63. Because the latter copy contains some misprints, as will be shown below, all references will be to the copy found in the Egyptian archives.

63 Cuno, *The Pasha's Peasants*, 191.

64 DWQ, MS, S/1/8/45, fol. 84 (no. 864) 9 Dhu al-Qaʿda 1272.

65 Al-Hitta's copy of the law states the opposite: that claimants had to support their request for their land with the relevant documents. See Al-Hitta, *Tarikh al-zira'a*, 359. Cuno was misled by Al-Hitta on this point. See Cuno, *The Pasha's Peasants*, 191, 252 (no. 56).

66 1847 Land Law, Article I.

67 For the government's use of this strategy in the past, see Cuno, *The Pasha's Peasants*, 103, 108, 110.

68 For a complete copy of the 1855 land law, see DWQ, Daftar nizam umur zira'iyya, no. 5004, fols. 38–45, 47–48. (All references concerning this law are to this copy.)

69 Regarding the second condition (verification of claims by the presentation of the proper documents), I point out that the 1847 law required peasant holders to document their land transfers on official paper, as will be shown below, with the aim of expanding the state's supervision of village land-tenure relations and ultimately ensuring that order and stability pervaded these relations. I believe that the inclusion of this condition in 1855 reflects this same aim; and so its inclusion should not be viewed as an attempt to disqualify and restrict claims to land.

70 1855 Land Law, Article I.

71 1855 Land Law, Article I.

72 DMU, Daftar al-athurat, jazirat al-a'jam, 1274, 1/1/20, fol. 17. Conversely without such evidence, the suit would not be heard; see for example, DMU, Daftar al-athurat, jazirat al-a'jam, fol. 4.

73 DWQ, MS, S/1/8/45, fol. 84 (no. 864) 9 Dhu al-Qa'da 1272.

74 For examples of recovery of pawned land that had occurred after *more* than fifteen years had elapsed, see DMU, Daftar al-athurat, jazirat al-a'jam, fol. 18.

75 1847 Land Law, Article II.

76 DWQ, MA, S/7/16/11, fol. 85 (no. 55) I Rabi II 1271.

77 1847 Land Law, Article II.

78 That wealthy villagers were known to do this prior to the implementation of the 1847 land law makes this a viable assumption. In Kafr al-Rajallat, for example, village notables Ibrahim and Ahmad al-Dib gave to Husayn al-Bayumi a small land plot (1 *faddan*, 2 *sahms*) in 1260/1844, and another (11 *sahms*) in 1263/1847. They declared that they had voluntarily given him (by *ramya* assignment) these land plots because "he was landless." See DMU, Daftar al-athurat, kafr al-rajallat, fol. 19.

79 1847 Land Law, Article II. For discussions on the tendency of village headmen to increase their wealth at the expense of powerless peasants, see Barakat, *Tatawwur al-milkiyya*, 231–60; Shalabi, *Al-Rif al-misri*, 156–69; Baer, *Studies in the Social History*, 48–49.

80 Hillal, *Al-Fallah wa al-sulta*, 164, 172.

81 1855 Land Law, Article II.

82 1847 Land Law, Article III.

83 1847 Land Law, Article IV.

84 1847 Land Law, Articles III and IV.

85 See chapter 4 below.

86 Cuno, *The Pasha's Peasants*, 19, 148. In her examination of the landholding patterns in the early Islamic period, Sijpesteijn does not mention the term *ramya*, but does describe one of the contexts for *ramya* distribution; see Sijpesteijn, "Landholding Patterns," 124, 126.

87 1855 Land Law, Articles III and IV.

88 This is specifically stated for the cases where claimants presented their suits after fifteen years had elapsed. (See 1855 Land Law, Articles III and IV). Although not explicitly specified for the cases where the reassigned land had been made part of another village's area, my reading of the archival sources leads me to believe that state officials also compensated these petitioners with subsistence plots.

89 Cuno preferred to translate the term *damin* as "surety fee," or the payment of a sum of money; see *The Pasha's Peasants*, 192–93. However, the archival sources suggest that what was meant was not the payment of a surety fee, but that an individual would stand as "guarantor" for the payment of the required taxes. For example, see: DWQ, DKH, S/2/8/16, fol. 51 (no. 48) 26 Muharram 1266; DWQ, DKH, S/2/8/16, fol. 67 (no. 63) 17 Safar 1266; DWQ, DD, L/19/15/5, fol. 82 (no. 311) 29 Muharram 1276; DWQ, DD, L/19/15/5, fol. 82 (no. 315) 29 Muharram 1276; DWQ, DD, L/19/15/5, L/19/15/6, fol. 40 (no. 34) 26 Safar 1276; DWQ, DD, L/19/15/5, fol. 147 (no. 91) 14 Rabi II 1276.

90 1855 Land Law, Article VIII. This land law did not only address the inheritance of peasant land, it also addressed the inheritance of *usya* land (see 1855 Land Law, Article VII), specifying that heirs of *usya* holders would henceforth be permitted to inherit these lands. Such land originally belonged to a *multazim* (tax farmer) in compensation for tax-collection and remittance services. Upon the abolition of the *iltizam* system in 1814, some *multazim*s were permitted to retain their *usya*s, as usufruct holdings, on a tax-free basis. Holders could dispose of this land as they wished, meaning they could farm it directly, rent it out, convert it into a *waqf*, and pass it on to heirs at the time of death. They had to accept one restriction, though, and this pertained to its sale, which had to be to the state. Thus, the 1855 land law was not granting *usya* holders a new right. (See Barakat, *Tatawwur al-milkiyya*, 25; Cuno, *The Pasha's Peasants*, 238, no. 15.) Instead, the change introduced by this law lies in the stipulation that the new holders (the heirs) of *usya* lands were henceforth to pay the same taxes borne by peasant lands, thus denying heirs the right to retain these lands on a tax-free basis as their predecessors had done.

91 See the "inheritance" section of an *athurat* register for evidence of these phenomena: inheritance was a customary practice; women were generally bypassed in the inheritance of land; however, there were circumstances in which women did inherit. For example, see DMU, Daftar al-athurat, kafr al-rajallat, fols. 22–23. Also see: Cuno, *The Pasha's Peasants*, 192–93; Tucker, *Women in Nineteenth-Century Egypt*, 43–52.

92 1847 Land Law, Article VI. According to Cuno, this article really "repeated an order issued two years earlier, requiring all land transactions to be

recorded on officially stamped paper, in order to be accepted as valid." He bases this view on a state decree issued on August 29, 1845. (See Cuno, *The Pasha's Peasants*, 191–92, 202, 252 (no. 57); Sami, *Taqwim al-Nil*, 534.) But I believe that the 1845 decree intended to target property (or *milk*) transactions; for if it had intended to include transactions in *miri* land, which was not property but was held on a usufructuary basis, it would have specifically mentioned *miri* land.

93 1855 Land Law, Article VI. The stipulation regarding the supervision of transactions by a recognized court targeted cessions only. On the other hand, Cuno states this stipulation pertained to all land transactions. See his *The Pasha's Peasants*, 202.

94 Cuno, *The Pasha's Peasants*, 193.

95 For the original copy of the 1858 Land Law (also known as Said's Law) see DWQ, MA, Mahafiz, Awamir no. 1 (no. 145) 24 Dhu al-Hijja 1274. For a published copy, see Hunayn, *Al-Atyan wa al-dara'ib*, 388–412. There are no discrepancies between these two copies.

96 However it was not to be applied retroactively. Thus all decisions issued prior to the promulgation of the 1858 law were to remain binding. See 1858 Land Law, Article VI.

97 Cuno, *The Pasha's Peasants*, 193. Also see: Jorgens, "A Comparative Examination," 94. In a similar vein, Aytekin reminds us of the place of the 1858 Ottoman Land Code in Ottoman land legislation; he states: "It was the first modern, comprehensive, and universally applicable land law enacted in the Ottoman Empire. It consisted of 132 articles in three sections and, in confirmation of its intended status as the sole source of land law in the Ottoman Empire, declared null and void all provisions of previous laws, regulations, decrees and legal opinions that conflicted with its provisions." See Aytekin, "Agrarian Relations, Property and Law," 935.

98 This view is elaborated by Gatteschi: "The order of the Viceroy of 1274 [Sa'id's Land Law] applied the imperial law of 1858 [to the conditions of Egypt]. . . . It was impossible to accept simply the laws of Constantinople for Egypt, where there did not exist a system parallel to that of Turkey. . . . It was therefore necessary to make special arrangements, which in taking into account these differences, would carry out in Egypt the broad and liberal reforms of the imperial laws." Cited in Baer, *Studies in the Social History*, 67. (The phrases in brackets are Baer's.)

99 Baer, *Studies in the Social History*, 66–71.

100 Jorgens, "A Comparative Examination" (for quoted phrases, 94, 111).

101 Cuno, *The Pasha's Peasants*, 189–97 (for quoted phrase, 197).

102 E. Attila Aytekin, who presents a more recent examination of the 1858 Ottoman Land Code, challenges the "state-centered approach" to the code developed by Islamolgu and others. Instead, he attributes the issuance of the 1858 Code to "the particular combination of the uneven development of the capitalist relations of production, various forms of agrarian conflict, and the complex matrix of the interests of ruling groups." See Aytekin, "Agrarian

Relations, Property and Law" (for quoted phrase, 936). (I do not address his argument, as my discussion of Egypt's 1858 Land Law largely subscribes to the "statist approach.")

103 Islamoğlu, "Property as a Contested Domain," 26; also see her "Politics of Administering Property," 279–80.

104 Jorgens makes a similar observation in regard to the 1858 Ottoman Code, but does not provide elaboration. See her "A Comparative Examination," 95.

105 I take this term (priority right) from Cuno; see his *The Pasha's Peasants*, 196.

106 1858 Land Law, Article I.

107 1858 Land Law, Article II.

108 Cuno, "Joint Family Households," 496. According to Cuno, the rural notables were dissatisfied with Article II of the 1858 law. Thus, they introduced the 1869 law, which, in effect, resulted in the imposition of "a regime of impartible inheritance in *miri* land" (for quoted phrase, 496).

109 See the inheritance section of this register: DMU, Daftar al-athurat, kafr al-rajallat, fols. 22–33.

110 1858 Land Law, Article II.

111 1858 Land Law, Articles VIII, IX, X.

112 Cuno, *The Pasha's Peasants*, 140–41, 147–48, 155–56.

113 This point will be discussed in greater detail in chapter 4.

114 1858 Land Law, Article III. (This fee constituted a tax for the issuance of the officially stamped paper on which the land transfer was to be recorded; see Article III.)

115 1858 Land Law, Article VII.

116 1858 Land Law, Article VIII.

117 1858 Land Law, Article XIX.

118 Artin, *Al-Ahkam al-mar'iyya*, 175; Hunayn, *Al-Atyan wa al-dara'ib*, 213, 405. (For a more detailed discussion of this phenomenon, see chapter 4.)

119 DWQ, DD, L/19/21/7, fol. 14 (no. 190) 15 Dhu al-Hijja 1274; DWQ, DD, L/19/21/3, fol. 146 (no. 40) 24 Rabi I 1274.

120 1858 Land Law, Article XXII.

121 DWQ, DD, L/19/21/3, fol. 91 (no. 27) 11 Rabi I 1274.

122 1858 Land Law, Article XXI. In the late 1850s, most of these land assignments came from *matruk* lands; for this, see: DWQ, DD, L/19/21/3, fol. 146 (no. 40) 24 Rabi I 1274.

123 DWQ, MA, S/7/16/7, fol. 37 (no. 61) 30 Rabi I 1270; DWQ, MA, S/7/16/6, fol. 71 (no. 273) 24 Muharram 1270. For another case see: DWQ, DD, L/19/21/5, fol. 91 (no. 202) 1 Sha'ban 1274.

124 DWQ, DD, L/19/21/3, fols. 130, 137 (no. 37) 19 Rabi I 1274.

125 For how the authorities in Ottoman Egypt addressed the problems pertaining to the erosion of land and the creation of new land that emerged due to the silting of the Nile, see Mikhail, *Nature and Empire*, 56–58. In discussing this phenomenon, Mikhail describes it as "one of the most common forms of environmental change in rural Egypt." (See his *Nature and Empire*, 56.) Mikhail highlights the authorities' reliance on "precedent and past

experience" to address the pertinent disputes, which aligns with my findings for mid-nineteenth-century Egypt. (For quoted phrase: *Nature and Empire*, 58.)

126 1858 Land Law, Articles XVI and XXIII.

127 DWQ, MA, S/7/16/7, fols. 1, 3 (no. 77) 2 Jumada I 1270.

128 Baer, *A History of Landownership*, 9.

129 DWQ, MS, S/1/8/41, fol. 209 (no. 30) 19 Rabi II 1272.

130 DWQ, DD, L/19/21/1, fol. 119 (no. 23) 7 Dhu al-Qaʿda 1273.

131 DWQ, MS, S/1/8/46, fol. 35 (no. 196) 24 Dhu al-Qaʿda 1272.

132 1858 Land Law, Articles X, XI, XVI.

133 See, for example: DWQ, MKH, Daʿawi wa ashhadat, no. 1, fols. 45–46 (no. 122) 15 Shawwal 1272.

134 1858 Land Law, Article V.

135 1858 Land Law, Articles XXIV and XXV.

136 1858 Land Law, Article XII. According to this article, peasants were to be granted property rights only if these activities had taken place after the introduction of the 1858 law. The *athurat* records suggest that if these activities occurred before the law, holders could only expect to be protected from competing claims to the land.

137 Artin, *Al-Ahkam al-mar'iyya*, 178.

138 DWQ, MS, S/1/8/16, fols. 99, 125 (no. 19) 26 Muharram 1268; also see DWQ, MA, S/7/16/7, fols. 1, 3 (no. 77) 2 Rabi I 1270.

139 The government addressed this request in the Memorandum of July 1856. See: DWQ, MS, S/1/8/45, fol. 84 (no. 846) 9 Dhu al-Qaʿda 1272.

140 DWQ, MS, S/1/8/45, fol. 84 (no. 846) 9 Dhu al-Qaʿda 1272. (Regarding point 2, the wording of this entry is actually vague: it merely states that governors were to deal with such lands according to a previous decree. Other entries suggest this involved the placement of these lands in auction; for this, see: DWQ, MS, S/1/8/42, fols. 524, 528 [no. 70] 26 Jumada II 1272.)

141 DWQ, DD, L/19/21/5, fol. 167 (no. 112) 28 Shaʿban 1274.

142 DWQ, MS, S/1/21/52, fol. 97 (no. 70) 20 Muharram 1278.

143 DWQ, DD, L/19/21/5, fol. 15 (no. 112) 14 Rajab 1274; DWQ, DD, l/19/21/6, fol. 147 (no. 249) 23 Dhu al-Qaʿda 1274; DWQ, MS, S/1/8/44, fols. 145, 155 (no. 350) 27 Ramadan 1272.

144 DWQ, DD, L/19/21/6, fol. 147 (no. 249) 23 Dhu al-Qaʿda 1274.

145 DWQ, DD, L/19/21/6, fol. 38 (no. 305) 2 Dhu al-Qaʿda 1274.

146 DWQ, DD, L/19/21/3, fol. 90 (no. 37) 5 Rabi I 1274; DWQ, DD, L/19/21/4, fol. 20 (no. 75) 25 Rabi II 1274; DWQ, DD, L/19/21/5, fol. 63 (no. 149) 19 Rajab 1274; DWQ, DD, L/19/21/6, fol. 1 (no. 122) 4 Shawwal 1274.

147 DWQ, DD, L/19/21/5, fol. 22 (no. 75) 7 Rajab 1274.

148 DWQ, MA, S/7/16/11, fol. 60 (no. 85) 18 Safar 1271; DWQ, MA, S/7/6/2, fol. 42 (no. 64) 24 Rabi II 1269; DWQ, DD, l/19/21/3, fol. 5 (no. 42) 28 Muharram 1274; DWQ, DD, L/19/21/5, fol. 194 (no. 127) 29 Ramadan 1274.

149 1858 Land Law, Articles XIII, XIV, XV.

150 DWQ, DD, L/19/21/1, fols. 1, 7 (no. 2) 19 Rajab 1273; also see DWQ, MA, Mahafiz, 7, (no. 80/99) 3 Dhu al-Qaʿda 1273.

151 The pre-1858 rules were specified in the June 1856 Decree, the July 1856 Memorandum and the decree of 16 July 1857. For June 1856 Decree: Hunayn, *Al-Atyan wa al-dara'ib*, 196–97; for July 1856 Memorandum: DWQ, MS, S/1/8/45, fol. 84 (no. 864) 9 Dhu al-Qaʿda 1272 (see point V). For the decree of 16 July 1857, see DWQ, MA, Mahafiz, Box no. 7, document no. 80/99, 3 Dhu al-Hijja 1273.
152 1858 Land Law, Article XXVI.
153 *Khirs* land: this is land on which esparto grass grows; cultivation cannot be undertaken until the land is cleared.
154 DWQ, MS, S/1/21/56, fols. 140, 153 (no. 88) 21 Ramadan 1278.
155 DWQ, DD, L/19/21/3, fols. 130, 138 (no. 37) 19 Rabi I 1274.
156 1858 Land Law, Article XV.
157 DWQ, DD, L/19/21/3, fol. 83 (no. 12) 8 Rabi I 1274; DWQ, DD, L/19/21/5, fol. 124 (no. 126) 11 Shaʿban 1274; DWQ, DD, L/19/21/5, fol. 135 (no. 189) 17 Shaʿban 1274. These same entries also reveal that the provincial authorities were uncertain about the scope of the 1857 decree, and they asked the center to clarify whether its instructions were to include *ushuriyya* lands (commonly held by the state elite) and personal property (like houses).
158 DWQ, MA, S/7/16/9, fol. 76 (no. 340) 20 Shawwal 1270; for another case: DWQ, MA, S/7/16/7, fols. 1, 3 (no. 77) 2 Rabi I 1270.
159 1858 Land Law, Articles VIII, IX, X, XI.
160 For a more detailed discussion, see ch. 4.
161 Foucault, "Governmentality," 87–104.
162 Islamoğlu, "Politics of Administering Property," 287–88; "Property as a Contested Domain," 21–22.

Chapter 2

1 Toledano, *State and Society*, 130.
2 Toledano, *State and Society*, 108.
3 Cited in Toledano, *State and Society*, 113.
4 Toledano, *State and Society*.
5 U.S., Department of State, De Leon to Marcy, vol. II, Oct. 19, 1854, p. 75.
6 For example, see: Richards, *Egypt's Agricultural Development*, 37; Richards, "Primitive Accumulation in Egypt," 233; Baer, *A History of Landownership*, 30; Rivlin, *The Agricultural Policy*, 119.
7 Levi, "The Predatory Theory of Rule," 438. For more detailed elaboration of these ideas, see her *Of Rule and Revenue*.
8 For the views of contemporary observers, see Toledano, *State and Society*, ch. 5. For an example of sweepingly negative comments about Abbas Pasha by scholars, see Baer, *A History of Landownership*, 7: "Agricultural developments ceased under Abbas I (1849–54), who opposed the modernization policy of his grandfather Muhammad Ali in every detail."
9 Cited in Toledano, *State and Society*, 43.
10 Toledano, *State and Society*, 132.
11 Toledano, *State and Society*.

12 For the start of the retrenchment process by Muhammad Ali, see Rivlin, *The Agricultural Policy*, 197–200, 253. For Abbas's retrenchment program, see Landes, *Bankers and Pashas*, 82. For reduction of the army (from 70,000 men in July 1848 to 20,000 men by May 1849), see Rivlin, *The Agricultural Policy*, 211.
13 Toledano, *State and Society*, 7; Rivlin, "The Railway Question."
14 PRO, FO 78/1401, Thompson to Malmesbury, April 6, 1852. On the other hand, Abbas's disinterest in seceding from the Ottoman Empire (viewed as a measure of his loyalty to the Porte) has also been documented. See: FO, 78/1401, Ross to Malmesbury, April 14, 1852: "Your Lordship will also be glad to learn that my relations with Abbas Pasha and the concurrent testimony of the Foreign Agents and other Parties here, convince me that the Viceroy has not an idea of raising the Standard of independence."
15 Hamza, *The Public Debt of Egypt*, 6.
16 Owen, *The Middle East in the World Economy*, 123; Hamza, *The Public Debt of Egypt*, 6. (For example, to pay for the construction of 131 miles of railway line between Alexandria and Cairo, he borrowed LE 400,000 from the Peninsular and Oriental Company.) For Abbas's interest in the revival of the monopoly system, also see chapter 1 above.
17 A "project" that may have contributed to Abbas's decision to raise land taxes was his interest in securing the throne of Egypt for his son: In May 1854, British Consul Bruce reported that Abbas Pasha "aims at changing in favor of his son the order of succession. He hopes that this change will be effected at his request by the Porte. . . . [Thus] the possession of wealth is necessary to him as a means of corrupting the sultan's advisors." See PRO, FO 78/1035, Bruce to Clarendon, May 30, 1854.
18 U.S., Department of State, De Leon to Marcy, no. 13, vol. 2, July 1854, pp. 68–69.
19 Landes, *Bankers and Pashas*, 83; Owen, *The Middle East in the World Economy*, 123; Hamza, *The Public Debt of Egypt*, 12.
20 Landes, *Bankers and Pashas*, 83, no. 4; 104, no. 2; Owen, *The Middle East in the World Economy*, 123; Hamza, *The Public Debt of Egypt*, 12.
21 Landes, *Bankers and Pashas*, 84; PRO, FO 78/1468, Colquhoun to Russell, Dec. 5, 1859.
22 PRO, FO 78/1156, Bruce to Clarendon, Dec. 3, 1854.
23 Mustafa, "The Breakdown of the Monopoly System," 306–307; Landes, *Bankers and Pashas*, 175; Holt, *Egypt and the Fertile Crescent*, 199.
24 Lawson, "Foreign Exploitation and Domestic Conflict," 61–70 (for quoted phrases, 62, 69).
25 On the other hand, Landes attributes Said's decision to accept the financial burden associated with the Suez Canal Company to de Lesseps's influence. Landes, *Bankers and Pashas*, 177. Also see Owen, *The Middle East in the World Economy*, 125.
26 Landes, *Bankers and Pashas*, 176–77 (for quoted phrase, 176).
27 Landes, *Bankers and Pashas*, 87.
28 PRO, FO 78/1401, Green to Malmesbury, March 29, 1858. Also see: PRO, FO 78/1401, Green to Malmesbury, May 11, 1858.
29 Abul-Magd, *Imagined Empires*, 97–101 (for quoted phrase, 98).

30 Abul-Magd, *Imagined Empires*, 100.
31 PRO, FO 78/1675, Colquhoun to Russell, June 9, 1862.
32 Said gave serious thought to the idea of declaring Egypt's independence from the Ottoman Empire, and he calculated that the success of this action would depend on European support, particularly that of France. See, for example: PRO, FO 195/618, Cowley to Malmesbury, June 17, 1859; PRO, FO 78/1467, Walne to Malmesbury, May 16, 1859; PRO, FO 78/1467, Walne to Russell, July 10, 1859. In addition, he wished to change the rule of succession to the throne of Egypt from the Ottoman rule of primogeniture to the rules of monarchy, which would allow his young son to succeed him; this also would require European support. See, for example: PRO, FO 78/1675, Cohen for Colquhoun to Russell, May 10, 1862.
33 For example, see: PRO, FO 78/1401, Green to Clarendon, Feb. 23, 1858; PRO, FO 78/1468, Colquhoun to Russell, Nov. 17, 1859; PRO, FO 78/1468, Colquhoun to Russell, Dec. 5, 1859; PRO, FO 78/1616, Barker to Headlam, Nov. 16, 1861; PRO, FO 78/1675, Cohen (for Colquhoun) to Russell, April 25, 1862.
34 PRO, FO 78/1467, Green to Hammond, Feb. 11, 1859.
35 PRO, FO 78/1715, Bulwer to Russell, Dec. 15, 1862.
36 PRO, FO 78/1477, T. B. Collinson to J. Burgoyne Bart, Nov. 12, 1858. For Said's pride in his army, also see U.S., Department of State, Thayer to Seward, no. 11, vol. 3, Nov. 19, 1861, p. 72.
37 PRO, FO 78/1467, Walne to Malmesbury, May 16, 1859.
38 PRO, FO 78/1467, Walne to Malmesbury, May 18, 1859.
39 PRO, FO 78/1467, Walne to Russell, July 26, 1859.
40 PRO, FO 78/1477, T.B. Collinson to J. Burgoyne Bart, Nov. 12 1858.
41 For the first opinion, see PRO, FO 78/1467, Walne to Russell, July 26, 1859; for the second opinion, see, for example: PRO, FO 195/618, Cowley to Malmesbury, June 17, 1859.
42 U.S., Department of State, Thayer to Seward, no. 26, vol. 3, Jan. 9, 1863, pp. 147–48; U.S., Department of State, Thayer to Seward, no. 27, vol. 3, Jan. 18, 1863, pp. 150–56.
43 PRO, FO 78/1156, Bruce to Clarendon, Dec. 3, 1854; also see PRO, FO 78/1156, de Redcliffe to Clarendon, Jan. 11, 1855.
44 Landes, *Bankers and Pashas*, 112–18.
45 For example, see: PRO, FO 78/1401, Green to Malmesbury, June 14, 1858.
46 Landes, *Bankers and Pashas*, 99; PRO, FO 78/1401, Green to Malmesbury, Nov. 19, 1858.
47 Landes, *Bankers and Pashas*, 106.
48 PRO, FO, 78/1468, Colquhoun to Russell, Oct. 6, 1859.
49 For the first foreign loan: Owen, *The Middle East in the World Economy*, 125; for the reissuance of treasury bonds: Landes, *Bankers and Pashas*, 106; for Minié rifles: U.S., Department of State, Thayer to Seward, no. 11, vol. 3, Nov. 19, 1861, p. 72.
50 Owen, *The Middle East in the World Economy*, 125; Marlowe, *Spoiling the Egyptians*, 96.

51 Lewis, "Ottoman Land Tenure," 120; Hancock, *Taxation*, 1–3.
52 Issawi, *The Economic History of the Middle East*, 72, 107.
53 Shaw, "The Nineteenth-Century Ottoman," 422. Also see Islamoğlu, "Politics of Administering Property," 302.
54 Hancock, *Taxation*, 3.
55 DWQ, MA, S/7/16/6, fol. 98 (no. 61) 5 Rabi I 1270; DWQ, MA, S/7/16/6, fol. 89 (no. 51) 19 Safar 1270; DWQ, MA, S/7/16/7, fol. 65 (no. 100) 25 Rabi II 1270; DWQ, MA, S/7/16/8, fol. 8 (no. 129) 19 Jumada II 1270.
56 DWQ, MS, S/1/8/42, fol. 413 (no. 65) 26 Jumada I 1272. Also see Daftar takmil al-dara'ib, rawdat al-bahrayn, 1271, 2209/109/22, introduction (Part I). (This *daftar*, or register, examines the two phases of the 1855 tax project. The problem is that the pagination of this register is not in consecutive order; for the second part of the register, which documents the second phase of the 1855 tax project, also starts with page 1. Thus, I distinguish between the two phases of the project by simply including an additional reference indicator—Part I or Part II in parentheses.)
57 DWQ, MS, S/1/8/42, fol. 413 (no. 65) 26 Jumada I 1272.
58 For a clear explanation of the revaluation guidelines, see DWQ, MS, S/1/8/42, fol. 413 (no. 65) 26 Jumada I 1272. Less clear explanations can be found in DMU, Daftar takmil al-dara'ib, rawdat al-bahrayn, 1271, fols: introductory page, 52 (Part I).
59 The unit of account of the Egyptian currency was the piaster, which was subdivided into 40 paras. For a discussion on Egyptian currency during the eighteenth and nineteenth centuries, see Issawi, *The Economic History of the Middle East*, 522–24.
60 DMU, Daftar takmil al-dara'ib, rawdat al-bahrayn, 1271, fol. 21 (Part I); DMU, Mukallafat atyan, al-jazira al-khadra, 1270, 3982/135/22.
61 DMU, Daftar takmil al-dara'ib, rawdat al-bahrayn, 1271, fol. 21 (Part I); DMU, Mukallafat atyan, al-jazira al-khadra, 1270, 3982/135/22.
62 DWQ, MS, S/1/8/42, fol. 413 (no. 65) 26 Jumada I 1272.
63 DMU, Daftar takmil al-dara'ib, rawdat al-bahrayn, 1271, fol. 5 (Part I).
64 DMU, Daftar takmil al-dara'ib, rawdat al-bahrayn, 1271, fol. 28 (Part I); DMU, Mukallafat atyan, kafr al-jarayda, 1270, 17002/305/22.
65 For example, see DMU, Daftar takmil al-dara'ib, rawdat al-bahrayn, 1271, fols. 1–4 (Part I).
66 For the monetary value of the jadid, see Hunayn, *Al-Atyan wa al-dara'ib*, 100.
67 Owen, *The Middle East in the World Economy*, 122–24; Hobsbawm, *The Age of Capital*, 125.
68 DMU, Daftar takmil al-dara'ib, rawdat al-bahrayn, 1271, fols. 51–52 (Part I) (for quoted phrase, fol. 51).
69 A few village *ib'adiyya*s were beyond the scope of this tax project because their holders had not obtained them under the favorable tax conditions specified by Muhammad Ali, but by auction. Thus these holders were to continue paying taxes at the rates specified by the auction. That these were much higher than the taxes of the nearby *ma'mur* land explains why the

government excluded them from this round of tax adjustment. For example, this was the case with a tract of *ib'adiyya* land consisting of 30 *faddans* in Birq al-Hajjar Village taxed at 70 piastres per *faddan*, while the cultivated *ma'mur* land (consisting of 342 *faddans*) was taxed at 27 piastres per *faddan*. DMU, Daftar takmil al-dara'ib, rawdat al-bahrayn, 1271, fol. 30 (Part I). For another example see fol. 40 of the same register.

70 For the shorthand term, see, for example: DMU, Daftar takmil al-dara'ib, rawdat al-bahrayn, 1271, fol. 52 (Part I).

71 DMU, Daftar takmil al-dara'ib, rawdat al-bahrayn, 1274, 2210/109/22, fol. 69.

72 For the entire estate of Jiflik Sabat, see DMU, Daftar takmil al-dara'ib, rawdat al-bahrayn, 1271, fols. 50–51 (Part I); for Dimira Village, see fol. 51 of the same register.

73 Here we recall that the *kharaji* lands of Jiflik Sabat that were marked for tax increase were not solely composed of *ib'adiyya* land.

74 One purse was worth 500 piastres. See Issawi, *The Economic History of the Middle East*, 523.

75 DMU, Daftar takmil al-dara'ib, rawdat al-bahrayn, 1271, fols.: introductory page; 51–52 (Part I); DWQ, MS, S/1/8/41, fols. 242, 244 (no. 89) 14 Rabi II 1272. The tax-reassessment register specifies that another 16 purses, 342 piastres, 35 para were to be temporarily remitted because two villages had not submitted their tax registers to the provincial authorities. It seems that this tax remission was to be revoked upon the submission of the tax registers. See DMU, Daftar takmil al-dara'ib, rawdat al-bahrayn, 1271, fol.: introductory page (Part I).

76 DMU, Daftar takmil al-dara'ib, rawdat al-bahrayn, 1271, fols.: introductory page, 51–52 (Part I); DWQ, MS, S/1/8/41, fols. 242, 244 (no. 89) 14 Rabi II 1272.

77 DMU, Daftar takmil al-dara'ib, rawdat al-bahrayn, 1271, 2209/109/22, fol. 48 (Part II).

78 DMU, Daftar takmil al-dara'ib, rawdat al-bahrayn, 1271, fol. 48 (Part II).

79 DMU, Daftar takmil al-dara'ib, rawdat al-bahrayn, 1271, fol. 48 (Part II).

80 As some of the entries were somewhat unclear and others seemed incomplete (this pertained to 21 percent of Gharbiyyia Province's *kharaji* land), I excluded them from my sample.

81 These *faddans* were part of Dimira Village's *ma'mur* land. This is the same village whose *ma'mur* land experienced a tax increase during the first stage of the 1855 land-tax project. Here we might recall that this was the only instance of a tax increase being imposed on *ma'mur* land in this province. Perhaps this village attracted so much official attention because it was part of the *jiflik* estate of the viceroy's son, and the 64 percent decrease was meant to cancel the effect of the earlier tax increase. See DMU, Daftar takmil al-dara'ib, rawdat al-bahrayn, 1271, fol. 51 (Part I); DMU, Daftar takmil al-dara'ib, rawdat al-bahrayn, 1271, fol. 47 (Part II).

82 I thank Professor Nicholas Hopkins for bringing this factor to my attention.

83 Rivlin, *The Agricultural Policy*, 126.

84 There were a few *ib'adiyya*s that did not undergo both reassessment processes: in some cases, phase II of the 1855 tax project maintained the same rate specified by phase I; and in others, the results of phase I were corrected in phase II, which specified a lower tax rate than had phase I. See DMU, Daftar takmil al-dara'ib, rawdat al-bahrayn, 1271, fols. 19–21, 50 (Part I); DMU, Daftar takmil al-dara'ib, rawdat al-bahrayn, 1271, fols. 36–38, 47 (Part II).

85 DMU, Daftar takmil al-dara'ib, rawdat al-bahrayn, 1271, fol. 52 (Part I). For the tract situated in Sirbay, see fol. 30 of this register; and for the tract in Kitama, see fol. 32 of this register.

86 DMU, Daftar takmil al-dara'ib, rawdat al-bahrayn, 1271, fol. 47 (Part II).

87 DMU, Daftar takmil al-dara'ib, rawdat al-bahrayn, 1271, fol. 48 (Part II).

88 DMU, Daftar takmil al-dara'ib, rawdat al-bahrayn, 1271, fols. 51–52 (Part I); DMU, Daftar takmil al-dara'ib, rawdat al-bahrayn, 1271, fols. 47–48 (Part II).

89 DMU, Daftar takmil al-dara'ib, rawdat al-bahrayn, 1271, fols. 51–52 (Part I); DMU, Daftar takmil al-dara'ib, rawdat al-bahrayn, 1271, fols. 47–48 (Part II).

90 DMU, Daftar takmil al-dara'ib, rawdat al-bahrayn, 1271, fols. 9–10 (Part I); DMU, Daftar takmil al-dara'ib, rawdat al-bahrayn, 1271, fol. 5 (Part II).

91 Hunayn, *Al-Atyan wa al-dara'ib*, 212–13.

92 For Sandbast Village, see DMU, Mukallafat atyan, sandbast, 1270, 12164/242/22. For another example of a village that bore a similarly high *suds* tax, see Abnahas Village: DMU, Mukallafat atyan, abnahas, 1270, 1847/190/25. On the other hand, the *suds* rate for al-Jazira al-Khadra Village is not specified by its land-tax register; I arrived at this figure (14 percent) by comparing between the 1270 (1853–1854) land-tax register for this village and the tax-reassessment register for Gharbiyya Province. See DMU, Mukallafat atyan, al-jazira al-khadra, 1270, 3982/135/22; DMU, Daftar takmil al-dara'ib, rawdat al-bahrayn, 1271, fol. 37 (Part II).

93 For example, see: DMU, Mukallafat atyan, shubra bakhum, 1270, 14227/15/27; DMU, Mukallafat atyan, sandbast, 1270, 12164/242/22; DMU, Mukallafat atyan, abnahas, 1270, 1847/190/25.

94 DMU, Daftar takmil al-dara'ib, rawdat al-bahrayn, 1271 (Parts I & II).

95 Merruau, *L'Egypte contemporaine*, 60–65; PRO, FO, 78/1660, Bulwer to Russell, November 25, 1862.

96 Upon Said's death in January 1863, the American consul-general listed the pasha's achievements, which included his agrarian reforms. The following observation most likely referred to the surcharge taxes: "Heavy taxes have been removed at the sacrifice of a large part of the Viceroy's revenue." U.S., Department of State, Thayer to W. H. Seward, no. 28, vol. 3, January 27, 1863, p. 159. However all these surcharge taxes had been reinstated by 1861(which will be shown below) and were certainly operative at the time of the pasha's death. Thus, it seems that Thayer's information was not always up-to-date.

97 DMU, Daftar takmil al-dara'ib, rawdat al-bahrayn, 1271, fol. 48 (Part II).

98 DWQ, MS, S/1/8/46, fol. 52 (no. 206) 2 Dhu al-Hijja 1272.

99 Artin, *Al-Ahkam al-mar'iyya*, 80, 82.

100 Cuno, *The Pasha's Peasants*, 171.
101 (The specified numbers were rounded in order to include *faddan* fractions.) DMU, Mukallafat atyan, al-jazira al-khadra, 1264, 3976/135/22, fol. 7. For other examples, see DMU, Mukallafaat atyan, ibyar, 1266, 2913/121/22; Mukallafat atyan, al-jazira al-khadra, 1266, 3978/135/22; Mukallafat atyan, kafr al-rajallat, 1266, 8203/110/20; Mukallafat atyan, jazirat al-aʿjam, 1266, 4571/61/20.
102 Ibyar Village, a large and prominent village in Gharbiyya Province, contained *masmuh al-mashayikh* but did not have *masmuh al-mastatib* lands. See, for example, DMU, Mukallafat atyan, ibyar, 1266, 2913/121/22; DMU, Mukallafat atyan, ibyar, 1270, 2917/121/22.
103 Cuno, *The Pasha's Peasants*, 172.
104 DWQ, MS, S/1/8/46, fol. 44 (no. 118) 4 Dhu al-Hijja 1272; DWQ, MS, S/1/8/46, fol. 57 (no. 59) 4 Dhu al-Hijja 1272; DWQ, MS, S/1/8/46, fol. 95 (no. 127) 29 Dhu al-Hijja 1272.
105 DWQ, MS, S/1/8/46, fol. 95 (no. 127) 29 Dhu al-Hijja 1272.
106 DWQ, MS, S/1/8/46, fol. 95 (no. 127) 29 Dhu al-Hijja 1272.
107 For the second factor, see Abul-Magd, *Imagined Empires*.
108 Baer, History of Landownership, 52; Hunayn, Al-Atyan wa al-dara'ib, 196; Barakat, Al-Qarya wa al-sulta, 24.
109 Barakat, *Tatawwur al-milkiyya*, 235–36.
110 Owen, *The Middle East in the World Economy*, 101.
111 PRO, FO, 78/1222, Bruce to Clarendon, September 18, 1856.
112 PRO, FO, 78/1313, Bruce to Clarendon, February 3, 1857.
113 DMU, Daftar takmil al-dara'ib, rawdat al-bahrayn, 1274, 2210/109/22, fol. 69.
114 DMU, Daftar takmil al-dara'ib, rawdat al-bahrayn, 1274, fol. 69.
115 The new governor submitted a report to the Viceregal Cabinet (dated March 24, 1858), wherein he stated that he had the opportunity to assess his predecessor's work while passing through some villages. He believed this work was appropriate, and so advised the introduction of the new land-tax code. (DMU, Daftar takmil al-dara'ib, rawdat al-bahrayn, 1274, fol. 69.)
116 DMU, Daftar takmil al-dara'ib, rawdat al-bahrayn, 1274, fol. 68.
117 DMU, Daftar takmil al-dara'ib, rawdat al-bahrayn, 1274, fol. 69.
118 DMU, Daftar takmil al-dara'ib, rawdat al-bahrayn, 1274, fol. 69.
119 The 1858 land-tax code largely focused on revising land taxes, while monetary reassessment, or specifically the "*takmil kusur al-para*," received minimal focus, probably because most of the necessary work had been completed earlier, as part of the 1855 land-tax code. Thus, only 5 percent of the peasant villages of Rawdat al-Bahrayn underwent monetary reassessment during this round of tax revaluation; and so the increase in a village's total tax sum can be largely attributed to increases in its land taxes. See DMU, Daftar takmil al-dara'ib, rawdat al-bahrayn, 1274, 2210/109/22.
120 For the 1855 tax rates, see DMU, Daftar takmil al-dara'ib, rawdat al-bahrayn, 1271, fol. 2 (Part II). For the 1858 rate see DMU, Daftar takmil al-dara'ib, rawdat al-bahrayn, 1274, fol. 31.
121 Artin, *Al-Ahkam al-mar'iyya*, 83; Hunayn, *Al-Atyan wa al-dara'ib*, 213.

122 Owen, *The Middle East in the World Economy*, 125–26.
123 Hamza, *The Public Debt of Egypt*, 54.
124 While Abbas Pasha did not increase the tax rates imposed on the village lands, it seems he imposed surcharge taxes. Specifically, Hunayn specifies that he imposed the *suds* surcharge tax. See his *Al-Atyan wa al-dara'ib*, 212.
125 Braun, "Taxation, Sociopolitical Structure," 304.
126 Braun, "Taxation, Sociopolitical Structure," 284, 286, 287.
127 Rivlin, *The Agricultural Policy*, ch. 7.
128 Rivlin, *The Agricultural Policy*, 135.
129 Braun, "Taxation, Sociopolitical Structure," 303.
130 Shaw, "The Nineteenth-Century Ottoman," 421–22 (for quoted phrases, 421). For state taxation of the peasant household on the basis of its annual income, see Islamoğlu, "Politics of Administering Property," 297.
131 Shaw, "The Nineteenth-Century Ottoman," 422.
132 For the Ottoman government's concern to enhance the productive capacity of the land during this period, see Islamoğlu, "Politics of Administering Property," 299.
133 DMU, Mukallafat atyan, abnahas, 1272, 1849/190/25.
134 DMU, Mukallafat atyan, abnahas, 1261, 1842/190/25.
135 DMU, Mukallafat atyan, abnahas, 1270, 1847/190/25, fols. 2, 5.
136 DMU, Mukallafat atyan, abnahas, 1271, 1848/190/25.
137 Cuno, *The Pasha's Peasants*, 131–32, 133; PRO, FO, 78/1222, Bruce to Clarendon, May 2, 1856.
138 Cuno, *The Pasha's Peasants*, 130.
139 Artin, *Al-Ahkam al-mar'iyya*, 112.
140 DWQ, MS, S/1/21/55, fol. 162 (no. 110) 28 Rajab 1278; DWQ, S/1/21/58, fols. 108, 109 (no. 121) 6 Muharram 1279. Artin states that the decree that introduced the new tax regulations for date trees was issued in 1861; and further writes that the calculations were to take place in 1861 and 1862 (Artin, *Al-Ahkam al-mar'iyya*, 112). Yet, he is mistaken: He miscalculates the date of the decree: 8 Safar 1277 corresponds to August 25, 1860. Also the first archival entry specified here states that the calculations were to take place in 1862 and 1863. Finally, the second archival entry specified here indicates that the 1.5-year gap between the issuance of the decree and the start of the calculations was intentional, as this was when the provincial administration was to recruit the local officials who were to be charged with this task.
141 DWQ, MS, S/1/21/55, fol. 1 (no. 27) 15 Jumada I 1278.
142 Cuno, *The Pasha's Peasants*, 131–32.
143 DWQ, DKH, S/2/8/17, fol. 3 (no. 123) 4 Shawwal 1266; DWQ, DKH, S/2/8/17, fol. 9 (no. 416) 11 Shawwal 1266.
144 DWQ, DKH, S/2/8/16, fol. 60 (no. 46) 7 Safar 1266.
145 For this explanation, see: 1847 Land Law, Article V.
146 Shalabi, *Al-Rif al-misri*, 206.
147 Land Law of 1847, Article V.

148 Land Law of 1855, Article V. Artin mistakenly states that the 1855 land law stipulated the continued imposition of the *firdat* tax. See Artin, *Al-Ahkam al-mar'iyya*, 77–78.
149 DWQ, DKH, Mahafiz, awamir no. 1, "Layha bi bayan ma yu'khadh alayhi awa'id wa ma yu'fa minha min al-muntajat al-mukhtalifa" (no. 148) 5 Muharram 1275, fols. 1–17. (The Privy Council was the Diwan al-Khususi, and should not be confused with the Diwan al-Khidawi. This document was stored with those of the Diwan al-Khidawi, the Department of Civil Affairs.)
150 "Layha bi bayan," fols. 1–17.
151 "Layha bi bayan," fols. 2, 3.
152 "Layha bi bayan," fol. 9.
153 "Layha bi bayan," fols. 5, 11.
154 "Layha bi bayan," fol. 17.
155 "Layha bi bayan," fols. 2–3.
156 "Layha bi bayan," fols. 1–6.
157 "Layha bi bayan," fols. 4, 6–7, 15.
158 "Layha bi bayan," fol. 17.
159 DWQ, DKH, Mahafiz, awamir no. 1 (no. 106) 26 Dhu al-Hijja 1275.
160 Mikhail discerns these sentiments in his examination of peasants' work on village irrigation systems in eighteenth-century Egypt. See his *Nature and Empire*, ch. 4.
161 Tucker, *Women in Nineteenth-Century Egypt*, 41; Richards, "Primitive Accumulation in Egypt," 218; Owen, *The Middle East in the World Economy*, 143; Mikhail, *Nature and Empire*, 280–83.
162 DWQ, Daftar nizam umur zira'iyya, no. 5004, fol. 26.
163 DWQ, MA, S/7/16/1, fol. 34 (no. 18) 16 Safar 1268.
164 DWQ, MA, S/7/16/7, fols. 1, 3 (no. 77) 2 Rabi I 1270.
165 DWQ, DWQ, MA, S/7/16/10, fol. 10 (no. 65) 3 Jumada I 1270. (But the punishment was not carried out because of a general pardon.)
166 DWQ, DD, L/19/15/5, fol. 59 (no. 300) 22 Muharram 1276.
167 PRO, FO 78/1313, Bruce to Clarendon, April 29, 1857.
168 DWQ, DD, L/19/15/5, fol. 13 (no. 980) 3 Muharram 1276; DWQ, DD, L/19/15/5, fol. 63 (no. 1025), 23 Muharram 1276; DWQ, MA, S/7/16/11, fols. 63–64, 66–67 (no. 94) 23 Safar 1271.
169 DWQ, DD, L/19/15/5, fol. 63 (no. 1025) 23 Muharram 1276.
170 DWQ, Daftar nizam umur zira'iyya, fol. 37.
171 Corvée Code of 1851, Article I (in DWQ, Daftar nizam umur zira'iyya, fol. 36).
172 This code specifies the following members of the provincial administrative hierarchy: the village watchman (*ghafir*), the village headman (shaykh), the district head (*nazir al-qism*), the head of a subdistrict (*hakim al-khut*), the inspector of *uhda*s (*mufattish al-uhad*), and the administrator of a number of villages (*qa'im maqam*).
173 Corvée Code of 1851, Article II.
174 See Owen, *The Middle East in the World Economy*, 143; Tucker, *Women in Nineteenth-Century Egypt*, 41.

175 Corvée Code of 1851, preamble. While the preamble describes the practice of recruiting women as unacceptable, the stipulations of this code specifically refer to pregnant women and those who were breastfeeding infants, disallowing their recruitment. This suggests that able-bodied young women outside of these two categories could be recruited.
176 DWQ, Daftar nizam umur zira'iyya, fol. 37.
177 DWQ, Daftar nizam umur zira'iyya, fol. 37.
178 DWQ, DD, L/19/15/6, fol. 30 (no. 13) 24 Safar 1276. For the official tendency to exempt villages from corvée duty (pertaining to major public works sites) when they had experienced ruination, see DWQ, MA, S/7/16/1, fol. 42, 16 Muharram 1269.
179 DWQ, MA, S/7/16/6, fol. 57 (no. 53) 1 Safar 1270. For other examples, see: DWQ, MA, S/7/16/6, fol. 94 (no. 77) 10 Rabi I 1270; DWQ, MA, S/7/16/7, fol. 17 (no. 83) 15 Rabi I 1270; DWQ, MA, S/7/16/7, fol. 20 (no. 98) 19 Rabi I 1270; DWQ, MA, S/7/16/7, fol. 25 (no. 105) 23 Rabi I 1270.
180 For *jiflik* holders: DWQ, MS, S/1/8/20, fol. 614 (no. 143) 8 Sha'ban 1268. For foreign landholders: DWQ, MS, S/1/8/19, fol. 779 (no. 37) 13 Sha'ban 1268; DWQ, MS, S/1/8/20, fol. 776 (no. 303) 26 Ramadan 1268.
181 PRO, FO, 78/1035, Bruce to Clarendon, May 30, 1854.
182 Abbas and Dessouky, *The Large Landowning Class*, 108.
183 DWQ, MS, S/1/8/17, fol. 334 (no. 142) 10 Jumada I 1268. For other examples, see: DWQ, MS, S/1/8/18, fol. 466 (no. 202) 21 Jumada II 1268; DWQ, MS, S/1/8/18, fols. 411, 418 (no. 73) 3 Jumada II 1268; DWQ, MA, S/7/16/6, fols. 5, 12 (no. 7) 14 Jumada I 1269; DWQ, MA, S/7/16/6, fols. 76, 82 (no. 59) 8 Safar 1270. In Qina Province (in Upper Egypt) provincial officials were also known to recruit "cheap workers to provide private services to the European consuls and consular agents." See Abul-Magd, *Imagined Empires*, 98.
184 For example, see: DWQ, MA, S/7/16/9, fol. 26 (no. 495) 24 Ramadan 1270; DWQ, MA, S/7/16/1, fols. 6, 16 (no. 4) 27 Safar 1268; DWQ, DD, L/19/15/5, fol. 52 (no. 1013) 21 Muharram 1276. Also see: Barakat, *Al-Qarya wa al-sulta*, 108–10.
185 DWQ, MS, S/1/8/45, fol. 81 (no. 338) 8 Dhu al-Qa'da 1272; DWQ, MS, S/1/8/41, fol. 270 (no. 43) 20 Rabi II 1272.
186 During the early eighteenth century, it seems that the peasants could depend on some form of payment (wages, food provisions, shelter). And in one case documented by Mikhail, he notes that the pertinent corvée arrangements were "likely quite welcome by many peasants, as they could make a significant amount of money and receive extra foodstuffs for their families while not being separated from them for an extended period." Mikhail, *Nature and Empire*, 178–84 (for quoted phrase, 182).
187 Tucker, "Decline of the Family Economy," 252.
188 Viceregal Cabinet entry: DWQ, MS, S/1/8/20, fol. 766 (no. 303) 26 Ramadan 1268; Toledano, *State and Society*, 189.
189 PRO, FO 78/1313, Bruce to Clarendon, April 29, 1857. Abul-Magd cites a case where the governor of Qina Province (Upper Egypt) had sent four

laborers to a European consul, and then asked him to confirm that he would pay their wages. It seems, though, that the governor was not looking out for these laborers, but for himself; as he did not want them to "turn to him for payments." See: Abul Magd, *Imagined Empires*, 98.

190 DWQ, MS, S/1/8/45, fol. 81 (no. 338) 8 Dhu al-Qaʿda 1272; DWQ, MA, S/7/16/11, fols. 63–64, 66–67 (no. 94) 23 Safar 1271.

Chapter 3

1 Shaw, "The Nineteenth Century Ottoman," 422–23. For the state's reliance on tax farmers throughout the nineteenth century, see: Salzmann, "An Ancien Régime Revisited," 411, 421 (no. 98).

2 The *uhda* system, introduced by Muhammad Ali in the 1830s, was rooted in peasant insolvency. Thus, it cannot be considered a resurrection of the *iltizam* (tax-farm) system.

3 Baer, *Studies in the Social History*, 26.

4 For example, Baer cites John Bowring's observation that "A well-grounded cause of complaint . . . is the making a district responsible in mass for the amount of its taxes." See Baer, *Studies in the Social History*, 23.

5 Cuno, *The Pasha's Peasants*, 141.

6 Cuno, *The Pasha's Peasants.*

7 DWQ, MA, S/7/16/8, fol. 14 (no. 157) 5 Jumada II 1270.

8 DWQ, MS, S/1/8/42, fol. 414 (no. 72) 2 Jumada II 1272. (The summer crops that the report referred to may have included: green fava beans, *al-ra's* sugar cane, rape. See: Cooper, "The Assessment and Collection of Kharaj Tax," 376–77.) I also point out that the date on which this report was recorded in the state registers (Feb. 9, 1856) and the date of the report itself (Feb. 1, 1856) are not the same.

9 DWQ, MS, S/1/8/42, fol. 504 (no. 76) 20 Jumada II 1272.

10 DWQ, MS, S/1/8/18, fol. 516 (no. 99) 7 Rajab 1268. (The rubric "villages under the jurisdiction of the provincial government" referred to freeholder peasant villages, or villages where the cultivators answered to state and provincial authorities, and unlike *uhda* villages, were not managed by officially appointed caretakers, or *muta'ahhid*s.)

11 DWQ, MA, S/7/16/8, fol. 14 (no. 157) 5 Jumada II 1270.

12 The following, rather speculative, discussion is based on James C. Scott's ideas regarding peasants' fear of impoverishment and their subsistence options. See his *The Moral Economy of the Peasant*, 27, 40–44, 162.

13 Shalabi, *Al-Rif al-misri*, 160, 175–76; Cuno, *The Pasha's Peasants*, 5–6, 155–56.

14 Ghalwash, "Land Acquisition by the Peasants," 127.

15 Cuno, "The Origins of Private Ownership," 264.

16 Cuno, *The Pasha's Peasants*, 156. (The archival sources refer to land assignments as *ramya* or *tawzi*.)

17 DMU, MT, Madabit murafaʿat, 333/186/46, fol. 3, 1 Jumada I 1273.

18 For these two cases, see Ghalwash, "Land Acquisition by the Peasants," 128.

19 Ghalwash, "Land Acquisition by the Peasants," 132–33.

20 DWQ, MS, S/1/8/42, fol. 498 (no. 71) 20 Jumada II 1272.

21 DWQ, MS, S/1/8/42, fol. 414 (no. 72) 2 Jumada II 1272. The following entry suggests that the Buhayra officials sent their observations to the Viceregal Cabinet less than two weeks after the introduction of the January 8, 1856, decree: DWQ, MS, S/1/8/41, fol. 374 (no. 171) 14 Jumada I 1272.

22 Ghalwash, "Land Acquisition by the Peasants," 127.

23 For low wages: peasants received 1 piastre/day for work on the Mahmudiyya Canal in 1849 (Toledano, *State and Society*, 189); in 1873, peasants working on *izba*s could receive between 1½—2 piastres per day (Owen, "The Development of Agricultural Production," 538). Thus, as it is reasonable to assume that these wage levels probably "represented no more than was necessary to keep the worker and his family alive" (Owen, "The Development of Agricultural Production," 526), it is also reasonable to conclude that landless peasants were unable to save enough money to pay the required fee for the acquirement of *ramya* land. For an adequate labor pool: studies on the Egyptian population conclude that it grew at a yearly rate of increase that exceeded 1 percent by the mid-nineteenth century. (McCarthy, "Nineteenth-Century Egyptian Population," 1–39; Panzac, "The Population of Egypt," 11–32. Also see Cuno and Reimer, "The Census Registers," 193.) In addition, the number of workers in the Delta increased during peak times due to seasonal migration of peasants from Upper and Middle Egypt (see Owen, "The Development of Agricultural Production," 538). Thus, the combination of population growth and seasonal migration into the Delta (where perennial irrigation supported cultivation of important cash crops and required high man-hours in labor) meant that the supply of labor was adequate and did not allow for wage increases.

24 For wheat and cotton prices: Owen, *Cotton and the Egyptian Economy*, 80; Richards, "Primitive Accumulation in Egypt," 227; Cuno, "The Origins of Private Ownership," 275 (no. 133); El-Darwish, "Note on the Movement of Prices," 448.

25 DWQ, MS, S/1/21/55, fol. 90 (no. 39) 15 Jumada II 1278. Also see Ghalwash, "Land Acquisition by the Peasants," 134.

26 Baer, *Studies in the Social History*, 17–29.

27 Owen, *The Middle East in the World Economy*, 142.

28 DWQ, MA, S/7/16/1, fol. 15 (no. 4) 7 Safar 1268.

29 DWQ, MA, S/7/6/2, fol. 27 28 Rabi I 1269.

30 DWQ, MA, S/7/16/11, fol. 41 (no. 31) 23 Muharram 1271.

31 DWQ, MS, S/1/8/41, fol. 208 (no. 59) 5 Rabi II 1272.

32 DWQ, MS, S/1/8/42, fol. 498 (no. 71) 20 Jumada II 1272. (I point out that the date of the report [Feb. 18, 1856] differs from the date of the recording of this document in the state registers [Feb. 27, 1856].)

33 DWQ, DD, L/19/21/6, fol. 15 (no. 175) 29 Dhu al-Qaʿda 1274.

34 Casson, "Tax-Collection Problems," 280.

35 See Cooper, "The Assessment and Collection of Kharaj Tax," 365–82. Cooper constructed a table that shows the months in which each of the eight installments was to be paid; see pp. 376–77.

36 Cooper's observation on this issue is the following: "However, the information given by Ibn Hawqal is not a reference to the number of installments, but more likely is a measure of the completion of the entire *kharaj* collection." (See his "The Assessment and Collection of Kharaj Tax," 382.) The second part of his statement appears vague to me, so I presented my interpretation instead of his.

37 DMU, Daftar takmil al-dara'ib, rawdat al-bahrayn, 1274, 2210/109/22, fol. 69.

38 Once every four years 1 Tut corresponds to September 11. See Al-Hitta, *Tarikh al-zira'a*, 365.

39 DMU, Daftar takmil al-dara'ib, rawdat al-bahrayn, 1274, 2210/109/22, fol. 69; DWQ, DKH, S/2/8/18, fol. 17 (no. 12) 25 Dhu al-Qa'da 1266; DWQ, MS, S/1/8/20, fols. 654, 658 (no. 119) 20 Sha'ban 1268.

40 DWQ, MS, S/1/8/17, fol. 240 (no. 86) 3 Rabi II 1268. This report (dated Jan. 15, 1852) was submitted by the Katkhuda Pasha, or the First Lieutenant of the Viceroy. I also point out that the date of entry of this report into the state registers (Jan. 25, 1852) is not the same as the date of its composition (Jan. 15, 1852).

41 DWQ, Daftar nizam umur zira'iyya, no. 5004, fol. 32.

42 DWQ, Daftar nizam umur zira'iyya, no. 5004, fol. 32; also see: DWQ, MS, S/1/8/17, fol. 375 (no. 102) 27 Jumada I 1268; DWQ, MA, S/7/16/2, fol. 24 (no. 44) 11 Rabi I 1269.

43 DWQ, MA, S/7/16/2, fol. 24 (no. 44) 11 Rabi I 1269; (1 purse = 500 piatres).

44 See DWQ, MA, S/7/16/2, fol. 24 (no. 44) 11 Rabi I 1269; DWQ, MS, S/1/8/17, fol. 375 (no. 102) 27 Jumada I 1268. (From this latter entry, we further learn that the Viceregal Cabinet instructed the officials of Gharbiyya Province to honor the terms of the agreement between the creditor and the debtors: the Khawaja Jubran and the shaykhs of Bilah village, the brothers Ghunaym and Musa. Thus, the officials were to oversee the shaykhs' payment of the debt. Failing that, they were to oversee the sale of the pawned jewelry held by Khawaja Jubran, and then give Khawaja Jubran his money from the proceeds of the sale.)

45 DWQ, MS, S/1/8/17, fol. 375 (no. 102) 27 Jumada I 1268.

46 DWQ, MA, S/7/16/11, fols. 27, 52 (no. 27) 10 Safar 1271.

47 DMU, Daftar nizam umur zira'iyya, fol. 32; also see DWQ, MS, S/1/8/42, fol. 498 (no. 71) 20 Jumada II 1272.

48 DWQ, MS, S/1/8/41, fol. 208 (no. 59) 5 Rabi II 1272.

49 For official instructions for retroactive tax payments, see: DMU, Daftar takmil al-dara'ib, rawdat al-bahrayn, 1271, 2209/109/22, fol. 48 (Part II). Here it is necessary to point out that according to the 1855 (AH 1271) land-tax registers of Gharbiyya Province, the peasants began paying their taxes at the new rates in September 1854; see, for example, DMU, Mukallafat atyan, mahalit abu ali al-gharbiyya, 1271, 22075/361/22. But this would mean that the government had introduced and begun the collection of taxes at the revised rates before it had completed the reassessment work. This seems highly implausible. A more likely explanation could be that the central government instructed the village accountants to write up new registers for the 1271/1855 fiscal year showing the new rates.

50 DWQ, MS, S/1/8/46, fol. 52 (no. 206) 2 Dhu al-Hijja 1272. (Baer, following Artin, mistakenly states that this decree was issued in April 1856. See Baer, *A History of Landownership*, 29; Artin, *Al-Ahkam al-mar'iyya*, 78–79.)

51 The final major land-tax code of the period was that of 1862. The land-tax registers of five villages show that the peasants paid their taxes in 1862 at the newly revised rates; while only the register of al-Jazira al-Khadra Village specifies that these new rates were introduced in 1861. This evidence initially led me to think that the latter register had really recorded retroactive tax payments made in 1862. On the other hand, it is more likely that the 1277/1861 register was a duplication of the 1278/1862 register. This leads me to conclude that the problematic posed by the al-Jazira al-Khadra register can be attributed to a difficulty at the time of documentation by the village accountants. (I am indebted to Kenneth Cuno for this interpretation.) Finally, this allows me to state that the government probably issued instructions for the 1862 land-tax increases in Aug. 1861 and that it did not require any retroactive tax payments. (For the five land-tax registers, see: DMU, Mukallafat atyan, kafr al-jarayda, 1278, 17009/305/22; DMU, Mukallafat atyan, mahalit abu ali al-gharbiyya, 1278, 22081/361/22; DMU, Mukallafat atyan, al-qini wa bani bakar, 1278, 6256/164/22; DMU, Mukallafat atyan, al-hayatim, 1278, 7203/176/22; DMU, Mukallafat atyan, ibyar, 1278, 2924/121/22. For the land-tax register of al-Jazira al-Khadra Village, see: DMU, Mukallafat atyan, al-jazira al-khadra, 1277, 3988/135/22.)

52 Ergene, "On Ottoman Justice," 68. (Ergene adopts the term *symbolic power* from Bourdieu, "Structures, Habitus, Power," 155–200. The other terms that I placed in quotations are Ergene's.)

53 Studies show that this applied to peasants from various parts of the Ottoman Empire; see Ergene, "On Ottoman Justice," 66–69; Islamoğlu-, *State and Peasant in the Ottoman Empire*; Chalcraft, "Engaging the State"; Singer, *Palestinian Peasants*.

54 This fiscal year (1855) is suggested by the following entry: DWQ, MS, S/1/21/57, fol. 103 (no. 311) 16 Dhu al-Qaʿda 1278.

55 DWQ, MS, S/1/8/41, fol. 208 (no. 59) 5 Rabi II 1272.

56 Shalabi, *Al-Rif al-misri*, 209.

57 DWQ, MA, S/7/16/6, fols. 76, 82 (no. 59) 8 Safar 1270.

58 These are (i) the fiscal year of 1260, which started in September 1843 and ended in August 1844; (ii) the fiscal year of 1267, September 1850–August 1851; (iii) the fiscal year of 1269, September 1852–August 1853; (iv) the fiscal year of 1271, September 1854–August 1855.

For the fiscal year of 1260: DWQ, DKH, S/2/8/18, fol. 21 (no. 14) 18 Dhu al-Qaʿda 1266; DWQ, MA, S/7/16/6, fols. 76, 82 (no. 59) 8 Safar 1270. **For the 1267 fiscal year:** DWQ, MA, S/7/16/6, fol. 20 (no. 16) 29 Jumada I 1269; DWQ, MA, S/7/16/9, fols. 83, 86 (no. 185) 2 Dhu al-Qaʿda 1270; DWQ, MA, S/7/16/9, fol. 35 (no. 283) 25 Ramadan 1270. **For the 1269 fiscal year:** DWQ, MS, S/1/8/46, fol. 23 (no. 191) 19 Dhu al-Qaʿda 1272; DWQ, MS, S/1/8/46, fols. 31, 70 (no. 152) 5 Dhu al-Hijja 1272; DWQ,

MS, S/1/21/57, fol. 103 (no. 311) 16 Dhu al-Qaʿda 1278. **For the 1271 fiscal year:** DWQ, MS, S/1/21/57, fol. 103 (no. 311) 16 Dhu al-Qaʿda 1278.

59 DWQ, MS, S/1/21/57, fol. 103 (no. 311) 16 Dhu al-Qaʿda 1278.

60 DWQ, MS, S/1/8/42, fol. 495 (no. 22) 22 Jumada II 1272.

61 DWQ, DKH, S/2/8/18, fol. 21 (no. 14) 18 Dhu al-Qaʿda 1266. Also see: DWQ, MA, S/7/16/6, fols. 76, 82 (no. 59) 8 Safar 1270.

62 DWQ, MS, S/1/8/46, fol. 23 (no. 191) 19 Dhu al-Qaʿda 1272; also see Hunyan, *Al-Atyan wa al-dara'ib*, 212.

63 DWQ, MA, S/7/16/6, fol. 20 (no. 16) 29 Jumada I 1269.

64 DWQ, MA, S/7/16/6, fols. 76, 82 (no. 59) 8 Safar 1270.

65 DWQ, MA, S/7/16/6, fols. 76, 82 (no. 59) 8 Safar 1270.

66 For *sharaqi* land: DWQ, DD, L/19/21/1, fol. 40 (no. 3) 29 Shaʿban 1273; DWQ, DD, L/19/15/6, fol. 167 (no. 79) 19 Rabi II 1276. For ruined rice crop: DWQ, MS, S/1/21/54, fol. 133 (no. 24) 25 Rabi II 1278; DWQ, MS, S/1/21/52, fol. 10 (no. 287) 15 Dhu al-Hijja 1277.

67 Shalabi, *Al-Rif al-misri*, 209.

68 DWQ, MS, S/1/8/46, fol. 84 (no. 222) 22 Dhu al-Hijja 1272.

69 DMU, Daftar al-athurat, al-jazira al-khadra, 1276, 27/77/22, fol. 1. (This register, compiled in 1859, states that the village had observed this strategy during the past twenty years, without specifying the exact date of its introduction.)

70 DWQ, MS, S/1/21/57, fol. 58 (no. 165) 5 Dhu al-Qaʿda 1278.

71 For Palestine: Singer, *Palestinian Peasants*, 39–42.; For Syria: Rafeq, "Land Tenure Problems," 373.

72 For earlier discussions on the village shaykh, see Cuno, *The Pasha's Peasants*, 85–99, 166–78; Baer, *Studies in the Social History*, 30–61; Azbawi, *Umad wa mashayikh*. For a recent discussion on the responsibilities of the village shaykh, as well as his tendency to abuse his power, see Barakat, *Al-Qarya wa al-sulta*, 101–13.

73 For example, see the following land-tax registers: DMU, Mukallafat atyan, ibyar, 1272, 2919/121/22; DMU, Mukallafat atyan, al-jazira al-khadra, 1272, 3984/135/22.

74 Cuno, *The Pasha's Peasants*, 89–91.

75 For insightful discussions on the shaykh's official responsibilities, see sources specified in n. 72 above.

76 The importance of the latter duty is illustrated by an entry in the records of the Department of Civil Affairs: In January 1851, Hassan al-Sharqawy complained that "he had been dismissed from the position of shaykh without good reason even though he had overseen the remittance of all the taxes required of him." In response, the government ordered his reinstatement. See: DWQ, DKH, S/2/8/18, fol. 112 (no. 157) 11 Rabi I 1267.

77 Hillal, *Al-Fallah wa al-sulta*, 166–67.

78 DWQ, DKH, S/2/8/16, fol. 25 (no. 21) 14 Dhu al-Qaʿda 1265. Also see: DWQ, DHK, S/2/8/18, fol. 21 (no. 17) 20 Dhu al-Qaʿda 1266.

79 Hakim, *Ayam Muhammad Ali*, 110.

80 DWQ, MS, S/1/8/16, fols. 95, 108 (no. 58) 14 Muharram 1268.

81 DWQ, DKH, S/2/8/16, fol. 58 (no. 92) 21 Rabi I 1266.

82 DWQ, DKH, S/2/8/16, fol. 117 (no. 12) 13 Jumada I 1266.
83 DWQ, DD, L/19/15/6, fol. 121 (no. 46) 29 Rabi I 1276. (The village *shaykhs*, however, did not appreciate this solution; for they stressed that the problematic arrears "belonged to people who were deceased or penurious." That the headmen made this complaint indicates that most of the village population was poor, and that they could not easily reassign the debt-laden land to others.)
84 DWQ, DD, L/19/15/6, fol. 54 (no. 13) 9 Rabi I 1276.
85 DWQ, DKH, S/2/8/17, fol. 24 (no. 316) 24 Shawwal 1266. Also see: DWQ, DKH, S/2/8/16, fol. 19 (no. 11) 17 Dhu al-Qaʿda 1265; DWQ, DKH, S/2/8/16, fol. 89 (no. 92) 4 Rabi II 1266.
86 DWQ, DD, L/19/15/6, fol. 77 (no. 60) 9 Rabi I 1276. For another case see: DWQ, DD, L/19/15/6, fol. 2 (no. 6) 16 Safar 1276.
87 DWQ, MA, S/7/16/1, fol. 34 (no. 18) 16 Safar 1268.
88 For other types of money-related infractions committed by headmen, see Hillal, *al-Fallah wa al-sulta*, 122–24.
89 DWQ, DD, L/19/15/6, fol. 11 (no. 5) 23 Safar 1276. For other cases see: DWQ, MA, S/7/6/2, fol. 5 (unnumbered) 4 Rabi I 1269; DWQ, MA, S/7/16/8, fol. 31 (no. 28) 19 Jumada II 1270; DWQ, MA, S/7/16/8, fol. 31 (no. 27) 17 Jumada II 1270.

Chapter 4

1 Owen, *The Middle East in the World Economy*, 116.
2 Owen, *The Middle East in the World Economy*, 118.
3 For a review of this literature, see: Aytekin, "Cultivators, Creditors," 292–313.
4 For onerous tax loads: Issawi, *The Economic History of the Middle East*, 65. For peasants' failure to register their lands, see: Owen, *The Middle East in the World Economy*, 119. For state's attitude to peasants, see: Aytekin, "Cultivators, Creditors," 303.
5 Issawi, *The Economic History of the Middle East*, 19.
6 PRO, FO 78/1222, Harris to Bruce, Dec. 19, 1856.
7 PRO, FO 78/1660, Bulwer to Russell, Nov. 25, 1862.
8 The analysis of the different modes of peasant land acquirement in Ibyar and al-Jazira al-Khadra Villages required the examination of their *athurat* registers only, as their registers provided a complete record of these villages' holders. This was not the case for Kafr al-Rajallat and Jazirat al-Aʿjam Villages, which necessitated the examination of both their *athurat* registers, compiled in 1857, and the 1274 (1857–1858) land-tax registers, as the latter helped me to develop complete lists of the smallholders' names.
9 Muhammad Hakim confirms the same finding for Kamshish Village; he notes that 43.31 percent of the lands in the possession of the villagers had been acquired by inheritance. (See his *Ayam Muhammad Ali*, 107.) On the other hand, Hakim does not try to discern the importance of this mode of land acquirement for the different village strata, which I do in the ensuing discussion. (Other scholars who consulted the *athurat* registers were

not concerned with the issue of land acquirement by smallholders: For example, Shalabi relied on this source to investigate the comparatively large landholdings of the village headmen; see his *Al-Rif al-misri*, 177–78. Also, Barakat, depending on this book by Shalabi and Ali Mubarak's *Al-Khitat* [vol. 9], does little more than briefly mention this source when referring to the impact of the 1858 land law on peasants; see his *Al-Qarya wa al-sulta*, 25.)

10 The exception here is al-Jazira al-Khadra Village, as the small strata holders obtained 67.80 percent of their lands by inheritance (table 4.2). This is because they relied far less than did the peasants of the other villages on land assignment in the acquirement of land. In turn, this can be attributed to the general quality of the land that was reassigned in their village, as much of it was marginal land that was difficult to farm and roughly another 71 *faddans* constituted *'atil* or waste land. (See DMU, Daftar al-athurat, al-jazira al-khadra, 1276, 27/77/22, fol. 1) The possession of such land was financially burdensome, mostly because peasants were expected to regularly pay its taxes as well as underwrite the costly reclamation efforts. This being the case, poorer peasants infrequently took possession of such lands. (For the examination of the circumstances that called for *ramya* distribution, see the following section of this chapter.)

11 The *masmuh* lands for these villages:
Kafr al-Rajallat: medium holders: 5 *faddans*; wealthy holders: 16 *faddans*.
Jazirat al-Aʿjam: medium holders: 5 *faddans*; wealthy holders: 10 *faddans*.
Ibyar: wealthy holders: 126.5 *faddans*.
Al-Jazira al-Khadra: wealthy holders: 50 *faddans*.

12 DWQ, MKH, Daʿawi wa ashhadat, no. 1, fol. 1 (no. 1) 5 Dhu al-Qaʿda 1268. (What is noticeable here is that the plaintiff referred to the mode by which he had acquired the land as "*irth*" or inheritance, as if the land were his private property, and not as *intiqal* or transmission, as he should have, considering the *miri* status of the land. While this gives us a sense of how peasants really viewed their lands (as their property), it also suggests that the authorities did not insist on legal niceties when errors dovetailed with state policy—in this case ensuring that heirs were not illegally dispossessed of their land legacies.)

13 DWQ, MKH, Daʿawi wa ashhadat, no. 1, fol. 55 (no. 138) 30 Muharram 1273.

14 DWQ, MA, S/7/16/16, fol. 103 (no. 99) 7 Rabi II 1274.

15 For example, see: DMU, MQ, Madabit murafaʿat, 77/98/46, fols. 85–86, 16 Shaʿban 1279; DMU, MT, Madabit murafaʿat, 335/186/46, fols. 121, 26 Rabi I 1275; DMU, MT, Madabit murafaʿat, 335/186/46, fols. 94–95, 29 Muharram 1275; DMU, MT, Madabit murafaʿat, 335/186/46, fols. 56–57, 62, 11 Shaʿban 1276.

16 For rural notables: Cuno, "Joint Family Households," 485–502 (for quoted phrase, 485). For poor peasants: According to Eric Wolf, peasants were likely to prefer this arrangement (joint households and joint holdings) when "the tasks of cultivation and the pursuit of part-time specialties both permit and require a larger labor force" (Wolf, *Peasants*, 65). With the change to perennial irrigation and the cultivation of profitable, yet labor-intensive

crops, poor peasants likely expanded their labor force by forming joint households rather than relying on hired labor. That peasants relied on this arrangement as a strategy for poverty alleviation is also suggested by the *athurat* registers: At mid-century, approximately 57 percent of the agricultural land of al-Jazira al-Khadra Village had not been adequately leveled or cleared of trees, making its cultivation a costly undertaking. At the time of the compilation of the *athurat* register of this village (1859), the *athurat* committee found that 56 percent of holders who had inherited land over the previous thirty to forty years did not divide their land legacy, and had instead formed joint households and joint holdings. In contrast, the figure for joint households and landholdings for Ibyar Village, made up of excellent agricultural land, was much lower, 34 percent. (See DMU, Daftar al-athurat, al-jazira al-khadra; DMU, Daftar al-athurat, ibyar.) Thus, as the retention of marginal land proved costly, its holders were more likely to pool resources and consolidate holdings (in an effort to better manage these lands) than were those who possessed good quality lands.

17 DWQ, MKH, Daʿawi wa ashhadat, no. 1, fol. 69 (no. 158) 8 Shawwal 1273.

18 Sijpesteijn, "Landholding Patterns," 124.

19 DMU, Daftar al-athurat, kafr al-rajallat, fol. 4.

20 DMU, Daftar al-athurat, al-jazira al-khadra, fol. 16.

21 DMU, Daftar al-athurat, kafr al-rajallat, fol. 11. (This same holder acquired another land plot, which consisted of a few *sahms*, by the same method for the exact same reason; that is, because the original holder, Muhammad Biyash, had died without leaving behind a resident heir.)

22 For al-Jazirah al-Khadra, see DMU, Daftar al-athurat, al-jazira al-khadra, fol. 1. For Jazirat al-Aʿjam, compare between DMU, Daftar al-athurat, jazirat al-aʿjam and DMU, Mukallafat atyan, jazirat al-aʿjam, 1274, 4576/61/20.

23 Barakat, *Al-Qarya wa al-sulta*, 25.

24 Shalabi, *Al-Rif al-misri*, 160; Cuno, *The Pasha's Peasants*, 5–6, 155–56; Hakim, *Ayam Muhammad Ali*, 109.

25 DMU, Daftar al-athurat, kafr al-rajallat; DMU, Mukallafat atyan, kafr al-rajallat, 1274, 8208/110/20.

26 DMU, Daftar al-athurat, kafr al-rajallat, fol. 19.

27 DWQ, MA, S/7/16/6, fol. 63 (no. 8) 22 Muharram 1270.

28 DMU, Daftar al-athurat, ibyar.

29 DMU, Daftar al-athurat, jazirat al-aʿjam; DMU, Mukallafat atyan, jazirat al-aʿjam, 1274, 4576/61/20.

30 For such cases, see: DWQ, MA, S/7/16/8, fol. 8 (no. 129) 19 Jumada II 1270; DWQ, MA, S/7/16/11, fol. 31 (no. 33) 9 Muharram 1271.

31 Compare between: DMU, Daftar al-athurat, kafr al-rajallat; DMU, Mukallafat atyan, kafr al-rajallat, 1274, 8208/110/20.

32 In his examination of the sources of peasants' landholdings in Kamshish Village, Hakim attributes 22.08 percent to *ramya* assignment (See his *Ayam Muhammad Ali*, 107), which was a comparatively low proportion, as was that of Kafr al-Rajallat and Jazirat al-Aʿjam. But Hakim does not try to explain

this figure. Perhaps the scenario outlined for the two sample villages specified here similarly applied to Kamshish Village.

33 For a more detailed examination of the *ramya* system during the mid-nineteenth century, see Ghalwash, "Land Acquisition by the Peasants."

34 Cuno, *The Pasha's Peasants*, 153–56; Shalabi, *Al-Rif al-misri*, 160, 163–64, 166.

35 DMU, Daftar al-athurat, ibyar.

36 DMU, Daftar al-athurat, al-jazira al-khadra, fol. 33. For other examples, see: DMU, Daftar al-athurat, ibyar, fols. 37–38, 41. On the other hand, Hakim claims that the *athurat* registers designated a mode of acquirement as "*athar*," which, he claims, meant that the concerned land portion that had been acquired by "*athar*" had been in the possession of the peasant holder since the time of the 1813–1814 cadaster. (See his *Ayam Muhammad Ali*, 107.) It seems that Hakim arrived at this conclusion because the Kamshish register did not include any explanation of this mode of land acquirement (though other registers did, like that of Ibyar.)

37 For impoverishment of *multazims*: DWQ, MA, S/7/16/9, fol. 23 (no. 170) 21 Ramadan 1270. For impoverishment of heirs of *multazims*: DWQ, MA, S/7/16/6, fol. 22 (no. 7) 17 Jumada I 1269. For lack of issue: DMU, Daftar al-athurat, kafr al-rajallat, fol. 33.

38 DMU, Daftar al-athurat, kafr al-rajallat, fols. 33–36.

39 DMU, Daftar al-athurat, ibyar, fol. 9. (Sometimes, peasants documented this type of land transfer in official land deeds. See: DWQ, MA, S/7/16/8, fol. 77 (no. 223) 26 Rajab 1270.)

40 For an examination of the role of the *wakil* in commercial affairs and disputes, see Cheta, "A Prehistory of the Modern Legal Profession," 649–68.

41 DMU, Daftar al-athurat, ibyar, fol. 187.

42 DMU, Daftar al-athurat, ibyar, fol. 9.

43 See DMU, Daftar al-athurat, ibyar.

44 For land cession: DMU, Daftar al-athurat, ibyar, fol. 173. For land rental: DMU, Daftar al-athurat, ibyar, fol. 44. For land pawn: DMU, Daftar al-athurat, kafr al-rajallat, fol. 1.

45 DMU, Daftar al-athurat, kafr al-rajallat, fols. 1–6. (I point out that the *athurat* registers often do not specify the reason for the execution of a land transaction; and so they do not provide us with direct confirmation of this point.)

46 DWQ, MA, S/7/16/9, fol. 76 (no. 340) 25 Shawwal 1270.

47 DWQ, MA, S/7/16/11, fol. 73 (no. 110) 7 Rabi I 1271. Also see: DWQ, MA, S/7/16/11, fol. 59 (no. 40) 30 Safar 1271; DWQ, DD, L/19/21/6, fol. 145 (no. 119) 25 Dhu al-Qaʿda 1274; DWQ, DD, L/19/21/6, fol. 43 (no. 286) 23 Shawwal 1274.

48 DMU, MT, Madabit murafaʿat, 335/186/46, fol. 87, 4 Muharram 1275.

49 DMU, MT, Madabit murafaʿat, 334/186/46, Part II, fol. 55, 29 Safar 1274; DMU, MT, Madabit murafaʿat, 333/186/46, fols. 2–3, 11 Jumada I 1273.

50 Fahmy, "The Police and the People," 353–54.

51 DMU, MT, Madabit murafaʿat, 337/186/46, fol. 51, 28 Jumada I 1277.

52 Baer, *A History of Landownership*, 28–29; Richards, "Primitive Accumulation in Egypt," 232–34; Barakat, *Tatawwur al-milkiyya*, 310–13; Artin, *Al-Ahkam al-mar'iyya*, 175–77.

53 Abbas and El-Dessouky, *The Large Landowning Class*, 24.

54 Baer seems to confuse between *tasahhub* and *matruk* lands. For when he explains what happened to *matruk* land, he starts by specifying the legislation developed by the three major land laws of the mid-century period that applied to *tasahhub* land. (See Baer, *A History of Landownership*, 29.) For the state decision that disallowed original holders from recovering *matruk* land, see: DWQ, DD, L/19/21/3, fol. 146 (no. 40) 24 Rabi I 1274; DWQ, DD, L/19/21/7, fol. 14 (no. 190) 15 Dhu al-Hijja 1274.

55 Artin, *Al-Ahkam al-mar'iyya*, 175; Hunayn, *Al-Atyan wa al-dara'ib*, 213. Abbas and El-Dessouky accepted Hunayn's figure. See their: *The Large Landowning Class*, 23–24.

56 Barakat, *Tatawwur al-milkiyya*, 311.

57 DWQ, DD, L/19/15/6, fols. 96, 114 (no. 39) 27 Rabi I 1276.

58 DWQ, DD, L/19/15/6, fol. 3 (no. 1) 13 Safar 1276; DWQ, DD, L/19/15/6, fol. 121 (no. 48) 30 Rabi I 1276; DWQ, DD, L/19/15/6, fol. 44 (no. 15) 27 Safar 1276; DWQ, DD, L/19/15/6, fol. 52 (no. 18) 27 Safar 1276; DWQ, DD, L/19/15/6, fol. 138 (no. 55) 4 Rabi II 1276; DWQ, DD, L/19/15/6, fol. 187 (no. 83) 3 Jumada I 1276; DWQ, DD, L/19/15/6, fol. 114 (no. 45) 29 Rabi I 1276; DWQ, DD, L/19/15/6, fol. 176 (no. 69) 21 Rabi II 1276; DWQ, DD, L/19/15/6, fol. 187 (no. 82) 3 Jumada I 1276.

59 For Qalyubiya Province: DWQ, DD, L/19/15/5, fol. 33 (no. 706) 11 Muharram 1276; DWQ, DD, L/19/15/5, fol. 78 (no. 730) 29 Muharram 1276. For Bani Suwayf Province: DWQ, DD, L/19/15/5, fol. 68 (no. 150) 6 Safar 1276; DWQ, DD, L/19/15/6, fol. 110 (no. 14) 26 Rabi I 1276. For al-Jiza Province: DWQ, DD, L/19/21/3, fol. 131 (no. 54) 24 Rabi I 1274.

60 Barakat, *Tatawwur al-milkiyya*, 311.

61 DWQ, MA, S/7/16/6, fol. 73 (no. 58) 8 Safar 1270; DWQ, MA, S/7/16/6, fol. 93 (no. 74) 26 Safar 1270; DWQ, MA, S/7/16/7, fol. 6 (no. 80) 9 Rabi I 1270; DWQ, DD, L/19/15/5, fol. 78 (no. 730) 29 Muharram 1276.

62 DWQ, MA, S/7/16/7, fol. 33 (no. 115) 5 Rabi II 1270; also see DWQ, MS, S/1/8/46, fol. 84 (no. 222) 22 Dhu al-Hijja 1272.

63 DWQ, DD, L/19/15/5, fol. 68 (no. 150) 6 Safar 1276; DWQ, DD, L/19/15/5, fol. 78 (no. 730) 29 Muharram 1276.

64 Abbas and El-Dessouky, *The Large Landowning Class*, 24. Instead of salaries: DWQ, DD, L/19/21/3, fol.131 (no. 54) 24 Rabi I 1274.

65 Instead of money pensions: DWQ, DD, L/19/21/3, fol. 188 (no. 75) 13 Rabi II 1274; DWQ, DD, L/19/21/4, fol. 169 (no. 150) 24 Jumada II 1274.

66 DWQ, DD, L/19/21/3, fol. 146 (no. 40) 24 Rabi I 1274.

67 Barakat, *Al-Qarya wa al-sulta*, 24.

68 DWQ, DD, L/19/21/4, fol. 21 (no. 92) 25 Rabi II 1274. For other examples, see: DWQ, DD, L/19/21/4, fol. 60 (no. 110) 14 Jumada I 1274; DWQ, DD, L/19/21/4, fol. 169 (no. 149) 18 Jumada II 1274; DWQ, DD, L/19/21/3, fol.

110 (no. 43) 11 Rabi I 1274; DWQ, DD, L/19/21/3, fol. 131 (no. 54) 24 Rabi I 1274; DWQ, DD, L/19/21/5, fol. 30 (no. 104) 20 Rajab 1274; DWQ, DD, L/19/21/5, fol. 35 (no. 143) 13 Rajab 1274.

69 DWQ, MA, S/7/16/6, fol. 93 (no. 74) 26 Safar 1270. For other examples, see: DWQ, MA, S/7/16/6, fol. 73 (no. 58) 8 Safar 1270; DWQ, MA, S/7/16/7, fol. 6 (no. 80) 9 Rabi I 1270.

70 DWQ, DD, L/19/21/3, fol. 131 (no. 54) 24 Rabi I 1274.

71 DWQ, DD, L/19/21/3, fols. 85, 90 (no. 32) 3 Rabi I 1274.

72 DWQ, DD, L/19/21/3, fol. 137 (no. 37) 23 Rabi I 1274.

73 For the official rule that disallowed the conferment of *matruk* lands on members of villages that had originally abandoned them, see n. 54 above.

74 DWQ, DD, L/19/21/7, fol. 14 (no. 190) 15 Dhu al-Hijja 1274.

75 DWQ, DD, L/19/21/6, fol. 32 (no. 50) 26 Shawwal 1274. This entry begins by specifying the complaint lodged by the headmen of al-Nazla Village; that is, that the governor forced them to cultivate land they had previously abandoned. Then it reports the outcome of the government's investigations of this complaint, which is that the villagers did not have the right to make this complaint because they had accepted the *matruk* land willingly. Whichever the case, the point I want to highlight is that the peasants ended up cultivating land they had abandoned earlier, something the government had expressly forbidden. This confirms the point I made just above—that officials did not hesitate to disregard government instructions if this ensured the regular cultivation of the land (and the payment of its taxes.)

76 DWQ, MS, S/1/21/58, fols. 126, 137 (no. 212) no date. This entry specifies the land categories that were to be sold. These were the *ziyada* (surplus) lands and the *matruk* lands.

77 Baer, *A History of Landownership*, 30.

78 For this decree, see: DWQ, MS, S/1/21/57, fol. 42 (no. 110) 29 Shawwal 1278; DWQ, MS, S/1/21/57, fol. 127 (no. 325) 23 Dhu al-Qaʿda 1278.

79 DWQ, DD, L/19/21/3, fol. 137 (no. 37) 23 Rabi I 1274.

80 DWQ, DD, L/19/21/5, fol. 85 (no. 3) 28 Rajab 1274; DWQ, DD, L/19/21/5, fol. 62 (no. 82) 22 Rajab 1274; DWQ, DD, L/19/21/5, fol. 112 (no. 38) 7 Shaʿban 1274.

81 See n. 68 above.

82 DWQ, DD, L/19/21/3, fol. 35 (no. 143) 13 Rajab 1274. For other examples: DWQ, DD, L/19/21/3, fol. 110 (no. 43) 11 Rabi I 1274; DWQ, DD, L/19/21/3, fol. 131 (no. 54) 24 Rabi I 1274.

83 Although Barakat does not specify the kind of land the peasants abandoned, the fact that these two villages left 84 percent of their combined arable area suggests that much of the *matruk* land was *ma'mur* land. (See n. 56 above.)

84 DMU, Daftar takmil al-dara'ib, rawdat al-bahrayn, 1271, 2209/109/22, Part I, fol. 28; DMU, Mukallafat atyan, kafr al-jarayda, 1278, 17009/305/22.

85 In one such case, dated Nov. 11, 1857, state employees adamantly refused to accept *matruk* lands in lieu of money payments and instead requested *ziyada* lands; see DWQ, DD, L/19/21/3, fol. 131 (no. 54) 24 Rabi I 1274. For other

cases, see: DWQ, DD, L/19/21/3, fol. 166 (no. 67) 5 Rabi II 1274; DWQ, DD, L/19/21/3, fol. 188 (no. 75) 13 Rabi II 1274.

86 For settlement of land claim: DWQ, MS, S/1/8/42, fols. 524, 528 (no. 70) 26 Jumada II 1272. For peasant volition: DWQ, DD, L/19/21/3, fol. 131 (no. 54) 24 Rabi I 1274. For peasants turned informants: DWQ, MA, S/7/6/2, fol. 19 (unnumbered) 21 Rabi I 1269.

87 In 1854, As'ad Atallah informed the Council of Justice that Husayn Agha, head of Ashmun District, was secretly cultivating an *ib'adiyya*. Official investigations of this report revealed that Husayn was fully within his rights, as the *ib'adiyya* was a land grant of 50 *faddans* given to him by a state order of January 4, 1835, but that he had neglected to obtain the requisite title deed. These findings prompted the government to send As'ad to Alexandria prison for one year while directing Husayn to obtain his title deed. See: DWQ, MA, S/7/16/8, fol. 51 (no. 202) 5 Rajab 1270.

88 Artin, *Al-Ahkam al-mar'iyya*, 178.

89 DWQ, DD, L/19/21/3, fols. 130, 138 (no. 37) 19 Rabi I 1274. This entry does not specify the number of *faddans* that appeared as surplus land, only focusing on the disposal of this land. For 1854 survey: Artin, *Al-Ahkam al-mar'iyya*, 178; Cuno, *The Pasha's Peasants*, 194. For 1821 land survey: Cuno, *The Pasha's Peasants*, 130.

90 Artin, *Al-Ahkam al-mar'iyya*, 178.

91 DWQ, DD, L/19/21/3, fols. 130, 138 (no. 37) 19 Rabi I 1274.

92 DWQ, DD, L/19/21/1, fols. 1,7 (no. 2) 19 Rajab 1273. (The Department of Interior referred to the Dec. 3, 1856 decree when examining the demand of informant Muhammad al-Kirdasi in March 1857.)

93 DWQ, MA, S/7/6/2, fol. 19 (unnumbered) 21 Rabi I 1269.

94 For the June 11, 1856, decree: Hunayn, *Al-Atyan wa al-dara'ib*, 196–67. For disposal of fractions of a *faddan*: Hunayn, *Al-Atyan wa al-dara'ib*, 196–67; DWQ, MS, S/1/8/45, fol. 84 (no. 864) 9 Dhu al-Qa'da 1272.

95 DWQ, MS, S/1/8/46, fols. 18, 20 (no. 188) 19 Dhu al-Qa'da 1272.

96 DWQ, MA, Mahafiz, Box no. 7, document no. 80/99, 3 Dhu al-Hijja 1273. (Artin mistakenly gives the date for this decree as July 20, 1857; see Artin, *Al-Ahkam al-mar'iyya*, 178.)

97 DWQ, DD, L/19/21/1, fol. 36 (no. 10) 20 Sha'ban 1273; DWQ, DD, L/19/21/1, fol. 56 (no. 17) 7 Shawwal 1273; DWQ, DD, L/19/21/1, fol. 18 (no. 7) 13 Sha'ban 1273; DWQ, DD, L/19/21/6, fol. 28 (no. 224) 17 Shawwal 1274.

98 DWQ, DD, L/19/21/6, fol. 28 (no. 224) 17 Shawwal 1274; DWQ, DD, L/19/21/4, fol. 128 (no. 128) 4 Jumada II 1274.

99 DWQ, DD, L/19/21/1, fol. 36 (no. 10) 20 Sha'ban 1273; DWQ, DD, L/19/21/6, fol. 28 (no. 224) 17 Shawwal 1274. In one case, the informant was a high state official, as he was referred to by the title "*bek*"; see DWQ, DD, L/19/21/4, fol. 128 (no. 128) 4 Jumada II 1274.

100 DWQ, DD, L/19/15/6, fol. 111 (no. 23) 5 Rabi II 1276. The threat of such treatment notwithstanding, peasants did not passively stand by while others took what was rightfully theirs. For example, in one case, a peasant

informant uncovered the existence of a surplus tract and upon reporting it to the provincial authorities, was dismayed to see it awarded to the headman of his village. He reported his situation to the Department of Interior and demanded its rectification. For this, see DWQ, DD, L/19/15/6, fol. 87 (no. 56) 21 Rabi I 1276. For another similar case see DWQ, DD, L/19/15/5, fol. 68 (no. 149) 25 Muharram 1276.

101 DWQ, DD, L/19/15/6, fol. 98 (no. 22) 23 Rabi I 1276; DWQ, DD, L/19/15/6, fol. 53 (no. 40) 29 Safar 1276.

102 DWQ, DD, L/19/21/5, fol. 167 (no. 112) 28 Shaʿban 1274. Also see: DWQ, DD, L/19/21/3, fol. 157 (no. 36) 25 Rabi I 1274.

103 DWQ, MA, S/7/16/11, fol. 83 (no. 70) 30 Rabi I 1271.

104 DWQ, DD, L/19/21/3, fol. 141 (no. 15) 19 Rabi I 1274.

105 DWQ, MS, S/1/8/42, fols. 524, 528 (no. 70) 26 Jumada II 1272.

106 We should recall that the small lots specified here referred to the *mutafarriqa* lots (roughly consisting of 1–5 *faddans*), not the lots that were less than a *faddan*, which were regulated by the June 1856 decree.

107 DWQ, DD, L/19/21/3, fol. 123 (no. 53) 22 Rabi I 1274; DWQ, DD, L/19/21/3, fol. 156 (no. 29) 24 Rabi I 1274; DWQ, DD, L/19/21/3, fol. 152 (no. 24) 12 Rabi II 1274.

108 DWQ, DD, L/19/21/3, fol. 141 (no. 15) 19 Rabi I 1274.

109 DWQ, DD, L/19/21/3, fol. 157 (no. 36) 25 Rabi I 1274.

110 DWQ, DD, L/19/21/3, fol. 156 (no. 29) 24 Rabi I 1274.

111 DWQ, L/19/21/5, fol. 167 (no. 112) 28 Shaʿban 1274.

112 Land Law of 1858, Article XV.

113 Artin, *Al-Ahkam al-mar'iyya*, 194–95.

114 DWQ, MS, S/1/21/56, fol. 132 (no. 75) 10 Ramadan 1278.

115 DWQ, MS, S/1/21/56, fol. 132 (no. 75) 10 Ramadan 1278; DWQ, MS, S/1/21/52, fol. 132 (no. 357) 27 Muharram 1278. Also see: Artin, *Al-Ahkam al-mar'iyya*, 195; Cuno, *The Pasha's Peasants*, 209.

116 DWQ, MS, S/1/21/56, fol. 132 (no. 75) 10 Ramadan 1278. (I thank Kenneth Cuno for explaining this point to me.)

117 DWQ, MS, S/1/21/52, fols. 20, 71 (no. 70) 3 Muharram 1278.

118 DWQ, MS, S/1/21/54, fols. 27, 78 (no. 7) 24 Rabi I 1278.

119 DWQ, MS, S/1/21/54, fols. 122, 132 (no. 64) 24 Rabi II 1278.

120 DWQ, MS, S/1/21/57, fol. 182 (no. 104) 1 Dhu al-Hijja 1278.

121 For Jirja: DWQ, MS, S/1/21/54, fol. 137 (no. 18) 1 Jumada I 1278. For al-Jiza: DWQ, MS, S/1/21/54, fol. 71 (no. 10) 4 Rabi II 1278.

122 DWQ, MS, S/1/21/56, fol. 9 (no. 54) 25 Rajab 1278.

123 DWQ, MS, S/1/21/54, fol. 137 (no. 18) 1 Jumada I 1278; DWQ, MS, S/1/21/54, fol. 143 (no. 10) 28 Rabi II 1278; DWQ, MS, S/1/21/54, fol. 148 (no. 23) 27 Rabi II 1278.

124 DWQ, MS, S/1/21/57, fol. 117 (no. 105) 22 Dhu al-Qaʿda 1278; DWQ, MS, S/1/21/58, fol. 179 (no. 423) 4 Safar 1279. For monetary compensation of informants: DWQ, MS, S/1/21/55, fol. 90 (no. 42) 22 Jumada II 1278.

125 DWQ, MS, S/1/21/56, fol. 184 (no. 122) 11 Shawwal 1278.

126 DWQ, MS, S/1/21/57, fol. 48 (no. 145) 12 Dhu al-Qaʿda 1278; DWQ, MS, S/1/21/57, fol. 124 (no. 152) 24 Dhu al-Qaʿda 1278.

127 1858 Land Law, Article XXIII.

128 DWQ, MS, S/1/21/55, fols. 90, 142 (no. 41) 22 Jumada II 1278. This entry reveals that the Qina-wa-Asna authorities worried about the intention of such winners to respect the tax obligations they had specified. So to preempt cases of retraction or abandonment by these winners, the provincial government required these auction winners to demonstrate good intent. Thus if the winning bid had specified a tax rate of 100 piastres/*faddan*, this winner was to present a reliable guarantor (who would pay the required taxes if the holder could not) before the authorities would release the land to him. But if the winner had specified a very high tax rate of 200 piastres or more per *faddan*, he was to pay three years' taxes in advance before the authorities would release the land to him. (Regarding the latter situation, the provincial authorities reminded the central government that they were merely observing the September 2, 1858, decree issued by the Council of Justice.)

129 DWQ, MS, S/1/21/57, fol. 67 (no. 70) 2 Dhu al-Qaʿda 1278.

130 DWQ, MS, S/1/21/58, fol. 181 (no. 430) 7 Safar 1279.

131 Richards, "Primitive Accumulation in Egypt," 224; Tucker, "Decline of the Family Economy," 256; Barakat, *Tatawwur al-milkiyya*, 300.

132 Baer, *A History of Landownership*, 20.

133 Abbas and El-Dessouky, *The Large Landowning Class*, 20–32, 38–41.

134 Barakat, *Tatawwur al-milkiyya*, 34, 72. Relying on Artin, Baer specifies that the first land grant was conferred on December 1, 1829. (Baer, *A History of Landownership*, 17.) But Barakat, drawing his information from the Egyptian archival records, specifies this first date as 29 Safar 1242, which he then converts into the Gregorian date, specifying this first date as September 4, 1826 (see p. 34). I rely on Barakat's data, but disagree with him on one point, the Gregorian date he gives, as it is incorrect: the correct Gregorian date is October 2, 1826.

135 Artin, *Al-Ahkam al-mar'iyya*, 53–54; Baer, *A History of Landownership*, 16; Cuno, *The Pasha's Peasants*, 162.

136 For Baer's assumption, see his *A History of Landownership*, 20.

137 Richards, "Primitive Accumulation in Egypt," 226.

138 Owen, *Cotton and the Egyptian Economy*, 80–81 (for quoted phrase, 81). Regarding the measurement specified here: 1 *ardab* equals approximately 5.5 bushels.

139 See chapter 2 above.

140 Barakat, *Tatawwur al-milkiyya*, 78–79.

141 This number is based on Barakat's data: it refers to the 66,758 *faddans* specified in table 4.5 plus the 70,414 *faddans* Said gave in lieu of pensions (just mentioned in this discussion). See Barakat, *Tatawwur al-milkiyya*, 75–79, 265–68.

142 Aharoni, *The Pasha's Bedouin*, 57–58 (for quoted phrases, 58).

143 Barakat, *Tatawwur al-milkiyya*, 263; Baer, *A History of Landownership*, 58–59.

144 Baer, *A History of Landownership*, 58.
145 Barakat, *Tatawwur al-milkiyya*, 265.
146 Artin, *Al-Ahkam al-mar'iyya*, 163–64.
147 Barakat, *Tatawwur al-milkiyya*, 101–10; Baer, *A History of Landownership*, 13–16; Hakim, *Ayam Muhammad Ali*, 116–21.
148 According to Baer, the *uhda* lands "covered more than 1,200,000 faddans" by the end of 1844 (for quoted phrase: Baer, *A History of Landownership*, 14). The specification of this proportion of *uhda* land (that is, one-third) is based on Cuno's statement: "In all of Egypt in the 1830s and 1840s a median of some 3.7 million faddans were cultivated." (See Cuno, *The Pasha's Peasants*, p. 115.)
149 Baer assumes that the peasants retained their lands while the village was under care of a *muta'ahhid*. See Baer, *A History of Landownership*, 13. It seems that scholars have commonly accepted Baer's view. For this see Cuno, *The Pasha's Peasants*, 158; Tucker, "Decline of the Family Economy," 256.
150 DWQ, MA, S/7/16/6, fol. 71 (no. 47) 5 Safar 1270.
151 DWQ, MS, S/1/8/46, fols. 6, 11 (no. 887) 14 Dhu al-Qaʿda 1272.
152 While I found only one entry belonging to the former type of case (see n. 150), the archival sources are replete with mentions of the abuses of *uhda* holders. For entries that focus on the unfair distribution of lands between the villagers and the *muta'ahhid*, see, for example: DWQ, MS, S/1/8/41, fols. 232, 251 (no. 35) 14 Rabi II 1272; DWQ, MS, S/1/8/41, fol. 213 (no. 47) 13 Rabi II 1272.
153 See above: ch. 1, n. 26.
154 Barakat, *Tatawwur al-milkiyya*, 103–104.
155 Barakat, *Tatawwur al-milkiyya*, 106.
156 DWQ, MA, S/7/16/6, fols. 34, 35 (no. 24) 26 Jumada I 1269. (This entry does not specify the name of the village or in which province it was located.) Also see: DWQ, MS, S/1/8/42, fols. 444, 464 (no. 58) 10 Jumada II 1272.
157 DMU, Daftar al-athurat, ayjul, 1276, 1/77/22; Daftar al-athurat, abstu, 1276, 2/77/22; Daftar al-athurat, abtu, 1276, 4/77/22; Daftar al-athurat, billa, 1276, 106/77/22.
158 DMU, MT, Madabit murafaʿat, 340/186/46, fols. 57–58, 11 Dhu al-Qaʿda 1279.
159 DWQ, MA, Mahafiz, 6 (no. 162/13) 17 Dhu al-Qaʿda 1270.
160 DWQ, MA, S/7/16/8, fol. 98 (no. 139) 26 Shaʿaban 1270.
161 DWQ, MS, S/1/8/41, fol. 232 (no. 31) 9 Rabi II 1272.
162 Barakat, *Tatawwur al-milkiyya*, 105; Barakat, *Al-Qarya wa al-sulta*, 24.
163 Artin, *Al-Ahkam al-mar'iyya*, 206–207.
164 DMU, Daftar takmil al-dara'ib, rawdat al-bahrayn, 1271, 2209/109/22, (Parts I, II); DMU, Daftar takmil al-dara'ib, rawdat al-bahrayn, 1274, 2210/109/22.
165 Baer, *A History of Landownership*, 17.
166 For this date, see Barakat, *Tatawwur al-milkiyya*, 85.
167 Barakat, *Tatawwur al-milkiyya*: For land composition (ma'mur/ib'adiyya) of *jifliks*: 85–95. For status of peasant villagers: 293–94. For the number of *jiflik faddans*: 94. Also, the figure of 9 percent is based on the total number of *jiflik faddans* specified here and the 3.7 million *faddans* specified by Cuno as

the extent of the arable area of Egypt during the 1830s and 1840s. (See above, n. 148.) For the status of peasants, also see: DWQ, MS, S/1/21/55, fols. 159, 180 (no. 81) 23 Rajab 1278. This entry reveals that Zanqar Village was part of Jiflik Sabat, and that the peasants of this village were tenants who rented the lands in their possession.

168 Barakat, *Tatawwur al-milkiyya*, 96–99.

169 DWQ, MS, S/1/21/55, fol. 20 (no. 134) 22 Jumada I 1278.

170 DWQ, MS, S/1/21/52, fol. 141 (no. 330) 9 Safar 1278; DWQ, MS, S/1/21/54, fol. 51 (no. 13) 24 Rabi I 1278.

171 For dates of *jiflik* conferrals, see Barakat, *Tatawwur al-milkiyya*, 85–94.

172 DWQ, MS, S/1/8/46, fols. 38, 44 (no. 202) 27 Dhu al-Qaʿda 1272.

173 DWQ, MS, S/1/8/41, fol. 245 (no. 99) 15 Rabi II 1272.

174 Scott, *Weapons of the Weak*.

175 DWQ, DD, L/19/21/6, fol. 28 (no. 222) 16 Shawwal 1274.

176 DWQ, MS, S/1/8/46, fol. 28 (no. 104) 27 Dhu al-Qaʿda 1272.

177 DWQ, MS, S/1/8/21, fol. 831 (no. 198) 19 Shawwal 1268.

178 First petition: DWQ, MS, S/1/8/21, fol. 868 (no. 118) 8 Dhu al-Qaʿda 1268. Second petition: DWQ, MS, S/1/8/22, fol. 77 (no. 14) 28 Dhu al-Hijja 1268. For other cases of terrorization: DWQ, MS, S/1/8/19, fol. 738 (no. 83) 23 Rajab 1268; DWQ, MA, S/7/16/9, fol. 36 (no. 252) 4 Shawwal 1270.

179 For depriving land of water resources: DWQ, MS, S/1/8/22, fol. 46 (no. 2) 21 Dhu al-Hijja 1268; DWQ, MS, S/1/8/21, fol. 886 (no. 381) 8 Dhu al-Qaʿda 2168; DWQ, MS, S/1/8/18, fols. 411, 418 (no. 73) 3 Jumada II 1268. For refusal to send corvée contingents: DWQ, MA, S/7/6/2, fol. 12 (unnumbered) 20 Rabi I 1269.

180 DWQ, DD, L/19/21/3, fol. 180 (no. 28) 15 Rabi II 1274.

181 DMU, MT, Madabit murafaʿat, 336/186/46, fol. 43, 6 Rajab 1276.

182 For reduced government control of the countryside, see Cuno, *The Pasha's Peasants*, 194, 253 (n. 64).

183 DMU, MT, Madabit murafaʿat, 336/186/46, fol. 15, 26 Rabi II 1276; DMU, MT, Madabit murafaʿat, 336/186/46, fol. 16, 28 Rabi II 1276.

184 For other cases see: DMU, MT, Madabit murafaʿat, 336/186/46, fol. 7, 12 Rabi II 1276; DMU, MT, Madabit murafaʿat, 336/186/46, fols. 25–26, 16 Jumada I 1276.

185 DMU, MT, Madabit murafaʿat, 335/186/46, fol. 133, 15 Jumada I 1275.

186 DMU, MT, Madabit murafaʿat, 339/186/46, fols. 20–22, 27 Muharram 1278.

187 DMU, MT, Madabit murafaʿat, 339/186/46, fols. 30–31, 12 Safar 1278.

188 DMU, MT, Madabit murafaʿat, 339/186/46, fol. 48, 4 Rabi I 1278.

189 DMU, MT, Madabit murafaʿat, 339/186/46, fol. 74, 13 Jumada I 1278.

190 See Hallaq, *An Introduction to Islamic Law*, 59; Schacht, *An Introduction to Islamic Law*, 148.

191 DMU, MT, Madabit murafaʿat, 336/186/46, fols. 56–57, 11 Shaʿban 1276; DMU, MT, Madabit murafaʿat, 336/186/46, fol. 62, 29 Shaʿban 1276.

192 DMU, MT, Madabit murafaʿat, 336/186/46, fol. 43, 6 Rajab 1276. For a similar case, see: DMU, MQ, Madabit murafaʿat, 77/98/46, fols. 85–86, 16 Shaʿban 1279.
193 DMU, MT, Madabit murafaʿat, 338/186/46, fols. 53–54, 14 Rabi I 1278.
194 Land Law of 1858: Article III, Article XXVIII.
195 Land Law of 1858: Article XXI.
196 DWQ, DD, L/19/15/6, fols. 116, 135 (no. 78) 2 Rabi II 1276.
197 As Abbas Pasha became viceroy in November 1848 (the beginning of the mid-nineteenth-century years), I should have started this discussion with the examination of the tax registers of 1265/1848–1849. But I did not because I could not locate the register of one of my sample villages for that year. Hence, I decided to rely on the registers of the following year 1266/1849–1850.
198 This was the case for al-Jazira al-Khadra Village, which can be seen by comparing its *athurat* register with its land-tax registers.
199 For example, in 1266/1849–1850, some peasants of Ibyar Village had been assigned insolvent lands of neighboring villages; when these lands were made the responsibility of the Ibyar villagers, they were referred to as *mudaf* (added) lands. (See for example: DMU, Mukallafat atyan, ibyar, 1266, 2913/121/22, fols. 11, 12, 36, 75.)
200 Cuno's discussion on distribution of land relies on cadastral registers as well as land-tax registers; and as neither reveals joint-holding arrangements, Cuno too uses the term *holding* instead of "holder." Cuno, *The Pasha's Peasants*, 69–74.
201 Appendix A presents the distribution of land in the sample villages according to this set of categories.
202 DMU, Mukallafat atyan, jazirat al-aʿjam, 1266, 4571/61/20. Here I point to the discrepancy between the total area of Jazirat al-Aʿjam Village specified by the 1266 land-tax register (385.5 *faddans*) and that specified by table 4.6 (397 *faddans*). This discrepancy emerged because of the difficulties involved in adding up the fractions of a *faddan*, which are explained in the notes of table 2.1.
203 For a discussion on "category" suitability, see Abbas and El-Dessouky, *The Large Landowning Class*, 15–20.
204 Cuno, *The Pasha's Peasants*, 67–69 (for quoted phrase, 67).
205 For a detailed examination of the impact of the three land-tax codes on the four sample villages, see appendix B.
206 For quoted phrase: Cuno, *The Pasha's Peasants*, 69. For the 1896 data: Radwan, *Agrarian Reform and Rural Poverty*, 5.

Chapter 5

1 Tucker, "Decline of the Family Economy," 267–70.
2 While some writers, (for example, Tucker, Cuno, Baer) claim that these laws aimed to grant women inheritance rights to arable land, Abul-Magd specifies the opposite, as she asserts that the aim of these laws was to deprive women of their inheritance rights to land. See her *Imagined Empires*, 115.

3 Cuno found such cases when examining the religious court registers. See his *The Pasha's Peasants*, 75–76. Also, Marsot discusses peasant women's access to land during the eighteenth century; see her *Women and Men*, 123, 128–29.
4 DWQ, MA, S/7/6/2, fol. 65 (unnumbered) 14 Jumada I 1269.
5 DWQ, MKH, Daʿawi wa ashhadat, no. 3, fol. 24 (no. 144) 13 Dhu al-Hijja 1273.
6 Abul-Magd, *Imagined Empires*, 115.
7 For first two quoted phrases: Cuno, *The Pasha's Peasants*, 76. For last quoted phrase: DWQ, MA, S/7/16/14, fol. 52 (no. 44) 27 Rabi II 1273.
8 Gerda Lerner presented a hypothesis on why this sexual division of labor emerged in early agrarian societies; see her *The Creation of Patriarchy*, 49–51. (I thank the blind reviewer for *Journal of Social History* who helped me understand this point when reviewing my article for this journal.) This paragraph, as well as the following three, basically follow Ghalwash, "Peasant Women and Rights," 31–32.
9 Pena, Maiques, and Castillo develop a similar argument to explain why land distribution systems in modern Nicaragua are informed by the idea of male dominance in land control, and tend to bypass women. Specifically they state: "The land distribution system has not favored women because it is assumed, even by women themselves, that they are not the producers, but are simply 'helping out' their husbands." See Pena, Maiques, and Castillo, "Using Rights-Based and Gender-Analysis Arguments," 63.
10 DMU, Daftar al-athurat, al-jazira al-khadra, fol. 5. For other examples, see fols. 5, 9, 13, 17, 22, 24, 34, 35, 39, 41, 47, 76. In other cases, the family chose to keep the land patrimony registered in the name of the deceased patriarch rather than transferring it to the name of the eldest son; see: fols. 10, 13.
11 1858 Land Law, Article II; Cuno, "Joint Family Households," 495–96.
12 Mundy, "The Family, Inheritance and Islam," 62–64; Cuno, *The Pasha's Peasants*, 74.
13 DWQ, MKH, Daʿawi wa ashhadat, no. 1, fol. 69 (no. 158) 8 Shawwal 1273.
14 DMU, Daftar al-athurat, al-jazira al-khadra, fols. 1, 76.
15 DMU, Daftar al-athurat, al-jazira al-khadra, fols. 2–4.
16 DMU, Daftar al-athurat, al-jazira al-khadra, fol. 76.
17 DMU, Daftar al-athurat, al-jazira al-khadra, fols. 2–4.
18 DMU, Daftar al-athurat, kafr al-rajallat, fol. 29.
19 DMU, Daftar al-athurat, kafr al-rajallat, fols. 4, 9, 10, 19, 24, 27, 28, 32, 33. (In two of these cases, the land was not transferred to one woman, but to a mother and her daughters.)
20 Croll, "The Exchange of Women," 47.
21 Aswad, "Women, Class and Power," 475. The same applied to Morocco roughly during the same time; see Maher, "Women and Social Change," 102.
22 Maher, "Women and Social Change," 102.
23 Goodnow and Lawrence, "Inheritance Norms," 76.
24 Goodnow and Lawrence, "Inheritance Norms," 76–77 (for quoted phrase, 77).
25 Backhouse, "Married Women's Property Law," 211.

26 Backhouse, "Married Women's Property Law," 211. Also see Combs, "A Measure of Legal Independence," 1031.
27 For examples of married women registering their lands in the names of their husbands, see DMU, Daftar al-athurat, kafr al-rajallat, fols. 7, 24, 29, 33.
28 DMU, Daftar al-athurat, jazirat al-aʿjam, fol. 9. For other examples, see: DMU, Daftar al-athurat, al-jazira al-khadra, fols. 6, 37; DMU, Daftar al-athurat, kafr al-rajallat, fol. 7.
29 For a more extensive discussion of women's consignment of land to male relatives, see Ghalwash, "Peasant Women and Rights."
30 Razavi, "Liberalisation," 1487.
31 For Kafr al-Rajallat: DMU, Daftar al-athurat, kafr al-rajallat, fols. 2, 4, 7–10, 19, 24, 27–29, 32–33. For Fatma: fol. 2. For Fatuna: fol. 32. For Jawhara: fol. 24. For al-Jazira al-Khadra: DMU Daftar al-athurat, al-jazira al-khadra, fols. 6, 10, 12, 20, 24–27, 30, 32–33, 37–38, 47, 51, 62, 75, 82, 87.
32 Tucker, *Women in Nineteenth Century Egypt*, 49.
33 DMU, Daftar al-athurat, kafr al-rajallat, fol. 8. For other examples: fols. 10, 19, 29.
34 DMU, Daftar al-athurat, kafr al-rajallat, fol. 19. For another example of women receiving marginal land in inheritance: DMU, MQ, Madabit murafaʿat, 77/98/46, fols. 70–71, 8 Jumada I 1279.
35 DWQ, MA, S/7/16/16, fol. 103 (no. 98) 7 Rabi II 1274.
36 DMU, Daftar al-athurat, kafr al-rajallat, fol. 28; DMU, Daftar al-athurat, al-jazira al-khadra, fol. 87.
37 DWQ, MA, S/7/16/16, fol. 103 (no. 99) 7 Rabi II 1274.
38 For a similar conclusion, see Tucker, *Women in Nineteenth Century Egypt*, 48.
39 Tucker, *Women in Nineteenth Century Egypt*, 51.
40 DWQ, MA, S/7/16/7, fol. 47 (no. 67) 15 Rabi II 1270.
41 For this case, see n. 13 above.
42 DWQ, MKH, Daʿawi wa ashhadat, no. 3, fol. 43 (no. 302) 29 Safar 1274.
43 DMU, MT, Madabit murafaʿat, 335/186/46, fol. 68, Dhu al-Qaʿda 1274.
44 DWQ, DD, L/19/21/1, fol. 28 (no. 9) 17 Shaʿban 1273.
45 DWQ, MA, S/7/16/14, fol. 169 (no. 137) 25 Rajab 1273.
46 DWQ, MA, S/7/16/14, fol. 52 (no. 44) 27 Rabi II 1273.
47 DMU, MT, Madabit murafaʿat, 333/186/46, fol. 40, 23 Shaʿban 1273.
48 For cases where women received the amount specified by Islamic law, see Cuno, *The Pasha's Peasants*, 193.
49 DWQ, MA, S/7/16/14, fol. 169 (no. 137) 25 Rajab 1273.
50 For examples of cases of dispossession, see: DMU, MQ, Madabit murafaʿat, 77/98/46, fols. 89–90, 28 Ramadan 1279; DMU, MQ, Madabit murafaʿat, 77/98/46, fols. 70–71, 8 Jumada I 1279.
51 DWQ, MA, S/7/16/14, fol. 169 (no. 137) 25 Rajab 1273.
52 DMU, Daftar al-athurat, al-jazira al-khadra, fol. 5.
53 For the thirty women who inherited land, see n. 31 above. These conclusions were also discussed in Ghalwash, "Peasant Women and Rights."
54 DMU, MT, Madabit murafaʿat, 336/186/46, fol. 116, 6 Muharram 1277.

55 For additional examination of this point, see: Ghalwash, "Peasant Women and Rights."

56 DMU, MT, Madabit murafaʿat, 336/186/46, fol. 64, 5 Ramadan 1276. For another similar case: DMU, MT, Madabit murafaʿat, 336/186/46, fols. 8–9, 13 Rabi II 1276.

57 DMU, MT, Madabit murafaʿat, 336/186/46, fol. 140, 17 Safar 1277.

58 DMU, MT, Madabit murafaʿat, 335/186/46, fol. 112, 8 Rabi I 1275; DMU, MT, Madabit murafaʿat, 335/186/46, fol. 118, 18 Rabi I 1275; DMU, MT, Madabit murafaʿat, 335/186/46, fol. 119, 19 Rabi I 1275; DMU, MT, Madabit murafaʿat, 335/186/46, fol. 121, 25 Rabi I 1275.

59 DMU, MT, Madabit murafaʿat, 337/186/46, fol. 107, 24 Ramadan 1277; DMU, MT, Madabit murafaʿat, 337/186/46, fol. 116, 13 Shawwal 1277.

60 DMU, Daftar al-athurat, al-jazira al-khadra, fol. 76. For other examples, see: fols. 2, 34.

61 DMU, Daftar al-athurat, al-jazira al-khadra, fols. 32–33, 62.

62 DMU, MT, Madabit murafaʿat, 335/186/46, fol. 121, 25 Rabi I 1275.

63 Abul-Magd, *Imagined Empires*, 116.

64 Jackson, "Gender Analysis of Land," 453–80.

65 Ghalwash, "Peasant Women and Rights."

66 Thus, society generally expected sisters to comply with their brothers' wishes regarding their land inheritances. An example can be seen in the sister–brother dispute that occurred in the late 1940s in the village of Batra. When Ali Fakhri tried to buy his sister's share of the land they had inherited from their father, she refused and tried instead to sell to an outsider. The anthropologist (Malak Rouchdy) who was researching the history of this village reported the following: "The matter turned into a severe dispute and was taken to court. Many villagers thought that the sister had no right to sell the land to 'a stranger.' Shaykh al-balad told me, commenting on this event, 'A sister has no right to disobey her brother and to scatter the family's land. We do not inherit the land, it is the land that inherits us.'" Rouchdy, "Change and Continuity," 246.

67 DMU, MT, Madabit murafaʿat, 337/186/46, fol. 97, 1 Ramadan 1277.

68 DMU, MT, Madabit murafaʿat, 337/186/46, fol. 104, 16 Ramadan 1277.

69 For another similar case, see DMU, MT, Madabit murafaʿat, 335/186/46, fol. 210, 22 Muharram 1276.

70 It was certainly for this reason that Yusif al-Barad'i, one of the shaykhs of Ibyar Village, decided to cede close to half his land (101 *faddans*) to his eldest son Yusif, starting the paperwork a short time before his death on January 18, 1859. The court issued the deed two days later, which meant that the cession deed carried the date of January 20, 1859. And it was on the basis of this deed that Yusif informed the *athurat* committee visiting his village that his nine siblings, of whom five were men, did not have any right to this land. On the other hand, the remainder of the land, which constituted roughly 126 *faddans*, was to be divided among all the heirs (Yusif included) according to the Islamic inheritance rules. This meant that Yusif was entitled to about

117 *faddans* of his father's land. At the time of the visit of this committee, though, the heirs had not divided the estate, but chose to keep the entire holding registered in their father's name as one unit. See DMU, Daftar al-athurat, ibyar, fols. 173–80. Also see Cuno, "Joint Family Households."

71 DMU, MT, Madabit murafa'at, 336/186/46, fol. 116, 6 Muharram 1277.

72 DMU, MT, Madabit murafa'at, 340/186/46, fol. 102, 22 Safar 1280.

73 DWQ, DD, L/19/15/8, fol. 44 (no. 168) 19 Jumada I 1276.

74 An example of a woman preferring to accept a reconciliation offer: DMU, MQ, Madabit murafa'at, 77/98/46, fols. 70–71, 8 Jumada I 1279.

75 For example see: DWQ, DD, L/19/15/5, fol. 38 (no. 712) 16 Muharram 1276; DWQ, DD, L/19/15/5, fol. 83 (no. 733) 30 Muharram 1276; DWQ, DD, L/19/15/6, fol. 172 (no. 98) 20 Rabi II 1276.

76 DMU, MT, Madabit murafa'at, 339/186/46, fols. 92–93, 22 Jumada II 1278. Another similar case: DMU, MT, Madabit murafa'at, 335/186/46, fols. 147–48, 21 Rajab 1275. Tucker makes the same observation for post-1858; see her *Women in Nineteenth Century Egypt*, 51. Cuno discerns peasant holders' dependence on this strategy before 1858; see his *The Pasha's Peasants*, 76.

77 I base this view on the following. In a final search for women-land cases after the introduction of the 1858 law, I looked at one of the registers of the Department of Interior; this register disclosed twenty-two cases. On the other hand, when searching three registers of the Council of Justice for women's land cases after the introduction of the 1855 law, I found only three entries. Department of Interior register: DWQ, DD, L/19/15/8, 1276. Council of Justice registers: DWQ, MA, S/7/16/14, 1273; DWQ, MA, S/7/16/15, 1273; DWQ, MA, S/7/6/16, 1273.

Conclusion

1 Toledano, *State and Society*, 249.

2 The title of this section is taken from the title of Chalcraft's article, "Engaging the State."

3 Abul-Magad, *Imagined Empires*; Barakat, *Al-Qarya wa al-sulta*.

4 Baer, *Studies in the Social History*, 99.

5 Scott, "Resistance without Protest," 419.

6 Waterbury, "Peasants Defy Categorization," 4–5, 18.

7 Scott, "Resistance without Protest," 419. Also see his *Weapons of the Weak*.

8 Adas, "From Avoidance to Confrontation," 217. For application of the ideas on peasant resistance in Asia to Middle Eastern contexts, see Waterbury, "Peasants Defy Categorization"; Brown, *Peasant Politics*, ch. 1.

9 Chalcraft, "Engaging the State," 304. In addition, Kerkvliet alerts us to another dimension of peasant politics: it was not limited to resistance and complaint/petitioning, but also involved "everyday forms of *support and compliance* with government authorities and prevailing political systems." Kerkvliet, "Everyday Politics," 227–43 (for quoted phrase, 235).

10 Hillal, *Al-Fallah wa al-sulta*, 343.

11 Ghalwash, "On Justice."

12 In a similar vein, while Brown's study on peasant politics focuses on the peasants' hostility to the state, it also notes that they depended on it for the correction of local abuses; see Brown, *Peasant Politics*, 173–74.

13 For peasants' specification of their shaykh's misdeeds and their insistence on his dismissal: DWQ, MA, S/7/16/9, fol. 26 (no. 495) 24 Ramadan 1270. For peasants banding together against the village officials: DWQ, MA, S/7/16/7, fols. 91, 98 (no. 145) 21 Jumad I 1270. For peasants who demanded the replacement of the *qadi* of their area with another: DWQ, DKH, S/2/8/16, fol. 168 (no. 91) 3 Sha'ban 1266. For the peasants who specified the names of the men they wished to have installed as the village shaykhs: DWQ, DD, L/19/15/5, fol. 52 (no. 1014) 21 Muharram 1276.

14 Hillal, *Al-Fallah wa al-sulta*, 344.

15 According to Hillal, peasants began to lose faith in the "petition instrument" toward the end of Khedive Ismail's reign, at which time they considered it an ineffective political instrument. See his *Al-Fallah wa al-sulta*, 344.

16 Hillal, *Al-Fallah wa al-sulta*, 344–45.

Appendix C

1 I specify only the registers pertaining to the four sample villages that were systemically examined. All other registers, being less closely examined, are not included in this list; instead, these are cited in the pertinent endnotes only.

2 Cartons hold loose-leaf documents.

Select Bibliography

Archival Sources

Egypt, Ministry of Finance Archives (Dar al-Mahfuzat al-Umumiyya), Cairo

Village land-tax registers (*Dafatir mukallifat al-atyan*), AH 1266–1279.

Village *athurat* registers, AH 1273, 1274, 1276.

Tax-reassessment registers (*Dafatir takmil al-dara'ib*), AH 1271, 1274.

Religious court registers of Tanta (*Sijillat mahkamat tanta al-ibtida'iyya al-shar'iyya*), AH 1273–1280.

Religious court registers of Qalyub (*Sijillat mahkamat qalub al-ibtida'iyya al-shar'iyya*), AH 1273–1280.

Egypt, National Archives (Dar al-Watha'iq al-Qawmiyya), Cairo

Department of Civil Affairs registers (*Dafatir diwan al-khidawi*), AH 1265–1267.

Department of Civil Affairs cartons, "Decrees" (*Mahafiz diwan al-khidawi*, "*awwamir*"), No. 1.

Viceregal Cabinet registers (*Dafatir diwan al-ma'iyya al-siniyya*), AH 1267–1269, 1272–1273, 1277–1279.

Council of Justice registers (*Dafatir majlis al-ahkam*), AH 1268–1274.

Council of Justice cartons, "Decrees" (*Mahafiz majlis al-ahkam*, "*awwamir*"), AH 1269–1279.

Department of Interior registers (*Dafatir diwan al-dakhiliyya*), AH 1273–1276.

Religious court registers of al-Khanka (*Sijillat mahkamat al-khanka al-ibtida'iyya al-shar'iyya*), AH 1268–1276.

Agricultural Affairs register (*Daftar nizam umur zira'iyya*), No. 5004.

United Kingdom, London

Foreign Office Dispatches, Public Records Office, Parts of the following series were examined: F.O./76, F.O./78, F.O.141, F.O.195.

United States, Washington, D.C.

Department of State, Dispatches from United States Consuls in Alexandria, National Archives, 1848–1863.

Published Works

Abbas, Raouf, and Assem El-Dessouky. *The Large Landowning Class and the Peasantry in Egypt, 1837–1952*. Translated by Amer Mohsen with Mona Zikri. Edited by Peter Gran. Syracuse, NY: Syracuse University Press, 2012.

Abul-Magd, Zeinab. *Imagined Empires: A History of Revolt in Egypt*. Berkeley: University of California Press, 2013.

Adas, Michael. "From Avoidance to Confrontation: Peasant Protest in Precolonial and Colonial Southeast Asia." *Comparative Studies in Society and History* 23, 2 (1981), 217–47.

Aharoni, Reuven. *The Pasha's Bedouin, Tribes and State in the Egypt of Mehemet Ali, 1805–1848*. London: Routledge, 2007.

Artin, Yaʿqub. *Al-Ahkam al-mar'iyya fi sha'in al-aradi al-misriyya*. Translated by Said Amun. Cairo, Bulaq: al-Matbaʿa al-Kubra al-Amiriyya, AH 1306/1886–1887.

Aswad, Barbara C. "Women, Class and Power: Examples from the Hatay, Turkey." In *Women in the Muslim World*. Edited by Lois Beck and Nikki Keddie. Cambridge, MA: Harvard University Press, 1978.

Aytekin, E. Attila. "Agrarian Relations, Property and Law: An Analysis of the Land Code of 1858 in the Ottoman Empire." *Middle Eastern Studies* 45, 6 (Nov. 2009), 935–51.

———. "Cultivators, Creditors and the State: Rural Indebtedness in the Nineteenth Century Ottoman Empire." *The Journal of Peasant Studies* 35, 2 (2008), 292–313.

Azbawi, Abd Allah Muhammad. *Umad wa mashayikh al-qura wa dawruhum fi al-mujtama al-misri fi al-qarn al-tasi ashar*. Cairo: Dar al-Kitab al-Jamiʿi, 1984.

Backhouse, Constance B. "Married Women's Property Law in Nineteenth-Century Canada." *Law and History Review* 6, 1 (Autumn 1988), 211–57.

Baer, Gabriel. *A History of Landownership in Modern Egypt, 1800–1950*. Oxford: Oxford University Press, 1962.

Baer, Gabriel. *Studies in the Social History of Modern Egypt*. Chicago, IL: University of Chicago Press, 1969.

Barakat, Ali. *Al-Qarya wa al-sulta fi Misr fi al-qarn al-tasiʿʿashar*. Cairo: al-Hay'a al-Amma lil-Kitab, 2018.

Barakat, Ali. *Tatawwur al-milkiyya al-zira'iyya fi Misr wa atharuhu ala al-haraka al-siyasiyya, 1813–1914*. Cairo: Dar al-Thaqafa al-Jadida, 1977.

Bourdieu, Pierre. "Structures, Habitus, Power: Basis for a Theory of Symbolic Power." In *Culture/Power/History: A Reader in Contemporary Social Theory*. Edited by Nicholas Dirks, Geoff Eley, and Sherry Ortner. Princeton, NJ: Princeton University Press, 1994.

Braun, Rudolf. "Taxation, Sociopolitical Structure, and State-Building: Great Britain and Brandenburg-Prussia." In *The Formation of National States in Western Europe*. Edited by Charles Tilly. Princeton: Princeton University Press, 1975.

Brenner, Robert. "Agrarian Class Structures and Economic Development in Pre-Industrial Europe." *Past and Present* 70 (Feb. 1976), 30–75.

Brown, Nathan J. *Peasant Politics in Modern Egypt: The Struggle Against the State*. New Haven, CT: Yale University Press, 1990.

Casson, Lionel. "Tax-Collection Problems in Early Arab Egypt." *Transactions and Proceedings of the American Philological Association* 69 (1938), 274–91.

Chalcraft, John. "Engaging the State: Peasants and Petitions in Egypt on the Eve of Colonial Rule." *International Journal of Middle East Studies* 37, 3 (2005), 303–25.

Cheta, Omar Youssef. "A Prehistoy of the Modern Legal Profession in Egypt, 1840s–1870s." *International Journal of Middle East Studies* 50, 4 (Nov. 2018), 649–68.

Combs, Mary Beth. "'A Measure of Legal Independence': The 1870 Married Women's Property Act and the Portfolio Allocations of British Wives." *The Journal of Economic History* 1, 4 (Dec. 2005), 1028–57.

Cooper, Richard S. "The Assessment and Collection of Kharaj Tax in Medieval Egypt." *Journal of the American Oriental Society* 96, 3 (1976), 365–82.

Corrigan, Philip, and Derek Sayers. "How the Law Rules: Variations on Some Themes in Karl Marx." In *Law, State and Society*. Edited by Bob Fryer, Alan Hunt, Doreen McBarnet and Bert Moorhouse. London: Routledge, 1981.

Croll, Elisabeth. "The Exchange of Women and Property: Marriage in Post-Revolutionary China." In *Women and Property: Women as Property*. Edited by Renee Hirschon. London: Croom Helm, 1984.

Crouchley, A. E. *The Economic Development of Modern Egypt*. London: Longmans, Green, 1938.

Cuno, Kenneth M. "Joint Family Households and Rural Notables in 19th-Century Egypt." *International Journal of Middle East Studies* 27, 4 (1995), 485–502.

Cuno, Kenneth M. "The Origins of Private Ownership of Land in Egypt: A Reappraisal." *International Journal of Middle East Studies* 12 (1980), 245–75.

Cuno, Kenneth M. *The Pasha's Peasants: Land, Society and Economy in Lower Egypt, 1740–1858*. Cambridge, MA: Cambridge University Press, 1992.

Cuno, Kenneth M., and Michael J. Reimer. "The Census Registers of Nineteenth-Century Egypt: A New Source for Social Historians." *British Journal of Middle Eastern Studies* 24, 2 (Nov. 1997), 193–216.

Darling, Linda. *A History of Social Justice and Political Power in the Middle East: The Circle of Justice from Mesopotamia to Globalization*. New York: Routledge, 2013.

Darling, Linda. *Revenue-Raising and Legitimacy: Tax Collection and Finance Administration in the Ottoman Empire, 1560–1660*. Leiden, the Netherlands: E. J. Brill, 1996.

El-Darwish, Mahmoud. "Note on the Movement of Prices of Egyptian Cotton, 1820–1899." In *The Economic History of the Middle East, 1880–1914*. Edited by Charles Issawi. Midway Reprint. University of Chicago Press, 1975.

Debs, Richard A. *Islamic Law and Civil Code, The Law of Property in Egypt*. Columbia University Press, 2010.

Dodwell, Henry. *The Founder of Modern Egypt: A Study of Muhammad Ali*. Cambridge: Cambridge University Press, 1931.

Ener, Mine. "At the Crossroads of Empires: Policies toward the Poor in Early- to Mid-Nineteenth Century Egypt." *Social Science History* 26, 2 (Summer 2002), 393–426.

Ener, Mine. *Managing Egypt's Poor and the Politics of Benevolence, 1800–1952*. Princeton: Princeton University Press, 2003.

Ener, Mine. "Prohibitions on Begging and Loitering in Nineteenth-Century Egypt." *Die Welt des Islams* 39, 3 (Nov. 1999), 319–39.

Ergene, Boğaç A. "On Ottoman Justice: Interpretations in Conflict (1600–1800)." *Islamic Law and Society* 8, 1 (2001), 52–87.

Fahmy, Khaled. *All the Pasha's Men: Mehmed Ali, His Army, and the Making of Modern Egypt*. Cambridge: Cambridge University Press, 1997.

Fahmy, Khaled. "The Anatomy of Justice: Forensic Medicine and Criminal Law in Nineteenth-Century Egypt." *Islamic Law and Society* 6, 2 (1999), 224–71.

Fahmy, Khaled. *Mehmed Ali: From Ottoman Governor to Ruler of Egypt*. London: Oneworld Publications 2009.

Fahmy, Khaled. "The Police and the People in Nineteenth Century Egypt." *Die Welt des Islams*. 39, 3 (Nov. 1999), 340–77.

Fahmy, Khaled, and Rudolph Peters. "The Legal History of Ottoman Egypt." *Islamic Law and Society* 6, 2 (1999), 129–35.

Foucault, Michel. "Governmentality." In *The Foucault Effect: Studies in Governmentality*. Edited by Graham Burchell, Colin Gordon, and Peter Miller. Chicago: University of Chicago Press, 1991.

Gerber, Haim. *State, Society and Law in Islam*. Albany: State University of New York Press, 1994.

Ghalwash, Maha A. "On Justice: Peasants, Petitions and the State in Mid-Nineteenth-Century Egypt." *British Journal of Middle Eastern Studies* 43, 4 (2016), 523–40.

Ghalwash, Maha A. "Land Acquisition by the Peasants of Mid-Nineteenth Century Egypt: The *Ramya* System." *Studia Islamica*, 88 (1998), 121–39.

Ghalwash, Maha A. "Peasant Women and Rights to Land in Nineteenth Century Egypt: Sites of Resistance?" *Journal of Social History* 52, 1 (2018), 26–53.

Goldberg, Jan. "On the Origins of *Majalis Al-Tujjar* in Mid-Nineteenth Century Egypt." *Islamic Law and Society* 6, 2 (1999), 193–223.

Goodnow, Jacqueline J., and Jeanette A. Lawrence. "Inheritance Norms for Distribution of Money, Land, and Things in Families." *Family Science* 1, 2 (April 2010), 73–82.

Green, Anna, and Kathleen Troup, eds. *The Houses of History, A Critical Reader in Twentieth-Century History and Theory*. New York: New York University Press, 1999.

Hakim, Muhammad. *Ayam Muhammad Ali: al-tamayz al-ajtima'i wa tawzi furas al-haya*. Al-Majlis al-aʿla lil-thaqafa, 2007.

Hallaq, Wael B. *An Introduction to Islamic Law*. Cambridge: Cambridge University Press, 2009.

Hamid, Ra'uf Abbas. *Al-Nizam al-ijtima'i fi Misr fi zill al-milkiyyat al-zira'iyya al-kabira, 1837–1914*. Cairo: Dar al-Fikr al-Hadith lil-Tibaʿa wa-al-Nashr, 1973.

Hamza, Abdel-Maksud. *The Public Debt of Egypt, 1854–1876*. Cairo: Government Press, 1944.

Hancock, Dora. *Taxation, Policy and Practice*. 3rd. ed. London: International Thomson Business Press, 1995.

Hillal, Imad. *Al-fallah wa al-sulta wa al-qanun: misr fi al-nisf al-thani min al-qarn al-tasi ashar.* Cairo: Matba'at Dar al-Kutub wa al-Watha'iq al-Qawmiyya bi-al-Qahira, 2007.
al-Hitta, Ahmad Ahmad. *Tarikh Misr al-iqtisadi fi al-qarn al-tasi ashar.* Cairo: Maktabat al-Nahda al-Misriyya, 1955.
al-Hitta, Ahmad Ahmad. *Tarikh al-zira'a fi Misr fi ahd Muhammad Ali al-kabir.* Cairo: al-Jam'iyya al-Malakiyya li-l-Dirasat al-Ta'rikhiyya, 1950.
Hobsbawm, Eric. *The Age of Capital.* London: Vintage Books, 1996.
Holt, P. M. *Egypt and the Fertile Crescent, 1516–1922.* Ithaca, NY: Cornell University Press, 1966.
Humphreys, Sally. "Law as Discourse." *History and Anthropology* 1, 2 (February 1985), 241–64.
Hunayn, Jirjis. *Al-Atyan wa al-dara'ib fi al-qutr al-Misr.* Cairo: Bulaq, 1904.
Hunter, F. Robert. *Egypt under the Khedives, 1805–1879: From Household Government to Modern Bureaucracy.* Pittsburgh, PA: University of Pittsburgh Press, 1984.
Hunter, F. Robert. "State-Society Relations in Nineteenth-Century Egypt: The Years of Transition, 1848–79." *Middle Eastern Studies* 36, 3 (2000), 145–59.
Hurewitz, J. C. *Diplomacy in the Near and Middle East.* Vol. I. Princeton: Princeton University Press, 1956.
İnalcik, Halil. "The Ottoman Economic Mind and Aspects of the Ottoman Economy." In *Studies in the Economic History of the Middle East.* Edited by M. A. Cook. Oxford: Oxford University Press, 1970.
Islamoğlu, Huri. "Politics of Administering Property: Law and Statistics in the Nineteenth-century Ottoman Empire." In *Constituting Modernity: Private Property in the East and West.* Edited by Huri Islamoğlu. London: I. B. Tauris, 2004.
Islamoğlu, Huri. "Property as a Contested Domain: A Reevaluation of the Ottoman Land Code of 1858." In *New Perspectives on Property and Land in the Middle East.* Edited by Roger Owen. Distributed by Harvard University Press, 2000.
Islamoğlu, Huri, and Çağlar Keyder. "Agenda for Ottoman History." In *The Ottoman Empire and the World Economy.* Edited by Huri Islamoğlu-Inan. Cambridge: Cambridge University Press, 1987.
Islamoğlu-Inan, Huri. *State and Peasant in the Ottoman Empire.* Leiden, the Netherlands: E. J. Brill, 1994.
Islamoğlu-Inan, Huri. "State and Peasants in the Ottoman Empire: A Study of Peasant Economy in North-Central Anatolia during the Sixteenth Century." In *The Ottoman Empire and the World Economy.* Edited by Huri Islamoğlu-Inan. Cambridge: Cambridge University Press, 1987.
Issawi, Charles. "The Economic Development of Egypt, 1800–1960." In *The Economic History of the Middle East, 1880–1914.* Edited by Charles Issawi. Midway Reprint. University of Chicago Press, 1975.
Issawi, Charles, ed. *The Economic History of the Middle East, 1800–1914.* Midway Reprint. University of Chicago Press, 1975.
Itzkowitz, Norman. *Ottoman Empire and Islamic Tradition.* Chicago: University of Chicago Press, 1972.

Jackson, Cecile. "Gender Analysis of Land: Beyond Land Rights for Women?" *Journal of Agrarian Change* 3, 4 (October 2003), 453–80.

Jorgens, Denise. "A Comparative Examination of the Provisions of the Ottoman Land Code and Khedive Sa'id's Law of 1858." In *New Perspectives on Property and Land in the Middle East*. Edited by Roger Owen. Distributed by Harvard University Press, 2000.

Kerkvliet, Benedict J. Tria. "Everyday Politics in Peasant Societies (and Ours)." *The Journal of Peasant Studies* 36, 1 (2009), 227–43.

Landes, David S. *Bankers and Pashas*. London: Heinemann, 1958.

Lawson, Fred H. "Foreign Exploitation and Domestic Conflict in Mid-Nineteenth-Century Egypt: A Reevaluation of the Suez Canal Concessions of 1854 and 1856." *Journal of the American Research Center in Egypt* 24 (1987), 61–70.

Lerner, Gerda. *The Creation of Patriarchy*. Oxford: Oxford University Press, 1986.

Levi, Margaret. *Of Rule and Revenue*. Berkeley: University of California Press, 1988.

Levi, Margaret. "The Predatory Theory of Rule." *Politics & Society* 10, 4 (1981), 431–65.

Lewis, Bernard. "Ottoman Land Tenure and Taxation in Syria." *Studia Islamica* 50 (1979), 109–124.

Maher, Vanessa. "Women and Social Change in Morocco." In *Women in the Muslim World*. Edited by Lois Beck and Nikki Keddie. Cambridge, MA: Harvard University Press, 1978.

Mardin, Serif. *The Genesis of Young Ottoman Thought: A Study in the Modernization of Turkish Political Ideas*. Princeton: Princeton University Press, 1962.

Marlowe, John. *Spoiling the Egyptians*. London: A. Deutsch, 1974.

Marsot, Afaf Lutfi Al-Sayyid. *A Short History of Modern Egypt*. Cambridge: Cambridge University Press, 2000.

Marsot, Afaf Lutfi Al-Sayyid. *Women and Men in Late Eighteenth-Century Egypt*. Austin: University of Texas Press, 1995.

McCarthy, Justin. "Nineteenth-Century Egyptian Population." *Middle Eastern Studies* 12, 3 (Oct. 1976), 1–39.

Merruau, Paul. *L'Egypte contemporaine de Mehemet-Ali à Said Pacha, 1840–1857*. Paris: Libr. Internationale, 1858.

Mikhail, Alan. *Nature and Empire in Ottoman Egypt: an Environmental History*. Cambridge: Cambridge University Press, 2011.

Mundy, Martha. "The Family, Inheritance and Islam: A Re-Examination of the Sociology of Fara'id Law." In *Islamic Law: Social and Historical Contexts*. Edited by Aziz al-Azmeh. London: Routledge, 1988.

Mustafa, Ahmed Abdel-Rahim. "The Breakdown of the Monopoly System in Egypt after 1840." In *Political and Social Change in Modern Egypt*. Edited by P. M. Holt. Oxford: Oxford University Press, 1968.

Najm, Zayn al-Abidin Shams al-Din, ed. *Dafatir Majmu Idara wa-Ijra'at, 1240–1280/1825–1863: Watha'iq Tarikh Misr wa al-Arab al-Hadith*. Cairo: Dar al-Fikr al-Arabi, 2003.

Owen, Roger (E. R. J.). *Cotton and the Egyptian Economy, 1820–1914: A Study in Trade and Development*. Oxford: Oxford University Press, 1969.

———. "The Development of Agricultural Production in Nineteenth-Century Egypt: Capitalism of What Type?" In *The Islamic Middle East, 700–1900: Studies in Economic and Social History*. Edited by A. L. Udovitch. Princeton: Princeton University Press, 1981.

———. *The Middle East in the World Economy, 1800–1914*. London: I. B. Tauris, 2011.

Panzac, Daniel. "The Population of Egypt in the Nineteenth Century." *Asian and African Studies* 21 (1987), 11–32.

Pena, Nuria, Mar Maiques, and Gina E. Castillo. "Using Rights-Based and Gender-Analysis Arguments for Land Rights for Women: Some Initial Reflections from Nicaragua." *Gender and Development* 16, 1 (March 2008), 55–71.

Peters, Rudolph. "Administrators and Magistrates: The Development of a Secular Judiciary in Egypt, 1842–1871." *Die Welt des Islams* 39, 3 (1999), 378–97.

Peters, Rudolph. "For His Correction and as a Deterrent Example for Others: Mehmed Ali's First Criminal Legislation (1829–1830)." *Islamic Law and Society* 6, 2 (1999), 164–92.

Radwan, Samir. *Agrarian Reform and Rural Poverty, Egypt 1952–1975*. Geneva: International Labour Office, 1977.

Rafeq, Abdul-Karim. "Land Tenure Problems and Their Social Impact in Syria around the Middle of the Nineteenth Century." In *Land Tenure and Social Transformation in the Near East*. Edited by Tarif Khalidi. Beirut: American University in Beirut Press, 1984.

Razavi, Shahra. "Liberalisation and the Debates on Women's Access to Land." *Third World Quarterly* 28, 8 (2007), 1479–1500.

Reilly, James A. "Women in the Economic Life of Late-Ottoman Damascus." *Arabica* 42, 1 (March 1995), 79–106.

Richards, Alan. *Egypt's Agricultural Development, 1800–1980: Technical and Social Change*. Boulder, CO: Westview Press, 1982.

Richards, Alan. "Primitive Accumulation in Egypt, 1798–1882." In *The Ottoman Empire and the World Economy*. Edited by Huri Islamoğlu-Inan. Cambridge: Cambridge University Press, 1987.

Rivlin, Helen A. B. *The Agricultural Policy of Muhammad Ali in Egypt*. Cambridge: Cambridge University Press, 1961.

Rivlin, Helen A. B. "The Railway Question in the Ottoman-Egyptian Crisis of 1850–1852." *Middle East Journal* 15, 4 (1961), 365–88.

Rouchdy, Malak S. "Change and Continuity in the Village of Batra: Family Strategies." In *Directions of Change in Rural Egypt*. Edited by Nicholas S. Hopkins and Kirsten Westergaard. Cairo: American University in Cairo Press, 2001.

Salzmann, Ariel. "An Ancien Régime Revisited: 'Privatization' and Political Economy in the Eighteenth-Century Ottoman Empire." *Politics & Society* 21, 4 (Dec. 1993), 393–423.

Sami, Amin. *Taqwim al-Nil*. Vol. II. Cairo: Matbaʿat Dar al-Kutub al-Misriyya, 1932.

Schacht, Joseph. *An Introduction to Islamic Law*. Oxford: Oxford University Press, 1964.

Scott, James C. *The Moral Economy of the Peasant: Rebellion and Subsistence in Southeast Asia*. New Haven, CT: Yale University Press, 1976.

Scott, James C. "Resistance without Protest and without Organization: Peasant Opposition to the Islamic Zakat and the Christian Tithe." *Comparative Studies in Society and History* 29, 3 (July 1987), 417–52.

Scott, James C. *Weapons of the Weak: Everyday Forms of Peasant Resistance*. New Haven, CT: Yale University Press, 1985.

Senior, N. W. *Conversations and Journals in Egypt and Malta*. Vol. II. London: S. Low, Marston, Searle and Rivington, 1882.

Shalabi, Ali. *Al-Rif al-misri fi al-nisf al-thani min al-qarn al-tasi ashar, 1847–1891*. Cairo: Dar al-Maʿarif, 1983.

Shaw, Stanford J. "The Nineteenth-Century Ottoman Tax Reforms and Revenue System." *International Journal of Middle East Studies* 6, 4 (Oct. 1975), 421–59.

Sijpesteijn, Petra. "Landholding Patterns in Early Islamic Egypt." *Journal of Agrarian Change* 9, 1 (January 2009), 120–33.

Singer, Amy. "New Trends in Agrarian History." *Asian and African Studies* 26, 3 (1992), 263–73.

Singer, Amy. *Palestinian Peasants and Ottoman Officials*. Cambridge: Cambridge University Press, 1994.

Toledano, Ehud R. *State and Society in Mid-Nineteenth-Century Egypt*. Cambridge: Cambridge University Press, 1990.

Tucker, Judith E. "Decline of the Family Economy in Mid-Nineteenth Century Egypt." *Arab Studies Quarterly* 1, 3 (Summer 1979), 245–71.

Tucker, Judith E. *Women in Nineteenth-Century Egypt*. Cambridge: Cambridge University Press, 1985.

Turner, Bryan S. *Weber and Islam*. London: Routledge and Kegan Paul, 1974.

Waterbury, John. "Peasants Defy Categorization (as Well as Landlords and the State)." In *Peasants and Politics in the Modern Middle East*. Edited by Farhad Kazemi and John Waterbury. Gainesville: University Press of Florida, 1991.

Weber, Max. *Economy and Society: An Outline of Interpretative Sociology*. Vol. I. New York: Bedminster Press, 1968.

Wolf, Eric. *Peasants*. Englewood Cliffs, NJ: Prentice Hall, 1966.

Index

Page numbers in italics refer to tables.

Ingram Content Group UK Ltd.
Milton Keynes UK
UKHW051652170423
420130UK00006B/34/J

9 781649 032775